Cognitive Governance and the Historical Distortion of the Norm of Modern Development:

A Theory of Political Asymmetry

Renny Rueda
American University in the Emirates, UAE

IGI Global
PUBLISHER of TIMELY KNOWLEDGE

A volume in the Advances in Public Policy and Administration (APPA) Book Series

Published in the United States of America by
IGI Global
Information Science Reference (an imprint of IGI Global)
701 E. Chocolate Avenue
Hershey PA, USA 17033
Tel: 717-533-8845
Fax: 717-533-8661
E-mail: cust@igi-global.com
Web site: http://www.igi-global.com

Library of Congress Cataloging-in-Publication Data

Names: Rueda, Renny, 1980- author.
Title: Cognitive governance and the historical distortion of the norm of modern development : a theory of political asymmetry / Renny Rueda.
Description: Hershey, PA : Information Science Reference, [2024] | Includes bibliographical references and index. | Summary: "In this book, the idea of political asymmetry is embraced as a depictive strategy to represent institutional settings that interfere with viable practices of governance, and thus, communication and coordination"-- Provided by publisher.
Identifiers: LCCN 2023035045 (print) | LCCN 2023035046 (ebook) | ISBN 9781668497944 (hardcover) | ISBN 9781668497951 (paperback) | ISBN 9781668497968 (ebook)
Subjects: LCSH: International relations--Philosophy. | Communication in politics. | International organization. | Political science--Philosophy.
Classification: LCC JZ1305 .R82 2024 (print) | LCC JZ1305 (ebook) | DDC 327.101--dc23/eng/20230810
LC record available at https://lccn.loc.gov/2023035045
LC ebook record available at https://lccn.loc.gov/2023035046

This book is published in the IGI Global book series Advances in Public Policy and Administration (APPA) (ISSN: 2475-6644; eISSN: 2475-6652)

British Cataloguing in Publication Data
A Cataloguing in Publication record for this book is available from the British Library.

Advances in Public Policy and Administration (APPA) Book Series

ISSN:2475-6644
EISSN:2475-6652

Mission

Proper management of the public sphere is necessary in order to maintain order in modern society. Research developments in the field of public policy and administration can assist in uncovering the latest tools, practices, and methodologies for governing societies around the world.

The **Advances in Public Policy and Administration (APPA) Book Series** aims to publish scholarly publications focused on topics pertaining to the governance of the public domain. APPA's focus on timely topics relating to government, public funding, politics, public safety, policy, and law enforcement is particularly relevant to academicians, government officials, and upper-level students seeking the most up-to-date research in their field.

Coverage

- Government
- Law Enforcement
- Political Economy
- Politics
- Public Administration
- Public Funding
- Public Policy
- Resource allocation
- Urban Planning

IGI Global is currently accepting manuscripts for publication within this series. To submit a proposal for a volume in this series, please contact our Acquisition Editors at Acquisitions@igi-global.com or visit: http://www.igi-global.com/publish/.

The Advances in Public Policy and Administration (APPA) Book Series (ISSN 2475-6644) is published by IGI Global, 701 E. Chocolate Avenue, Hershey, PA 17033-1240, USA, www.igi-global.com. This series is composed of titles available for purchase individually; each title is edited to be contextually exclusive from any other title within the series. For pricing and ordering information please visit http://www.igi-global.com/book-series/advances-public-policy-administration/97862. Postmaster: Send all address changes to above address.

Titles in this Series

For a list of additional titles in this series, please visit: http://www.igi-global.com/book-series/advances-public-policy-administration/97862

Financial Evaluation and Risk Management of Infrastructure Projects
Kleopatra Petroutsatou (Aristotle University of Thessaloniki, Greece) and Constantin Zopounidis (Technical University of Crete, Greece & Audencia Business School, France)
Information Science Reference • © 2024 • 248pp • H/C (ISBN: 9781668477861) • US $225.00

Policies, Practices, and Protocols for International Commercial Arbitration
Basheer Ahmed Mohammed Khan (Supreme Court of India Bar Association, India) and Kaushal Kishore (Supreme Court of India Bar Association, New Delhi, India)
Information Science Reference • © 2023 • 271pp • H/C (ISBN: 9781668440407) • US $225.00

Governmental Power Market-Ing in the VU-CHAOS World
Kittisak Jermsittiparsert (University of City Island, Cyprus) Srirath Gohwong (Universitas Muhammadiyah Sidenreng Rappang, Indonesia) Shayut Pavapanunkul (Universitas Muhammadiyah Sidenreng Rappang, Indonesia) and Nasaran Mahittichatkul (Universitas Muhammadiyah Sidenreng Rappang, Indonesia)
Information Science Reference • © 2023 • 296pp • H/C (ISBN: 9781668472804) • US $205.00

Historical and Political Analysis on Power Balances and Deglobalization
Emily Brynn Stacey (Rose State College, USA)
Information Science Reference • © 2023 • 253pp • H/C (ISBN: 9781668456330) • US $205.00

Juvenile Justice in African and Western Criminal Justice Systems
Simeon Peter Sungi (United States International University-Africa, Kenya) George Rugaimukamu Kakoti (Tennessee State University, USA) and Deneil D. Christian (Tennessee State University, USA)
Information Science Reference • © 2024 • 300pp • H/C (ISBN: 9781668493434) • US $215.00

Public Policy's Role in Achieving Sustainable Development Goals
Mahani Hamdan (Universiti Brunei Darussalam, Brunei) Muhammad Anshari (Universiti Brunei Darussalam, Brunei) Norainie Ahmad (Universiti Brunei Darussalam, Brunei) and Emil Ali (Universiti Brunei Darussalam, Brunei)
Information Science Reference • © 2023 • 370pp • H/C (ISBN: 9781668489031) • US $235.00

Governance Quality, Fiscal Policy, and the Path to a Low-Carbon Future Perspectives From Developing Economies
Ibrahim Nandom Yakubu (University for Development Studies, Ghana)
Engineering Science Reference • © 2023 • 284pp • H/C (ISBN: 9781668492727) • US $240.00

IGI Global
PUBLISHER of TIMELY KNOWLEDGE

701 East Chocolate Avenue, Hershey, PA 17033, USA
Tel: 717-533-8845 x100 • Fax: 717-533-8661
E-Mail: cust@igi-global.com • www.igi-global.com

Table of Contents

Preface

This book proposes a new theoretical approach to the study of norms and normative meaning on international relations and political science. It is directed to contextualize and account how "political asymmetry" affects the processes of production of normative interventions of international institutions of governance such as the World Bank or the International Monetary Fund. In addition, it aims to reconstruct and explain how norms of highly contradictory nature, reproduce historically within the ordinary institutional practice of organizations with atypical biographical and political settings.

From the outset, in late modern social systems, the asymmetric interaction of actors take place both, at the level of systemic settings as well as at the level of formal subsystems of organization. Also, the concept of asymmetry doesn´t take actors as equal but as unequal entities. Thus, every *referentiation* of relations within interactions includes both systemic and/or sub systemic settings. Asymmetry therefore can be defined if two assumptions are taken into account:

1. Agents are unequal in factual and ideational (informational) settings.
2. For asymmetry or symmetry to be declared agents should hold a relation within a settled systemic or sub systemic structure.

Asymmetry therefore holds a power relations nature[1], but at the same time, a cognitive role in the process of communication, representation and coordination that takes place in multi agent environments (subsystems) such as organizations or institutions. In these two levels, *political asymmetry can be depicted as the material (factual) capacity of actors to operate within the system in accordance with the structure resources of base., and the capacity of actors to formalize normative constructions (information) into systemic structures*. As it is further explained in this work, these features of the concept, aim to restore the notion of "the political" in the realm of deontology and dialogical interaction as well as in plain power politics relations. As such, the scope detach the political realm from factual or ideational settings of actors, to factual or ideational relational patterns of actors within a systemic or sub systemic structure. Over the recent decades, this endeavor has been customarily avoided on international relations theory and political science, carrying out the limitation of social analysis to conduct inquiry on the study of the meaning and origin of normative interventions of institutions, as well as to diagnose how unbalanced relations of actors within structures[2] can be empirically accounted.

Since the study aims to operationalize and depict the consequences that settings of international encounters have on norms production, the ontological assumption of the book embraces a rather realist assumption on the study of norms. Thereby, while the book stresses the social character of institutions, it highlights the conflicting historicity and role that power[3], coordination and dialogical interaction has over the process of construction of meaning.

The case study of the book deals with the construction of a "norm of modern development" at the Bretton Woods Institutions, a composite made up of discursive interventions induced from the outside into domestic policies and political architectures. Such constructions, customarily produced and endorsed on the official record of the World Bank and the IMF, have been chosen for a variety of reasons. One of them is the relevant influence of western economic academia in assigning cognitive constructions in today's social systems. During recent years, the prominence of such conceptions have acquired ubiquitous roles in the definition of political agendas of high income countries, which for the most part of the 20th century remained isolated from the negative impacts of the expansion of the global economy. On the other hand, the discussion on the historical expansion of the "*developmental*" process has been at the core of international relations literature on the global south. These topics have acquired special relevance on more recent contributions on IR sociology (Escobar, 1995) (Escobar, 2008) (Barro, 2005), yet, a coherent theory solution to this international puzzle has not taken distance from embracing a single ideological or epistemological turn. While it is clear that international institutions such as the World Bank and the International Monetary have been able to reconfigure politically and ideologically the global arena, it is not clear to which extent they are narrowed by means of self-referential processes of "development", and the exercise of sovereignty within single epistemic an unbalanced international architecture.

The theory of political asymmetry, aims also to highlight how normative constructions of international institutions have systematically addressed critical norms affected from their origin by clear functional settings adopted within defined historical global transitions. This particular assumption implies that the process of data collection in the present study, remains necessarily attached to a macro level and historical structure.

The decision to call this theory a "general" theory, aims to dispute the limitations of single ontological categories -realist and constructivist international relations literature- problematizing the critical normative dimension of international relations and international politics. As a result, the definition of "political asymmetry" developed in this book seeks to disentangle the empirical limitations of constructivism when embracing the task of accounting the role of the structure in the process of norms production, while at the same time the false legitimacy of the realist tradition in upholding critical assumptions that avoid the communicational institutional architecture and remain on the individual.

THE STATE OF THE CONCEPT OF POLITICAL ASYMMETRY ON IR

The concept of political asymmetry in political science and international relations has often been influenced by research on realism, yet theoretical and empirical engagement is absent from modern research. Customarily, it has been characterized by the role that *asymmetrical* arrangements have over the definition of *unfair* or uneven political and social settings. In such representations, asymmetry is frequently understood as inequality. However, this assumption cut in the roots the significant contributions of the subject as an entity in itself that constructivist research has systematically endorsed on recent decades. In any case, neither a semantic depiction, nor a theoretical contextualization has been rigorously addressed -much less an operationalization for the study of the meaning of normative interventions of actors on governance architectures-.

Arguably, the most consistent recent attempt to define the concept of political asymmetry was carried out by Philip Kitcher (2001). In his view on the relationship between science and democracy, he stresses that societies tend to favor positions that are not only "scientifically" accountable, but belong to a defined epistemic approach. Thus, agreements between individuals frequently take place on arenas that differ from each other within decision taking procedures. This natural feature of societies, highlights the existence of *political asymmetries* that are also further reproduced within different epistemological communities[4]. While this analysis contributed to stressing the role of science and knowledge in the field of governance, it focuses solely in solving ethical dilemmas in democratic systems. This frames the potential for further research on global governance and the study of norms.

On social sciences, political asymmetry has been represented as divergent "interests" within relations of "political equality" (Alonso Et. Al, 2011, p. 8). This approach emphasizes the role that participation of individuals on social institutions that aim to safeguard rights and aspirations of agents have on a membership environment such as the nation state. While this notion is valuable for grasping the participatory nature of the concept, the approach doesn't explain its role within the production of normative agreements (Wray, 2001), which in turn preclude any attempt to carry out empirical or theoretical inquiry.

On international relations and international politics, political asymmetry has been characterized as an spontaneous relation of countries that collude on unbalanced power relations. This approach has frequently been used to depict the interaction between cultures and territories (Hadi, 1998) (Nandy, 1989), political economic structures (Buchanan, 1977) (Galbraith, 1998), IR political strategy (Brantly, 2006) (Thomas, 2001), international communities such as the European Union (Ehrenfeld, 2012) (Ágh, 1998), transnational relations between the rule of law and democracy (United Nations, 2009), and research oriented to discuss policies beyond the nation-state (Keohane & Raustiala, 2008) (Deutch, et al., 2004), among others.

The most recent endeavor to theoretically frame the concept of political asymmetry on IR theory was carried out by Brantly Womack. His research focuses on reconstructing features that characterized the historical interaction between two highly unequal Asian actors (China and Vietnam). This attempt detaches from classical[5] interpretations of asymmetric relations by turning to the "imbalance of capacities and power, (…) a disequilibrium that creates either subordination or a competition for domination". Instead, asymmetry implies not only unequal power, but also perspective-differentiations that increase the risk of misunderstandings and agenda *subjectification*; "asymmetric relationships must be analyzed in terms of their two sub-relations, that of the stronger to the weaker and that of the weaker to the stronger". This attempt to depoliticize asymmetry on international relations, overcome the frequent moral categories given to the existence of scenarios of inequality[6]. Thus asymmetry theory is not a syncretic sampling of what appears attractive from each of the other theories, "but rather a reinterpretation"[7]. In this approach, the historicity of the subjective relations that condition the role and evolution of actors and structures, remains to be a fundamental concern that is ignored in customary research. Thus, ideas of political advantage or paranoia, don´t necessarily represent diametrical standpoints, but the existence of shared patterns in a relation observed from two subjective reflections on a similar language. In this approach however, the lack of a general illustration on the concept makes it to focus too much on depicting scenarios of political inattention, over attention, deference, autonomy, misperception, stalemate and normalization, making it more a descriptive analysis than a theory as a whole.

CONSIDERATIONS ON THE SELECTION OF THE CASE STUDY: THE NORM OF "MODERN DEVELOPMENT"

Deciding the choose the normative concept of development, derives from its unexpected ambiguity due to the active role that the United Nations, NGO´s, the academia, governments, and communities have had in claiming a voice on its definition. On the other hand, the concept is selected due to the mainstream criticism it has on the academia, often being related to crisis over the life, interests, environmental and cultural assets of populations along the globe. This recent trend follows the experience of the 1972 Conference on the Human Environment (Stockholm) and its further General Assembly of the United Nations commission, founded in 1982. Under the name of the "Word Commission on Environment and Development", it drafted the earlier institutional guidelines for the future of a world with an environment "not separate from human ambitions". From that moment, customary publications on "development" of international institutions regularly addressed the idea of the harmonization of economic growth with systemic concerns such as the relation of the society with the atmosphere, all of them variables associated with the notion of "development".

Beyond the subject of the environment (Sachs., 1993) (Srivastava, 2011), "development" was lately and gradually reformulated as a political category. Moreover, it was institutionally and forcefully endorsed to signatories of the United Nations in order to address issues concerning not only the economy, but diverse fields of the living experience of populations and the society as a whole. Since the Brundland Commission[8]. the ambiguity of the concept has frequently raised ordinary criticism due to the fact that its definition is institutionally difficult to grasp besides the imperatives of economic growth, often being referred to as a term to "green-wash socially or environmentally destructive activities" (Wade, 2003) (Sachs., 1993) (Stiglitz, 2003) (Sutcliffe, 2004) (Wei, 2006).

Most recently, during the 2000 summit of the United Nations, the Bretton Woods Institutions adopted in their historical record the objective to achieve by 2015 the "Millennium Development Goals". These goals were categorized in three defined thematic spheres; material, environmental and political. a) Material goals were bounded to the capacity of contemporary structures of governance to provide services, and to cope with life-scoping demands such as eradicating extreme poverty and hunger, achieving universal primary education, reducing child mortality rates, improving maternal health, and combating HIV/AIDS, malaria and other diseases. b)Environmental goals were bounded to the biodiversity, the cultural value of the nature on social systems, and the geopolitical role of global resources and its consumption in a process of economic development of contemporary societies "ensuring environmental sustainability". c) Finally, political goals embraced the dignity of individuals, their normative values, rights, liberties and their overall human moral demands. They included the promotion of gender equality, the empowering of women and the enlargement of a "global partnership for development" (United Nations, 1983).

Despite the attempts to propose a coherent representation of the idea of "development", the limitations of the institutional categories in encompassing structural flaws and international urgencies derived from the process of globalization, led to an erosion of the political and ideological scope from which the norm of "modern development" built up. In the historical record of the World Bank or the IMF, such situation represented the existence of robust theoretical and political restrictions within which the norm nurtured semantically. As a consequence, this book explains that such tendency legitimated a discursive global crisis in which the core nations, share burdens and responsibilities, with a 20th century periphery (Sachs., 1993) (Wade, 2003) (Stiglitz, 2003) (Stiglitz, 2004) (Stiglitz, 2006) (Rodrik, 2001).

This research stresses that with the institutional practice and the normalization of the regulatory settings of the Bretton Woods Institutions, they have being able to bring into the political realm a norm of "modern development"; a discursive intervention consistently used into political and academic scholarly. Such event is carried out through the systematic publication of an institutional record, reinforced by the customary praxis of organizations such as the International Monetary Fund or the World Bank. This shift in the normative dimension of international institutions, has affected not only economic, but also institutional (domestic), cognitive, functional and cultural spheres of societies that are influenced by recommendations, policies, guidelines, procedures, language and direct political pressure (Finnemore & Barnett, 1999) (Finnemore, 1994).

The central argument of this book relies in disentangling the relationship between the normative constructions of modern development with the asymmetric settings of highly influential international organizations. In this endeavor, the study attempts to explain how conditions of political asymmetry boosted the characterization of fundamental representations of development within selected historical periods; normalizing critical arrangements with the production of a biased historical record. In attaining this objective, the study aims to shed lights on two fundamental dimensions of the discourse on development at the Bretton Woods Institutions; the thematization and topical structures of linguistic interventions, and the ideological dimension of normative constructions such as the norm on "modern development". In doing so, the case study aims to account empirically two questions:

A. Within historical interventions on "development", which normative constructions have been formalized along grey literature of these institutions on defined semantic fields/areas? How it is possible to account its historical evolution?
B. In addition to semantic evolutions or plain informational features, how can power relations be depicted, explained and contextualized within the progression of the norm historically?

WHY THE RECONSTRUCTION OF A NORM OF "MODERN DEVELOPMENT" IS IMPORTANT

The difficulties that national structures of governance had with keeping pace with the expanding spheres of political interaction aroused within globalization, led to functional gaps that were to be legally coped with private or specialized law[9]. After the Second World War, the most ambitious attempt to establish a common regulatory and institutional body, was reached through the foundation of the United Nations and the Bretton Woods Institutions (Eichengreen, 2004) (Boughton, 2002). The functional limitations of the international architecture, the unequal power relations (Lombardi, 2006) (Swedberg, 1986) (Mikesell, 1994) (Leech, 2003), and the historical events that surrounded the institutions during the second half of the 20th century (Eichengreen, 2004, p. 92) (Mikesell, 1994), increased the role of private or cognitively specialized law into global politics (Park & Vetterlein, 2010) (Finnemore & Sykkink, 2001). Such settings highlighted the influence of power and money as mediators of political interaction (Thacker, 1999) (Dreher et. al., 2010) (Rowlands & Bird, 2006), thus, the irruption in the political sphere of global institutions that besides regulating fragmented ranges of social relations -such as the economy, technology, science or intellectual property-, also embraced a normative quality, defining institutional paths of modernization and development of a highly uneven global arena. In such circumstances, within the normative dimension of contemporary private law, the Bretton Woods Institutions lead the path as creators of meaning nurtured from a defined epistemic community - the economy- (Vetterlein, 2010) (Vetterlein and others, 2010) (Escobar, 1995), normalizing arrangements otherwise rejected if suggested within symmetric political architectures.

STRUCTURE OF THE BOOK

This book is divided in two parts. The first section encompasses the necessary theoretical and methodological considerations to present a theory on "political asymmetry" and to further conduct research within these institutional conventions. It includes the definition and operationalization of the theory, the necessary ontological assumptions of the study of norms, the definition of the epistemological conventions of the book, and the methodology to conduct empirical research directed to reveal how asymmetries at the level of the Bretton Woods Institutions affect discursive and normative interventions. The second part of the book carries out the above-described conventions into a single qualitative and quantitative case study.

FIRST PART

Chapter one aims to disentangle the ontological dichotomies that problematize research directed to the study of norms. On the one hand it describes the limitations, resemblances and consequences branching out from the opposition between the two original ontological theoretical schools. On the other, it brings philosophy, and particularly the notion of historicity as a fundamental link amidst the two conflicting ontologies. It argues that both materialism and cultural subjectivism can be appropriately understood and bounded once they are contextualized historically within the above two ontological domains. Finally, it analyzes the consequences of this theoretical approach on research directed to reconstruct meaning of normative interventions on international relations and political science.

Chapter two introduces the concept of political asymmetry. It draws on contributions of critical constructivism to exemplify how in contemporary social systems, political asymmetry can be adequately grasped in the public domain. The first part of the chapter introduces ordinary approaches to the notion of symmetry, asymmetry and politics in dissimilar fields of science. The second part attempts to suggest a characterization of political asymmetry for further operationalization into political analysis. In conclusion, political asymmetry in contemporary social systems is given by the capacity of actors to formalize normative constructions into systemic structures (cognitive/informational system) and the capacity of actors operate within the system in accordance with the structure resources of base (resources of base such as culture and formal power).

Chapter three presents the theoretical approach to my dissertation project. It addresses the scope, strengths and limitations of current political theory to explain the development of the normative construction of "modern development" at international institutions, as well as offering a further conceptual framework to be implemented within the study. In modern late capitalist societies, the discourse on development has frequently entailed opposite narratives that ranges between an economic rationality, to an entirely moral one. While the economic approach sustains that economic growth and markets evolution allow higher stages of wealth and thus of overall material wellbeing as development; the moral one raises criticism about how the current model of modern development affects peripheral actors and interests. This discussion, I argue, has structural flaws that can be only grasped through studying "development" as a sociological and political category. In that sense, development is considered as a "norm" to be explored using a framework for political and discourse analysis. The section elaborates in a theoretical structure within which with the contributions of critical constructivism and historical institutionalism, inquiry over meaning of institutional narratives on the concept of "modern development" should be draw upon. Finally, it presents preliminary conventions to further explore how normative constructions such as "development" evolve into contexts pervaded by strong conditions of political asymmetry such as those taking place in the IMF or the World Bank.

Chapter four describes, explain, operationalize and contextualize, how critical discourse analysis, together with secondary approaches to qualitative and quantitative research; develops a coherent methodological resource for the enquiry of ideology and the political economy behind cultural normative constructions. The chapter focuses in carrying out this task within a suggested case study of discursive interventions at the level of institutions on defined historical periods. Moreover, it provides the method within which the study of the "norm of modern development" is to be conducted along the case study.

Chapter five operationalizes the concept of political asymmetry at the level of the Bretton Woods Institutions.

SECOND PART

Chapter six carries out the historical reconstruction of selected discursive interventions on the concept of "development" at the IMF and the WB. It also serves as a theoretical –research tool to analyze the role of political asymmetry on the evolution of ideological (chapter 7-8) and cognitive (chapter 9-10) constructions.

Chapter 7 reconstructs the social implications of the historical evolution of the norm of modern development within the three decades selected in the methodological section. It opens up with the chronological depiction of the norm of "modern development" over a global core and a periphery increasingly interdependent since the end of the Second World War, to further stress the similarities that take place within such ideological conventions in either capital importing or capital exporting nodes.

Chapter eight depicts the historical evolution of the ethical dimension of the norm, entrenched within the institutional approach to "Justice" at the level of the World Bank and the International Monetary Fund. The chapter explains the ideological foundation and more sophisticated development of such theoretical approach to justice, by bounding the evolution of this convention with more recent contributions in *contractualism* and public philosophy on law.

Chapter 9 and 10 operationalize the methodological approach to the study of the cognitive and informational evolution of the norm. As it is explained in detail in the methodological section, both final chapters aim to depict the two selected topical representations of discourse production over grey literature of the Bretton Woods institutions. For this section of the study, the book draw on two of the three main thematic spheres on "development" established on the institutional literature of the United Nations; material goals of signatories and environmental and systemic goals. This public policy and political fields are further used as the original framework for the idea of development by member organizations such as the World Bank and the International Monetary Fund. On chapter 9, the research focuses on the environmental field, by depicting the evolution of the semantic context of land and land acquisition within the normative construction of "modern development" since 1945. On chapter ten, the chapter analyses the role of corporations of the global south within the economic and institutional demands on "development" that both institutions stressed over the last seven decades.

REFERENCES

Ágh, A. (1998). *From Democratization to Modernization in Hungary: The Political Preconditions for the Full Membership in the European Union.* NATO Fellowships Programme 96-98.

Alonso, S. J. K. W. M. (2011). *Introduction. The Future of Representative Democracy.* Cambridge University Press. doi:10.1017/CBO9780511770883

Barnett & Duvall. (2005). Power in International Politics. *International Organization, 59*(1). doi:10.1017/S0020818305050010

Barro, R. J. a. J.-W. L. (2005). IMF Programs: Who Is Chosen And What Are The Effects?. *Journal of Monetary Economics, 52*, 1245-1269.

Bird, G., & Rowlands, D. (2006). D. a. G., 2006. IMF quotas: Constructin an international organization using inferior building blocks. *The Review of International Organizations, 1*(2), 153–171. doi:10.100711558-006-8342-x

Boughton, J. M. (2002). Why White, Not Keynes? Inventing the Postwar International Monetary System. (IMF Working Paper). IMF.

Buchanan, J. M. (1977). Democracy in Deficit: The Political Legacy of Lord Keynes. In *The Collected Works of James M. Buchanan in 20 vols* (pp. 1999–2002). Liberty Fund.

Deutch, J., Arnold, K., Ernest, M. & Daniel, P. (2004). Making the World Safe for Nuclear Energy. *Survival, 46*(4).

Dreher. (2010). *Do the IMF and the World Bank influence voting in the UN General Assembly.* Public Choice. . doi:10.1007/s11127-010-9750-2

Dunoff L, J. (2009). *RULING THE WORLD? Constitutionalism, International Law, and Global Governance.* Cambridge University Press.

Ehrenfeld, W. (2012). *Climate Innovation - The Case of the Central Chemical Industrie. April 2012. No. 2.* IWH-Diskussionspapiere.

Eichengreen, B. (2004). *Global Imbalances and the Lessons from Bretton Woods.* National Bureau of Economic Research.

Escobar, A. (1995). *Encountering Development. The making and unmaking of the third world.* Princeton University Press.

Escobar, A. (2008). The Problematization of Poverty; the tale of three worlds and development. In *The development reader* (pp. 131–140). MPG, Books Ltd. Bodmin.

Finnemore, M. (1994). International organizations as teachers of norms: the United Nations Educational, Scientific, and Cutural Organization and science policy. *Intemational Organization, 47*(4).

Finnemore & Barnett. (1999). The politics, power and pathologies of International Organizations. International Organization, 53.

Finnemore & Sykkink. (2001). TAKING STOCK: The Constructivist Research Programin International Relations and Comparative Politics. Annual Review of Political Science. Vol. 4: 391-416 (Volume publication date June 2001). DOI: doi:10.1146/annurev.polisci.4.1.391

Galbraith, J. K. (1988, April - June). 1998. The Political Asymmetry of Economic Policy. *Eastern Economic Journal, 14*(2), 125–128.

Haas, P. (1992). Introduction. Epistemic communities and international policy coordination. MIT Press. International Organization, Vol. 46, No. 1 [Online]. *Knowledge, Power, and International Policy Coordination*, (Winter), 1–35.

Habermas, J. (1984). *The Theory of Communicative Action, Volume 1: Reason and the Rationalization of Society. Translated by Thomas McCarthy. Boston: Beacon Press*, s.l.:s.n.

Hadi, M. A. (1998). *Dialogue on Jerusalem.* Palestinian Academic Society for the Study of International Affairs.

Keohane & Raustiala. (2008). *Toward a Post-Kyoto Climate Change Architecture: a Political Analysis.* The Harvard Project on International Climate Agreements.

Kitcher, P. (2001). *Science, Truth, and Democracy.* Oxford Studies in the Philosophy of Science. doi:10.1093/0195145836.001.0001

Leech, D. &. R. (2003). *Voting power in the Bretton Woods institutions.* In: Development Studies Association Conference, Glasgow, Scotland..

Lombardi, N. W. &. D. (2006). Uneven patterns of governance: how developing countries are represented in the IMF. *Review of International Political Economy, 13*(3), 480-515.

Mikesell, R. F. (1994). The Bretton Woods debates. A memoir. Essays in International Finance, 192.

Nandy, A. (1989). Science as a Reason of State. *Science as Culture, 1*(7), 69–83. doi:10.1080/09505438909526260

Park & Vetterlein. (2010). Do policy norms reconstitute global development? Owning Development: Creating Policy Norms in the IMF and the WB. Cambridge University Press.

Riles, A. (2010). *Collateral Expertise: Legal Knowledge in the Global Financial Markets.* The Wenner-Gren Foundation for Anthropological Research.

Rodrik, D. (2001). *Trading in Illusions.* Foreign Policy. *Washington post Newsweek Interactive, LLC.*

Sachs., W. (1993). Global Ecology and the Shadow of Development. *Global Ecology: A New Arena of Political Conflict. Zed Books.*

Srivastava, J. (2011). Norm "on Sustainable Development. Predicament and the Problematiqze. *India Quarterly: A Journal of International Affairs, 67*(2). doi:10.1177/097492841006700201

Stiglitz, J. (2003). *Globalization and Its Discontents.* Penguin.

Stiglitz, J. (2004). Capital-market Liberalization, Globalization, and the IMF. *Oxford Review of Economic Policy, 20*(1), 57–71. doi:10.1093/oxrep/grh004

Stiglitz, J. (2006). *Making Globalization Work*. W W. Norton & Company, Inc.

Sutcliffe, B. (2004). World Inequality and Globalization. Oxford University Press. . s.l.:s.n. doi:10.1093/oxrep/grh002

Swedberg, R. (1986). The Doctrine of Economic Neutrality of the IMF and the World Bank. *Journal of Peace Research, 23*(4), 377-390.

Thacker, S. C. (1999). The High Politics of IMF Lending. *World Politics, 52*(1), 38–75. doi:10.1017/S0043887100020025

Thomas, T. L. (2001). Academic journal article from Military Review, 81(4).

United Nations. (1983). *Process of preparation of the Environmental Perspective to the Year 2000 and Beyond*. UN.

United Nations. (2009). *Global Compact International Yearbook*. UN.

Vetterlein., & Associates. P. (2010). Owning Development: Creating Policy Norms in the IMF and the World Bank. Cambridge: Cambridge University Press.

Vetterlein, S. P. (2010). *Owning development: creating policy norms in the IMD and the World Bank*. World Bank.

Wade, R. H. (2003). *The World Trade Organization and the schrinking of the development space*. (Working Paper No.31). London School of Economics.

Wei, S. A. &. S.-J. (2006). *The WTO Promotes Trade, Strongly But Unevenly. January 12*. World Bank.

Womack, B. (2006). China and Vietnam: The Politics of Asymmetry. Cambridge University Press,.

Wray, B. (2001). *Science, Biases, and the Threat of Global Pessimism*. University of British Columbia.

ENDNOTES

1 Aka. Factual

2 I endorse to a rather broad definition of the concept of "structure", to differenciate it from the concept of system. When I speak about structure, I don´t only refer to the socially constructed patterns (culture), but also to physical contingencies of the environment that determine societal behaviour.

3 In an attempt to attribute to the concept of power a constructivist lens, Barnett defines it as "the production, in and through social relations, of *effects* that shape the capacities of actors to determine their circumstances and fate". Yet conflicting, such critical dimension of social systems is indeed one of the reasons by which the present book aims to create a bridge between the abovementioned two ontological positions. (Barnett & Duvall, 2005)

4 This view has been extensively documented both in social science as well as in recent international relations research. Such approach stresses the epistemic character of knowledge besides institu-

tional or structural provitions, making "ideas and experiences (…) shared and debated" composites "accross professional, ideological and political positions" (Escobar, 1995, p. 149) . On the role of epistemic communities in recent social science and international relations research, see specially (Haas, 1992). See also (Srivastava, 2011) (Riles, 2010).

5 In his criteria on international relations, asymmetry branches out into two basic theses; "first, that disparities in capacities create systemic differences in interests and perceptions between the stronger and weaker sides of the relationship. (…) Rather, mutual perceptions and interactions in an asymmetric relationship will be fundamentally shaped by the different situation of opportunity and vulnerability that each side confronts. (…) Second, although asymmetric relations are rarely unproblematic, they tend to be robust. "Stability" might not be the right word to describe asymmetry, because the differences in interests and perceptions between A and b are a constant source of tensions. (…) The learning process in an asymmetric relationship involves the acceptance of the relationship as normal" (Womack, 2006, p. 18)

6 This explains why Lenin´s or Wallerstein theories of critical hegemonies don't allow a higher understanding of the rationality behind the interaction.

7 ((Womack. 2006. P. 21.))

8 Created by the General Assembly in 1983 [Res.38/161] (United Nations, 1983), which coined the most recognized definition of sustainable development in the chapter "Our Common Future". Namely; "...the "environment" is where we live; and "development" is what we all do in attempting to improve our lot within that abode. The two are inseparable."

9 This evolution is clearly endorsed by a critical constructivist tradition that sustains that modern structures of consciousness are nurtured within the boundaries historically settled on private law. Historically, this process was institutionally endorsed by the three formal properties of such construction into contemporary structures of governance; positivity, legality and formality. (Habermas, 1984, p. 259). See (Dunoff L, 2009, p. 24) (Finnemore & Barnett, 1999)

Acknowledgments

The content of this book is highly indebted to the research on norms of the Centre for Globalization and Governance of the University of Hamburg, and particularly to the members of the Forschungskolloquium on Global Governance, Constitutionalism and World Society research area, leaded by Prof. Antje Wiener, PhD FAcSS. I want to also thank Prof. Dr. Anita Engels for her time and support as advisor. This book wouldn't have been possible without the support of the team of the Graduate School of the Faculty of economy and social sciences at the University of Hamburg, in charge of Dr. Ulf Beckmann. This book wouldn't also be possible without the support of Richard Rueda.

Chapter 1
Societal "Development" and the Ontological Assumptions for Exploration of Normative Meaning:
An Alternative Approach

ABSTRACT

Within the theory of political asymmetry, this chapter provides an alternative approach to the dilemma between constructivism and realism, so that further research on the idea of a norm on modern development can be coherently addressed. The chapter depicts features and common weaknesses of fundamental contributions on both schools on IR and political science theory, to further provide an alternative approach, able to contextualize along the ontological dilemma, the development of norms on late modern social systems.

INTRODUCTION

The present chapter drafts an alternative approach to the ontological dilemma between realism and constructivism by bounding them as composites of stages of social systems. The content is based on the fact that a common place on IR is to dispute about the ontological assumptions from which the study of normative meaning should be grasped theoretically. Such disagreements often define the ideological and political conventions from which social science research customarily draws conclusions and interpretations, stressing the fundamental opposition between the notion that norms are defined by the material environment -and therefore are natural or given-, or entirely social constructions. In this dilemma, if norms are entirely social constructions there should be a narrow scope for defending political positions that claim moral, intellectual, or political objectivity. Conversely, if the environment and the material

DOI: 10.4018/978-1-6684-9794-4.ch001

world are the substantive composite from which norms are constituted, the possibility of societies accepting "political perspectives" is out of the table, transforming politics into a zero-sum game.

International relations literature has made fundamental contributions to the study of this ontological dilemma -labeled as the "fourth debate"- and enhanced the antagonism between rationalist and constructivists[1] scholars (United Nations, 1983). Since rationalists lean toward positivism, they tend to stress the relevance of empirical methods directed at *explaining* political phenomena, boosting up theoretical doctrines such as realism and neorealism. Constructivists, in contrast, have argued that political interaction is shaped primarily by ideational factors (Finnnemore & Sikkink, 2001) "employing ontologies that invoke mutual constitution and transformation" and founded through historical processes of construction and reconstruction of shared beliefs (Farrel & Finnemore, 2009, p. 59). For the sake of this book, this ontological dilemma remains as a fundamental problem when speaking about the idea of the "development" of social systems or norms production; in any case, the question about the origin from which norms meaning arises remains.

When speaking about normative meaning, the chapter explains that while previous stages of social organization are characterized by a sense of formal systemic demands, later stages are characterized by increasing cognition about the social sphere and the inclusion of the *subjective experience* into the cognitive horizon of individuals. This explains why, in the first case, norms are prone to be raised within teleological representations about the contingencies of the material environment, making a materialist ontology decisive in defining boundaries to the *ecosistemic* nature of individuals. With the overcoming of systemic contingencies and the increasing overlap of processes of discursive negation concerning human nature, societies generate norms that overcome material boundaries, building up the "social" as a symbolic subjective expression and bringing into social systems a sense of historicity acquired through sophistication, which is nurtured by interaction in later stages of social organization. For this section of the chapter, meaning is the composite from which social relations and political interaction nurture, allowing actors to act together, based on common mutual assumptions and cognitive horizons[2] (Mendelson, 1979) As such, in the absence of a set of shared expectations, communication between actors is fruitless or broken, becoming a practice unable to maintain or retain what social systems built upon cognitive structures or values.

INTERNATIONAL RELATIONS, CONSTRUCTIVISM AND REALISM

Norms and IR Constructivism

Constructivist approaches to international relations and international politics have consistently shared a set of principles that bond their multifold perspectives in a well-defined theoretical school (Campbell, 1998) (Finnemore & Sykkink, 2001) (Finnemore, 1996) (Wiener, 2007) (Kratochwil, 2000) (Checkel, 1998). This approach is largely organized by the relevance that scholars give to the ideational factors in the process of production of a *norm*, as well as the roles that identity, socialization, contestation, and structure play in the life cycle of it. Martha Finnemore argues that what makes constructivism effective as a method of social analysis lays in the outstanding relevance of culture, identities and ideas,[3] yet, when it comes with the definition of methods of empirical scrutiny to clarify clear cut differentiations between actors, or to suggest measurable tendencies or normative outcomes in regard with their behavior, she personally stresses the boundaries of her own analysis (Finnemore & Sikkin, 1998, p. 898). In her view,

"Constructivism does not (…) make any particular claims about the content of social structures or the nature of agents at work in social life. Consequently, it does not, by itself, produce specific predictions about political outcomes that one could test in social science research" (Finnnemore & Sikkink, 2001, p. 2). Addressing these challenges has become a fundamental source of theoretical and methodological discussion, drawing even on Foucault´s power theory, communicative action theory, organizational behavior or agency, and culture, among others[4] (Finnnemore & Sikkink, 2001, p. 4).

Most recently, an increasing amount of social science research has adopted the relevance of intersubjectivity and cultural backgrounds as fundamental sources of meaning for assessing behavior[5] (Checkel, 1998), reducing the influence that utilitarian[6] or goal-oriented conducts of agents have in defining decisions (Steinhoff, 2009) (Niiniluoto, 1991) (Srivastava, 2011). This is how, in this regard, decisions are deeply embedded on ideological or ideational frontiers, built upon the context, information, language, the cultural environment of the subject. This creates institutional or organizational culture, and opposes the applicability of modern institutionalist perspectives that highlight the fact that institutions -particularly international institutions- were prone to be aseptic to any influence of cultural or subjective rationality, due to their formal bureaucratic[7] (Thelen, 1999) (Finnnemore & Sikkink, 2001) (Finnemore, 1996).

While "conventional wisdom" asserts that "bureaucratic organization was seen as the only way to divide labor, specify responsibilities, and institutionalize coordination and decision making in rational and efficient ways", the alternative explanation argues that they "exist, proliferate, and have the form they do not because they are efficient but because they are externally legitimated"[8] (Finnemore, 1996). In this fashion, the path taken by the constructivist approach has turned to the analysis of the evolution, spreading and development of international organizations from an historical and cultural perspective, addressing for instance, in terms of the development of social systems, normative values of late modern societies expanded in relatively short periods of time through the reproduction of institutional practices.

"The Western cultural agenda of promoting expanding gross national product and equality through expanding and deepening bureaucracies and markets has spread to dominate global political and social life over the past several centuries. One prominent artifact of Western cultural dominance is the organization of the world into Western-style bureaucratic states"… "(…) one central feature of Western culture is the value it places on rationality and purposive action. By rationality, institutionalisms mean simply the structuring of action in terms of ends and means"[9] (Finnemore, 1996).

Assumptions such as this have been further endorsed on studies conducted by Campbell and Barnett[10] (Campbel, 2002) (Campbell, 1998) (Barnett & Duvall, 2005), who concluded that dynamics of norms diffusion can be very well distinguished in the behavior of international organizations such as the Word Bank and the International Monetary Fund, who act as norms transmitters to less developed economies. Moreover, in advanced stages of international coordination, aside from being granted with a regulatory and political authority to steer relations of the international system, institutions embraced the role of being actors of cultural diffusion within members. This is why institutions, aside from managing functional spheres of the economic system, performed "a major role in arbitrating the meaning of development and norms of behavior appropriate to the task of developing oneself"[11] (Finnemore & Barnett, 1999, p. 714).

One of the most relevant studies conducted to analyze how institutions and norms spread internationally, was conducted by Martha Finnemore[12], who sought to define the history of how the United Nations "educational, scientific and cultural organization and science policy" spread (Finnemore, 1994). She detailed how external pressure from international organizations played an outstanding role in the choices made by regimes influenced by these organizations. Such findings shed lights on the role played by UNESCO, in emphasizing guidelines, policies and recommendations to be exerted in numerous countries, despite displacing the agenda that low budget regimes possessed internally. In conclusion, while institutions such as UNESCO were originally constituted to serve science and scientists all over the world, its influence was further bounded with the implementation of predefined structures of organization among very different national systems. In this case, the history of this shift includes marginalizing local agendas that frequently listed much more compelling priorities[13] (Finnemore, 1994).

As far as international norms are fundamentally embodied in agendas and institutions, ideas about the impartiality of norms lose strength, due to the conditions in which they evolve to conform shared beliefs. In this fashion, constructivists -rather than suggesting directions toward which the behavior of actors should point - take part in setting the fundamental relevance of the historical and political context in which meaning spreads. This is how rather than functional or teleological goals, institutions embrace as customary praxis an organizational culture, "understood as the rules, rituals, and beliefs that are embedded in the organization [with] important consequences for the way individuals who inhabit the organization make sense of the world" (Finnemore & Barnett, 1999, p. 719). Finally, this shift explains the difficulty in attributing to contemporary institutions and international norms, a character of universalism that they frequently claimed to embrace discursively.

In contrast, the capacity for constructivist literature to highlight the role of culture as a *leit motiv* for action has questioned the controversial assumptions of realists[14]. This is how rationalist or positivist assumptions that tended exclusively to suggest the pivotal role carried by "objective" predictions under defined political circumstances, have recently lost strength by means of sociological inquiry. On the other hand, while the findings of constructivism have been able to raise awareness about the role of subjectivity and culture in the definition of normative meaning, one cannot isolate the difficulties of this theoretical paradigm in demonstrating a clear differentiation about what can be considered *true* or *false* scientific analysis, so this is a major weakness[15] of the approach (Niiniluoto, 1991).

Defining the ontological assumptions of the meaning of norms is in fact the capacity of societies to give an explanation about the origin of knowledge and the course of politics. In this endeavor, constructivism has endorsed this challenge by enhancing the relevance of the social environment in which knowledge is created, diluting the idea of behavior or meaning as a rational composite redeemable by empirical analysis. In contrast with an empiricist tradition, it argues that the discussion about the meaning of fundamental norms, has to be done in light of the cultural background of the actors that make use of them. Thus, they don't only create meaning by shaping norms but also by interpreting them[16] (Wiener, 2008) (Wiener & Pueter, 2009). As such, norms only have not only an active attribute -in the sense that they tend to regulate or to dictate the behavior of those they are expected to affect-, but also have a passive role in which actors *read between their lines* in accordance with a pre-defined cultural background. Norms are also constituted through the behavior of the community which is embracing them or towards which the norm is addressed or forcefully exerted. This means that the constitutive character of the norm is built upon the asymmetric perspectives of those who collectively construct the meaning-baggage of it. Most recently, in this fashion, the idea of contestation has become a fundamental component of the process of construction and legitimation (Wiener, 2014). While difficult to distinguish from the other stages upon which norms are validated by dialogical interaction, *contestedness* represents a phase of reinforcement or legitimation of normative meaning beyond customary social feedback. Hence, there are three fundamental scenarios in which norms meaning is enhanced through this medium; first, when in times of crisis social feedback is reduced yet norms are capable enough of being considered as social institutions; second, in scenarios in which their meanings persist upon processes of change of governance; and third, when they remain relevant beyond historical contingencies (Wiener, 2007, p. 7). In this approach, by virtue of contestation, the assumption that norms are only customary constructions loses strength. In contrast, the persistence of the norms and the development of their meaning are shared by traditions and perspectives in permanent transformation.

On a transnational level, this feature is reinforced by the fact that, while norms are supposed to be universal, in local arenas, they are constituted through cultural and legal practices meshed with international or global principles (Burca, 2009). Conversely, the validity of the international norm is not *given* according to the interpretation or suggestion of one or another cultural group. Instead, an international norm constitutes itself, and remains relevant due to its capacity of lasting in scenarios in which diverse cultural perspectives collaborate on its meaning. As it has been described by Wiener, "While in supranational contexts actors might well agree on the importance of a particular norm (…) the agreement about a kind of norm does not allow for conclusions about the meaning of that very norm. As in different domestic contexts, that meaning is likely to differ according to experience with norm-use" (Wiener, 2007, p. 12).

Indeed, the relevance of constructivism is two-fold: first, its capacity for settling the middle point between polarized ontological IR theory, dismantling the weaknesses of realism for addressing the relevance of the cultural background as an attributor of norm meaning; second, the rejection of reflectivism in digging into empirical research[17]. As previously explained, the approach can be depicted by stressing three fundamental features; first,

…"a preference of ontology over epistemology, second, a distinction from the incommensurable positions of rationalism and reflectivism yet the ability to engage in talk with both, and, third, the variation in preferences for methodological tools (e.g. identity, speech-act, learning, persuasion, discourse) (….) [K]eep[ing] a distance from the poles, they allow for variation amongst themselves, and they share the crucial role of ontology" (Thomas & Knud Erik Jørgensen, 2001, p. 11).

These distinctions do not imply that constructivists are not prone to argue with regard to the plausibility of the assumptions of actors concerning the outside world; instead, the focus of the approach is keen to assign logical, empirical, or persuasive plausibility to some interpretations rather than others[18] (Finnnemore & Sikkink, 2001). Finally, aiming to be located between two ontological poles -exclusive material assumptions and all social assumptions (Wiener, 2006) - this distinctive feature of the approach cannot exclude the fact that some authors simply consider it as a branch of *reflectivist* perspectives at the pole of rationalism or realism[19] (Schouten, 2008).

Realism and the Source of Normative Meaning

Realist approaches are keen to give theoretical validity to the assumption that the meaning of a norm is attributed to material circumstances; thus meaning can be derived from the permanent link between the material outside world and the rationalization of *objective* externalities. Realism dates back to the end of the Second World War, where the influence of the Soviet Union in the post war period, generated anxieties about how ideas highlighted in the public domain would help to reformulate the dominant approaches to international relations and international politics. In such historical settings, defined faculties lead the reformulation of the realist traditions to the study of bipolar IR theory in opposition to the idealist perspectives that dominated the field during the first decades of the 20th century. At the time, postwar statements about the role of international politics were very clear in sustaining the idea that additional international scientific branches were required to provide something of "interest" to the former global tension. Moreover, the worries also relied upon the necessity of reconstructing political science as an academic field open to the claims of scholars who argue against the common "antipositivist and antitechnocratic impetus behind IR" (Guilhot, 2008, p. 283).

An important milestone in this conversation was a series of regional conferences organized by the Council on Foreign Relations in April and May 1946[20] *(...) whose conclusions were summarized in a volume later published by Grayson Kirk (1947(...)characterized by its criticism of the infatuation of academics with Wilsonianism: (in which) a ''disproportionate amount of time and energy was given to discussion 'international cooperation, (...) It certainly emboldened the active minority that opposed the widespread acceptance of value-relativism and rationalism in the study of politics that resulted from the methodological subordination of IR to other disciplines (Guilhot, 2008, p. 289).*

Such circumstances outlined the ideological trends that shaped International Relations theory since the post war period, leading to a theoretical division between "scientific" and "idealist" internationalism. While the former claimed the urgency for setting rigorous empirical methods capable of disentangling the fundamental motivations of the human being, and predicting universal properties of societies by scientific enquiry, the second embraced a tradition nurtured through theories of the surrounding behavioral sciences. After the Second World War however, political realism became the representative of a new widespread positivism, and indeed, the single most fundamental theoretical shift in understanding 20th century United States politics.

The Realist Agenda

For realism, the cultural context from which a claim is uttered lacks the relevance customarily embraced by constructivist analysis. In contrast, realism suggests that empirical methods and research on objective causations are methodological instruments capable of describing the paths of human rationality. This focus embraces the conviction that knowledge, and therefore meaning, arouses from the material environment and is discovered by the cognition rather than interpreted or constructed through socialized inquiry and analysis. This helped realism to explain human behavior as a natural ego-oriented pattern of conduct, and, therefore, the source from which normative meaning nurtures. Concerning international relations, realism has settled upon two core ideological traditions; individualism and materialism (Wendt, 1999, p. 3). Individualism has been attributed to the influence of economic conventions of maximization and rationality. Therefore, as humans in an environment of scarcity tend to rationalize their behavior and to maximize transaction relations in the economic sphere, states behave following this same criteria. In this manner, state behavior appears as a permanent condition of rationalization of choices under conditions of scarcity, maximizing the outcome in accordance with the settings of the environment. This focus stresses the role of individualism on International Relations, relying on the dominium of power and interests as fundamental *leitmotiv* for state behavior. Such assumptions endorse a rather new theoretical conception of the original framework of individualism, meaning that processes of decision-taking in the national sphere, are permanently disposed to making use of a conduct prone to accumulate power through permanent stages of bargaining. "Interests" therefore –as the vector orienting goals-, supposes for realists not only a reinforcement of a self-benefit rationality but also a fundamental assumption to quantify outcomes of human patterns or social behavior. Relying upon the conviction that behavior can not only be reduced but also measured, estimated and quantified; realist inquiry customarily justifies the application of empirical quantitative tools in social analysis, a turn that has boosted a bifurcation in transatlantic social science inquiry.

Since material conditions represent a highly influential variable in the behavior of the state, material capabilities and the search for them exemplify the single most fundamental direction in the process of construction of normative meaning. For the realist, the cultural context is not the core assumption of state or human behavior; in this fashion, power determines the set of goal oriented values that will constitute the ontological source of normative meaning. While structures can be seen as a complex mixture of cultures, ideas or historical transitions, neorealism may view them as outsources of historical bargaining of material forces, implying the erosion of the social context within which communities built institutions up, and giving "claims for power", attributes of meaning creation.

Realism steps out from the legalist tradition that continued to characterize political science in the beginning of the 20th century. This feature remains for decades, even after the formalization of relevant international political institutions such as "international arbitration, customary law, and disarmament and peace conferences"[21] (Boyle, 1999.) (Guilhot, 2008, p. 290). It claims that, as political culture, legal culture tends to a *value-laden relativism* that prevented the social science from establishing differentiations between political systems. Thus "a true science did not pronounce upon ultimate ends, only on the causal sequences allowing for their realization. As long as science was considered to be part of a modernizing historical process that could be described as progress, value-relativism *[was]* not an issue" (Guilhot, 2008, p. 285).

When it comes to ontology, in opposition to constructivism, realism´s assumptions are not prone to conceive an interaction between actors based on mutual consensus, but, instead, they are mainly based on forms of reification of the other. This assumption suggests that "consensus", as a mechanism by which norms on the international sphere gain validity, are prone to be subjected to a predetermined material structure. In such a view, normative meaning exists even before the community discusses or reaches agreements about what is *normative* by social inquiry. For them, "the construction of new physical phenomena in a laboratory is not a social construction, since the potential for their existence 'has always been there… [so] all theoretical statements and beliefs about reality are always conjectural" (Niiniluoto, 1991, p. 148).

While recent decades have seen the origin of norms branching out in scholarly approaches incompatible with one another, the definition of the ontological source of normative meaning remains fragmented. The strong theoretical differentiation between the two traditions advances a dilemma that has implications not only for scientific research, but also for political analysis. Whereas most part of the 20th century saw scientific inquiry directed to constitute a theoretical structure from which international relations and international politics should contribute to the understanding of the outside world; the conflicting claims of moral relativism endorsed by the realist perspective generated an unexpected division, both theoretically and geographically. This is why current mainstream realist studies come from the United States.

Rationality and History

The *social*, as the dimension in which human subjectivities take place, is the representation of the historical project of societies to operationalize overlapped stages of cognition. If societies lose their constitutive traditions, or the cognitive abridgements from which they nurtured cognitively, they lose meaning, and therefore embrace an historical setback. With growing levels of information and social complexity, communicative action becomes a fundamental necessity for systemic preservation and reproduction. This is why the inclusion of subjectivities, rather than being an isolated practice in modern social organization, becomes a customary demand of almost all societies, frequently enjoined into the system through mechanisms of public debate, deliberation and participation. Modern structures of social organization, due to systemic necessities of reproduction, are prone to being constituted through cooperation and reason rather than ceremonial, metaphysical or supernatural practices[22] (Habermas, 1984, p. 52). The praxis of dialogical agreements over time, constitutes patterns formally endorsed as normative. Contrariwise, rules, principles of organization, or institutions erected by different channels than communicative action, tend to be highly contested if spaces of deliberation offer the possibilities of doing so. On the other hand, norms within historical stages of societies, tend to be adopted as legitimate as they cope with autonomous expectations of individuals. Embraced between two ontological opposites, they divide the sphere of the formal systemic reality with the individual as a member of a society. While teleological action defines the boundaries through which social organization don't threatens its systemic reproduction; communicative rationality and dialogue ensure the paths through which the individual enhance its role within the social dimension. This is why just societies that have overcome the contingencies of the environment are capable enough of setting normative agreements from which actors can recognized themselves as member of a social sphere. Manifestations like justice, righteousness, solidarity, liberty, equality, fairness, and complex ethical presuppositions are therefore ontologically constructed *socially. History* sets the path that belongs to the relation of teleological reflection to dialogical interaction. While the first recreates itself upon a physical universe gradually discovered through information about the objective world, the second is constructed upon permanent processes of representation and mutual understanding of individuals as members of the social sphere. In contemporary societies, this last task is fulfilled by subsystems of knowledge that compile, reproduce and codify this information with increasing levels of (sub)systemic sophistication.

The Modern Society

Increasing levels of sophistication can only be reached by encompassing previous historical processes of coordination. This knot presents fundamental pathologies in modern societies in which spheres of communication have been replaced by economic and functional power imperatives. As such, current institutional arrangements look to steer these pathologies through the institutionalization of the political sphere[23]. While *de facto* institutions contain the levels of conflict produced in the social sphere, they don't necessarily guarantee the fulfillment of the demands that arise from subjective experiences of cognition.

In the case of higher contestation concerning normative meaning, modern societies tend to overcome political tension via law[24] (Habermas, 1996, p. 40).

"The development of the constitutional state can be understood as an open sequence of experience-guided precautionary measures against the overpowering of the legal system by illegitimate power relations that contradict its normative self- understanding. From inside the legal system, this appears as an external relation between facticity and validity, the familiar tension between norm and reality that again and again provokes a normative response. Modern societies are integrated not only socially through values, norms, and mutual understanding, but also systemically through markets and the administrative use of power."[25] (Habermas, 1996, p. 40)

At the point in which societies acquire higher levels of complexity, and must therefore coordinate the evolution of professional and scientific knowledge with the demands of subjective experiences, institutionalization of meaning through law, replace mechanisms of communicative rationality and action. If mechanisms of reproduction of the normative constitutive traditions -as well as the cognitive abridgment that conforms the social sphere- can't overcome the demands of the complexity of the environment, meaning of norms concerning the social sphere diffuses into systemic contingencies.

Figure 1. Relevance of subjective representations

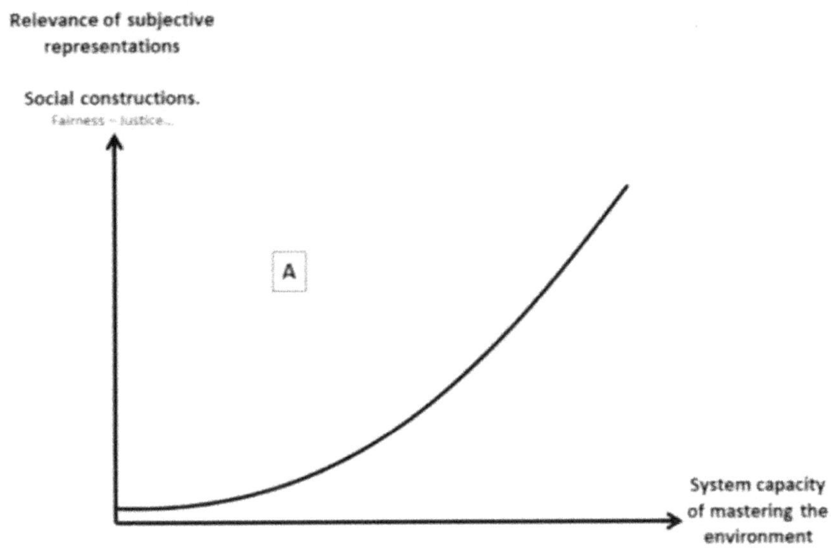

Figure 2. Relevance of systemic demands

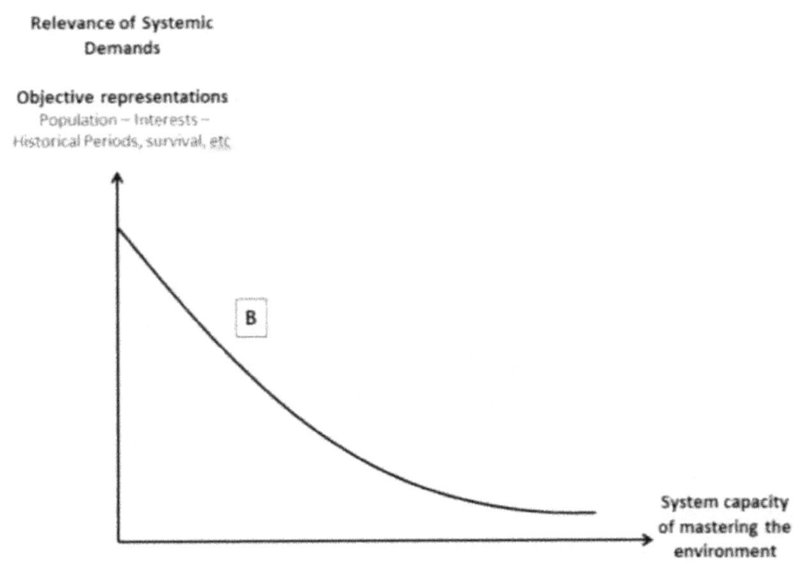

In this setting, social progression develops through increasing stages of mutual understanding between individuals once contingencies of the structure or the environment are overcome. It is upon this condition that the ontological substrate of normative meaning in higher historical stages of social evolution, replaces formal systemic representations by each time more complex symbolic subjective expressions. The capacity of societies of master the environment or to steer structural material boundaries, enables the construction of the identity of the individual beyond de facto contingencies. The economic structure, the behavior associated with an instinctive nature, relations of power aroused under conditions of political asymmetry, overexploitation relations, resource crisis, and cognitive limitations about the outside world, are phenomena prone to being isolated and replaced by either political, ethical, and social claims for higher stages of coordination and organization; or agreements about the definition of the "living experience". Four fundamental assumptions about these phenomena can be suggested.

First, that processes of contestation of norms that take place in political arenas, rather than being a concern for realist assumptions, represent, in fact, a natural transition of societies from stages in which both subjective experiences and rationality prone to being cognitively constructed by social consensus were excluded. Second, contemporary cognitive and political settings on subsystems of organization have a fundamental role in defining the ontological subtract from which norms are nurtured. From and historical perspective, one can suggest that, organizational asymmetries rather than being a de facto contingency of societies, represent weaknesses of social environments in which processes of a rationality prone to communicative action are not yet exercised. Third; that social systems with asymmetrical subsystems of organization, in which subjective experiences are marginalized through institutional and political practices, represent distorted or undeveloped stages of normative meaning. Finally; if development of societies from an historical perspective, is determined by stages of maturation of dialogical interaction, it is just upon effective practices of public rational debate that one can suggest the development of a society, rather than by structural (institutional) or systemic guidelines. It is not the goal of the present section to elaborate these four suggestions, but it is important to bear in mind that the present approach understands the fact that, contemporary schools of thought in which social and cultural backgrounds are increasingly being influential, rather than being an academic or theoretical phenomena, are an unavoidable historical one.

CONCLUSION

In the present section we have elaborated theoretical and philosophical discussions concerning the ontology of normative meaning and the idea of societal development. From the beginning, two opposite schools of international politics and international relations were to be approached, realism, and constructivism. We have described how the role of actors in the process of construction of normative meaning, rather than being an isolated practice, represents a continuous, highly influential parameter that is increasingly covered through social research. Moreover, we have asserted, that in international relations and international politics, this role has been highly externalized in the figure of international institutions, due to their highly influential spheres of action, and these have settled what is and what is not to be considered appropriate normative behavior. We have contrasted how constructivism, rather than being an opposite of realism, has served as a linking point between materialist, and ideational/social ontologies. Finally, we have briefly described some fundamental assumptions that belong to the sphere of the realist school.

In an effort to elucidate more clearly the distinctions between the two schools, we have preliminarily reflected on how the role of actors distorts the traditional consistency in which classical typologies of norms theoretically rested. In this regard, we have analyzed to what extent, social and individual behavior serve as the fundamental link between materialist and social ontological assumptions. Finally, we have explored how, in the process of norms construction, actors operate both upon material/cognitive and cultural boundaries. This has been done by analyzing three theoretical contemporary contributions; 1) Finnemore, 2) Wiener and 3) Steve Smith, Patricia Owens, Wendt and Wight. Whereas we agree that the role of actors is relevant in all approaches, our conclusion is that, while positivist perspectives are based on processes of empirical induction through which normative meaning is revealed, there is no contemporary agreement about the existence of a category to validate cultural and cognitive constructions. It is upon this condition that we suggest Habermas framework of communicative action to suggest a theory of rationality. Embracing the role of communication upon an historical structure, we explored the possibility of assigning a direction to normative constructions and normative meaning. Our conclusions are that:

A. Norms are a function of information. Information interpreted by individuals is always codified. Codification takes places via symbolic subjective expressions (social sphere) or formal scientific information about the outside world (material sphere).
B. In low stages of social organization, systemic interests are established by the demands of the environment. Survival, reproduction, offspring protection, risk of starvation, health maintenance, and customary behavior are constitutive of an ecosystem pattern, rather than a socially-constructed agreement. Through communicative interaction, social groups set systemic goals. Mastery over the environment becomes the single most important object subject correlation. Social demands are displaced by formal systemic exigencies. Norms are constituted upon material contingencies. Higher stages of social organization are outcomes of communicative interaction. Mastery over the structure demands increasing the validation of subjectivities. Individual concerns regarding norms of social organization are taken into account. Communicative action replaces teleological rationality, and norms increasingly acquire social, rather than systemic character.
C. *Complex symbolic subjective expressions* take place in the social sphere. Subjective expression can only be interpreted through communicative interaction. On the other hand, formal scientific information about the outside world is teleologically codified sub-systemically. Subjectivities, negation (critizability, contestedness, validity claims), and formally codified information about the outside world, increases the cognitive horizon of societies. The increasing of the cognitive horizon of societies determines a path of historical evolution -*development*-. With the professionalization and codification of information about the outside world, norms are increasingly constituted by agreements between individuals, and formal systemic contingencies are displaced by social demands.
D. A sense of history of societies is given by the inclusion of processes of rationalization that take into account knowledge organized systemically about previous stages of cognition. Modern societies generate subsystems of conservation of previous stages of cognition by professionalizing codification and scientific organization of knowledge. Societies that are highly affected by the limitations of the environment, or by formal systemic structures, are prone to displacing the relevance of the information that is raised upon subjectivities of the social sphere by institutional mechanisms of definition of normative arrangements. In the event in which communicative interaction is deterred by higher stages of social complexity, systemic measures are fundamentally prone to institutionalize normative arrangements via law. Finally, institutions in modern, highly complex environments are

to replace the public sphere by standardized meaning and professionalized/institutional procedures, rather than communication. This last shift, following the above-mentioned conditions, rather than being a step forward in the process of modernization, represents a fundamental weakness of arrangements settled in asymmetric agent environments.

E. With a framework on the progression of the material and ideational sphere of social systems, normative interventions are ontologically indebted to the interrelation between communicative and goal-oriented practices of rationalization. Interrelation is embedded within a sense of history whose meaning is defined by the role of formal subsistemic constrains such as political organizations, and social demands along processes of communication and coordination.

REFERENCES

Barnett & Duvall, M. (2005). *Power in International Politics, 59*(1). Cambridge. , doi:10.1017/S0020818305050010

Brown, V. (2011). *The Reflectivist Critique of Positivist IR Theory*. Cardiff University. http://www.e-ir.info/2011/02/27/the-reflectivist-critique-of-positivist-ir-theory/.

Burca, G. d. (2009). The European Court of Justice and the International Legal Order After Kadi. [s.l.:s.n.]. *Harvard International Law Journal, 1*(51).

Campbel, J. L. (2002). Ideas, politics, and public policy. [s.l.:s.n.]. *Annual Review of Sociology, 28*(1), 21–38. doi:10.1146/annurev.soc.28.110601.141111

Campbell, J. L. (1998). *No. 3 (Jun., 1998)* (Vol. 27). Institutional Analysis and the Role of Ideas in Political Economy. Theory and Society. Springer. https://www.jstor.org/stable/657900

Checkel, J. (1998, January). The Constructivist turn in International Relations Theory. Review Article. *World Politics, 50*, 324–348. doi:10.1017/S0043887100008133

Farrel & Finnemore. (2009, February). Ontology, methodology and causation in the American school of international political economy. George Washington University,Washington, DC, USA. *Review of International Political Economy, 16*(1), 58–71.

Finnemore, M. (1994). International organizations as teachers of norms: the United Nations Educational, Scientific, and Cutural Organization and science policy. *International Organization, 47*(4), 565-597.

Finnemore, M. (1996). Norms,culture, and world politics: insights from sociology's institutionalism. *Intemational Organization 50*(2).

Finnemore & Barnett. (1999). The politics, power and pathologies of International Organizations. International Organization, 53(4).

Finnemore & Sikkin. (1998). International Norm Dynamics and Political Change. *International Organization 52*(4).

Finnemore & Sykkink. (2001). TAKING STOCK: The Constructivist Research Programin International Relations and Comparative Politics. Annual Review of Political Science, 4, 391-416 doi:10.1146/annurev.polisci.4.1.391

Gibbs, J. P. (1965). *No. 5 (Mar. 1965)* (Vol. 70). Norms: The Problem of Definition and Clasiffication. American Journal of Sociology. The University of Chicago Press. https://www.jstor.org/stable/2774978

Guilhot, N. (2008). The realist Gambit: Postwar American Political Science and the Birth of IR Theory. International Studies Association. *International Political Sociology*, *2*(4), 281–304. doi:10.1111/j.1749-5687.2008.00052.x

Haas, P. (1992). Introduction. Epistemic communities and international policy coordination. *International Organization*, 46(1), 1–35.

Habermas, J. (1984). The Theory of Communicative Action, Volume 1: Reason and the Rationalization of Society. [T. McCarthy, trans.]. Boston: Beacon Press.

Habermas, J. (1985). Theory of communicative action.: Vol. 2. *Lifeworld and System. A critique of functionalist reason* [T. McCarthy, Trans.]. Beacon Press.

Habermas, J. (1996). Between Facts and Norms. Contributions to a Discourse Theory of Law and Democracy. [W. Rehg, trans.] Massachusetts Institute of Technology. doi:10.7551/mitpress/1564.001.0001

Habermas, J. (1996). *Habermas Jürgen. Between Facts and Norms. Contributions to a Discourse Theory of Law and Democracy*. Massachusetts Institute of Technology. doi:10.7551/mitpress/1564.001.0001

Habermas, J. (2008). Freedom and Determinism. In *Between Naturalism and Religion: Philosophical Essays. Ciaran Cronin (trans.)*. Polity Press.

Kant, I. (1793). *Prolegomena*. University of Washington.

Kojeve, A. (1969). *Introduction to the reading of Hegel*. [J. H. Nichols. Jr., trans.]. Cornell University Press.

Kratochwil, D. (2000). Constructing a New Orthodoxy? Wendst's Social Theory of International Politics and the Constructivist Challenge. Milennium. *Journal of International Students*, *29*, 73.

Lawson, G., (2012). The eternal divide?: history and International Relations. *European journal of International Relations.*

Mendelson, J. (1979). The Habermas-Gadamer Debate. *New German Critique, 18,* 44–73. . doi:10.2307/487850

Morris, R. T. (1956). A typology of Norms. *American Sociological Review, 21*(5), 610-613. American Sociological Association. https://www.jstor.org/stable/2089098.

Niiniluoto, I. (1991). *No. 1. Scientific knowledge and Scientific Practice (Oct., 1991)* (Vol. 89). Realism, relativism and constructivism. Synthese. Springer.

O'Neill Surber, J. P. (2003). The "End of History" Revisited: Kantian Reason, Hegelian Spirit, and the History of Philosophy. In Hegel's History of Philosophy. New Interpretations. State University of New York Press.

Passmore, J. (1965). *The idea of a history of philosophy. History and Theory: The historiofraphy of the historiy of philosophy.* Wiley-Blackwell for Wesleyan University.

Schouten, P. (2008). 'Theory Talk #3: Alexander Wendt on UFO's, Black Swans and Constructivist International Relations Theory.' *Theory Talks.* http://www.theory-talks.org/2008/04/theory-talk-3.html.

Srivastava, J., 2011. *Norm" on Sustainable Development. Predicament and the Problematiqze. India Quarterly: A Journal of International Affairs June 2011 vol. 67 no. 2. 93-110..* s.l.:s.n. doi:10.1177/097492841006700201

Steinhoff, U., 2009. *"Communicative" versus Purposive Rationality. 2009 Print ISBN-13: 9780199547807 Published to Oxford Scholarship Online: September 2009 DOI: ..* s.l.:s.n. doi:10.1093/acprof:oso/9780199547807.001.0001

Thelen, K. 1999. "Historical Institutionalism in Comparative Politics" edited by Sven Steinmo, Kathleen Thelen, and Frank Longstreth. Annual Review of Political Science 2(1):369–404. Retrieved (https://www.annualreviews.org/doi/abs/10.1146/annurev.p

Thomas, C. (2001). *Knud Erik Jørgensen, u. A. W., 2001. The Social Construction of Europe*. SAGE.

Thompson, K. (2003). Systematicity and Experience: Hegel and the Function of the History of Philosophy. In.*Hegel's History of Philosophy. New Interpretations.* State University of New York Press.

United Nations. (1983). *Process of preparation of the Environmental Perspective to the Year 2000 and Beyond.* Resolution 38 / 161. UN.

Wendt, A. (1999). Social Theory of International Politics. *Social Theory of International Politics.* Cambridge University Press. doi:10.1017/CBO9780511612183

Wiener, A. (2006). Constructivist Approaches in International Relations Theory: Puzzles and Promises. *The Constitutionalism Web-Paper.* University of Bath, Department of European Studies and Modern Languages. http://ideas.repec.org/p/erp/conweb/p0025.htm

Wiener, A. (2007). *Constructivist Approaches in International Relations Theory: Puzzles and Promises Constitutionalism Webpapers, ConWEB No 5/2006.* Queen's University Belfast.

Wiener, A., (2007). *Contested Meanings of Norms: A Research Framework. Comparative European Politics.* Palgrave Macmillan.

Wiener, A. (2007). The Dual Quality of Norms and Governance beyond the State: Sociological and Normative Approaches to 'Interaction'. *Critical Review of International Social and Political Philosophy, 10*(1), 47-69.

Wiener, A. (2008). *The invisible constitution of politics. Contested norms and international encounters. Cambridge University Press.* Cambridge.

Wiener, A. (2008). The Invisible Constitution of Politics. Contested Norms and International Encounters. Cambridge University Press. doi:10.1017/CBO9780511490408

Wiener, A. (2014). *A Theory of Contestation.* Springer Berlin Heidelberg.

Wiener & Pueter. (2009). The quality of Norms is what actors make of it. Critical constructivism research on norms. *Journal of International Law and International Relations, 5*(1).

ENDNOTES

1 Sometimes referred to as "The Third Great Debate" in the literature by authors rejecting the previous inter-paradigm debate as a Great Debate.

2 I make use of the concepts of cognitive or informational „horizon" not to parafrase Gadamer´s hermeneutic horizon. Yet in the process of reconstruction of meaning, a fundamental condition is determined by the role traditions play in the knower interpretation. See (Mendelson, 1979).

3 In the scope of the relevance of ideas, it is worth to mention her references about the binding relations of ideational shared believes. In her studies concerning the motivations behind norm entrepreneurship, his view is focused on demonstrating the greater relevance of common ideological views. "Ideational commitment is the main motivation when entrepreneurs promote norms or ideas because they believe in the ideals and values embodied in the norms, even though the pursuit of the norms may have no effect on their well-being" (Finnemore & Sikkin, 1998, p. 898)

4 "To frame research designs on these questions, scholars have supplemented constructivism's minimalist social-theoretic claims with a variety of more specific, often more substantive, theories about the mutual constitution process and the behavior that results from it (...)Constructivists are skeptical about claims to all-encompassing truth [what Price& Reus-Smit (1998) call "Big-T" claims] and instead produce and evaluate "small-t" contingent claims". On (Finnnemore & Sikkink, 2001, p. 4).

5 On the historical process of the event, see (Checkel, 1998).

6 On the debate between rationalities, see for example (Steinhoff, 2009) (Niiniluoto, 1991). On the effects of the problematization of phenomena's, in accordance with different cultural and professional cognitions upon given normative issues. See (Srivastava, 2011)

7 Ibid.

8 Ibid.

9 Ibid.

10 Ibid.

11 Ibid.

12 Ibid.

13 See more in (Finnemore, 1994)

14 Of considering normative constructions as universalistic paradigms.

15 This dilemma raised originally by David Bloor has been discussed in what is known as the strong program, or the sociology of scientific knowledge. See more in (Niiniluoto, 1991)

16 Ibid.

17 And to make universal statements about the outside world.

18 See more in (Finnnemore & Sikkink, 2001)

19 See Wendt in (Schouten, 2008)

20 Supported by the Rockefeller Foundation.

21 (Boyle, 1999.) In (Guilhot, 2008, p. 290)

22 "Mythical worldviews hold sway over cognition and orientations for action, a clear demarcation of a domain of subjectivity is apparently not possible. Intentions and motives are just as little separated from actions and their consequences as feelings are from their normatively fixed, stereotyped expressions. In this connection it has been observed that the members of archaic societies tie their own identities in large measure to the details of the collective knowledge set down in myths and to the formal specifications of ritual prescriptions. They do not have at their disposal a formal concept of the world that could secure the identity of natural and social reality in the face of the changing interpretations of temporalized cultural traditions..." (Habermas, 1984, p. 52)

23 In this manner, for instead, the practice of "democracy" is reached by the institutionalization of procedures that marginalize the political identity of the citizenship by the formalization of isolated voting practices.

24 "Money and administrative power are systemic mechanisms of societal integration that do not necessarily coordinate actions via the intentions of participants, but objectively, "behind the backs" of participants" (Habermas, 1996, p. 40). (Habermas, 1996, p. 40)

25 Ibid.

Chapter 2
Political Asymmetry:
A Characterization for Social Science Research Inquiry

ABSTRACT

This chapter aims to develop a taxonomy and further the definition of the concept of political asymmetry for operationalization into social science research inquiry. On the one hand, the chapter covers the single main categories to offer a taxonomy of the concept, exposing the semantic context of symmetry and asymmetry, and depicting the idea of the political sphere from a classical Aristotelian tradition as well making use of public political science and philosophy of law. Later on, drawing on contributions of critical constructivism, and particularly Habermas communicative action theory, the chapter addresses how political asymmetry can be found in contemporary social structures at the level of subsystems of administration, such as institutions, as well as at the level of individual interaction.

INTRODUCTION

The concept of asymmetry refers to either a subjective impression that a structure generates upon the senses or to the recognition of inconsistencies between patterns belonging to a structure, inequality to a material direct differentiation. Two or more actors can relate to a structure equally, even if they are unequal. For instance, the right to equality before the law, found in the fourteenth amendment of the US Constitution that views persons as legal rights holders (Convention, 1788) (Rosenfeld, 2001) (Balkin, 2011). Contrariwise, relations with a structure of correlated actors can be unequal, even if the actors are equal, such as the 1865 Jim Crow Laws that prevented black citizens from voting in the US, though acknowledging them as equal individual political entities (Crespino, 2003). In the interaction between actors, their relation cannot be unequal or equal, because one is portraying and not comparing an interaction; thus, in such cases, their relation can be symmetric or asymmetric. It is only by considering the role and the identity of an actor upon a structure, that it can be said whether a relation has symmetry or sensorial harmony[1].

DOI: 10.4018/978-1-6684-9794-4.ch002

The concept of political asymmetry in political science and international relations has often been influenced by research on realism, yet theoretical and empirical engagement is absent from modern research. Customarily, it has been characterized by the role that *asymmetrical* arrangements maintain over the definition of *unfair,* or uneven, political and social settings. In such representations, asymmetry is frequently understood as inequality. This inadequate assumption, however, undermines the significant contributions of the subject as an entity in itself, that constructivist research has systematically revealed during the recent decades. In any case, by now, neither a semantic depiction, nor a theoretical contextualization has been rigorously addressed, much less an operationalization for the study of the role and the praxis of actors with diverse normative baggage within governance architectures.

This paper aims to address this issue by offering a characterization of the concept of political asymmetry for further operationalization into social science research inquiry. The paper builds on sociology, public philosophy, and, particularly, Habermas´ contributions on communicative action theory to address the topic from a systemic dimension, aiming to stress how contemporary structures of governance are highly indebted to architectural settings that end up defining further stages of system organization. The goal of the paper is to offer a coherent framework to further address research on political science and international relations theory, especially concerning the relation between macrostructures and norms production. On the other hand, from a critical constructivist perspective, the paper also aims to offer explanation on the evolution of power relations indebted to organizational arrangements that end up been replicated over time.

The chapter is divided in two parts. The first offers a semantic depiction of the conception of *asymmetry,* as well as the notion of the political sphere, to further provide a characterization of the concept of political asymmetry. The second part, operationalizes the contribution of the depiction within late modern social systems. The implications for further research of the present paper are given by the necessity, within social science inquiry, to offer a coherent characterization of asymmetry, stressing both the systemic and the political implication of such settings along organizations. The chapter also aims to enhance research directed at increasing scrutiny on the outcome of normative interventions of institutions, and, to diagnose how unbalanced relations of actors within structures can be empirically measured. On the issue of best practices to organizational culture, the papers offers fundamental conventions for digging out coherently about the implications of normative constructions that affect plural agencies interactions, which are further internalized within formal institutions. Finally, the characterization of the concept of political asymmetry provides guidance for further study of both, organizational normative constructions, and the practical implications of power and cognitive relations along informational structures, such as formal systems or societal subsystems of governance.

PART ONE

Social Science Research Contributions On Asymmetry

Arguably, the most consistent recent attempt to define the concept of political asymmetry was carried out by Philip Kitcher (Kitcher, 2001). In his view on the relationship between science and democracy, he stresses that societies tend to favor positions that not only are "scientifically" accountable, but at the same time, belong to a defined epistemic approach. In this fashion, agreements between individuals frequently take place on arenas that differ from each other within decision making procedures. This natural feature of societies, highlights the existence of *political asymmetries* that are further reproduced within different epistemic communities[2] (Haas, 1992) (Srivastava, 2011) (Riles, 2010). This view has been extensively documented both in social science as well as in recent international relations research. Such approach stresses the epistemic character of knowledge external to institutional or structural provisions, making “ideas and experiences… shared and debated” composites “across professional, ideological and political positions” (Escobar, 1995, p. 149) . While this analysis contributed to stressing the roles of science and knowledge in the field of governance, it focuses solely on solving ethical dilemmas in democratic systems, framing the potential for further research around global governance, and the study of how normative constructions evolve in international relations.

Within social sciences, political asymmetry has been represented by divergent “interests” within relations of “political equality” (Alonso Et. Al, 2011, p. 8). This view emphasizes the role of the participation of individuals in social institutions that aim to safeguard rights and aspirations of agents in a membership environment such as the nation state. While valuable for grasping the participatory nature of the concept, the approach does not explain its role within the production of normative agreements, which, in turn, precludes any attempt to carry out empirical or theoretical inquiry (Wray, 2001).

Concerning international relations and international politics, political asymmetry often has been characterized as an ordinary condition between countries belonging to a diverse power relation. This approach has been frequently used to depict the interaction between cultures and territories (Hadi, 1998) (Nandy, 1989), political economic structures (Buchanan, 1977) (Galbraith, 1998), IR political strategy (Brantly, 2006) (Thomas, 2001), international communities -such as the European Union- (Ehrenfeld, 2012) (Ágh, 1998), transnational relations between the rule of law and democracy (United Nations, 2009), and research oriented toward discussing policies beyond the nation-state, among others (Keohane & Raustiala, 2008) (Deutch, et al., 2004). From these schools, the most recent endeavor to theoretically frame the concept of political asymmetry on IR theory was carried out by Brantly Womack. The research focused on reconstructing features that characterized the historical interaction between two unequal actors in Asian -China and Vietnam-. This attempt, in particular, moves away from classical interpretations of asymmetric relations as “an imbalance of capacities and power, a disequilibrium that creates either subordination or a competition for domination”. In Womack´s criteria on international relations, asymmetry branches out into two basic theses:

“First, that disparities in capacities create systemic differences in interests and perceptions between the stronger and weaker sides of the relationship. (…) Rather, mutual perceptions and interactions in an asymmetric relationship will be fundamentally shaped by the different situation of opportunity and vulnerability that each side confronts. (…) Second, although asymmetric relations are rarely unproblematic, they tend to be robust. “Stability” might not be the right word to describe asymmetry, because the differences in interests and perceptions between A and B are a constant source of tensions (Womack, 2006, p. 18)”.

Thus, asymmetry implies not only unequal power but also perspective-differentiations that increase risks for misunderstandings and agenda subjectification. In this fashion “Asymmetric relationships must be analyzed in terms of their two sub-relations, that of the stronger to the weaker and that of the weaker to the strong”. This attempt to depoliticize asymmetry in international relations, overcome the frequent moral categories given to the existence of *diversity*, if scenarios branch out from conditions of inequality. Furthermore, this explains why Lenin´s or Wallerstein´s theories of critical hegemonies, do not permit a higher understanding of the rationality behind the interaction. Thus, asymmetry theory, is not a syncretic sampling of what appears attractive from each of the other theories, "but rather a reinterpretation" (Womack, 2006, p. 21). In this approach, a fundamental concern is often ignored in customary research is addressed; namely, the historicity of the subjective relations that condition the role and evolution of actors and structures. Thus, ideas of political advantage or paranoia represent not necessarily diametrical standpoints, but the demonstration of the existence of common patterns, in a relation observed from two subjective reflections with a similar language. Finally, the lack of a general conjectural structure of this approach leads it to over-focus on depicting scenarios of political inattention, over attention, deference, autonomy, misperception, stalemate and normalization, becoming more a descriptive analysis than a theory.

In customary international relations and political science, realism describes asymmetry as a pattern to be maintained between actors striving to acquire influence. Asymmetry thereby is represented as "significant disparities" after "calculating the resultant of the various vectors of power" (Thomas, 2001, p. 34). In this same approach, it has been recently added that in order to analyze political relations, one has to start from the fact, that rather than perspectives, they are defined by material settings (Morgenthau, 1950). While such a view has been highly adopted in international relations research, it has serious limitations for explaining how rather than plain power, social normative arrangements, such as actor's interests, frequently emerge in accordance with defined cultural and historical features.

Constructivist literature on political science customarily addresses asymmetry as diversity, branching out in two main categories: critical and conventional. In the first, asymmetry is represented as a dissimilarity of interests, later being reproduced within political, ideological, institutional or normative discourses. This perspective is indebted to the rather elusive notion of multiplicity, stressing the social character of the concept of symmetry but somehow diminishing the political relevance of the influence over political architectures and social structures. In the second, it stresses that the nature and distinctive characteristics of actors always have a social component, taking "the selves, or identities of states, [as] a variable" that "likely depend on [a] historical, cultural, political, and social context (Hopf, 1998) (Wiener, 2007).

"Conventional" constructivism highlights the qualities of social asymmetries as features of a state of anarchy, emerging from unsystematic structures, and "having multiple meanings for different actors, upon their own communities of inter subjective understandings and practices". This approach imagines different domains and issue areas of international politics that are regarded by actors as more or less "anarchic" (Hopf, 1998, p. 5); highlighting the importance of the "identity" as a leitmotiv for "action" (Wiener, 2007). Finally, it avoids assigning ethical or deontological assumptions to interactions of actors within a structure, such as an international organization, or to structures made upon conditions of asymmetry, because, on "conventional" constructivism, any moral or political categorization of asymmetry should be embedded within the productions of *plurality*.

In the absence of research directed at contextualizing the concept of political asymmetry, the next section of this chapter develops fundamental distinctions between the meaning of *the political* and the idea of asymmetry. In what follows, *political asymmetry* is defined by drawing on a critical constructivist framework. This attempt aims to operationalize the concept for inquiry directed toward the study of governance practices, structures, and procedures, such as the production of norms on international organizations. This process is carried out by first exploring the meaning of both symmetry and asymmetry, as well as the notion of the "political sphere" within the nation-state. Building up this discussion, the paper will proceed to schematize how this definition of asymmetry can be operationalized at the institutional and individual level. The idea is to exemplify how asymmetry can be part of further research on subsystems of organization, such as international institutions, how it plays a fundamental role in the process of production of norms, and how it is further exerted within actors making use of institutional, cultural or plain political power.

A CHARACTERIZATION OF THE CONCEPT OF POLITICAL ASYMMETRY

Symmetry and Asymmetry

The absence of research directed at contextualizing the concept of political asymmetry between ideological traditions, can raise diverse and overall contradictory interpretations on the concept. In the present work, therefore, it is necessary to establish preliminary differentiations between the meaning of the "*political*" and the idea of *asymmetry*, in order to later develop the definition of *political asymmetry* as a category of analysis.

In a customary exploration of the notion of "politics", two main ideological traditions emerge. On the one hand, politics related to power, in which the reification of the individual through a process of rationalization of objectives and goals shape constructions and relations. On the other, there is a classical interpretation of the political arena as the field where opposite or conflicting views meet in the definition of the *best society*. In contrast with the former, the latter approach to "politics" has been conventionally represented within the guidelines of the Aristotelian tradition, highlighting how, in society, "mankind always act in order to obtain that which they think good", and if so, "all communities aim at some good the state or *political* community, which is the highest of all, and which embraces all the rest"[3] (Aristotle et al., 2000). Such a semantic feature reconfigures the role of the individual to an idealist, transcendentalist perspective that set itself in the goal of reaching the "best form of government"[4] (Lang, 2005, p. 13)..

While functioning as opposites, the two branches constitute a composite by complementing each other in an historical perspective. While power relations have shaped and determined fundamental episodes of the construction of the political sphere, social interaction through reason has nurtured the conception of higher stages of consciousness about societies and the outside world. The question that remains is to what extent and under which circumstances this interaction between power and Aristotelian politics is possible, and what the consequences are of this dichotomy in modern societies, which are required to steer the tensions that branch out from those normative assumptions about politics. In an attempt to preliminarily address the question, as it can be described in the previous sections, political relations depart from pre-institutional conditions of social organization, moving to an institutional one, in which the "organization", is recreated through a common tacit, asserted or coercive set of principles, ideas, meanings and norms. Philosophically, this notion of political relations can be conceived through the scope of a modern Hegelian depiction of history, through which human beings live in the imperative of establishing moral and ethical claims, in an effort to identify themselves beyond material natural contingencies. In contemporary societies, this state of alienation can be explained from a Habermasian perspective, upon which social relations, particularly those related to the material economic sphere, are ""“institutionalized"[5] (Mc. Carthy, 1984, p. 33) and the world of labor "tamed" through a "normalization" of occupational roles and an enhancement of consumer roles" [6] (Mc. Carthy, 1984, p. 35).

In recent decades, the concept of asymmetry and the analysis of symmetry as a phenomena has speeded from math and game theory research to the study of theory of art and biology (Rosen, 2008).

Unlike the concept of equality, symmetry allows a more widely theorical interpretation and therefore a more complex and rich epistemological explanation. Symmetry, as a notion, can be predominantly found in the study of art, pure and natural sciences. The representation of the concept between these perspectives differs semantically, but keeps a coherent structure from which asymmetry as an abstraction can be reconstructed for political science and international relations theory.

In geometry, for instance, symmetry is given by the faculty of any object or figure to be projected on to different planes or dimensions. In this fashion, symmetry is "not a number or a shape, but a special kind of transformation, a way to move an object. If the object looks the same after being transformed, then the transformation is symmetrical. For instance, a square looks the same if it is rotated through a right angle" (Stewart, 2008, p. 8). Within this approach, objects hold a set of features and properties that can be projected on-to planes and further represented by geometrical or mathematical categories. Such is the case of representations that make possible the existence of spherical, radial, or bilateral symmetry. In geometry, the necessity of projecting objects within a common space was nurtured in the scientific potential of representing abstractions in uni- or multidimensional surfaces. The existence of symmetry throughout representations boosted scientific inquiry, from which the study of advanced geometry began[7]. The late evolution of geometry, and specifically of projective geometry, has been largely attributed to Évariste Galois, from whom the concepts of projective transformations and perspective came (Lord, 2013).

In applied mathematics, particularly economics, the idea of symmetry is frequently attributed to Nash´s contributions on games theory (Mariotti, 2000). Symmetry or asymmetry, as a formal condition of a social setting, was developed in his studies on the rationality behind cooperative strategies. In this view a game in its normal form is "symmetric if all agents have the same strategy set, and the payoff to playing a given strategy depends only on the strategies being played, not on who plays them" (Cheng et. al, 2005). The relation of games theory and groups theory with economics, has enhanced the scope of development and research within diverse fields of applied sciences. For instance, these theories have been operationalized to numerically exemplify symmetry in mathematical problems[8] (Kessler, 2003). This progress, often considered exclusive to pure sciences, has been further implemented in biological, social and natural sciences.

In biology, symmetricity, has formally enhanced the interpretation and contextualization of forms that reproduce within geometrical patterns in the natural world. These forms have been associated with the formation of structures that create life through chemical compatibility combinations. The existence of symmetricities within the natural world, has increased research on analyzing how life and the physical universe itself were formed through different forms of symmetry, catalogued within the field through concepts like as chirality, parity or isometry (Guijarro & Yus, 2009) (Riehl., 2010).

From an entirely aesthetic standpoint, symmetry is strongly related to the notion of equilibrium, beauty, pleasure, and a sense of the *appealing*. Upon those symbolic expressions, the mind differentiates and recreates mental patterns, moral categories of shapes, forms, sounds, flavors, feelings, ideas, and customary depictions of harmony. By their nature, these foundations encompass a broader semantic content than that attributed to the customary scientific approach to the idea of symmetry and its many features. Finally, the attribution of moral categories founded upon the notion of symmetry, allows individuals to make deontological differentiations in terms of proportionality, justice, correctness, ethics, fairness, and collective values. On the contrary, asymmetry remains as a subjective, qualitative or quantitative construction for the opposite of what is considered "good", "fair" or aesthetically pleasing.

The Political Sphere

Considering that from an entirely political standpoint, the idea of asymmetry is determined by each one of the abovementioned ideological traditions within politics, the upcoming section will proceed first by analyzing the most significant features of the realist and classical perspectives, digging further into the analysis of political asymmetry as a composite of the approaches of the various social sciences. The goal of this section is to provide a clear characterization of mainstream ontological approaches to political science, in order to further provide a standpoint from which to develop for a suitable definition.

The Political Sphere as the Realm of Deontology and Dialogical Interaction

Social systems are formed by overlapping stages of interaction, from which they formalize progressively new constitutive traditions. This process, rather than being entirely random, is fulfilled by increasingly adhering to the cognitive acquis of actors, new symbolic expressions and social constructions. The sources for these are the sophistication of dialogical interaction and the formal reproduction of expected behaviors. Upon the action of communication, societies further recreate normative assumptions that originally built their discursive and political spheres. Interaction plays a fundamental role in the process of the construction of normative meaning. It is upon this idea that the political dimension of a social system is erected, fostering formal structures of power with symbolic expressions aroused in the communicational sphere. Without information, or codification and socialization of information, social systems are prone to limit, distort, or curb their processes of development.

The existence of a political sphere, beyond the reification suffered by the concept of the power-politics perspective, is nurtured in the Aristotelian tradition of the notion of "the good life" (Kratochwil, 2000, p. 81). This approach bears in mind that social systems are founded in strong "structures of cognition", upon which they can assign value-laden assumptions for examining the consequences and causes of social arrangements. Politics, therefore, is in this manner represented as an outcome of the progressive evolution of joints between semantic units of societies and their formal meaning, shared and constructed dialogically by rational interaction. In communicative action theory, this process takes places in the arena of argumentation, which operates as a procedure for contemporary societies to be set apart from traditional, mythological conceptions about life experiences[9] (Habermas, 1992, p. 37). In discourse theory, this assumption is recognized as operative, as far as individuals in the public arena interact with each other under the perception of conditions of general symmetry, where the ideal speech situation takes place "when every competent speaker presuppose (they) are sufficiently satisfied insofar as he intends to enter into argumentation at all"[10] (Habermas, 1984, p. 25)

. The Aristotelian tradition of politics, therefore, presupposes the political sphere as a space in which individuals behave not only as individual entities, but also as entities that maintain a sense of belonging to a defined social group, orienting their actions toward those activities where common values *make sense*. This is why, in social systems, the political life is formed by a combination of interests that can be characterized as a) teleological behavior, aroused by formal structures that harmonize the relations of the individual with the environment; and b) normative expectations, that evolve coherently through communication[11] (Habermas, 1998, p. 46). Thus, the political sphere arises as an outcome of the processes of agenda definition and goals settled into differentiated social domains.

From the necessity of the reproduction of the material capabilities of the system, to the demarcation of the duties and rights of members of the social order, modern social systems are characterized by increasingly sophisticated levels of organization, formed upon processes of interaction and the formal administration of institutional subsystems. In western societies, this phenomenon takes place through the implementation of symbolic structures of legitimation that steer potential pitfalls between the facticity of political structures and their inner validity. Democracy, as a notion jointed with defined symbolic presuppositions, counts among many others, as a fundamental source of legitimation of the political sphere; this is done through deliberative or participative consensus. In political theory, however, devices such as this, have not been absent of criticism, especially when it comes to addressing to what extent formal procedures replace processes of interaction and agreement inherent to social systems. As it has been pointed out; "at present it is unclear how [procedural concepts of democracy] can link up with empirical investigations that conceive politics primarily as an arena of power processes" (Habermas, 1996, p. 287). This is due to the fact that, even in the presence of formal structures of collective decision, claims for authority and legitimacy are prone to being isolated from the limitations of such mechanisms[12] (Haas, 1992).

When it comes to the analysis of the definition of *politics* in contemporary social systems, it is necessary to mention that a great extent of the assumptions made in the traditional approach, have undergone a process of demystification, derived from the role of postindustrial economic relations in the political sphere. While this assumption has been previously discussed in more detail, it is worth mentioning that modern state systems, in the challenge of steering higher processes of social complexity, have replaced previous conventions from the arena of rational debate for standardized procedures. As such, the late modern individual becomes a client of the state, on behalf of a political arena that tends to steer tension via institutions, formal procedures, law or redistributive justice (welfare systems).

To the extent that the economic system subjects private households, employees, and consumers to its imperatives (…) The communicative practice of everyday life is one-sidedly rationalized into a specialist-utilitarian lifestyle; and this media-induced shift to purposive-rational action orientations calls forth the reaction of a hedonism freed from the pressures of rationality. As the private sphere is undermined and eroded by the economic system, so is the public sphere by the administrative system (Mc. Carthy, 1984, p. XXXII).

This shift in the customary convention of politics, rather than representing a structural disagreement from the traditional notion, can be better explained as a condition arising from the difficulty of highly complex social systems legitimating normative traditions via agreement and communicative interaction. While it may be suggested that the phenomenon is explanatory of a change of paradigm in the definition of the political sphere, our preliminary assumption is to suggest its appearance as a non-forecasted, non-steered event of formal modern structures of governance. It is upon such a new organizing nature of late modern societies, that further research directed to address the idea of political asymmetry can be operationalized both at the level of structures of governance such as organizations, and at the level of ordinary, individual interaction.

The Political Sphere as Power

The concept of power, always suggests the existence of a relation between two active edges. On the one hand, that from which certain action is executed; on the other, that in which the executed action is imposed or exerted. In social science, three broad characterizations of the concept of power can be proposed: a) a phenomenological approach, in which power is studied as an active or passive event of effective domination through multiple human relations domains. In Luke's characterization, power can be interpreted as a "potentiality", rather than physically proved phenomena in which the will of an actor can be effectively imposed over the will of other. In his *tridimensional stages*, power is represented in the social sphere by performing Meta and phenomenological roles, such as cohesion, influence, authority, force, manipulation, and finally, agenda definition.

The theoretical construction of power as a phenomenon beyond formal violence, intimidation, or dissuasion, has its roots in the classical interpretation of power politics that goes back to Machiavelli and is further recreated theoretically in the hegemonic-politics tradition. The idea of the enactment of the *Realpolitik* as the practice of reaching, maintaining, and reproducing power is one that regularly rejects the evolution of modern societies from the multitude to the notion of the "people"; a concept that belongs to a social science tradition that highlights communitarian wills and socially shared goals rather than force or influence. The transition of power from a plain, coercive force, to divergent qualitative symbolisms -such as power as manipulation, or to fields such as agenda definition or alienation-, can be well explained in modernity by the role exerted by hegemonic actors[13]. This requires a shift from the elucidation of power as the capacity of applying context, based force, to the notion of power as the capacity of actors to shape opposition, and therefore political discourse and agenda (Barnett & Duvall, 2005) . Finally, the approach can be found in the work of critical theory from the most classical to recent traditions: Weber, Marx, Gramsci (hegemony), and Foucault (bio politics), among others. In this tradition:

"violence and force presuppose a condition where the vivere politico e civile[14] are not the operative and defining principles of political action, a condition where the hegemonic relation is not yet universalized (…)The moment of force becomes transformed into the moment of hegemony only within …[a] new political structure, where speech and discourse are possible. (…) [R]ather subordinated to the public and political space created by the new subject" (Fontana, 1993, p. 131).

b) In a turn from Luke's views, Parsons and Arendt enhance the discussion by reflecting upon the quality of power within social relations[15] (Fontana, 1993, p. 132). For Arendt, "power corresponds to the human ability not just to act but to act in concert." Therefore, it is "never the property of an individual: it belongs to a group and remains in existence only so long as the group keeps it together" (Arendt, 1972, p. 143). Her reflection is inspired by a skeptical approach to endorsing somewhat Universalist traditions within social science, that, after the end of the Second World War, permeated theories of political analysis. In her view, social interaction carries the quality of reaching, via praxis, social arrangements. In this fashion, the very idea of power in modern social systems, remains bounded within previous definitions of authority, hierarchy, normative arrangements, and overall *agreements* reached early on in the social sphere. In the face of disruption of constitutive traditions upon which this sphere is built, power dilutes into the masse, as long as it is further harvested by interaction and coordination[16] (Habermas, 1996, p. 147) .

In an attempt to distinguish herself from the influence of Habermas´ theory of communicative action, Arendt argues that power doesn't fit within the borders of a sense of universal rationality. This precondition, for her, rather than being an improvement toward new stages of human organization, meticulously, hides the seed for further practices of despotism. This is why, in her overall book, the role of truth is hindered by her refusal to claim a superior or a higher argumentative position. While communicative interaction takes place in the sphere of transaction of information and linguistic intercourse, rather than embracing the notion of *dialogue*, she endorses the role of *debate*, suggesting the impossibility of setting agreements based on higher stages of human cognition. Power, in this perspective, does not reach levels of *consensus omnious* as an outcome of dialogical situations, but more as a result of the faculty of persuasion certain utterances possess to generate momentary cohesion among diversity[17] (Luban, 1979, p. 89). In her view, the differentiation of power from the classical approach, is pivotal determining the role of force in political relations. Indeed, the assumption of conceiving an actor capable of establishing a factual relation of dominance over the other actor, is rather a demonstration of force but not of power. Finally, inspired in the Aristotelian tradition of praxis, Arendt envisions power as a phenomenon linked to the capacity of the *people* to set ethically binding individual appeals, rather than the capacity of an entity to exert an agenda upon others. This conception, however, is not only different from a highly traditional acceptance of the outstanding role of power politics in political science, but also from the simple necessity of conceptualizing Arendt´s approach in a well-articulated theoretical body[18].

c) In Habermas, power in modern societies is embedded within values created in the social sphere, in accordance with a dialogical theory of action. In this regard, society sets the spaces through which power can be embraced by individuals prone to act, according to social expectations, or to fulfill a performative role on societal institutions[19] (Haas, 1992) (Riles, 2010). In his view, power is created not just as an outcome of a structure founded through democratic or institutional presuppositions - or under conditions of coercive institutional or implicit relations of dominance-, but also as a reconstruction of human cognitive boundaries within the exercise of communicative interaction. He bears in mind that power is formed by "common will" through the practice of "a communication directed to reaching agreement" (Luban, 1979, p. 4/17). It is important, thought, to bear in mind that *praxis* mechanisms are in need of permanent redefinition.

While Arendt´s perspective on power appears to have a spontaneous quality upon which individual wills are temporarily bounded, Habermas´ approach aims to explain to what extent modern political systems have increasingly constituted structures of authority that appear to be not as less planned, nor illegitimate than Arendt´s view (Luban, 1979, p. 82). Rather, they are consubstantial to a defined set of biographical events within complex social systems. In this perspective, Arendt conviction that political structures remain detached from *logical* patterns on view of customary analysis, set loose when it comes to explain the permanent develop of each time highly overlapped constitutive traditions of unbounded societies that sophisticate through interaction and communication. This is why, the assumption of societies as entities that act in concert, rather than entities that also communicate in concert, is limited for portraying power beyond spontaneous social wills. In Habermas analysis, this dilemma is addressed by the role of consensus in modern social systems, and thus the creation of a sphere of politics beyond individual or collective will. Hence, power is also a sphere mediated by social structures and processes of both construction and reconstruction of constitutive traditions via practices of dialogical interaction and coordination.

Table 1. Symmetry and asymmetry

1.1 Symmetry & Asymmetry	
1.2 The political Sphere	
1.2.1 The political sphere as the realm of deontology and dialogical interaction	Classical Aristotelian tradition of the notion of the "good life"
	Politics as an outcome of the progressive evolution of formal meaning, shared and constructed dialogically
1.2.2 The political sphere as power	The Realpolitik as the practice of reaching, maintaining, and reproducing power
	Parsons and Arendt- Reflections upon the quality of power into social relations
	Habermas. Power in modern societies is embedded within values created in the social sphere in accordance with a dialogical theory of action.

Asymmetry and The Political Sphere

In the definition of the concept of political asymmetry, it is necessary to outline that societies rather than being open systems, are enclosed structures that interact within cognitive boundaries. In this fashion, the contribution of traditional sociology and constructivist theory to schematize processes of reproduction within the social sphere, stress the relevance of the communicative character that distinguishes societies from any other systemic environment in which actors establish relations.

Language in social systems operates both as an instrument for interaction -from the use of the most primitive to the most complex forms of symbolic constructions- as well as a tool of cognitive referentiation of individuals in higher stages of system sophistication. As with any other cognitive product, it is formed by symbolic expressions and normative expectations that, simply from the faculty of recognition from the receptor, are able to be codified and internalized into a cognitive acquis. While it may be possible to suggest that language is customarily conceived within the boundaries of semantic constructions, it is necessary also to establish that, processes of communication in social systems are not limited to these structures, and, that any interaction between individuals is inherently and act of communication. That is, information that posits a particular impression about what constitutes the political sphere.

Following the previous assumptions on the definition of the political sphere, it is necessary to say that asymmetric interaction of actors within a communicative or a power politics tradition, take place through different channels. While asymmetry as a setting of political organization based on communication is represented by the capacity of actors to affect from diversity normative constructions, in power politics, conversely, it is represented within the institutions formally created in the political realm. Institutions, however, don't only represent given structures of human organization[20] (Taylor, 1996), but also normative constructions that further formalized upon principles, and recognized shared cognitions[21] about how the world should operate in accordance with an historical legacy firmly attached to the figure of the nation state (Finnemore, 1996) (Campbell, 1998) (Thelen, 1999) (North, 1991).

In the elaboration of a theory of political asymmetry, this dichotomy of the relation between agent and structure can be grasped from two approaches. The first is an ontological one, in which it is possible to argue that, in early stages of human organization, the environment as the structure, determines extensively the identity of actors. In political analysis, however, this dimension tell us nothing about how social relations develop into the evolution of the social sphere. In a second approach, we alternatively hold that both definitions about the evolution of the political sphere, are valid in contemporary political analysis, and, therefore, when we speak about social relations we mean that these take place in formal subsystems of organization and communication (governance), and also individual interaction (power). It is in both features of modern social systems in which such a definition of the concept can be embraced, and, therefore, at the point in which both asymmetries take place at the individual or sub systemic level, it can be represented as:

1. The capacity of actors to formalize normative constructions (information) into social systemic structures.
2. The material (factual) capacity of actors to operate within the system in accordance with the structure *resources of base*.

PART TWO

a. Political asymmetry in formal subsystems of organization

In contemporary societies, formal subsystems of organization are erected upon the structure of the modern nation-state, in which law determines institutionally regulated behavior for confined social relations. Resource administration, migration, rights and duties of citizens, public order, private property and the pillars of a global market oriented economy, are institutionalized and rationalized upon structures that aim to derive their functions from a sense of authority spread cognitively and forcefully into the community. The transition of normative constitutive traditions, through their development into official regulations, is made primarily via law at the national realm. This feature is further extended globally by making national law to interrelate semantically and procedurally with foreign agendas, traditions, and codes. Through this condition, regulation in a global sphere, acquires a fragmented yet articulated structure that aims to establish formal normative patterns that steer separate domains of the political life[22] (Teubner et. al, 2004, p. 6) . In customary political analysis, while this phenomenon is considered apparently as a spontaneous transition of the nation state, it has been broadly affected by the increasing influence of the economic system, the implementation of international law and institutions -via coercion or force-, and the faculty of individuals to regulate private interactions upon transnational relations (Finnemore, 1996). These events have, in turn, accelerated the production of regulation for the steering of market oriented relations, replacing[23] (Mc. Carthy, 1984, p. XXXIII) socially-produced values, with those that are economically produced[24] (Frericks et.al., 2009) (Frericks et. al., 2010) (Frericks et. al., 2010.).

While the formal sovereignty of the nation state from international structures of governance looks to maintain levels of autonomy of isolated social systems; the tendency of countries to regulate increasingly complex interactions, leads to the reinforcement of patterns on the international realm that are *imposed* legally (law and institutions), or refined cognitively (norms). Yet, in recent decades, this phenomenon has been experienced both in the political and the economic spheres, it has increasingly developed normative and law robustness in private relations between individuals or actors. Attempting to outline the phenomenon, it is possible to affirm, that the weak steering structures of governance of formal national and international institutions have led to the erosion of a political realm, in which normative traditions

-that are to be further formalized into regulation-, have fallen short on the level and number of decisions to be addressed upon dialogical communicative interaction.

The economic steering mechanisms of the Nation-State have supposedly been unable to keep pace with the creation of distinct global markets; instead, a variety of competing global regulation regimes have been established, each with their own legal decisional instances... The primary motor for this development is an accelerated differentiation of society into autonomous social systems, each of which springs territorial confines and constitutes itself globally (Teubner et. al, 2004, p. 8).

In the transition from the a) processes of communication, to the b) definition of normative constitutive traditions, onward to the c) establishment of formal structures of governance, social systems are prone to make use of coherent assumptions that justify cognitively the evolution of subjective perspectives into norms or suitable institutions. In this progression, however, it is just upon the assumption of validity under common agreement in which the process is prone to be considered legitimate. Since social systems mature through dialogical interaction nurtured by different perspectives, it is expected that the process of construction of normative assumptions includes the information of the commonality assembled as a whole -collective arrangements-. In such circumstances, each member of the social sphere has the possibility of postulating views about his role into the system, and, thus, to formalize normative constructions into systemic structures. If this is not the case, norms that branch out from that settings are constructed with asymmetric inputs of information, due to the fact that, while all members of the social sphere are capable of affecting the structure setting, information upon which normative constructions are nurtured is partial or biased.

Formal subsystems are created by the necessity of societies to regulate and organize increasingly articulated spheres of life, such as the legal system, the systems of participation, the economic system, and the administrative/bureaucratic system among others. Such fields define their own normative structure and, thus, validate their role via articulation with the system as a whole. As individuals are prone to enter into communication, conditions of cognitive and power symmetry are expected. They can be based on either a) the capacity of interacting upon previous normative constitutive traditions, or b) the capacity of reproducing equally their own perspective by following the conditions settled by the communality. Symmetry, therefore, enhances the faculty of each actor to recodify internally others´ views, and to input the information of their own subjective experience in to the system, so others can apply the same self-referential process[25] (Fink & Yolles, 2015). In this relation all participants are capable of locating their own singular experiences and elaborating new cognitive constructions that are to be further socialized. This is why, during the process of creation of normative constructions, the outputs of dialogical interaction are to be further constitutive of normative meaning. This is because shared meaning makes conceivable the capacity of reproducing previous constructions upon which consensus is tacitly pre-established. As Kjaer has stated on common ethical constructions; with the "insights contained in the system theoretical concepts of morality and critique, (…) the function of meaning is to re-introduce symmetry into the relation between the two sides, so creating a two-dimensional form which, at the same time, is characterized by symmetry and asymmetry"[26] (Kjaer, 2006, p. 76). As such, the expected symmetry suggested in the process of formalization of normative constructions, is to be guaranteed by the assumption that all members are capable enough to perceive, and take into consideration others subjectifications; allowing the society to operate in a coordinate manner.

The most important contributions on the relevance of distribution of information on structures of coordination can be found in studies on the uncertainty of markets by Akerlof, Spence and Stiglitz. Coordination based on symmetric levels of information have been fundamentally studied in information economics, which has established that increasing levels of uncertainty, based upon the idea of high levels of asymmetric information, lead to processes of distortion of market efficiency. In markets theory, as well as in economic development theory, patterns of asymmetric information have been characterized as fundamental constraints to levels of mutual interaction. In game theory, this array has been also demonstrated in the Prisoner´s dilemma, upon which, contrary to traditional economic theory, cooperation upon limited shared information, lead to increasing levels of collective outcomes, weakening the argument of self-oriented competition as a condition for production maximization. In the words of Stiglitz, in his Nobel Prize acceptance lecture;

"The argument of Adam Smith [1776], the founder of modern economics, that free markets led to efficient outcomes, "as if by an invisible hand" has played a central role in these debates: it suggested that we could, by and large, rely on markets without government intervention. There was, at best, a limited role for government (…)(Stiglitz, 2001) [T]he reason that the hand may be invisible is that it is simply not there – or at least that if is there, it is palsied"[27] *(Akerlof, 1970).*

Upon the idea of shared meaning, and symmetric information, it is expected that social systems are capable to increase the levels of coordination necessary for higher stages of organization. Moreover, the strengthening of the areas of communication warrants the maintenance of constitutive traditions from which deontological purposes[28] of formal institutions are to be nurtured. Symmetry thus corresponds to an ethical claim that is to be reconstructed institutionally on structures that permit sophistication of processes of collaboration and synchronization of systemic and individual goals. It is in this evolution, where modern subsystems of formal administration make permanent appeals to open channels for prospected new information that converge in the subsystem via inclusion[29] (Habermas, 1996, p. 127).

On a social organizational level, distribution of inputs of information is customarily established by the regulatory framework of organizations that are to fill the unoccupied gaps left by the nation-state. In this analysis, beyond the nation-state, organizations acquire a character of legitimacy by the conformation of decision-taking boards that look to include formally the higher number of member states. Administration on a global level is therefore increasingly conformed by international organizations that by force of habit acquire institutional normative character. At an increasing rate, organizational meaning conformed by resolutions, assessment, legal decisions, reports, formal suggestions, and public records, such as institutional publications, acquire a normative character that is later replicated by custom or force at the national level. In recent decades, this phenomenon has increasingly created a disjunction between the level of coordination of nation-states and global institutions, due to the increased autonomy of international organizations on contemporary political relations (Finnemore, 1994).

At the global level of contemporary social systems, institutions are prone to make appeals to legitimacy by the formalization of regulation conceived to make nation-states, formal participants of institutional boards directed to steer and control the sphere of governance. states have a capacity for generating informational input to the dialogical processes of deliberation that takes place in organizations: Built upon this feature, the idea of governance becomes an exercise of rational analysis of information gathered through channels of participation. While the qualitative differences of nation-states make them extensively heterogeneous subjects of political action, at the level of the institutions, they are expected to be taken into account as *equals*. For the sake of a sense of authority that derives from processes of integration of different world perspectives and interests into the organization, symmetrical conditions are to be fulfilled by mechanisms of deliberation and decision making. If this is not the case, internalization of information in institutions conceived for governance beyond the state reproduces limited representation of the *outside*. This is why, if some actors have a superior capacity to formalize normative constructions into systemic structures via formal organizational meaning[30], a distortion in the process of development of meaning is seen evidently (Finnemore, 1994) (Finnemore & Barnett, 1999). Consequently, in formal subsystems of organization and communication, political asymmetry can be represented in the unequal capacity of actors to formalize normative constructions into systemic structures.

b. Individual interaction.

Contemporary structures of governance are set upon arrangements built upon the rationalization of expected upcoming social/environmental contingencies and historical institutionalized events. Internationally, they frequently carry normative patterns of personnel engaged in diplomatic practices at the global level, whose decisions are further operationalized on normative constructions, or formally embedded into social systems via law. At diverse levels of social organization, such structures are represented in institutions, which aim to formalize in advance, elite interaction procedures driven to generate political outcomes. All representations that take place at the level of the institutions carry a cognitive baggage that follows previous processes of construction of socially shared norms.

Aside from traditions, in contemporary societies, private law has been embraced as the customary formal attempt to transpose individual relations to a communitarian sphere. This shift was carried out within the properties that modern structures of governance offered to market relations, at both local and transnational levels. As such, formal structures of political administration steer relations at the level of governments, international institutions, bureaucratic apparatuses, and authority assemblies, among others; fostering the formation of an effective legal system constricted to the maintenance of private property. This single feature of modern institutions, isolated all further attempts to formalize normative constructions conflicting with a legal system aimed at fostering the market economy and making "property rights, unambiguous, secure and freely alienable" (Rapaczynski, 1996, p. 83) . This is why today, rather than an exception, all property rights regimes enhance the maintenance and enforcement of market relations, which are determined by an economic system entrenched into the political sphere of individuals.

The increasing robustness of the legal regulatory system of the modern nation state, rather than being entirely formed upon dialogical interaction, is embedded into an evolutionary progression "through which economic forces shape the legal system [that] is itself a form of competitive and evolutionary mechanism" (Rapaczynski, 1996, p. 88). This progression in modern legal systems set the enforceability of private property rights as a fundamental dimension for the further *refinement* of the same legal structure. Whereas in early stages of economic development, the legal structure was prone to ensure the protection of private interests by the safeguard of possession upon "lineage, marriage and patronage"; in further stages of organization, such arrangements are replaced by market forces (Greif, 1994, p. 17). These are focused to ensure not only the expansion of private relations, but the avoidance of the erosion of the local settings for production, due to the interaction of the nation-state with transnational economies and societies. In such events, the regulatory boundaries aim always to defend relations of property of the private sphere by ensuring the existence of competitiveness, stressing the maintenance of a system free from price controls, a stable currency, and open markets (Konrad, 1980).

The ethical claim of law on market encounters is nurtured by the principle of equal rights between two private parties. In such settings, individual capabilities are frequently given by the capacity of actors to operate within the system, making use of the system base resources, such as social recognition and hierarchy, information or money. While actions of individuals or actors are decoupled by the role of mediated regulatory principles such as morality or law, structures of power end up determining the formal capacities to operate in the system. In such a setting, in late modern societies, the concept of political asymmetry on individual interaction is carried out within the relation of the political with the economic arena. Thus, it is depicted as the capacity of an actor to operate into the system in accordance with two system structures:

1. Cultural cognitive sphere (INDIVIDUAL ACTION): The institutionalization of political relations within individuals, came to be formed by the appropriation of each one to recognize the settings given by the form of production and organization, and to behave accordingly to the demands of the system. Individual action is customarily focused on stressing the capacity of the actor to recognize the patterns of the system, the structures and the previous socially endorsed agreements, and to adhere culturally to the demands of the production apparatuses.
2. Formal power sphere (INSTITUTIONS-MONEY-POWER-): At the national level, tensions between individual life projects and asymmetric distribution of roles and capabilities are frequently steered through mechanisms of redistributive justice (welfare state). At the international level, outcomes of asymmetric relations lack any regulatory or institutional control to steer tensions. Power is customarily given by the combination of violence in the form of dissuasion, or the capacity to operate in a structure with the medium of money or political influence.

Table 2. Policital sphere

1.2.1 The political sphere as the realm of deontology and dialogical interaction	*The capacity of actors to formalize normative constructions (information) into social systemic structures.*	1.3.1 Formal subsystems of organization
1.2.2 The political sphere as power	*The material (factual) capacity of actors to operate within the system in accordance with the structure resources of base.*	1.3.2 Individual interaction

CONCLUSION

In the goal to operationalize the concept of political asymmetry for further empirical research, this chapter has carried out an account of customary semantic representations of asymmetry and symmetry, as well as a taxonomy of the political sphere in late modern social systems for a further characterization of the concept. The chapter is motivated by conflicting and failed previous attempts to schematize similar concepts so fundamental to international relations. This underscore the necessity to carry out the task within a defined theoretical view. In this endeavor, the aim of this paper lays in making use of necessary conventions of critical constructivism, and, fundamentally, Habermas contributions of communicative action theory to define the paths through which asymmetry can be explained within a late modern societal sphere. Such a view, embraces the capacity of power to affect interaction but also stresses the communicative role of societies as the single character from which further normative interventions are nurtured. This alternative theoretical stand relies on the robust capacity of the theory to mix up structural and factual power settings with constructivist assumptions that highlight the role of ideas, communication and subjectivity as sources of norms and overall structures of governance.

The chapter first explored how the idea of symmetry has been sufficiently analyzed in the realm of pure and social sciences, economics, and international relations, among others, digging into the semantic content of the concept and clearing up necessary considerations for giving a further definition -one that is able to be operationalized for social science research-. Next, the chapter depicted the idea of the political sphere from a classical Aristotelian tradition and a power politics tradition, drawing on public political science and philosophy of law. While the first tradition is bounded to the conception of politics as the realm of deontology and dialogical interaction, the second is frequently given by the shape that settings and features of both, contemporary structures of governance and formal subsystems of organization -such as institutions of modern social systems-, give to contemporary governance architectures. Finally, drawing on contributions of critical constructivism and particularly communicative action theory, the chapter discussed how political asymmetry can be found in contemporary social structures at the level of subsystems of administration -such as formal institutions-, as well as at the level of individual interaction. In conclusion, political asymmetry in contemporary social systems is given by the capacity of actors to formalize normative constructions into systemic structures (informational system), and the capacity of actors to operate within the system in accordance with the system structures and base resources (culture/cognition and formal power). On the one hand, asymmetry generates a distortion in the process of dialogical interaction, upon which formal systems of governance are informationally nurture (cognitively). On the other, asymmetry is given by the unequal capacity of actors to interact with the system within two properties, individual interaction (cognition about rules, rationalities and procedures) and a formal power sphere highly affected in late modern societies by the relations of the economy on politics.

While the mere notion of political asymmetry is not capable of giving details about underlying facts related to the existence of structures of information and social organization, it can foster research which is able to offer a more measurable standard to deduce how settings and normative outcomes of asymmetric institutions, define the terms of the distribution of power, and the anachronism between global and domestic structures of governance, policies, and goals. The present chapter stresses both the relevance of studying from a critical perspective, and how discourses at the level of asymmetric organizations can be later institutionalized in the process of construction of settings and norms beyond domestic cultural environments. Our assumption is that the theoretical contributions of this chapter can raise awareness about how contemporary processes and structures of creation of normative meaning, pretend to present themselves as aseptic narratives and communicational architectures that belong to actors who intervene in asymmetric bargaining scenarios.

Frequent discussions in politics and sociology have addressed critically the study of the unevenness of the foundational settings of contemporary global and domestic political systems, yet a clear characterization which depicts the construction of normative outcomes of asymmetric information flow and interaction along formal organizations is frequently avoided. By now, it is recurrent in customary analysis to consider that normative interventions represent outcomes of dialogical interaction. By making use of a clear taxonomy and characterization of the concept of political asymmetry, such assumptions can be revealed as highly problematic or even false. Finally, this chapter aimed to draw attention to the cognitive sphere of institutional practices, and the implications of such conflicting settings in framing the language, goals, interests, discourses, and the overall functional practices of the contemporary policy-making process.

REFERENCES

Ágh, A. (1998). *From Democratization to Modernization in Hungary: The Political Preconditions for the Full Membership in the European Union Final Report*. NATO Fellowships Programme.

Akerlof, G. A. (1970, August). The Market for "Lemons". Quality Uncertainty and the Market Mechanism. [s.l.:s.n.]. *The Quarterly Journal of Economics, 84*(3), 488–500. doi:10.2307/1879431

Alonso Et Al, S. J. K. W. M. (2011). *Introduction. The Future of Representative Democracy*. Cambridge University Press. doi:10.1017/CBO9780511770883

Arendt, H. (1972). *Crises of the Republic: Lying in Politics; Civil Disobedience; On Violence; Thoughts on Politics and Revolution*. Harcourt Brace Jovanovich.

Aristotle, B. J. (2000). *Politics*. Dover Publications.

Balkin, J. M. (2011). *Living Originalism. Equality before the law*. Harvard University Press.

Barnett & Duvall. (2005). Power in International Politics. *International Organization, 59*(1). . doi:10.1017/S0020818305050010

Brantly, W. (2006). *China and Vietnam The Politics of Asymmetry*. Cambridge University Press.

Buchanan, J. M. (1977). Democracy in Deficit: The Political Legacy of Lord Keynes. In *The Collected Works of James M. Buchanan in 20 vols* (pp. 1999–2002). Liberty Fund.

Campbell, J. L. (1998). *No. 3 (Jun., 1998)* (Vol. 27). Institutional Analysis and the Role of Ideas in Political Economy. Theory and Society. Sprynger. https://www.jstor.org/stable/657900

Carthy, M. (1984). Introduction. The theory of communicative action, 1(1). Beacon Press.

Cheng. (2005). *Notes on equilibrium in symmetric games*. University of Michigan Artificial Intelligence Lab..

Convention, P. (1788). *The Constitution of the United States*. National Archives.

Crespino, J. (2003). The History of Jim Crow; Remembering Jim Crow. [s.l.:s.n.]. *The Journal of American History, 90*(2), 750–752. doi:10.2307/3659600

Deutch, J., Arnold, K., Ernest, M. & Daniel, P. (2004). Making the World Safe for Nuclear Energy. *Survival, 46*(4), 65-79. Routledge, part of the Taylor & Francis Group..

Ehrenfeld, W. (2012). *Climate Innovation - The Case of the Central Chemical Industrie. April 2012. No. 2*. IWH-Diskussionspapiere.

Escobar, A. (1995). *Encountering Development. The making and unmaking of the third world*. Princeton University Press.

Fink, G., & Yolles, M. (2015). Collective emotion regulation in an organization - a plural agency with cognition and affect. *Journal of Organizational Change Management, 28*(5), 832–871. doi:10.1108/JOCM-09-2014-0179

Finnemore, M. (1994). International organizations as teachers of norms: the United Nations Educational, Scientific, and Cutural Organization and science policy. *Intemational Organization 47*, 4.

Finnemore, M. (1996). Norms,culture, and world politics: insights from sociology's institutionalism. *IntemationalOrganization 50*(2)..

Finnemore & Barnett. (1999). The politics, power and pathologies of International Organizations. International Organization 53(4).

Fontana, B. (1993). *Hegemony and Power. In the relation between Gramsci and Machiavelly.* Univ Of Minnesota Press.

Frericks et.al., P. (2009). Toward a Neoliberal Europe?: Pension Reforms and Transformed. *Administration & Society, 41*(135). doi:10.1177/0095399708328874

Frericks. (2010). Capitalist Welfare Societies' Trade-Off Between Economic Efficiency And Social Solidarity *European Societies, 12*(5), 719–741. doi:10.1080/14616696.2010.483010

Frericks, P. (2010). *Patricia Frericks, Mark Harvey and Robert Maier The 'paradox of the shrinking middle': The central dilemma of European social policy. Critical Social Policy.* Sage. doi:10.1177/0261018310367671

Galbraith, J. K. (1988, April - June). 1998. The Political Asymmetry of Economic Policy. *Eastern Economic Journal, 14*(2), 125–128.

Greif, A. (1994). On the Political Foundations of the Late Medieval Commercial Revolution: Genoa During the Twelfth and Thirteenth Centuries. The Journal of Economic History. *53rd Annual Meeting of the Economic History Association.* Springer.

Guijarro & Yus. (2009). The origin of chirality in the molecules of life. A revision from awareness to the current theories and perspectives of this unsolved problem. University of Alicante, The royal society of Chemistry.

Haas, P. (1992). Introduction. Epistemic communities and international policy coordination. MIT Press. International Organization. *Knowledge, Power, and International Policy Coordination*, (Winter), 1–35.

Habermas, J. (1984). The Theory of Communicative Action, Volume 1: Reason and the Rationalization of Society. [T. McCarthy]. Boston: Beacon Press

Habermas, J. (1992). *Legitimation Crisis*. Polity.

Habermas, J. 1996. Between Facts and Norms. Contributions to a Discourse Theory of Law and Democracy. Translated by William Rehg. Massachusetts Institute of Technology. doi:10.7551/mitpress/1564.001.0001

Habermas, J. (1998). The Inclusion of the Other Studies in Political Theory. The MIT Press.

Hadi, M. A. (1998). *Dialogue on Jerusalem*. Palestinian Academic Society for the Study of International Affairs.

Hopf, T. (1998, Summer). The Promise of Constructivism in International Relations Theory. [MIT Press.]. *International Security*, *23*(1), 171–200. doi:10.1162/isec.23.1.171

Keohane & Raustiala. (2008). *Toward a Post-Kyoto Climate Change Architecture: a Political Analysis*. The Harvard Project on International Climate Agreements.

Kessler, A. S. L. C. M. G. M., Lülfesmann, C., & Myers, G. M. (2003). (2003), Economic versus political symmetry and the welfare concern with market integration and tax competition *Journal of Public Economics*, *87*(5-6), 847–865. doi:10.1016/S0047-2727(01)00155-4

Kitcher, P. (2001). *Science, Truth, and Democracy*. Oxford Studies in the Philosophy of Science. doi:10.1093/0195145836.001.0001

KjaerP. (2006). Systems in Context. On the outcome of the Habermas/Luhmann-debate. ANCILLA IURIS (anci.ch). SSRN.

Konrad, Z. (1980). *The Origin of the German Social Market Economy. The leading ideas and their intellectual roots*. Adam Smith Institute.

Kratochwil, D. (2000). Constructing a New Orthodoxy? Wendst's Social Theory of International Politics and the Constructivist Challenge. Milennium – *Journal of International Students*, *29*, 73.

Lang, A. F. (2005). *Hannah Arendt and International Relations: Readings Across the Lines. New York: Palgrave Macmillan.*

Lord, E. (2013). *Symmetry and Pattern in Projective Geometry*. Springer.

Luban, D. (1979). On Habermas on Arendt on Power. *Philosophy and Social Criticism, 6*(1).

Mariotti, M. (2000). Maximal symmetry and the Nash solution. *Social Choice and Welfare*, *17*(1), 45–53. doi:10.1007/PL00007174

Morgenthau, H. J. (1950). *Politics among nations: the struggle for power and peace. New York: Knopf.* s.l.:s.n.

Nandy, A. (1989). Science as a Reason of State. *Science as Culture*, *1*(7), 69–83. doi:10.1080/09505438909526260

North, D. C. (1991). Institutions. *The Journal of Economic Perspectives*, *5*(1), 97–112. doi:10.1257/jep.5.1.97

Rapaczynski, A. (1996). The roles of the State and the Market in Establishing Property Rights. *Journal of Economic Perspectives, 10*(2).

Riehl, J. P. (2010). *Mirror-image asymmetry. An introduction to the origin and consequences of chirality*. John Wiley & Sons, Inc. doi:10.1002/9780470588888

Riles, A. (2010). *Collateral Expertise: Legal Knowledge in the Global Financial Markets*. The Wenner-Gren Foundation for Anthropological Research.

Rosen, J. (2008). *Symmetry Rules. How science and nature are founded on symmetry*. Frontiers Collection.

Rosenfeld, M. (2001). *The rule of law and the construction of constitutional democracy*. Jacob Burns Institute for Advanced Legal Studies.

Srivastava, J. (2011). Norm on Sustainable Development. Predicament and the Problematiqze. *India Quarterly: A Journal of International Affairs*. doi:10.1177/097492841006700201

Stewart, I. (2008). Why Beauty Is Truth: The History of Symmetry. New York; London: BasicBooks.

Stiglitz, J. E. (2001). Nobel Prize Lecture, December 8, 2001, Information And The Change In The Paradigm In Economics. Columbia Business School, Columbia University.

Taylor, P. A. H. R. R. (1996). Political Science and the Three New Institutionalism. *Polilical Studies Associalion*, *XLIV*, 936–957.

Teubner, G. (2004). Fischer-Lescano, Andreas. Regime-Collisions: The Vain Search for Legal Unity in the Fragmentation of Global Law. *Michigan Journal of International Law*, *25*(4).

Thelen, K. (1999). Historical Institutionalism in Comparative Politics. *Annual Review of Political Science*, *2*(1), 369–404. doi:10.1146/annurev.polisci.2.1.369

Thomas, T. L. (2001). Deciphering Asymmetry's Word Game. Academic journal article from Military Review, 81(4).

United Nations. (2009). *Global Compact International Yearbook*. UN.

Wiener, A. (2007). *Constructivist Approaches in International Relations Theory: Puzzles and Promises Constitutionalism Webpapers, ConWEB No 5/2006*. Queen's University.

Womack, B. (2006). China and Vietnam: The Politics of Asymmetry. Cambridge University Press.

Wray, B. (2001). *Science, Biases, and the Threat of Global Pessimism*. University of British Columbia. Philosophy of Science.

ENDNOTES

1 Countries, individuals and overall actors are frequently unequal between each other. It has been a common error to make use of the idea of equality in social science and modern politics as a measure for validating standardizes policies and approaches to ethical dilemmas. It is just upon the limitations and complexities that arise from highly unequal actors that one can reflect upon the structural limitations of international institutions and contemporary standardized legal constructs.

2 On the role of epistemic communities in recent social science and international relations research, see specially (Haas, 1992). See also (Srivastava, 2011) (Riles, 2010).

3 In (Aristotle et al., 2000). Chapter One.

4 It is worth to mention Anna Arendt definition. For her: "real politics is the highest form of human action, the noblest pursuit in which people can engage and the realm in which they can discover and display their truly human character". In (Lang, 2005, p. 13).

5 (Mc. Carthy, 1984, p. 33)

6 In this view, the consequences are that the "complex economic-political system penetrates ever deeper into the symbolic reproduction of the life-world, drawing ever-new spheres of communicatively structured interaction into the vortex of capitalist growth" (Mc. Carthy, 1984, p. 35).

7 Evolving from the necessity of measuring planes, shapes or volume figures, to the more abstract study of mathematical patterns.

8 See also (Kessler, 2003).

9 Although highly relevant in the overall approach to Habermas, this perspective is no longer completely valid to interpret the evolution of contemporary social systems, in which state and society experience a rupture that is further replaced by systemic demands fundamentally established by the economic system. In sum, the traditional relation that remained as an outcome of the state as a source of political authority in local and isolated systems of production, is lately turned into the construction of the civil society, upon which the individual is "his own end". In his words "This conceptual framework no longer fits modern societies. in which the commodity exchange (organized under civil law) of the capitalist economy has detached itself from the order of political rule. Through the media of exchange value and power. (WO systems of action that are functionally complementary have been differentiated out. The social system has been separated from the political, a depoliticized economic society has been separated from a bureaucratized state" (Habermas, 1992, p. 37)

10 (Habermas, 1984, p. 25)

11 Not even necessarily in further theoretical paradigms of political science the idea of societies as entities that evolve through rationality and communication is eroded in its natural robustness. This is why on the evolution of the Aristotelian tradition, Kantian contributions on political science, and philosophy of law fit adequately when it comes with the validity of rationality to justify normative traditions. Habermas acknowledge this predisposition an furthermore, considers it as a step further in the discussion about the validity of norms and the ontological presuppositions of this validity. In his words "Strong cognitivist seeks in addition to take account of the categorical validity claim of moral obligations. It attempts to reconstruct the cognitive content of the moral language game across its full scope. The Kantian tradition, unlike neo-Aristotelianism, is not just concerned with clarifying a practice of moral justification that unfolds within the horizon of received norms, but seeks to justify a moral point of view from which such norms can themselves be judged in an impartial fashion" (Habermas, 1998, p. 46).

12 Nonetheless even in the face of the recognition of actors "with recognized expertise and competence in a particular domain and an authoritative claim to policy-relevant knowledge within that domain or issue-area", there is substantial criticism over how such epistemic constructions may rather erode democratic procedures. On epistemic communities see (Haas, 1992).

13 These cases can relate to domestic or supranational levels, such as lobbying corporations, or highly influential countries in the international system.

14 The civil and political life.

15 This differentiation about the origin of power in politics was previously well established even by Machiavelly who in his studies on "The art of war", already attempted to discuss about the origin of power and its consequences upon the act of government. " The organization and deployment of force—whether by the "new prince," whose power is based on the collective action of the people, or by the republic, which is the political space coextensive with the populo—is viewed by Ma-

chiavelli as a problem that the People as a Political Force requires the "resurgence" of the ancient virtu, without which the Romans would never have established a stable and successful "armed republic."To Machiavelli, the moment of force is always the moment of organized violence—that is, the deployment and organization of the popular masses". In (Fontana, 1993, p. 132)

16 For habermas, Arendt approach to power, although highly related to the role of communicative interaction, is somewhat dogmatic when it comes to explain the relation of power, legitimacy, and overall social organization with claims to authority or justice. In modern societies, this view is furthermore problematic in the effort of grasping a notion of justice that allow to propose to social systems, moral or ethical categorizations from which formal normative constructions are to be nurtured deontologically. As he adds; "According to this explanation [in the discussion about discourse-theoretic concepts of political autonomy], legislation depends on the generation of another type of power, namely, on the communicative power that, as Hannah Arendt says, no one is really able to "possess": "Power springs up between men when they act together, and it vanishes the moment they disperse." According to this model, both law and communicative power have their co-original source in the "opinion upon which many publicly were in agreement." This reading of political autonomy necessitates a differentiation in the concept of political power. *If the sources of justice from which the law itself draws its legitimacy are not to run dry*, then a jurisgenerative communicative power must underlie the administrative power of the government". (Habermas, 1996, p. 147)

17 In accordance with Luban study on the distinction between Habermas and Arendt on power and communication, there are four points in which he argues, Arendt departs from Habermas contributions on the topic; the first one has to be with the role of debate in Arendt, as a replace of dialog. The second with the irreconcilable relation between science and politics (potentially harmonic for Habermas). The third with the role of truth in the idea of power, and finally, the distinctions in the presuppositions of both authors when it comes to analyze "the notion of participation and consensus". In this point, he adds; "Habermas' *consensus omnium*, [was] indeed [what] Arendt feared more than anything else. Truth, she argues strikingly, is coercive, (…) even truth arrived at through Socratic dialogue forms the foundation of tyranny when it enters the political realm". (Luban, 1979, p. 89).

18 One can suggest that Arendt, in an attempt to propose a theory of power radical enough to contravene political configurations of dominance and inequality in societies, falls into the underestimation of the systemic dynamics by which social systems reproduce themselves even in the face of serious discursive, rational or ethical contradictions. Her intuition about the level of control that societies can exert upon highly rigid structures of concentration of power, is however extremely futile to explain the trends experienced globally in recent decades, when it has to be with an increasing phenomena of concentration of power of political actors amidst sterile claims for "democracy" and legitimacy. Or even forms of mixture of capitalism with authoritarianism, as the one implemented in China.

19 At this point is esential to bring into account, recent research on IR theory and social science, in which the role of epistemic communities play a substantial role in defining what power, whitin selected social spheres, means and represent. As Haas in his introduction on epistemic communities expresses, " control over knowledge and information is and important dimension of power" (Haas, 1992). See also (Riles, 2010).

20 On alternative contemporary debates on the discussion of institutional theory, see (Taylor, 1996).

21 In the relation between culture and institutions, see (Finnemore, 1996) (Campbell, 1998). In the discussion between path dependency in institutional sociology, see (Thelen, 1999). In a classical approach to institutions as formal structures see (North, 1991).

22 A phenomena not absent of criticism when it comes with the normative and legal outcomes of steering institutions that tend to govern increasingly new spheres of life on a global level, in an increasingly fragmented global law. In the questions concerning the coallision of national regimes, the discussion draws on the analysis of the level of division of heterogeneous political spheres into global law. Embracing fundamental assumptions of communicative action, the argument goes back to define to which extent global law operates upon a fundamental rationality defined by the economic sphere that runs in contradiction with other rationalities and interests constitutive of social systems. Teubner and others have suggested that the phenomenom can be problematized within three thesis; "1. The fragmentation of global law is more radical than any single reductionist perspective—legal, political, economic or cultural—can comprehend. Legal fragmentation is merely an ephemeral reflection of a more fundamental, multidimensional fragmentation of global society itself (…) 2. Any aspirations to a normative unity of global law are thus doomed from the outset (…) 3. Legal fragmentation cannot itself be combated. At the best, a weak normative compatibility of the fragments might be achieved". (Teubner et. al, 2004, p. 6)

23 "The economy cannot be treated as a closed system; to begin with, it is essentially interconnected with an administrative subsystem that fulfills market-complementing and market- replacing functions. Problems arising in the process of capital accumulation can be transferred to the political system and dealt with administratively; conversely, problems arising in the political sphere can be dealt with through the distribution of economically produced values" (Mc. Carthy, 1984, p. XXXIII).

24 This phenomenon constituted the basics of modern discussions concerning social systems, when it has to be with the effects of the economic system over the political sphere, as well as the consequences and dilemmas of regulation that can't be considered legit from a dialogical perspective, yet inhabit all spheres of life. In the discussion between market oriented values and public private legal transitions, see; (Frericks et.al., 2009) (Frericks et. al., 2010) (Frericks et. al., 2010.).

25 On the relation between cognition (& emotions)and plural agency interaction see (Fink & Yolles, 2015)

26 "It is against this background that Luhmann introduces his concept of morality, stating that "Moral ist immer symmetrisierter Sinn". In (Kjaer, 2006, p. 76).

27 In conclusion, increasing levels of asymmetric information lead to increasing levels of uncertainty in scenarios in which coordination based in the assumption of trust is imperative (used cars or labor markets-health insurance systems and formal credit market structures (lending shortages) in developed countries among others). Symmetricity of information on the contrary, increase levels of social coordination, allowing higher stages of system complexity based in the assumption of shared meaning and presuppositions about normative traditions and expectations. This is why formal systemic organization represents an inertial stage of social systems in the effort of rationally steering system complexity. See (Akerlof, 1970).

28 Such as fairness, morality, equality, efficiency, tolerance, ethical operation, participation and so on.

29 "… use of communicative freedoms require a legally structured deliberative praxis in which the discourse principle is applied. Just as communicative freedom prior to any institutionalization refers

to appropriate occasions for the use of language oriented toward mutual understanding, so also do political rights— in particular, entitlements to the public use of communicative freedom—call for the legal institutionalization of various forms of communication and the implementation of democratic procedures. These are meant to guarantee that all formally and procedurally correct outcomes enjoy a presumption of legitimacy. Rights of equal participation for each person thus result from a symmetrical juridification of the communicative freedom of all citizens" (Habermas, 1996, p. 127).

30 Resolutions, rules, assessment, legal decisions, institutional reports, formal suggestions, and informational mainstream material. See more on (Finnemore, 1994) (Finnemore & Barnett, 1999)

Chapter 3
Epistemological and Theoretical Assumptions for Carrying Out Research Directed to Study the Construction of the Norm of Modern Development: The Bretton Woods Institutions

ABSTRACT

Drawing on literature on critical constructivism, historical institutionalism and philosophy of law, this chapter identifies that customary discursive narratives on the idea of "modern development" at the World Bank and the IMF, entail severe flaws that can only be grasped by suggesting a theoretical framework to address the sociological background, power structure, and the fundamental historical biographical periods of these organizations. In this approach, the task of defining the meaning of discursive interventions on the public debate must merge the role that settings, interests, cognitive abridgments, and overall perspectives overlap conflictively in asymmetric structures of authority. The attempt to present this framework is to make use of a theoretical standpoint from which narratives entrenched on normative interventions at the Bretton Woods Institutions can be grasped coherently in the public debate.

INTRODUCTION

After the fall of the Berlin Wall, and the overall expansion of the free market-economy into the former Iron Curtain countries, discussions over the future of contemporary structures of governance and political organization frequently avoided stressing its economic character. The increasing role of the markets and the burdens of the economic system over the political boundaries of contemporary societies, led to a distortion of institutional narratives that attempt to bring out political demands that continuously col-

DOI: 10.4018/978-1-6684-9794-4.ch003

lide with trade imperatives (Rodrick, 2002) (Rodrik, 2001). In such settings, global institutions[1] (North, 1991) formerly isolated from the public opinion due to their specialized character (Hall & Taylor, 1996, p. 6), have acquired a voice in politics in which systematic interventions create normative constructions followed by social systems at risk of being displaced to marginal roles in the global power politics (Park & Vetterlein, 2010) (Finnemore, 1994) (Finnemore & Barnett, 1999). In such settings, the Bretton Woods Institutions, acquired a decisive role, managing historical inconsistencies of the global monetary and trade regime of the prewar periods (Black., 1960, p. 267) (Eichengreen, 2008) (Eichengreen, 2004) (Lewis, 2011) (Chang, 2002). Although they were originally conceived to cover regulatory gaps emerged by the increasing economic fragmentation of the global society, their influence settled consistently political relations that some have called constitutional (Peters, 2011) (Cass, 2001). At this point, a compulsory question to address is: how should such normative constructions be interpreted theoretically? And furthermore, how has the meaning of these norms evolved historically?

The limitations of the institutional categories in encompassing structural flaws and international urgencies derived from the process of globalization, led to an erosion of the discursive sphere from which the norm of "modern development" built up. In the historical record of the World Bank or the IMF, such situation represented the existence of robust theoretical and political restrictions within which such norm nurtured semantically. Thus, the system evolved legitimizing discursively, crisis in which core and periphery nations shared burdens and responsibilities (Sachs., 1993) (Wade, 2003) (Stiglitz, 2003). It is along such limitations that a theoretical framework to explore discursive interventions of the norm of "modern development" at the Bretton Woods Institutions, can turn the discussion from the political to the academic realm. The main goal of this turn, I claim, is to set a distance from customary research on political science and international relations, avoiding the ideological gaps of the official publications of the World Bank, the IMF and the WTO, and stressing the asymmetric character of a structure of governance that has operated within this setting for almost seven decades.

In this endeavor, the following chapter is divided into four parts. First, it draws on critical constructivism, to set a theoretical framework for the study of normative interventions of asymmetric structures of governance. This introduction deals with the limitations of alternative approaches on political science, giving validity to the idea of modernity, as a phenomenon that emerged within practices of dialogical interaction, yet merged within market forces and encounters of free market social systems. With this assumption, this section aims to describe how the contributions of critical constructivism can provide support for inquiry directed to reconstruct discourse in late modern societies. This task is carried out by stressing for further research, the relevance of three properties of discursive interventions; the influence of economic relations over ideological constructions, the relevance of subtle formal structures on discourse production, and the fabrication of normative constructions as a practice of symmetric interaction.

The second section of the chapter contextualizes how historical institutionalism and philosophy of law can further offer a working framework to analyze the relationship of social systems and the discursive interventions of contemporary institutions of governance. Bearing in mind that historical contingencies such as the end of the Second World War led to a transition of specialized regulative arrangements and structures into normative constructions, at the Bretton Woods Institutions this shift supposed a transposition of private law agreements into global norms. Drawing on historical institutionalism, the chapter aims to highlight three features of institutional discourse for further inquiry; the role of concrete temporal processes on the production of norms, the institutional control over superstructures and the role of institutional values on discourse fabrication.

In the third stage, the chapter briefly introduce the concept of political asymmetry to further explain how it should complement research directed to analyze normative constructions at the World Bank and the International Monetary Fund. This last attempt is made by bearing in mind the need of preliminary and alternative ontological assumptions for conducting research on normative meaning. Following literature on constructivism it argues that institutions, rather than being open assemblies, are structures enclosed into regulatory, cognitive and political boundaries. In the case of the Bretton Woods Institutions, these boundaries are present on defined periods of time, shaping relations between agents and the information produced at the executive level.

Finally, considering the ontological conflicts in addressing a norm of "development" entitled into "modernity", the fourth chapter combines a rather alternative stand between realist and constructivist theories for the study of norms at the level of the Bretton Woods.

CRITICAL CONSTRUCTIVISM AND INSTITUTIONAL DISCURSIVE INTERVENTIONS

The Properties of Economic Relations over Contemporary Normative Constructions

With the increasing levels of influence that the economy has over the political sphere of nation-states, the difficulties of contextualizing normative constructions influenced by economic phenomena dilute the objectivity of inquiry directed to reconstruct meaning. In international relations, this has carried out a lack of distinction of political events from economic imperatives, affecting thoroughly institutional narratives and normative interventions. This is how on the elaboration of a theoretical framework to reconstruct discourse, academic contributions on social analysis such as critical constructivism, can ease the difficulties in depicting linguistic interventions, otherwise normalized in customary public debate. In this strategy, it is possible to stress the historical role of the structure within the social institutions, discursive assemblies, and overall normative constructions of contemporary social systems. Rather than framing norms as constructions built up within the multiplicity of social systems, it embraces them as products of communicational patterns reproduced and produced dialogically within the influence of a superstructure such as the economy. This attempt highlights the role of language as an interaction mediated not only between individuals as political entities, but also as systemic agents of social systems, who aim to avoid gaps not covered by formal structures of governance yet claim the "legitimacy of their own interventions into social affairs" (Hopf, 1998) (Wiener, 2007) (Wiener & Pueter, 2009).

The existence of conditions of political asymmetry within a global governance architecture, holds for critical constructivism as a necessary assumption for understanding what "modernizing development" means. In such setting, *development as a project*, fosters the creation of a new cognitive standpoint from which institutions and societies nurture. In this sense, pre modern societies are able to achieve the sophistication of their social integration (Habermas, 2001) via norms and institutions; yet developing political provisions to control power relations triggered by capitalist patterns of economic and social modernization (Johnson, 2008) (Habermas, 1984). Following this tradition, in the decision making process of international institutions, the evolution of contemporary structures of governance, and the appropriation of highly legitimized normative procedures such as "voting", reveals the possibility of societies to smooth out the unevenness that appeared within the robustness of formal regulations. This is how political relations are recognized not just as settings influenced by the way actors relate with each other on the arena of regulation, but also at the level of values, interests and individual strategies. Accordingly, the customary social contract tradition used to reconstruct meaning of normative interventions of international institutions ignoring their economic (systemic) role, is arguably one of the main limitations of routine social inquiry directed to contextualize their discourse.

On a global level, the social demands for clarifying the legitimacy of norms endorses an even higher importance, since functional limitations of contemporary organizations erode the rights of political participation of nation states, depriving them of their sovereign autonomy (Barro, 2005) (Leech, 2012) (Dreher et. al., 2010) . Since norms are social constructions and contemporary structures of governance are highly asymmetric environments, the role of participation and the legitimacy of the relation between law and norms acquire a primary character in the study of meaning. As it has been pointed out, under pressure of globalized markets in today's world, "Keynesianism in one country" is no longer a possibility", because, "as markets drive out politics, the nation-state increasingly loses its capacities to raise taxes and stimulate growth, and with them the ability to secure the essential foundations of its own legitimacy" (Habermas, 2000, p. 79) . In the absence of an institutional architecture, capable of ensuring equal rights of participation, gaps left by the inability of the nation state are frequently occupied by private regulation (private law), the economy, and overall power-politics relations. It is in this state of affairs where the inclusion of the structure into the analysis of meaning of normative interventions on "development" plays a primary role. This property of discourse I argue, reveals the democratic flaws of the current structures of global participation, and disentangles the influence of economic relations in the process of construction of meaning (Bird-Pollan, 2010) (Rasmussen M, 1976) (Moore, 1985).

The Idea of Development and the Relevance of Subtle Formal Structures on Discourse Production

In adopting a theory on the evolution of "modern development", critical constructivism endorses a two dimensional approach. On the one hand, it suggests an increasing process of rationalization of social systems that has led to a permanent reconstruction of customary aspirations of individuals. Within such features, social systems were able to "master" their settings, redefining "'the collective patterns of life, progress, full employment, controllability and exploitation of nature' (Johnson, 2008, p. 76). These events eroded the role of the nation-state, unleashing the power of industrial or capital exporting nodes while generating increasing global interdependency. With this framework, this notion of "development" took place ensuring the early pivotal role of the nation state as the single actor for system steering. In such conjuncture, "a politics centered on the state and its institutions can no longer count on its own forces to provide citizens with adequate protection from the consequences of decisions taken elsewhere" (Johnson, 2008, p. 76). This is why any attempt to contextualize contemporary discourses on development, must consider the relationship between communitarian projects, such as nation-state policies, and formal structures of discourse production such as international organizations, NGO´s, or media corporations (Blommaert, 2005) (Blommaert & Bulcaen, 2000) (Fairclough & Chouliaraki, 1999). With these conditions, critical constructivism, rather than setting the fundamental principles through which modern societies evolve, stresses the role of western liberal values as normative standpoints from which contemporary national entities entitled their role as channels through which social tensions where functionally steered. During the 20th century, this feature of the nation state was epitomized in the conception of the *welfare*, and the implementation at the national level of policies directed to generate economic redistributive justice. Such arrangements restricted the contradictions of the systems, acknowledging the limitations of the contemporary state to control relations taking place at the economic sphere. In this manner, the limitations of the normative dimension of constructions such as redistributive justice, was revealed by the lack of global consensus to adopt the same "ethical-political" dimension transnationally. In absence of a global state, this is why contemporary meaning from which a norm of "modern development" nurtures is far away of a real cosmopolitan cultural background[2] (Habermas, 2000, p. 108) (Eichengreen, 2004) (Eichengreen, 2008) (Finnemore, 1994) (Wiener, 2014).

The lack of a real global participatory structure of consensus, stresses the restrictions of global politics to "catch up" with global markets. This flaw of the international system, has increasingly stressed during the resent years the pessimism of developing a real cosmopolitan democracy. In such conditions, it has been argued that attempts to solve the global gaps between politics and economics is likely to "proceed according to another model" (Habermas, 2000, p. 109). Such thoughts raise awareness over a highly conflictive international system not yet capable of realizing the limitations of their own institutional biography. In these settings, normative constructions produced at the global level are prone to carry contradictory baggage of an international bargaining architecture in permanent evolution (Rueda C, 2013). This is how reconstruction on discourse directed to stress the relevance of formal subtle settings, makes possible to stand in the core assumption of capturing the inter-subjective connotations that lay on the relation of the structure with the process of discourse production. In this strategy, inquiry directed to reconstruct meaning can be adequately embraced, by analyzing institutional literature, or official interventions biased by settings within which subtle arrangements such as economic power or an asymmetric structure of governance took place (Finnnemore & Sikkink, 2001).

Normative Constructions as a Practice of Symmetric Interaction

From a critical constructivist tradition, the existence of asymmetries on governance structures reveals critical flaws in the process of interaction, and are therefore discursive misrepresentation of the public sphere (Huckin, 2012) (Tenorio, 2011). Thus, with the formation of international institutions, such feature foster conflictive, incoherent or contradictory regulation of selected global social spheres. While it has been argued that on the constructivist tradition, the disengagement of populations from social to individual life projects had the liberatory effect of avoiding taming social risks into previously agreed goals of associated actors, such second stage of the *modernization of development* hid the seed for further phases of deregulatory measures. With the individualization of life projects, the lack of real structures of communication, and the increase of the erosion of social ties, "modern development" is no longer considered a "project committed to the rationalization of intertwined futures in accordance with goals determined by open-ended processes of reflection and negotiation", but as outcomes manufactured within asymmetries spread in the system (Johnson, 2008, p. 78) .

In the task of reconstructing the meaning of a norm of development in which international institutions play a leading role, these considerations enhance the scope of the discussion by offering a twofold property of societies. On the one hand they clear up the existence of norms as devices that emerge not only naturally but also dialogically. This endorses the idea that the development of social, political and cognitive arrangements of societies acting together, can produce normative interventions that can be further empirically grasped. Moreover, such assumption has proved to be fruitful in research of language scrutiny, such as studies directed to analyze the role of speech, argument and persuasion (Habermas, 1984), the emergence of norms entrepreneurship (Finnemore & Barnett, 1999) (Finnemore & Sikkin,

1998), the role of international organizations (Finnemore, 1994) and law, or the existence of "epistemic communities"[3] (Finnnemore & Sikkink, 2001). On the other hand, symmetric interaction endorses the idea that normative constructions need to sum up cooperative and coordinative practices -rather than bargaining-, making them functional devices through which meaning is harvested rather than imposed.

Following contributions on discourse theory and law, constructivism has revealed the weaknesses that frequently afflict approaches that elude the debate between the formal facticity of norms and their inner validity (Habermas, 1996) . In the case of the norm of "modern development", this tension can be characterized by the conflicting nature of regulation that tends to homogenize relations and interests of a highly asymmetric global realm. In this approach, norms "represent social facts demarcating areas within which success oriented individuals (actors) can choose and act as they wish; as [they are supposed to be] linked with a universal freedom, rights deserve the respect of moral subjects, and thus carry a claim to legitimacy"[4] (Habermas, 1996). Besides legal theory, this conflictive dichotomy of the facticity and the validity of norms is the reason by which customary contributions on international institutions set loose and detached from being capable of reconstructing meaning. Finally, this is why they cannot explain how normative constructions such as the idea of "modern development", are customarily embraced as legitimate –or at least reasonable-, despite being formed upon asymmetric global contexts isolated from open concrete criticism.

Criticism

Some of the constraints of critical constructivist approach as a framework to reconstruct discursive interventions, lay in the epistemological limitations of the theory to claim the legitimacy of its own perspective. This concern reveals the potential flaws of critical theory in establishing a coherent "relationship to scientific discourse" from its unilateral standpoint. Moreover, this feature generates a contradiction of the theory which generally claim to have a superior epistemological perspective "contest[ing] the coercive authority of reason with the aim of restoring a democratic plurality of knowledge's" (Koch, 1995, p. 1). Notably, this line of criticism rests in a kind of relativism in interpreting the relation between the structure and the behavior and interests of actors in the customary power politics. Actors do have interests, and as such, behave accordingly with them. Therefore rather than falling into the legitimation of arrangements, a critical constructive analysis to the study of a norm on development, is directed to stress their role within structures of interaction, stressing how they deviate or influence meaning production. This strategy, highlights how normative interventions are nurtured from world perspectives that overlook information that can be reached just dialogically (from a more *democratic* or participative environment), or that normalize actions developed on highly asymmetric governance structures.

In reconstructing the meaning of a norm of modern development, it is possible to suggest that the contemporary governance architecture has nothing to do with the construction of fundamental norms. Therefore, analysis concerning the role of the structure into the process of construction of norms is an unnecessary attempt to explain a political event as a source of meaning. Such reflectivism lay in the fact that constructivism puts emphasis in the description of observable phenomena such as social praxis, although "non-observable elements of social life might be important factors in explaining outcomes, [indeed] (…) without denying the importance of individuals in social explanation, (…) the most influential social processes are non-observable [aka. "scientific"] (Wight, 2007, p. 381) (Wendt, 1999). This line of argument goes along with the positivist approach of International Relations theory, adopting a radical ontological stand in conducting research (Brown, 2011) (Farrel & Finnemore, 2009). However, in order to disjoint the relationship between social constructions and mere facts, the assumption falls loose in explaining the role of context and culture in the process of construction of norms. In fact, it is upon such context and the recognition of the existence of subjectivities that the study of International Relations dropped out from the overall realist tradition of power politics that dominated the science during the last century (Checkel, 1998) . Critical constructivism thus, doesn't only reveal the importance of the structure as the framework through which meaning is produced, but also as a necessary point of research for implementing discourse analysis.

THE BRETTON WOODS INSTITUTIONS AND THE ROLE OF HISTORICAL INSTITUTIONALISM

Concrete Temporal Processes and the Development of Discourse

In the necessity of framing the evolution of norms at the level of the World Bank and the International Monetary Fund, the contributions of historical institutionalism allow us to encompass the reconstruction of influential arrangements that took place since the meeting of Bretton Woods in 1944. In a case study, the main reason for adopting the theoretical approach lay in the fact that the origin of the Bretton Woods Institutions took place on an exceptional historical moment, thus the meetings of New Hampshire represent a crucial event in which a few political participants were able to define, within exceptional contingencies, a global structure that regulated economic and political relations for the decades to come.

Research directed to analyze institutional behavior, emerged as a response to literature on political science and sociology, that frequently framed the study of organizations within structural and functional traditions. During the decades of the 70s, the use of institutions as actors able to be analyzed theoretically, were disrupted in three lines of inquiry, specifically, historical institutionalism, cultural institutionalism, and rational choice institutionalism (Taylor, 1996, p. 7) (Gandara, 2007, p. 5) (Haas, 1964). Historical institutionalism "emphasizes the asymmetries of power associated with the operation and development of institutions". It analyzes institutions from a perspective that joins up political context, outcomes, and the study of strategies and policies adopted by them on time frame scenarios. Cultural institutionalism looked after the implications of patterns and human behavior rather than human calculus and cost maximizing rationality on the mechanisms of institutional decision making. Finally, rational choice institutionalism "emphasize[s] the importance of property rights, rent-seeking, and transactions costs to the operation and development of institution". Within such subdivisions, the difficulties of elaborating an agent-reconstructive analysis[5] of the norm of "modern development", and the distinctive historic features of the Bretton Woods Institutions, reveal that historical institutionalism can fill the gap left by alternative theoretical schools that tend to overlook biographical contingencies of international organizations.

On the other hand, the relevance of "concrete historical processes", demonstrate the role of chronological moments through which institutions evolve and determine their T*emporality* function (Thelen, 1999, p. 382). These approach play a substantial role in explaining why institutions *frequently embrace changes and political circumstances that emerge within unforeseen events,* rather than behaving "rationally" or according to a defined functional goal. This feature of the theory reveals, that the study of discursive interventions, should take into account significant historical circumstances that shape the context of normative production at the level of international organizations. Moreover, it explains the selection of fundamental institutional values, linking them up with temporal events that emerge from particular historical "constellations".

Finally, in reconstructing a norm of "modern development", discursive interventions that share peculiar contexts are treated more as assemblies to be explored within the boundaries of *the historical*, that is to say; inquiry on the reconstruction of discursive interventions of international institutions, while carried out in between the settings of systemic constellations, should include in the analysis the extent to which contemporary structures of governance emerged within clearly defined chronological events.

Institutionalism and the Relation Between Institutions and Superstructures

In the analysis of normative constructions and the association of these with the customary operations that take place within the institutions, historical institutionalism adopts a rather pragmatic view of politics by relying in the contributions of rational choice institutionalism to explain actors intentionality's at the decision-making level of organizations. It builds up a tradition of international relations theory, that embraces the reality of power, as a complementary feature of the preferences of actors on a defined historical moment, stressing that "polity and economy structures conflict so as to privilege some interests while demobilizing others" (Eckstein & Apter, 1963).

While a significant branch of literature criticizing a norm of "development" has turned to the analysis of the role of the nation-state as the natural operational agent, historical institutionalism shifts the debate to the analysis of the global political economy, and thus to the role of the superstructure in constraining the nation-state by regulative and political arrangements that take place beyond the boundaries of otherwise "autonomous" social entities. As it has been explained:

[H]istorical institutionalists [are] influenced by the way in which structural functionalists saw the polity as an overall system of interacting parts. (...) [In reaction] they saw the intitutional organization of the polity or political economy (...) They emphasized the 'structuralism' implicit in the institutions of the polity rather than the 'functionalism' of earlier approaches that viewed political outcomes as a response to the needs of the system (Hall & Taylor, 1996, p. 96).

It is within such boundaries that contrary to customary assumptions in the analysis of today's international politics, encounters of countries on asymmetric international arenas are framed by operational, cultural, cognitive and organizational limitations of highly disfunctional architectures and institutional environments. In this sense, the nation state, rather than being enhanced by a given coordinating capacity, is bounded by the role of the structure, and the set of systemic features that have guided the system through decades.

Institutional Values and Meaning

Historical institutionalism enhances the level of explanation of conflicting interests in the global domain, without entering on the complex territory of assigning value laden assumptions on the relations between culture and the idea of development. Instead of judging the *structural functionalist* approach to institutions it´s "likely to be concerned with the origins" (Thelen, 1999, p. 382) . As such, it is not dependent on the "social, psychological or cultural traits of individuals as the parameters driving much of the system's operation" (Hall & Taylor, 1996, p. 96) . In the study of a normative construction created at global governance level, this feature, rather than demeaning the role of cultural values of actors, focuses in criticizing the strong limitations of conceiving the idea of "modern development" as a construction embedded within isolated epistemic communities or cultural encounters, such as those likely to take place at the World Bank or the IMF.

Institutions have a tendency to adopt patterns that are frequently repeated over time. Even when facing strong contradictions they rely on historical practices that emerge within historical stages that overlap unevenly. Indeed, traditions represent a substantial part of their cognitive boundaries and "cultural constrains".

The distinctions between a rational oriented approach to explain the emergence of institutions, and an approach that traces the historical and political features of asymmetric environments such as the Bretton Woods Institutions, has made historical institutionalism to branch out into two necessary approaches for further research on normative meaning. On the one hand, a functionalist (Thelen, 1999, p. 393), that highlights the incentives, in which policy feedback, is produced at the institutional level –previously discussed-. On the other hand; a systemic, making it a tool to analyze the "distributional effects of institutions". This last branch, turns to the discussion on how discursive interventions at the institutional level build over time -reconstructing along their own narratives relations that are closely embedded within biographical stages-. As Thelen has pointed out;

"institutions are not neutral coordinating mechanisms but (…) reflect, and also reproduce and magnify, particular patterns of power distribution in politics (…) [facilitating] the empowerment of certain groups while actively disarticulating and marginalizing others. The distributional biases in particular institutions or policies "feedback" so that "over time, some avenues of policy become increasingly blocked, if not entirely cut off" as "decisions at one point in time can restrict future possibilities by sending policy off onto particular tracks" (Thelen, 1999, p. 394) .IV

Following this perspective, further research on the reconstruction of discursive interventions on "modern development", ought to highlight the role of the "distributional effects" that take place during the policy making process; reproduced on biased normative interventions in the IMF and the World Bank. This strategy bears in mind that distributional effects are customarily affected by the unequal control and conflicting relations of actors over a structure, which in turn tends to reproduce over time anomalous patterns. In sum, by stressing the biographical settings of organizations, historical institutionalism can explain the evolution of contradictory normative interventions that take place at the level of international institutions. In this approach, research directed to reconstruct discourse and normative interventions on development at the level of the Bretton Woods organizations, ought to stress the role of concrete temporal processes (Thelen, 1999, pp. 371-382) (Taylor, 1996), the asymmetric control over the superstructures and the role of institutional values and politics in the production of meaning (Thompson, 1999) (Campbel, 2002) (Campbell, 1998).

POLITICAL ASYMMETRY AT THE BBWWII

In The Definition Of Political Asymmetry

Today, the foundational body of norms of the World Trade Organization and the International Monetary Fund represent the most legitimate source from which historically the policies for "development" were globally institutionalized. In such settings, the discourse on development was only possible to be carried out through the normative grid that standardized political and economic relations of countries, within the legal frontiers of the GATT, the Articles of Agreement, and the *By-Laws* rules and regulations of the IMF and the World Bank. At present, and since 1978, the customary approach to the idea of development derives from the official publications of the World Bank, and particularly from the World Development Report. This report, has arguably been the leading voice of the International Institutional Commerce System, "expanding" the capacity of marginal countries and populations to transit the path to become "modern economies and societies" (World Bank, 1978, p. 1). In recent decades, the construction of the concept through the use of institutional publications, has contributed not only to define a specific theoretical and ideological framework, but to establish power relations and ideological constrains that contribute to emphasize the same settings in accordance with the regulatory legacy of the organizations. While historical circumstances define the evolution of international organizations in contemporary societies, they themselves are not capable of explaining how the internal settings favor, distort or reproduce selected narratives. Frequently, the validity of their interventions is linked up with their capacity to legitimate normative constructions, assuming that members of their functional and political administration, are capable to perceive and interact with other members' views and subjectivities in a symmetric dialogical scenario. Since we assume that this is not the case, foundational purposes of organizations tangled into power relations, moving them away from their deontological aims.

As it has been mentioned above, in formal structures of administration, we define political asymmetry as the (RUEDA, 2013):

a. Unequal capacity of actors to relate within a structure while formalizing normative constructions into systemic structures.
b. Unequal capacity of actors to operate within the system structure in accordance with the structure resources of base.
    1. Cultural cognitive sphere
    2. Formal power sphere

a. **The capacity to formalize normative constructions into systemic structures:** At the level of the Bretton Woods, institutional imbalances are characterized by the relation between the representation and the level of influence of the actor's part of the institutions, since the foundational process enabled extensive influence of limited political players in the process of creation of executive and political boards (Eichengreen, 2004) (Eichengreen, 2008) . In this fashion, for the IMF and the WB, even after the last quota reform that took place in 2008 "voting power [of influential countries such as the United States] is always substantially much more than its weight, while for all other members, their voting power shares are slightly lower than their weights". This setting not only represent the allocation of voting influence one-sided from the "one person, one vote" rule -with many emerging markets seriously under-represented-, but reproduces a bias compounded by the inequality in the distribution of burdens of economic and political relations, and the overall voting rules" (Leech, 2012) (Dreher et. al., 2010) (Leech, 2004). Preliminarily, it can be said that rather than being isolated events, these types of pathologies are part of the Bretton Woods Institutions from their foundational constitution (Mikesell, 1994) and have reproduced historically within the diverse structures of representation of the institutional architecture (Lombardi, 2006) (Swedberg, 1986) (Mikesell, 1994) (Dennis Leech, 2004) .

1. **Cognitive sphere.** Cognitive asymmetries are represented in the cultural unevenness between representatives of international organizations that regulate political global arrangements such as international trade, or monetary and economic relations between highly uneven global actors, and are contextualized within three features of the WB and the IMF. On the one hand, they permeate the overall foundational values of the organizations, because defined actors have increasingly more information and access to spaces of participative and decision making power within the foundational events of the organizations that took place in New Hampshire in 1944 (Mikesell, 1994) (Eichengreen, 2004) (Boughton, 2002). Secondly, normative and regulatory outcomes of the institutions are further normalized and defined in accordance with the interests of strategic actors. From the foundation, such quality of governance originated on the goals of capital exporting nodes able to influence the decision making process of low industrialized territories, configuring a process of exploitation of their political, cultural and institutional vulnerabilities (Escobar, 1995) (Escobar, 2008) (Barro, 2005) (Lombardi, 2006). Third, because along the contemporary customary operation, access to information at the institutions, and epistemological practices continue to be framed in accordance with cultural backgrounds represented in specialized staff from defined countries (Riles, 2010) (Vetterlein and others, 2010).
2. Formal power: Represented in the role of money, staff, voting power and representation in the management and decision-making bodies of both the International Monetary Fund as well as the World Bank (Vetterlein, 2010) .

Asymmetry and the Analysis of Discursive Interventions

On the task of reconstructing a norm of modern development, it is pivotal to consider the different effects globalization has over core and periphery arenas (Stiglitz, 2003) (Spanu, 2003) (Khan Haider, 2008). This consideration highlights basic consequences derived from defined features of institutions, which in turn provide hints for further inquiry focused on the process of governance. On the other hand, research directed to reveal this distinction can generate contributions for the policy-making process of capital scarce, or low industrialized territories, which for the most part have historically endure the burdens of highly unbalanced political and economic environments. Finally, the implications of asymmetric relations along the process of construction of a norm on "development" expand the debate over the meaning of "development", and how biased cognitive abridgments from which public policies nurture, are bounded to conflicting interests within an uneven governance arena.

Research over the normative outcomes of deliberations that mis-rationalize (Habermas, 1984, p. 47) global defined norms, have avoided the institutionalization of paradigms aroused under unique periods of history[6]. The implications of asymmetric cultural backgrounds and power relations boosts theoretical and political concerns related to the spheres of the normative framing of principles of global constitutionalism, and deontological debates over the ordinary practices of institutions such as the World Bank, the WTO and the International Monetary Fund. These concerns are customarily related to the preeminence of the principle of growth over inequality and the idea of "development". This in turn has shaped discursive interventions of international institutions during the last century, creating norms with constitutional character permeated by predefined economic paradigms (Peters, 2011). In contemporary social contract theory, this legitimation of unbalanced relations as pre-contractual agreements can be associated to public institutional philosophy[7]. Despite their attempts to detach from a utilitarian perspective, it has emphasizes the *genuineness* of post-contractual institutional arrangements. After the Second World War, such conceptual tendencies, found their way in the contractual tradition to law and justice, assuming that normative interventions of highly influential institutions such as the World Bank or the IMF, were legitimate by the mere fact of being "official", or recognized as an outcome of a previous contractual agreement. However, this approach is not absent of criticism. A) On the one hand contractual theory leaves no room for further discussions about the legitimacy of international institutions. B) Secondly, attempts to change the arrangements of the global economic architecture could lead to the problem of political inertia, and the violation of the principle of *efficiency (Rawls, 1971, p. 65)* .

More recently, strong institutionalism is recognized as increasingly unsustainable[8]. This is because discursive interventions at the level of institutions, should not consider norms as a "states of affairs", but rather analyze their validity rationalizing them as devices that represent the "manifestation of [historical] subjective experiences" (Habermas, 1984, p. 57).

Bearing in mind the above mentioned conditions, research directed to highlight the consequences of political asymmetry, should also stress the existence of a subjectivity attached to power, or forms of interpretation of political relations entirely embedded in the modern asymmetric settings and the current economic global sphere. Such assumption makes possible the reconstruction of meaning of a *"life world"* rationalized under conditions of political and economic privilege or deprivation further linked to practices on governance[9] (Habermas, 1988, p. 26). Furthermore, it should consider that frequently, countries meet under unbalanced institutional scenarios, which in turn makes necessary to conduct inquiry directed to reveal the patterns taken by actors on these negotiations, and the contradictions of their expectations, discursive interventions and instrumental actions[10] (Heat, 2010). For further research, political and institutional phenomena can be considered not only as an event bounded by institutional or sociological practices, but also to philosophical conceptions that reify social relations between agents in defined international environments. Indeed, the pervaded existence of political asymmetries, carries out the assumption that the once constituted institutions, conceived to shape international scenarios for economic and political agreement, were later embedded in systemic dynamics of power that eroded their same original constitutive traditions.

In highlighting the role of asymmetries, research oriented to the analysis of discursive interventions stresses the problematic historicity contained within the process of maturation of such institutions. This demonstrates how customary normative interventions, rather than being formed upon participation, flow of free information or subject-oriented governance practices, sink instead into the entanglement of isolated interests competing through decades for thriving or surviving.

To stress the role of political asymmetry as a substantive quality of the process of production of norms, means to carry out the study of the relationship between perceptions (cognition) and formal power as correlated boundaries in the development of meaning. This twofold strategy can enhance the capacity to explain how the current institutional normativity of the Bretton Woods Institutions may have eroded fundamental practices of democracy, participation, and flow of information; narrowing the semantic boundaries from which a better understanding of modern development can nurture semantically. Finally, it can reveal how global governance procedures evolve to become bargaining practices, diluting fundamental principles of justice in a *for profit* rationality, and threatening to elevate to a constitutional category norms isolated from scientific knowledge and facts.

ASSUMPTIONS FOR THE STUDY OF A NORM ON *DEVELOPMENT*

Customarily, the idea of development is based upon the assumption that history is a deterministic project where normative constructions cannot take into account the role of socialization or subjectivity. This hypothesis however, usually presents flaws in the arena of politics, because any conjecture about the evolution of contemporary social systems, is to be drawn from conceiving modern societies as *democratic* or participative endeavors. Consequently, just upon the increasing levels of sophistication of their mechanisms of coordination, they are able to reach higher stages of "development". In this conditions, the attempt to conduct inquiry on the normative dimension of the concept of "development", should bear in mind that in contemporary societies norms are constructions that operate politically into social environments permeated by both, processes of coordination and socialization, and institutions. While social constructions remain heterogeneous, the operation into social environments is defined by organizational, historical, cultural and structural constraints. What makes the legitimation of social constructions possible, is the common capacity of participants to communicate by making use of rational statements, while adopting a set of shared beliefs about "something" in the outside world. In this regard, the environmental and historical conditions in which these dialogues operate, are frequently prone to evolve in accordance with their own shared political circumstances. Such view, nurtured in constructivist literature, built up in recent decades an approach to norms that confronted the realist and liberal wave that broadly dominated the debate from the second half of the 20th century. While the underlying conceptions of social structures as communicative structures, unchained the limitations of the common goal oriented rationalities, it also enhanced the role of the individual as an interpreter and conscious agent of the political life. This shift reallocated rationality at the core, jointing it to classical traditions of thinking in which social structures were established by bearing in mind cognitive boundaries from which the external world is rationalized. Due to the conflicting ontological dimension from which a norm on development can nurture, when we speak about *norms*, we do so by embracing a particular constructivist stand in which they are not considered as superstructures produced apart the outside material world, but as social constructions able to be raised dialogically, conceding to the material world attributes of source of meaning.

While the realist tradition has argued that norms rise up from teleological reflections of actors (*objective* goal orientations), it fails in explaining the limitations of the individual "human nature" as the predominant source of meaning of complex modern societies[11] (Section 3rd) (Habermas, 2006). In this dispute, recent constructivist literature directed to explain such handicaps have successfully demonstrated how institutional autonomy (epistemic communities), culture, and communication became in contrast dominant vectors of social sophistication and behavior. More than a dichotomy, these two features, can be better represented as a symbiotic relationship between the material environment and the social structure as cognitive origins from which normative abstractions nurture. This alternative stand, is widely explained in the first chapter of this book. It eases the difficulties of departing theoretically from the realist tradition, or of mixing it up with concepts such as the identity, the interpretation, the culture, the role of actors and the overlapping political structures as the variables that influence creation of normative meaning. As previously depicted, in research aimed to reconstruct a norm of *modern development*, we identify that reason and dialogical interaction of societies plays a complementary role to that of culture and subjectivity (Wiener, 2007) (Brown, 2011) (Wight, 2007) (Checkel, 1998). This means that the meaning of discursive interventions, can be also considered as a functional praxis of the Cartesian legacy, therefore, as a source of information that further develops on the idea of historical direction[12], yet stressing the social role of the identity of individuals (Wendt, 1999).

Thereby, research directed to reconstruct normative meaning, should acknowledge that norms are also information filtered by the senses, the intellect, the language, the culture, the historical moment and the cognitive capabilities of agents. Thus, regulative norms, are representations of communal or collective understandings of social agreements on historical and material circumstances, further embodied institutionally once they are embraced by actors through logics of appropriateness and argumentation (Clifford, 2009) (Wiener, 2007). Most recently, research on the analysis of discursive interventions, points out that norms are "enacted through (…);1) the degree of appropriateness depending on the potential for social recognition (…) 2) the perception of legitimacy depending on the degree of persuasion generated through deliberation; and 3) …the degree of understanding generated through the interactive process of cultural validation" (Wiener & Pueter, 2009). As with any other social construction, norms can be considered to be exteriorizations of context-framed communalities further parameterized into linguistic or symbolic utterances; playing a fundamental role in the assembly of social systems and grounding the beginning of the development of systems autonomy (Habermas, 1988, p. 11). As boundaries for social behavior, norms are to be permanently subjected to a dialectic relation with the outer nature so that they can be consistently exposed to processes of argumentative validity. This is why further research on normative constructions should acknowledge that norms constrain the process of thinking, and ground the restrictions through which the understanding of the outer nature acquires meaning. On the other hand, this societal "development", is supported in the assumption of the existence of socio historical stages that differentiate human political systems from other natural systems, thus providing them historicity. Finally, the recognition of the existence of developmental stages, represents the theoretical ground for conceiving history not as a disorderly set of events, but as a fundamental source of information from which later societies *rationalize acts and meaning*.

CONCLUSION

Aiming to contribute to research directed to reconstruct meaning of normative interventions, and particularly to inquiry on the norm of modern "development", the present chapter argues that such endeavor can be addressed by stepping out from customary approaches of political science, and international relations. After the fall of the Berlin Wall and the increasing influence of the global economy over the process of organization of the nation state, the debate on development consistently ignored the role of money and power as devices that steered functional gaps of the political spheres of societies. Moreover, customary literature on development increasingly fell in ambiguities in which worldviews of periphery actors were displaced to marginal roles in the global power politics. This stresses the necessity of addressing the topic by using an alternative framework, capable of defining the ideological patterns of current structures of governance and their operation within a highly unbalanced institutional arena. In contrast with institutional literature, this chapter concludes that any attempt to study normative interventions of international organizations in this field should highlight systemic distortions of the institutional narrative. Bearing in mind that the concept of development has acquired a mystification in a narrative of modernity, the chapter stresses that such norm frequently operate as an ideological device derived from economic relations that *greenwash* socially or *environmentally (aka. Systemic)*-destructive activities. This embrace the limitations of customary literature in offering a feasible methodological agreement in how to conduct research directed to the study of meaning. Drawing from historical contributions on sociology and political science, such as critical constructivism, as well as more recent theories on international relations with a focus on history, such as historical institutionalism, this chapter offers a theoretical starting point to conduct research of discursive interventions bearing in mind the following provisions:

a. In the task of proposing an alternative perspective to analyze critically discursive interventions of "development", this chapter stresses the necessity of reconstructing meaning by making use of two theoretical approaches; critical constructivism and historical institutionalism. It argues that the task to conduct research aimed to reconstruct such interventions, should be addressed using a sociological and historical perspective that disentangle the consequences of asymmetric relations that take place on the institutional discourse of the norm. Such focus can reveal the structural weaknesses of contemporary representations of the idea of "development", produced systematically in highly asymmetric environments such as the Bretton Woods Institutions.
b. By appropriating contributions on critical constructivism, the chapter notes the relevance of contextualizing normative constructions as byproducts of processes of communication, nurtured in between historical transitions of late modern societies. It argues, that critical constructivism, enhance the necessity of reflecting about the increasing role of the economy in the progression of a norm of "modern development". This process happens amidst the raise of new etico-political dimensions of individualization, that gain ascendancy threatening the project of a "democratic" social order. Finally, the chapter points to highlight three fundamental properties of text; *the role of economic relations over contemporary normative interventions, the relevance of subtle formal structures on discourse production, and the idea of normative constructions as a practice of symmetric interaction.*
c. In the task of explaining the role and the functional limitations of the Bretton Woods Institutions in addressing a chronological norm on "modern development" absent from robust criticism, the present chapter endorses to literature on historical institutionalism. It argues, that the evolution of the norm within a highly uneven structure of governance, rather than being clarified from a structural functionalist perspective, should be grasped by emphasizing the role that concrete historical processes played in the progression of such settings. It furthermore describes the limitations of functional perspectives, that frame norms production within the boundaries of concrete cultural backgrounds, isolating the historical circumstances that nurtured the ideological routes of a contemporary highly influential international architecture. Finally, the chapter also adheres to the idea that institutions reproduce and magnify patterns of power distribution in accordance with an internal narrative. Bearing in mind this quality of language, research directed to reconstruct meaning should stress the role of three feature of discourse, *the existence of concrete temporal processes, the relation between institutions and superstructures and the influence of institutional values and meaning in normative production.*
d. Finally, the chapter suggests preliminary methodological and ontological conventions. First, it briefly introduces the role of the concept of political asymmetry, and its relation with a norm on societal "development" within late modern societies. In this regard, it argues that asymmetry, as any other structural feature of organizations, is bounded to governance architectures such as those

taking place at the International Monetary Fund or the World Bank. Secondly, it sketches alternative ontological assumptions for the study of norms.

By proposing an alternative theoretical framework, this chapter aims to enhance the debate about the norm of "modern development", so frequently taken for granted in the public debate and in the historical record of international organizations such as the World Bank and the International Monetary Fund. Rather than suggesting the necessity of contributing to customary institutional or academic literature, it embraces the idea of conducting critical inquiry of discursive interventions, and therefore, the meaning of a norm from a serious theoretical standpoint. Finally, stressing the role of historical institutionalism and critical constructivism, this chapter aims to foster research within which the reconstruction of a norm on "development" at the Bretton Woods Institutions can be coherently grasped in the public and academic debate.

REFERENCES

Barro, R. J., 2005. and Jong-Wha Lee. IMF Programs: Who Is Chosen and What Are the Effects?. Department of Economics, Harvard University. Department of Economics, Korea University. April.

Barro, R. J. a. J.-W. L., 2005. IMF Programs: Who Is Chosen And What Are The Effects?. *Journal of Monetary Economics,* 7 October, Volume 52, pp. 1245-1269.

Bird-Pollan, S. M.-D. a. S., 2010. *Nation state, capitalism, democracy: Philosophical and political motives in European Journal of Social Theory. 13: 443 the thought of Jürgen Habermas DOI:* .. s.l.:s.n. doi:10.1177/1368431010382759

Black, E. R. (1960, June). The age of economic development. *Economic Journal (London), 70*(278), 266–276. doi:10.2307/2228727

Blommaert, J. (2005). *Discourse: A Critical Introduction. Key topics in sociolinguistics.* Cambridge University Press. doi:10.1017/CBO9780511610295

Blommaert, J., & Bulcaen, C. (2000). Critical Discourse Analysis. Annual Review of Anthropology. *VOl., 29,* 447–466.

Boughton, J. M. 2002. Why White, Not Keynes? Inventing the Postwar International Monetary System. *IMF Working Paper,* March.pp. 1-25.

Brown, V. 2011. The Reflectivist Critique of Positivist IR Theory. Cardiff University. http://www.e-ir.info/2011/02/27/the-reflectivist-critique-of-positivist-ir-theory/, February 27.

Campbel, J. L. (2002). Ideas, politics, and public policy. [s.l.:s.n.]. *Annual Review of Sociology, 28*(1), 21–38. doi:10.1146/annurev.soc.28.110601.141111

Campbell, J. L. (1998). *No. 3 (Jun., 1998)* (Vol. 27). Institutional Analysis and the Role of Ideas in Political Economy. Theory and Society. Sprynger., https://www.jstor.org/stable/657900

Cass, D. (2001). The "Constitutionalization" of International Trade Law: Judicial Norm-Generation as the engine of constitutional development on international trade. The Constitutionalisation of International Trade Law (2011). *European Journal of International Law, 12*(1), 39–75. doi:10.1093/ejil/12.1.39

Chang, H.-J. (2002). *Kicking Away the Ladder. Development Strategy in Historical Perspective*. Anthem Press.

Checkel, J. (1998, January). The Constructivist turn in International Relations Theory. Review Article. *World Politics, 50*, 324–348. doi:10.1017/S0043887100008133

Checkel, J. (1998, January). The Constructivist turn in International Relations Theory. Review Article. *World Politics, 50*, 324–348. doi:10.1017/S0043887100008133

Clifford, B. 2009. *New human rights issues. Understanding their contentious rise. Colombia Internacional 69, ene - jun 2009, Pp 228, ISSN 0121-5612, Bogotá, Pp. 14 - 35.* s.l.:s.n.

Dennis Leech, R. L., 2004. Voting Power in the Bretton Woods Institutions. *WARWICK ECONOMIC RESEARCH PAPERS*, November, Issue 718.

Dreher et. al., A. &. J.-E. S., 2010. *Do the IMF and theWorld Bank influence voting in the UN General Assembly. Public Choice. DOI* .. s.l.:s.n. doi:10.1007/s11127-010-9750-2

Eckstein, H., & Apter, D. 1963. *Comparative Politics. Glencoe, Free Press.* s.l.:s.n.

Eichengreen, B. 2004. Global Imbalances and the Lessons from Bretton Woods. *National Bureau of Economic Research*, May, Volume Working Paper No. 10497, p. 39.

Eichengreen, B. (2008). *Globalizing Capital:A History of the International Monetary System* (2nd ed.). Princeton University Press. doi:10.2307/j.ctt7pfmc

Escobar, A. (1995). *Encountering Development. The making and unmaking of the third world*. Princeton University Press.

Escobar, A. (2008). The Problematization of Poverty; the tale of three worlds and development. In *The development reader* (pp. 131–140). MPG, Books Ltd. Bodmin.

Fairclough & Chouliaraki. N. a. L., 1999. Discourse in Late Modernity. Rethinking Critical Discourse Analysis. Edimburgh University Press. Cambridge. ISBN. 0-7486-1082-0.

Farrel & Finnemore. (2009, February). H. a. M., 2009. Ontology, methodology and causation in the American school of international political economy. George Washington University,Washington, DC, USA. *Review of International Political Economy, 16*(1), 58–71.

Finnemore, M., 1994. International organizations as teachers of norms: the United Nations Educational, Scientific, and Cutural Organization and science policy. ntemational Organization 47, 4, Autumn 1993, pp. 565-597 ?3 1994 by The 10 Foundation and the MIT.

Finnemore, M., 1994. International organizations as teachers of norms: the United Nations Educational, Scientific, and Cutural Organization and science policy. ntemational Organization 47, 4, Autumn 1993, pp. 565-597 ?3 1994 by The 10 Foundation and the MIT.

Finnemore & Barnett. M. &. M., 1999. The politics, power and pathologies of International Organizations. International Organization 53. 4, Autumn, pp. 699-732. By the IO Fundation and the Massachusetts Institute of Technology. s.l.:s.n.

Finnemore & Sikkin, M. a. K., 1998. International Norm Dynamics and Political Change. nternational Organization 52, 4, Autumn 1998, pp. 887-917 . 1998 by The 10 Foundation and the Massachusetts Institute of Technology..

Finnnemore & Sikkink, M. &. K., 2001. *TAKING STOCK: The Constructivist Research Programin International Relations and Comparative Politics. Annu. Rev. Polit. Sci. 2001. 4:391–416 Copyright c ⟳ 2001 by Annual Reviews.* s.l.:s.n.

Gandara, P. 2007. *The Role of Energy for Regional Integration in the EMP:Working Paper Number 0712.* Berlín: Jean Monnet Centre of Excellence.Freie Universität Berlin. Germany. Date: 31/12/2007. The Sixth Framework Programme. Contract No. 028386.

Haas, E. B. (1964). *Beyond the Nation-State. Functionalism and International Organization.* Stanford University Press. Stanford. California.

Habermas, J. 1984. *The Theory of Communicative Action, Volume 1: Reason and the Rationalization of Society. Translated by Thomas McCarthy. Boston: Beacon Press,* s.l.:s.n.

Habermas, J. 1988. Legitimation Crisis. British Library Cataloguing in Publication Data. ISBN 0-7456-0609-1. First published in Great Britain by Heinemann Educational Books 1976.First published by Polity Press.: s.n.

Habermas, J. 1996. Between Facts and Norms. Contributions to a Discourse Theory of Law and Democracy. Translated by William Rehg. Massachusetts Institute of Technology. Faktizität und Geltung. Beiträge zur Diskurstheorie des Rechts und des demokratischen Rechtsstaats, ISBN 0-262-08243-8. ©: s.n. doi:10.7551/mitpress/1564.001.0001

Habermas, J. (2000). *The Postnational Constellation* (M. Pensky, Trans.). MIT Press.

Habermas, J., 2001. Why Europe Need a Constitution. New Left Review 11 sep oct 2001-5.

Habermas, J., 2006. Between Naturalism and Religion. Entre Naturalismo y Religión. Ediciones Paidós Ibérica, S. A..

Hall & Taylor. P. a. R., 1996. Political Science and the new three Institutionalisms. Political Studies Association. XLIV. 936-957. Blackwell publishers.

Heat, J. 2010. *'Legitimation crisis' in the later work of Jürgen Habermas. In* https://philpapers.org/rec/HEALCI. *University of Montreal. 15-04.* s.l.:s.n.

Hopf, T. (1998, Summer). The Promise of Constructivism in International Relations Theory. [MIT Press.]. *International Security, 23*(1), 171–200. doi:10.1162/isec.23.1.171

Huckin, T. A. J. &. C.-L. J. (2012). Critical discourse analysis and rhetoric and composition. *College Composition and Communication*, 107–129.

Johnson, P. (2008). Globalizing Democracy: Reflections on Habermas's Radicalism. *European Journal of Social Theory, 11*(1), 71–86. https://est.sagepub.com/content/11/1/71. doi:10.1177/1368431007085288

Khan Haider, Y. L. 2008. "Globalization and the WTO Dispute Settlement Mechanism: Making a Rules-based Trading Regime Work". MPRA Paper 7613, University Library of Munich, Germany, revised.: s.n.

Koch, R. (1995). The case of Latour. *Configurations, 3*(3), 319–347. doi:10.1353/con.1995.0020

Leech, D. &. L. R., 2004. "Voting Power and Voting Blocs," The Warwick Economics Research Paper Series (TWERPS) 716, University of Warwick, Department of Economics.

Leech, D. L. a. R., 2012. A New Analysis of A Priori Voting Power in the IMF: Recent Quota Reforms Give Little Cause for Celebration. WARWICK ECONOMIC RESEARCH PAPERS. No. 1001..

Lewis, N. 2011. 1971: Bretton Woods And The Four-Decade Trauma Of Its Collapse. https://www.forbes.com/2011/07/07/bretton-woods-collapse.html. 2011.

Lombardi, N. W. &. D., 2006. Uneven patterns of governance: how developing countries are represented in the IMF. *Review of International Political Economy,* August, 13(3), pp. 480-515.

Mikesell, R. F. 1994. The Bretton Woods debates. A memoir. Essays in International Finance, March, Volume 192, p. 76.

Moore, B. 1985. Authority and Inequality under Capitalism and Socialism. Oxford(Brasenose College): s.n.

North, D. C. (1991). Institutions. *The Journal of Economic Perspectives, 5*(1), 97–112. doi:10.1257/jep.5.1.97

Park & Vetterlein. S. a. A., 2010. Do policy norms reconstitute global development? In Susan Park & Antje Vetterlein. Owning Development. Creating Policy Norms in the IMF and the WB. Cambridge University Press.

Peters, A. 2011. The Constitutionalisation of International Trade Law (2011). THE PROSPECTS OF INTERNATIONAL TRADE REGULATION: FROM FRAGMENTATION TO COHERENCE, pp. 69-102, Cambridge University Press.

Peters, A. 2011. The Constitutionalisation of International Trade Law (2011). THE PROSPECTS OF INTERNATIONAL TRADE REGULATION: FROM FRAGMENTATION TO COHERENCE, pp. 69-102, Cambridge University Press.

Rasmussen M, D., 1976. *Advanced Capitalism and Social Theory: Habermas On the Problem of Legitimation: DOI: Philosophy Social Criticism 1976 3: 349.* s.l.:s.n. doi:10.1177/019145377600300402

Rawls, J., 1971. *A Theory of Justice. 0674017722, 9780674017726. Harvard University Press.* s.l.:s.n.

Riles, A., 2010. *Collateral Expertise: Legal Knowledge in the Global Financial Markets. The Wenner-Gren Foundation for Anthropological Research. All rights reserved. 0011-3204/2010/5106-0006..* s.l.:s.n.

Rodrick, D. 2002. *Feasible Globalizations. NBER Working Paper No. 9129. JEL No. F0. September.* s.l.:s.n.

Rodrik, D., 2001. *Trading in Illusions. Foreign Policy. No. 123 (Mar. – Apr., 2001), pp. 54-62. (article consists of 9 pages). Published by: Washingtonpost.Newsweek Interactive, LLC. Stable URL:* https://www.jstor.org/stable/3183155. s.l.:s.n.

RUEDA. (2013). *R.* POLITICAL ASYMMETRY.

Rueda, C. R. 2013. Global Crisis and History Repeating: Three Historical Stages of the Norm of „Modern Development" within the Regulatory Framework of the Bretton Woods Institutions. SSRN Scholarly Paper. Rochester, NY: Social Science Research Network, 24. Juli.

Sachs., W., 1993. *Global Ecology and the Shadow of „Development".. in Global Ecology: A New Arena of Political Conflict, pp3 – 21 Wolfgang Sachs (ed), London and New Jersey: Zed Books..* s.l.:s.n.

Spanu, V. 2003. Liberalization of the international trade and economic growth: implications for both developed and developing countries. John F. Kennedy School of Government. 79 Kennedy Street. Harvard University. Cambridge, MA 02138 May.: s.n.

Stiglitz, J., 2003. *Globalization and Its Discontents.* Penguin; Auflage: New Ed (3. April 2003). ISBN-10: 014101038X. ISBN-13: 978-0141010380.: s.n.

Swedberg, R., 1986. The Doctrine of Economic Neutrality of the IMF and the World Bank. *Journal of Peace Research,* December, 23(4), pp. 377-390.

Taylor, P. A. H. R. R. (1996). Political Science and the Three New Institutionalism. *Polilical Studies Associalion, XLIV*, 936–957.

Tenorio, E. H. (2011). Critical Discourse Analysis, an Overview. *Nordic Journal of English Studies, 10*(1), 183–210. doi:10.35360/njes.247

Thelen, K. 1999. "Historical Institutionalism in Comparative Politics" edited by Sven Steinmo, Kathleen Thelen, and Frank Longstreth. Annual Review of Political Science 2(1):369–404. Retrieved (https://www.annualreviews.org/doi/abs/10.1146/annurev.p

Thelen, K. (1999). Historical Institutionalism in Comparative Politics. *Annual Review of Political Science, 2*(1), 369–404. doi:10.1146/annurev.polisci.2.1.369

Thompson, A. (1999). Alexander Thompson and Duncan Snidal. The History of International Organizations. *University of Chicago., 9800*, 692–722.

Vetterlein., & Associates. P., 2010. Owning Development: Creating Policy Norms in the IMF and the World Bank. Cambridge: Cambridge University Press.

Vetterlein, S. P. a. A., 2010. Owning development: creating policy norms in the IMD and the World Bank..

Wade, R. H., 2003. *The World Trade Organization and the schrinking of the development space. Working Paper No.31. London School of Economics. Development Research Center..* s.l.:s.n.

Wendt, A., 1999. Wendt Alexander. Social Theory of International Politics. Wendt, A. (1999). Social Theory of International Politics.. PUBLISHED BY CAMBRIDGE UNIVERSITY PRESS. doi:10.1017/CBO9780511612183

Wiener, A., 2007. *Constructivist Approaches in International Relations Theory: Puzzles and Promises Constitutionalism Webpapers, ConWEB No 5/2006. Queen's University Belfast. Rivista Italiana di Scienza Politica.*. s.l.:s.n.

Wiener, A., 2007. *Contested Meanings of Norms: A Research Framework. Comparative European Politics, 2007, 5, (1–17). Palgrave Macmillan Ltd 1472-4790/07.* s.l.:s.n.

Wiener, A., 2014. *A Theory of Contestation. Springer Berlin Heidelberg.*. s.l.:s.n.

Wiener & Pueter, A. &. U., 2009. *The quality of Norms is what actors make of it. Critical constructivism research on norms. Journal of International Law and International Relations. Introduction. Volume 5, issue 1. Winter 2009. Special issue. Contested Norms iin International law and IR.* s.l.:s.n.

Wight, C. (2007, March). A manifesto for Scientific Realism in IR: Assuming the Can-Opener Won't Work. *Millennium, 35*(2), 379–398. doi:10.1177/03058298070350021601

World Bank. 1978. World Development Report. World Bank. Library of Congress Catalog Number: 78-67086.

ENDNOTES

1 As "the formal or informal procedures, routines, norms and conventions embedded in the organizational structure of the polity or political economy". This definition withdraw from customary functionalist perspectives such as North definition, namely: "Institutions are the humanly devised constraints that structure political, economic and social interaction. They consist of both informal constraints (sanctions, taboos, customs, traditions, and codes of conduct), and formal rules (constitutions, laws, property rights)" (North, 1991). This distinction is worth to mention due to the important role of the structure, in opposite from functional approaches.

2 This assumption found in Habermas carries out even major consequences (Habermas, 2000, p. 108). In absence of cultural transnational agreements directed to embrace domestic principles globally, nation state practices frequently fall into power politics relations that erode any attempt to transpose domestic principles beyond a single jurisdiction. The very difficulties in conceiving mechanisms of redistributive justice globally –that aim to steer domestic relations of exploitation-, is within this conjuncture one of the reasons behind the increasing levels of concentration of power and wealth of the international system. It also explains how and why in the last century a clearly defined global core and periphery formed up. See (Eichengreen, 2004) (Eichengreen, 2008) (Finnemore, 1994) (Wiener, 2014)

3 See. Mechanisms and Processes of Social Construction. In (Finnnemore & Sikkink, 2001)

4 William Rehg. Xii. On (Habermas, 1996).

5 Which makes problematic the use of cultural or rational choice institutionalism.

6 Such as the end of the Second World War, and the historical background that increased the political urgencies for creating an International Institutional Economic System.

7 Rawls agrees in accepting the necessity of shaping principles for arranging social distributive shares. He, however, don´t digs deeper in analyzing whether there is an asymmetric distribution of "rights" to define the scale of influence of certain actors among others in the process of creation

of social principles. The historical conditions in which principles have been created, recreated a systematically process of "institutional" truths that have come from more influential political actor to less influential political actors. In today's institutional global order, it is important to suggest that Rauwlsian universalism has served as a solid theoretical ground for the construction of a legitimacy of the Institutionalization of justice. His appeals operated in a philosophical frame that encourages the principle of fairness, in accordance with a set of material assets from which further social arrangements are to be implemented. He is probably considered one of the most influential philosophers of the United States, in the second half of the 20th century.

8 Perhaps in this direction, the irruption of Sen´s theory of justice, contrapone the importance of Rawls traditions, while enhances the debate about how justice is pivotal to define deontological practices of International Institutions.

9 "...The market secures for the owners of the means of production the power, sanctioned in civil law, to appropriate surplus value and to use it privately and autonomously. Naturally, in its crisis-ridden course, the process of accumulation surrenders the secret of the "contradiction" embedded in this mode of production. Economic growth takes place through periodically recurring crises because the class structure, transplanted into the economic steering system, has transformed *the contradiction of class interests into a contradiction of system imperatives"*. See (Habermas, 1988, p. 26)

10 "...because social order is not possible among agents who adopt purely instrumental orientations, society cannot shift organizational objectives over to systems of instrumentally rational action simply by abolishing normative controls. In order to harness the potential of instrumental rationality, it is necessary to design a set of institutions that will specifically channel and regulate these interactions. Habermas argues that the problem of introducing institutional constraints on systems of instrumental action is addressed at its most general level through introduction of the two situational steering media, money and power. (...)Institutional sanctions, once expressed in media units, provide a very simple way of imposing parametric constraints on strategic interaction problems in order to privilege socially desirable equilibria" See (Heat, 2010).

11 In line with the contributions on critical constructivism, this debate, both from a scientific as well as from a philosophical perspective, is well described in the Habermas essay "Liberty and Determinism" (Section 3rd), in (Habermas, 2006)

12 "... broad-gauge definitions of materialism and idealism constitute the hard cores of alternative research programs, ontologies, or "sociologies", and as such are not specific to IR. To some extent each can accommodate the insight of the other but only on its own terms"..." A truly synthetic position is hard to sustain, however, because materialists will always object to arguments in which the ideational superstructure bears no determinate relation to the material base, and idealistic will always object to arguments in which it does..." (Wendt, 1999).

Chapter 4
Methodological and Theoretical Assumptions for Conducting Research on the Cognitive Dimension of Narratives on "Development":
The Method

ABSTRACT

This chapter describes, explains, operationalizes, and contextualizes how critical discourse analysis together with secondary approaches to qualitative and quantitative research; develops a coherent methodological resource for enquiry of ideology, meaning and the overall semantic horizon of normative macrostructures at the level of international institutions. After explaining the adoption and the use of the methodology, the chapter further provides the method for conducting research on the two dimensions of political asymmetry, cognition and ideology (formal power sphere).

INTRODUCTION

This chapter constitutes a methodological section for conducting qualitative and quantitative analysis of normative constructions within selected biographical periods of international institutions. The long term goal of the project addresses the identification, deconstruction and theoretical framing of the norm of "modern development" at the Bretton Woods Institutions. This section is a complementary chapter of the ontological and theoretical assumptions of the book. For conducting a concrete case study research on normative meaning, this section elaborates in fundamental epistemological advantages in which Discourse semantics and Critical Discourse Analysis can potentiate the study of politics and ideology within grey literature of international institutions such as the World Bank and the International Monetary Fund.

DOI: 10.4018/978-1-6684-9794-4.ch004

The approach developed is complementary to the theoretical and historical contributions of the book, framed within the assumption of the problematization of the construction of norms under conditions of political asymmetry. Finally, the chapter aims to depict an operational path to dig further in the study of normative meaning, as well as to embrace this task within a defined empirical case study. This goal is oriented to reveal the rol of political asymmetry in both, the cognitive and the ideological dimension of the norm of "modern development".

Periods of Analysis

Considering the evolution of structural transitions at the Bretton Woods Institutions (Eichengreen, 2008) and following chapter 2 and chapter 3 of this book, the following chapter contextualizes this study upon three historical periods. First, the period between the end of the Second World War. This period covers the foundation of the institutional architecture, to the beginning of the 50´s decade. This era encompasses the global transition of the world in adopting an international institutionalized commerce system, formally established with the constitution of the World Bank, the International Monetary Fund and the approval of the General Agreement on Tariffs and Trade. It also takes into consideration the events that surrounded the reconstruction of Europe and the particular role of the western world in implementing the necessary policies to rebuilt their industrial capacity, acquiring the financial support of the United States and strengthening political relations at the back of a world deeply scarce of capital.

The second period goes back to the decade of the end of the Bretton Woods convertibility system. This decade formally began within the years 1971 and 1973 (Lewis, 2011) (Encyclopædia Britannica, 2013) (Eichengreen, 2004), tracing the ideological and political effects of the widest GATT round for the expansion and progressive liberalization of trade since the adoption of the treaty on the Tokyo round (1973-1979). This round was held with the representation of more than 100 countries, covering fundamental sectors of domestic political and economic institutions of the signatories. It was inspired by the 1974 declaration of the United Nations General Assembly for the "Establishment of a New International Economic Order" (Chimni, 2006) while during the same decade, the World Bank released for the first time the "World Bank Development Report", which settled the ground for further institutional approaches to the notion of "development" at the level of the Bretton Woods architecture (Weaver, 2010).

The third period of the study covers the last decade (2005-2015), which is characterized by the rise of new actors in the global political arena, the recognition of upcoming scenarios of global warming, global depletion of fundamental natural resources, new critical phenomena attached to the development of globalization (Wade, 2003), increasing levels of nation states uncertainty in dealing with a highly unstable global economic environment (Leiteritz & Moschella, 2010) (Stiglitz, 2004), complains over undemocratic conventions of the international institutional architecture (Sturm, 2006) (Leech, 2004) (Eichengreen, 2004) (Khan Haider, 2008) (Barro, 2005) (Rodrik, 2001), and a growing awareness of populations about how certain global policies are unable to be carried out solely by isolated nation-state entities (Park & Vetterlein, 2010).

Media Focus

The media focus of the present study is divided into three broad written sources. First: the institutional publications on "development" at the Bretton Woods Institutions. The decision to make use of this material lay in the high levels of accessibility and global influence of such institutional record issued by the World Bank and the International Monetary Fund. They can be broadly classified upon two types of documentation; a) the World Bank "development" prospects, which are a set of internal official reports of the institution -conducted since 1952 by the economic staff-. This collection of reports was designed to elaborate prognosis about perspectives and overall political and economic situations of countries that hold financial relations with the bank. b) The annual "Development" reports of the World Bank[1] and the International Monetary Fund -issued for the first time since 1978 and 1996-. These reports constitute up to date the single most influential institutional publications of these organizations.

Second, the foundational system of norms of the Bretton Woods Institutions, composed by the Agreement of the International Monetary Fund (22 July 1944), the World Bank Articles of Agreement (effective in Dec, 1945), the General Agreement on Trade and Tariffs (1947), and the Final Act of the Uruguay Round on multilateral trade negotiations - which embodies the constitution of the World Trade Organization (1994)-.

Third, the declassified cabinet reports of England previous the definition of the Bretton Woods Conference -open to the public decades after the end of the Second World War-. This material covers the period between January 22nd 1945, until September 20th 1949. This historical lap covers the moment when for the first time the proposal for the setting up of "an International Monetary Fund and an International Bank for Reconstruction and Development" at a conference to take place on Bretton Woods was mentioned, until the moment in which for the last time[2] the Bretton Woods Agreements were considered part of the agenda.

Preliminary Considerations For Implementing Discourse Analysis

Within the text corpus, reconstruction of meaning of normative interventions will be carried out by bearing in mind two qualitative caveats on the application of discourse analysis:

On the one hand, while the routinary use of critical discourse analysis (CDA) pays attention to reveal "the way social power abuse, dominance, and inequality are enacted, reproduced, and resisted by text and talk in the social and political context" (Djik, 1997, p. 352), for the present study, the assumption falls short in addressing fundamental dimensions of pivotal phenomena that explain normative constructions created under conditions of what in the research is introduced as political asymmetry. While this chapter doesn´t elaborate on the concept of political asymmetry, it is necessary to stress also within the analysis of discourse the role played by cognitive abridgments and biographical patterns, along normative constructions influenced by an exclusive progression of events in the global market oriented enterprise. This is why, while the relation between power and discourse represent a substantive task on the operationalization of CDA, in my research, it embraces partially the task of digging coherently about how cognition, information and formal architectures of political organization -such as the Bretton Woods Institutions- explain normative constructions. As it has been clarified in the theoretical section of this study, political asymmetry is determined by variables that embrace structures, cognition and customary power. This is why macro level analysis of discursive representations[3] (Djik, 1997, p. 70) held in the exploration of institutional records of social systems, are consistently dependent of a strong theoretical ground, capable to isolate the role power plays, upon a vastly robust cognitive and structural political setting.

In this use of semantic analysis, the book adheres to contributions on semantic macrostructures from which more contemporary approaches on critical discourse analysis has nurtured. This means, that it focuses specially in the way in which information is filtered through agent's environments, framing the knowledge and the development of normative constructions that have a multidisciplinary character such as the idea of development. This approach nurtures in the rather multifaceted concept of social *semantic memory*, that further develops over normative constructions or institutional guidelines issued at the executive board of prominent global institutions such as the World Bank or the International Monetary Fund. As it has been originally depicted, the concept of semantic memory "also represents group ideologies, norms and values, that is, any form of social cognition" (Van Dijk, 2014, p. 85), yet it original basis is "largely socially shared and presupposed in epistemic communities (Van Dijk, 2014, p. 225). As such, the approach of the research stresses the role that asymmetric institutions play in offering from a *one global speech act*, defined semantic information that further reproduces within global cognitive models that create "world knowledge". As depicted:

The role of knowledge in discourse comprehension is not only limited to the establishment of local coherence (…) the local coherence of discourse is a function of topic, that is, of macrostructures. The macro rules can apply only, however, if knowledge about the higher-order structuring of reality is available: (…) GENERALIZATION requires knowledge about the hierarchical relations between concepts; and CONSTRUCTION especially requires knowledge about the normal conditions, components, and consequences of global events and actions. Of course, this knowledge about the actual macroproposition of a sequence may be induced by explicit topical sentences or titles in the previous part of the discourse. But even then, the reader must know that the subsequent sentences are indeed dominated by the macroproposition, and he therefore needs world knowledge (Van Dijk, 1980, p. 239).

Second. On the distinction and clarification of normative constructions, the operationalization of CDA cannot in any way exclude fundamental contributions on sociology, history, and philosophy of law. In the present case study, the abovementioned theoretical assumptions play a relevant role in any attempt to reconstruct meaning of an institutional construction of the idea of "development". While CDA enhances the capacity of the researcher to outline a procedural setting for the analysis of texts in contexts pervaded by unequal access to social resources (Dijk, 1994, p. 30), this research also aims to draw attention about how certain phenomena are joined to symbolic constructions within a defined historicity in modern social systems. This means again, that the subtle ideological subtracts of discourse, can´t be assumed exclusively as an outcome of power interactions, but also as a cognitive setting that fit in a concrete intitutional biography. This presupposition holds necessarily ontological assumptions about normative meaning in need of further clarification. For the sake of consistency, this are considered in the theoretical section of this book. In short, I assume the existence of patterns of normative constructions that hold *claims to validity* able to be redeemed discursively, this is why ideology around a norm on "development" can´t be entirely socially constructed.

Structure of the Chapter

The goal of this chapter is twofold; on the one hand I attempt to provide an overview of key methodological issues of the following section of this research project. Accordingly, I conduct in the next section a summary exploration of discourse analysis as a customary methodology for the study of media with a focus of its application on research of regulation and institutional record in the form of text. In this section I also raise reflections about the weaknesses and strengths of CDA in relationship with the study of norms. Then I turn to provide a summary of the application of CDA, and particularly semantic macrostructures analysis on investigation conducted in relation with institutions and particularly, with international institutions. I highlight its applicability and potentials in disentangling critical components of normative constructions which aim to reproduce ideology, clear topical representations and cognitive abridgments within a defined political economy. I pay attention to semantic analysis as a problem oriented method whose strengths can be effectively applied to the study of norms, and which can be considered as a method of social inquiry. Finally, I endeavor to demonstrate that such potential can be translated to the macro level, therefore to the study of interventions of social structures such as the Bretton Woods Institutions.

On the other hand, I operationalize the approach within a case study directed to analyze a norm on institutional development entrenched on modernity. My conjecture is that conditions of political asymmetry on international institutions and the systemic division of spheres of life of social systems (modernity), have increasingly assigned to norms, meaning nurtured within an economic epistemic community. In this circumstance, privileged discursive constructions, which are frequently endorsed to a particular vision of global normative settings, are distortive of the political relations taking place at the system. This phenomenon is given by the isolation of social, economic, cultural (constitutive), legal, systemic and overall political events confronted by actors in a highly complex global environment. Following the tradition of the philosophical and sociological contributions of Habermas in the notion of the public sphere, my hypothesis is that while modern-day structures of governance -such as the Bretton Woods Institutions- carry the belief that international institutions are capable to rationalize social relations between highly asymmetric social environments, the stresses caused by normative constructions such as the idea of "modern development" points out to the inoperability of such hypothesis. Since my focus deals with the concept of political asymmetry, it follows that normative meaning raised upon such circumstance, frequently entail crisis that can be just hermeneutically grasped. In short, the section focuses on the method through which critical constructivist analysis will be operationalized in my research, stressing the role of political asymmetry as a polydimensional event beyond power, describing the steps to be carried out in research directed to disentangle the semantic fields of normative interventions (cognition), as well as the ideological trends of such discourse in a defined case study.

OBJECTIVE OF THE STUDY

Since the 80´s, the gradual evolution of social science has increasingly endured the task of confront, contextualize and understand the evolution of political phenomena entrenched within the omnipresence of market relations and globalization. At the theoretical level the last consistent endeavor to criticize the political features of this reality was made by postmodern authors, who warned about the limitations and pathologies derived from contemporary metanarratives (Habermas, 2000, p. 150) (Brown, 2011). Although embracing a different philosophical standpoint, it is upon these flaws of the idea of modernity that the study of contemporary discursive constructions acquires a renewed breath. In this endeavor, the present chapter is an attempt to show how one of this metanarratives has evolved, and how it is necessary to contextualize it. Based on contributions of critical constructivism and historical institutionalism, my research aims to explore the evolution and representation of an institutional norm of "modern development". The definitive assumption of the study deals with the fact that this single normative construction at the level of the Bretton Woods Institutions, has been built upon conditions of political asymmetry, therefore, it internalizes critical yet irremovable or static arrangements frequently endured by social entities marginalized from the decision making process at the governance domains of these institutions.

Most of the literature on development frequently features criticism or support to contemporary phenomena of global capitalism. This chapter however aims to detach from customary schools of development, to decompose discursively how this normative construction at the Bretton Woods Institutions has carried cognitive, ideological, political and structural constructions of a global asymmetric institutional environment. In contemporary formal systems of administration such as international institutions, political asymmetry is found along relations developed by agents and structures of organization. Within this background, asymmetry is reproduced on a cognitive and a political dimension. Upon such conditions, the case study tries to answer a set of three research questions. The first one is empirical; it looks to determine the paths through which the normative construction of modern development is mapped at the discursive level of the Bretton Woods institutions. The second and third questions are normative; they drew upon contributions on political theory and sociology to understand the thematic representations of "modern development" on asymmetric late modern social systems.

Cognitive

1. How conditions of political asymmetry at the Bretton Woods Institutions, affect the thematization, topical structure and representation of the norm of "modern development" along the diverse dimensions of contemporary social systems? How they change (if so) over time and how it is possible to track such changes consistently?

Political

2. How power relations variate or reproduced within the discursive construction of "modern development" at the global level?
3. What are the consequences over life spheres of social systems part of multi agents structure of governance such as the International Monetary Fund or the World Bank, once the implementation of such policies and norms are exerted?

The aim of this section of the book is to represent the topical and symbolic evolution of categories of normative constructions raised within highly influential international organizations, reproducing not only historical power relations but well-defined thematizations and representations. Finally, the chapter aims to offer research tools to dig out how such settings frame extensively the cognitive horizon of the exercise of governance, and reproduce historically critical arrangements frequently endured by actors isolated from the decision making process.

DISCOURSE SEMANTICS AND MACROSTRUCTURES AS A CRITICAL DISCOURSE STRATEGY

For conducting the present research, the distinctions between qualitative and quantitative methods are in essence epistemological and ontological[4]. Following Maxwell approach; quantitative research "define the problems of practice in their own terms, not the terms of the practitioners", while qualitative research "strives to understand the meaning of action to the participants", offering "improvement of arguments for practice" (Maxwell, 1996, p. 124). This means in sum that in the field of examination, the path to know what is "knowable", adopt between quantitative and qualitative research a divergent epistemology; where "knowledge" as a social construction containing the characteristics of a subject is built upon those two strands by descriptive and interpretative hypotheses.

In the field of the study of social phenomena however, the formation of scientific knowledge, carry the problematic ontological assumption that the "knowing subject" is unavoidably immersed within the subject context. In this fashion, any attempt to "know" the social phenomena holds the necessity of being further interpreted upon a paradigmatic approach. It is in this conjecture that the adoption of a qualitative approach to analysis broad the scope of comprehension of *the social*, carrying out theoretical perspectives which aim to "accumulat[e], reformulat[e], improv[e] and updat[e] (..) theories (…) produced within paradigms and their appearance associated with the presence of relevant social events" (Gialdino, 2009). Finally, in the field of methodology, in recent decades, discourse analysis has acquired a significant role in transposing critical social theory into scientific research. It has been frequently considered as being constituted by an *agglomeration* of approaches to the study of discourse (Haig, 2006, p. 52), whose roots can be found in the contributions of the Frankfurt school of social analysis before the Second World War, while Horkheimer and others aimed to produce knowledge capable to emancipate social actors upon self-reflection and the critical account of text in context (Tenorio, 2011, p. 187) (Djik, 1993, p. 251) (Sheyholislami, 2001) (Djik, 2008, p. 352) (Luke, 2008). I what follows, this chapter will offer a characterization of CDA as a composite of mainstream social science methodology to finally further address how, both CDA and semantic analysis, is to be incorporated in chapter 8 and 9 of the present book.

Characteristics of CDA

Critical discourse analysis pays special interest to "understand how social power, its use and abuse, is related to spoken and written language" (Haig, 2006, p. 52). It deals primarily with the "discourse dimension of power abuse and the injustice and inequality that result from it" (Djik, 1993, p. 252). It is a "type of discourse analytical research that primarily studies the way social power (…) dominance, and inequality are enacted, reproduced, and resisted by text and talk in the social and political context" (Djik, 2008, p. 352). It "aims at making transparent the connections between discourse practices, social practices, and social structures, connections that might be opaque to the layperson" (Sheyholislami, 2001); raising "awareness concerning the strategies used in establishing, maintaining and reproducing (a)symmetrical relations of power as enacted by means of discourse". It focuses on "those features contributing to the fabric of discourse in which dominant ideologies are adopted or challenged, and in which competing and contradictory ideologies coexist" (Tenorio, 2011, p. 184). Its purpose is to "analyze- "opaque as well as transparent structural relationships of dominance, discrimination, power and control as manifested in language-" (Blommaert & Bulcaen, 2000, p. 448). It´s objective is to "perceive language use as social practice [since] The users of language do not function in isolation, but in a set of cultural, social and psychological frameworks" (Horvath, kein Datum, p. 45), founding its operational source on discourse analysis, which embraces interdisciplinary approaches to the study of language drawing upon constructivist theories, "linguistics, literary theory and cultural studies, philosophy of language, sociology and psychology" (Luke, 2008).

CDA, Social And Institutional Representations

Given the role of power as a single dimension of political asymmetry, the working assumption of the research is to analyze how discourse enact, reproduce and legitimates domination at the institutional level, while at the same time reproduce framed social representations within ideology. In this strategy, I drew on previous contributions to discourse analysis to find out how knowledge is not only embedded upon the production of common symbolic expressions of social systems, but also socially constructed and actively performed upon categories, structures, contexts and agendas encompassed institutionally. Following customary contributions in the study of language, my study holds the assumption that in contemporary social systems, discourse holds the attribution to be embedded within structures, and therefore, to fulfill a role as a social practice. As it has been clearly exemplified by Fairclough and Wodak, this shift implies, "a dialectical relationship between a particular discursive event and the situation(s), institution(s) and social structures(s) which frame it (Wodak, 1997, p. 258).

In this transition, CDA aims to re-contextualize such meaning, taking an argument and "restating it in a new context" (Wodak & Krzyzynowski, 2008, p. 3). This is because every piece of text holds a meaning that is to be bounded with previous and future practices (intertextuality) upon which both, context and meaning evolve. This overall compendium of meaning in context, are thus considered as discursive practices that just by drawing on anthropology, history, cultural studies, philosophy and so forth, can be arranged, to analyze and detail how they should be embraced at the level of the public sphere (Wodak & Koller, 2010) (Fairclough & Chouliaraki, 1999).

In the reconstruction of discursive interventions, previous studies have made use of CDA to carry out research focused in relations taking place on institutional environments. This is because they often embrace the study of associations between power, language and social processes, which at the level of institutions are frequently found along customary practices. Blommaert argues, that such approach has its roots on historical surveys conducted at the University of East Anglia in the 1970´s, which focused their studies on the use of language in social institutions, offering a new strand of research for emancipatory agendas of linguistic analysis (Blommaert, 2005, p. 22). In his view, CDA rightly focuses on the critical analysis of normalization of discourse commonly embraced at the level of institutions, reacting against the "mundanization" of ideological discourse; "observed in many other branches of language studies" (Blommaert, 2005, p. 34)

Considering the role of history in shaping fundamental conceptions of contemporary social systems, it is pivotal to determine how discourse analysis can be applied to the identification of discursive transitions upon different periods of time. In the process of shaping normative meaning, historical events have carried not only necessary cognitive information, but also structural patterns that are reproduced along time. As it has suggested by Wodak, "utterances are only meaningful if we consider their use in a specific situation (…) if we know what the discourse relates to in the past" (Wodak, 1997, p. 276). Intertextuality therefore, plays a fundamental category to embrace the task to reconstruct meaning embedded in early periods, keeping the substantial relation of past constructions with contemporary norms.

Following studies carried on the field of rhetoric and composition, Huckin argues that CDA provides an "excellent methodological basis for archival work and ethnographic study" that considers "history as part and parcel of analysis" (Andrus, 2012, p. 111). In his view, the possibility of arrange the source of information upon sophisticate categories, allows to avoid the sacrifice of either theory or practice in the analysis of historical records. Moreover, "power abuse is most often centered in institutions", and indeed,

"CDA routinely engages in institutional analysis—especially, powerful institutions such as government, education, the law, or the mainstream news media" (Andrus, 2012, p. 123) .

To conclude, in their studies between power and knowledge within the field of social normative constructions, Pettenger highlights the role of CDA in following the chronological dialogue between power and knowledge. It is upon such assumptions that CDA plays a key role in examining how normative constructions evolve in epistemic communities such as those around the social construction of climate change (Pettenger, 2008, p. 2). Within this framework, the methodology adopted by critical discourse analysis can also reveal necessary choices made by actors upon "political interests" and "philosophical stances" (Pettenger, 2008, p. 8).

Weaknesses and Criticism of CDA

Hand in hand with the implementation of CDA as a methodological approach to social inquiry, criticism concerning their limitations calls our attention for the present study. In advance, it is necessary to say that detractors have frequently pointed out such assumptions, without distinction of the diversity of approaches and authors within the field of CDA, therefore, the aim of the present section is both, to operationalize briefly such weaknesses, as well as to give a glimpse to how they can be further solved in my research.

Following Blommaert distinctions, two kinds of criticism can be raised to CDA as a methodology for social inquiry; on the one hand "specific critical comments on method, methodology and analytical approaches". Second, criticism about the capacity of CDA "for becoming a critical study of language" (Blommaert, 2005, p. 34). Beforehand, it is worth to say that within research, the relation between operationalization and methodology has to be rigorously follows by theoretical assumptions which are to support the production of knowledge. Thus, before considering the methodological weaknesses of CDA, it is worth to mention Blommaert reflections on the capacity of CDA to contribute as a critical study of language.

In his view, weaknesses of such research approach on the study of language is prone to be related to three main problems; linguistic bias, a tendency of a closure to particular kind of societies and a tendency to a closure to a particular time-frame (Blommaert, 2005, p. 34). Concerning the potential limitation deriving from the linguistic bias of CDA, our assumption in the present research, deals with the role that systemic functional linguistics, rather than formal semiotics, can play in the definition of meaning in normative constructions. Since the focus of my study deals with the normative construction of an institutional approach to "modern development", our attempt is to stress the relevance of meaning upon highly robust social structures, bypassing considerations over the customary semantic study of the available discourse. In the reflections upon the role of the structure (time-frame-geography) over the analysis of discursive interventions, it is the aim of my research precisely to scrutinize how cognitive asymmetry shape and thematize norms, and how this unevenness is reproduced historically.

On the operationalization of CDA as an approach to embrace the study of discourse, criticism has been raised upon five fields: methodological eclecticism, biased outcomes, incompatibility of methods, and the isolation of the role of cognition into discourse. On the one hand, CDA has been criticized due to the limitations of interrelating "concepts, disciplines and methodologies", which carry the "vagueness of (…) concepts (…) as well as the vagueness of analytical models" (Blommaert & Bulcaen, 2000, p. 31). This position has been further endorsed by Keller, who argues that whereas linguistic methodological devices offered by CDA can be "well suited" for the analysis of the functionality of discourse, are hardly useful to grasp knowledge and the relation between knowledge and power (Keller, 2006, p. 5). Indeed, in this same fashion, "most critics" have argued that such conventional eclecticism can "be a source of contradiction" (Tenorio, 2011, p. 195); attempting to blur out "important distinctions between concepts, disciplines, and methodologies" (Blommaert & Bulcaen, 2000, p. 455).

When it comes to impartiality, Widdowson argues that CDA frequently tends to replace ideological frames within the selectivity of a defined theoretical interpretation of discours (Blommaert, 2005, p. 31) (Tenorio, 2011, p. 195), while Schegloff advocates that the approach tends to generate an over representation of "aspects of context", that project bias "onto their data, and analyze them accordingly" (Blommaert & Bulcaen, 2000, p. 32). This quality has been described as a tendency of CDA to move between ideology dominated interpretations "drawing on social theory" (Blommaert & Bulcaen, 2000, p. 33) (Keller, 2006, p. 2) and embracing the "shortcomings of the approaches it criticizes" (Tenorio, 2011, p. 196).

On the methodological incompatibility that may arise on the use of linguistic fields and social theory: it has been argue that CDA tend to fuse semantics and pragmatics, considering context "theory as truth", closing the dialogical process by the analyst and transforming the analyst in an "arbiter of meaning" (Blommaert & Bulcaen, 2000, p. 33). Whereas some authors have attempted to suggest "devices" to reveal "semantic meaning (or signification), In Widdowsons view such attempts have wrongly tended to isolate sentences, instead of utterances, which in turn generate context indetermination and imprecision (Tenorio, 2011, p. 195). Finally, CDA has been considered as an approach to discourse analysis that isolates the influence of cognition upon a theory of language[5] (Tenorio, 2011, p. 196). Indeed, it has been authors like van Djik and Wodak who have embraced the task of extending this worry to a theoretical level. In van Djik words, "CDA should also not limit itself to a study of the relationship between discourse and social structure, (…) [but] always presuppose the intervening mental models, goals and general social representations (knowledge, attitudes, ideologies, norms, values) of the language users. In other words, the study of discourse triangulates between society/culture/situation, cognition and discourse/language" (Wodak & Meyer, 2009, p. 14) (Horvath, kein Datum) (Van Dijk, 1993).

Strategies to Avoid Criticism. Implementation Of Discourse Analysis

In view of the opposition to CDA, it is necessary to begin with the reasonable weakness of the approach of raising conclusions upon the boundaries of the social paradigms it embraces. Since its key factor of analysis endorses to the book of the omnipresence of power and exploitation as a fundamental vector of societies, it is our goal to account this potential to a limited field of discourse analysis. While it is clear that contemporary normative constructions rely to a certain level with power relations embraced on ideology, our assumption is that the configuration of formal structures of administration, the historical transition of contemporary social systems, and the operational limitations of societies play a balancing role in the epistemology of meaning. On the other hand, rather than looking into concrete cases of exploitation relations within discourse, our attempt is to reveal the historical and cognitive implications that defined setting on structures of governance have over the process of construction of meaning. In this sense, the adequate semantic characterization of broad institutional literature, can reveal the evolution of political relations that take place at the macro level and not within just concrete grammatical structures. This is why the approach should rather endorse to analyze general categories of representation of discourse rather than single grammatical entrenched into fragments. In this sense, the research adheres to the developed ide of Van Dijk on Semantic Macrostructures, which as it has been addressed, they aim to "denote global properties of discourse (that) mainly pertain to the meaning or content of the discourse and not to the style of expression, the ordering of discourse parts, etc. This means that this kind of notion should be made explicit in semantic terms (;) to distinguish them from other kinds of global structures" (Dijk, 1980, p. 5).

From the outset, our purpose in the analysis of the discursive construction of the norm of "modern development", holds the assumption that one of the key categories of inquiry of discursive interventions made at the executive level of these institutions, is that related to the reproduction and legitimation of relations of exploitation. Nevertheless, this single assumption can't explain by itself, how a norm on "modern development" has evolved, what it means, nor the biographical paths it has covered along the almost 70 years of operation of the Bretton Woods Institutions.

On the other hand, the depiction of the concept of political asymmetry carried out in previous chapters of the present study, demands from us the operationalization of complementary vectors that will allow a demanding analysis of the text corpus. It is in this fashion, that the methodology of the research is directed to establish the paths through which the researcher can make accountable both the components[6] (Hansen, 2011) of the discourse to be studied, and the framing categories of depiction and analysis of the normative constructions it embraces. Situating the present section of the methodology as an explanation of the potential and weaknesses of CDA, our single convention at this point is given by the fact that unbalances of power and influence along the process of construction of norms matter; although they can't be accounted as the single vector to understand the meaning behind linguistic representations.

When it comes to eclecticism, the present study holds to the idea that carrying out the reconstruction of meaning behind discursive interventions, demands necessarily the embracement of selected theoretical contributions on social sciences. This assumption holds truth in any attempt to disentangle the epistemology of the "known subject", that is; to contextualize discursive representations upon systematic contributions on history, philosophy of law and sociology. While the theoretical chapter of this research describes the role of historical institutionalism and critical constructivism on this endeavor, the methodology below engages with the explanation of particular categories of analysis which are to support the role of CDA on interpreting representations found on the text corpus. When it comes with criticism regarding the tendency of CDA to bias towards particular kinds of societies and time-frames, it can be said that the goal of this research is precisely to explore the paths through which such phenomena took place along the second half of the 20th century.

From the beginning it is necessary to make a warning against taking for granted theory as discursive reconstruction. For this to be done, the analysis of discourse should set a distance from theory by framing its scope upon further suggested categories of analysis, adequate examination of the thematization of the text corpus and the selection of how certain transitions while consistent with the discursive interventions of the Bretton Woods institutions, are to be better explained by contributions on social science. Finally, the present study makes an exception in regard of the linguistic bias prone to arise along the process of research. The study rather than to stress the relevance of semantics, aims to make a critical approach to pragmatics and the outcomes of the ideological strands that over decades have embraced politics as meaning. Drawing attention on the abovementioned caveats as an introductory map to understand my decision to make use of CDA, and particularly the use of semantic macrostructure as an approach to account the "cognitive processes and representations" within which a define normative construction evolves, in what follows I turn to describe the method to be embraced on the first part of the case study.

THE METHOD

In the present study, the method is acknowledged as "the means to answering the research question" (Maxwell, 1996, p. 74). Bearing in mind this goal and following the definition of the concept of political asymmetry, this task is carried by analyzing discursive interventions while stressing how cognition and power shape normative constructions at the level of institutions. Our goal is to validate how cognitive and operational unevenness of actors in regard to a structure leads to a distortion of dialogical interaction, reproducing within time semantic areas and power relations of a highly asymmetric political arquitecture. In sum, we aim to explain quantitatively and qualitatively how in asymmetric environments, the production of normative constructions reproduces overtime framed interests, world perspectives, information and selected cultural backgrounds further normalized by discursive and legal contradictory arrangements.

The goal of the method to be presented in the following passages is inspired by the necessity of approaching analytically the ideological boundaries of normative interventions made at the institutional level in asymmetric organizations such as the World Bank, the International Monetary Fund and the World Trade Organization. The outcomes of the analysis of their discursive interventions strives to set a methodological and theoretical framework from which further research can enrich the discussion over institutional practices and normative meaning. Finally, the proposed method aims to cover inquiry over three fundamental dimensions of the practices of global governance. First, the cognitive dimension, focused in how cognition on normative constructions are institutionally thematized over fields, interests and spheres of contemporary social systems. Second, the deontological and ideological dimensions of institutions, which is given in the case study by the production of text in context. This stage aims to reveal the depiction of interventions framed by defined topical structures; known as discursive boundaries from which further and previous normative interventions nurture dialectically. Third, the ideological and theoretical dimension of norms; which shape the political spheres of contemporary social systems, reproducing cognitive constructions (1), and therefore legitimating relations and normative interventions(2) of asymmetric systems of administration.

Cognition

Thematization of Discourse and Semantic Macrostructures (Dijk, 2002, p. 68)

Discourse theory plays a pivotal role in easing the difficulties to operationalize the analysis of text corpus as a method for inquiry. Following the contributions of Fairclough, discourse can be schematized over three dimensions: Discourse as text, which encompass the "linguistic features and organization of concrete instances of discourse" such as "choices and patterns in vocabulary", grammar, modality and structure, among others. Discourse as "discursive practice" bearing in mind how societies produce and put into circulation discourse for its enlargement, consumption or distribution. And finally discourse as a social practice in which the ideological effects of its content upon structures of hierarchy, orders or hegemonies are embraced (Blommaert & Bulcaen, 2000). In our approach, it is within the third dimension of discourse that the study of language can be fruitful in the analysis of *intertextuality*, customarily isolated in the regular use of language.

In an effort to disentangle scrutiny of discourse as a social practice, one has to establish that discourse in form of text, is entrenched into linguistic interventions of actors. Language therefore, serves as a device to share subjectifications upon common symbolic constructions of a defined social context. On the other hand, language as a tool, is closely interrelated with cognition and the depiction of experience and perception by utterances. The building of a linguistic theme therefore, "unfold a textual strategy which [constitutes…] and iconic reflection of the reality perceived by the speaker of the message"[7] (McCabe & Alonso, 2001) (Haig, 2001).

The semantic macrostructures of broad utterances that made up institutional approaches to defined norms, broads the capacity to contextualize and extract the overall discursive meaning behind formal or informal discourse. Moreover, thematization of discourse is a customary practice on the production of language representations. As it has been previously studied:

"…macrostructures have an essential semantic function. They define higher level or global meaning derived from lower-level meanings. This process of derivation may involve the construction of new meaning (i.e., meaning that is not a property of the individual constitutive parts). Hence, as their crucial function, macrostructures allow additional ways of comprehension for complex information…" (Dijk, 1980, p. 15).

From a cognitive perspective, this single event is given by the fact that humans codify linguistically their reality following boundaries given by the senses. Thereby, following research on the elaboration of a framework for a suitable study of discursive interventions, every linguistic production should hold the relationship between discourse, cognition and society (Djik, 1997) (Djik, 1994 Oct). The role of cognition, is therefore pivotal to understand the linguistic strategies from which actors reconstruct "mental models" (Djik, 1997, p. 70) and project them onto semantic representations. Within this triad, we embrace cognition as the fundamental dimension that affects both linguistic practice and discourse representations.

Thematization carries out the focalization of discourse on structures of representation of the "objective" world. This phenomenon is customarily given in social systems aiming to arrange their own normative constructions upon discursive interventions embraced politically, culturally and institutionally. In the analysis of how societies reproduce their own traditions, thematization plays a fundamental role in ensuring representations upon cognitive frames that aim to steer potentially contradictory worldviews (Habermas, 1984, p. 395), easing the path to strengthen necessary communicative patterns to avoid misinterpretation or confusion. Finally, it reduces levels of dissension, playing a fundamental role in how knowledge and identification about the outside world *ought* to be embraced, and making it a device for the production of "behavior stabilizing" certainties (Habermas, 1996, p. 36) .

Throughout thematization, the text producer holds the role of create "reality" via language. This process is carried by the interrelation of a defined selection of themes, and the boundaries of the experiential content upon which actor's representations aim to describe something in the outside world. Inquiry on formal thematization of discourse, rather than focusing in the psychological processes that take place along a corpus creation, turns to the "linguistic outcome" of such process, that is, to the analysis of the compendium of symbolisms and "Iconicity" of the content of the linguistic product (McCabe & Alonso, 2001).

Accordingly, in analyzing norms created under conditions of political asymmetry, the first task to embrace on the study of discursive interventions holds the necessity of thematizing the original text corpus into semantic fields within which the norm of "modern development" is customarily represented. Such vector fields are given by conducting corpus linguistics and data driven analysis of selected institutional material of the Bretton Woods Institutions. This process takes place by running multiplatform tools focused in explore and produce first and foremost the semantic properties of the text, as well as concordance lines, linguistic clusters, collocation or search terms, keyword lists and n-gram linguistic sequences for further exploration.

In the study of the norm of modern development, the process implies fundamentally to operationalize for the study semantic and text analysis inquiry.

Semantic Analysis

Analysis of semantic content of large corpus carries out the compulsory difficulties of the manual categorization of the social spheres, grammatical facets, and cumulative qualitative features to which linguistic interventions allude. This is how assistance of natural language processing techniques eases the problem of scanning large amounts of data, which further can be explored individually or by comparison with large corpora. Probabilistic tools such as those executed on the study of semantic content doesn't replace the task of the researcher in analyzing the meaning of the text; but assist the labor of recognizing properties of the content -or contents- otherwise impossible to be carried without investing highly time consuming methods of semantic scrutiny of the corpus. Both, for the process of semantic as well as text analysis, standardization of the presentation qualities of the text has a significant role in avoiding biases. In the field of automatization of language inquiry, it is therefore recommended to use material formed by a single actor, or by different actors upon a similar data withdrawal context. On the other hand, annotation of the grammatical features of the content frequently carry the definition of clear semantic tagging systems, which can further give validity to the results. This process, which can wrongly be related to the definition of key categories or key words of the text, differs by the fact that frequently the production of linguistic interventions avoids the repetition of single terms, to mention content directed to a same or to similar topical categories. This is why subtle qualities of the corpus can be ignored by just making use of quantification of properties of the text such as frequency or keywords analysis.

In order to conduct the semantic analysis of the corpus, the methodology embraced in the research of the norm of "modern development" makes use of two interrelated tools. On the one hand, the USAS semantic Tag set[8], used and developed since 1990 on projects directed to conduct "content tag" of contemporary English. The tag set is composed by a structure that includes 21 major discourse fields, such as science and technology; the environment, social actions, states and processes; money & commerce; food and farming; or education, among others. Each one of the discourse fields is composed by multi-level subdivisions composed by prototypical word units. The lexicon contains over 37.000 words, with a template list of over 16.000 multi-word units (Archer et. al., 2002) . Second; the web-based corpus tool Wmatrix, which provides an interface for the automatization of USAS and "CLAWS" -which is a complementary speech (POS) tagging software for English text-. Wmatrix can conduct not only a computer based process of tagging of uploaded text corpus, but also customary linguistic methods of corpus analysis such as frequency lists and concordance (Rayson, 2008) (Rayson, 2003). Finally, it provides the possibility of conducting semantic and keywords frequency comparisons between corpus, which in turn allows for the researcher to recognize the differences and most significant key fields of the semantic structures of the text, and to provide statistical analysis of the tag frequency profiles.

Text Analysis

Exploration of Representations

Text analysis is carried out by the operationalization of three strategies of exploration of the corpus linguistic; Frequency of words, representative N-grams of linguistic sequences and concordance of highly frequent words into plots belonging to each one of the three period of study; namely the post II World War period, the decade after the end of the convertibility system and the publication of the "development" reports, and the last decade.

The production of the word list is followed by the selection of "keywords" that are most frequent in the target files. Transposition of keywords upon the plots belonging to each one of the periods, is followed by analysis and justificatory definitive selection of preferences of cognitive representations at the Bretton Woods institutions, and thus, to the further study of the text corpus into political fields or dimensions.

N-grams are created by the continuous sequence of items, symbolized numerically by the letter *n*, that represent a given combination of words. The n-grams are collected from the text corpus of each one of the periods, and are further crossed between each other to filter their frequency along time. This process allows identifying the cognitive changes on linguistic interventions through which the Bretton Woods Institutions carried out the foundational and institutional task of representing "development".

There is at this point a caveat to be made on the outcomes between the first and the two following chronological periods of the study. This warning is given due to the central importance of making clear the differentiation between the texts that compose the corpus on the first period, in qualitative comparison with the nature of further periods. On the one hand, the files to be used within the analysis of meaning of the two last periods are constituted by material that belongs to an institutional series of publications of the World Bank, the International Monetary Fund, and later on, the World Trade Organization. This institutional "collection" on the concept of development is guided with the same formal aim in each one of their issues, and therefore, imply a more accurate representation of the strategies endorsed by institutions when they carry out their discursive representations over defined historical intervals. This assumption however doesn't deter us to cross the outcomes of the linguistic interventions made by the Bretton Woods Institutions with the first period. This is because by now, none of the foundational objectives of the World Bank and the IMF have been replaced[9] (1965-1989), and summarizing the written material produced by them, especially the public available material of the World Bank after the Second World War, the "Development Prospects" -issued for internal circulation at the level of the institution- are the only single set of yearly publications[10] that cover the institutional approach to the concept of *development* openly[11].

With the outcome of the operationalization of the frequency and plots-distribution of words -with the cross analysis of the N-grams-; dimensions of thematization for the upcoming stages of the research are defined. Dimensions given by the data are distinguished as weak and strong, according to each one of the periods. This is because, our assumption, is that representations of the concept of development at the level of the Bretton Woods Institutions have changed over time, and therefore, policy fields or social dimensions upon which such representations take place, frequently acquire different levels of importance between periods.

Topical Structures and the Context Dimension of the "Norm of Modern Development": An Approach to the Text Corpus

Cognitive representations of the norm of modern development are given by the linguistic extraction of keywords, dimensions, policy fields, and intensity of the thematization carried by international institutions. Thematization eases the manipulation of the text, and allows conducting the analysis of the context (Wodak & Krzyzynowski, 2008, p. 11) in which the notions of "modernity" and "development" are operationalized in the historical record of the Bretton Woods institutional discourse.

Drawing discourse studies as a theoretical approach to the analysis of language as a social practice, the study implies that the scrutiny of discursive interventions can contextualize the emergence of representations, roles, dominion, resistance, ideology and overall hierarquical dimensions within which modern development is represented. This analysis is conducted by studying the text as a discursive practice rather than as a linguistic device. In this task, I embrace the operationalization of topical structures (Dijk, 1994, p. 16), concordance and clusters formation of the concept of "modern development". My assumption is that the gathering of the context allows the further implementation of CDA, as an approach to extract the meaning of normative interventions.

The production of topical structures is a mechanism of syntactic production upon which phrases and linguistic constructions acquire diverse interpretations, boundaries and roles onto semantic structures. The customary questions given on the analysis of these structures are: About which topics institutions produce knowledge when they refer to development? In which manner they impose theoretical, philosophical, political or thematic limitations when it comes to represent what modernity and development means? In answering such questions, the arrangements that take place on linguistic constructions define the intensity, the style, the treatment and overall grammatical strategies to present and to represent discourse.

The selection of text in context can be joined if necessary with the gathering of concordance and clusters on "modernity" and "development", as well as in all their deviations found in linguistic interventions at the institutional level. For the present research however, this strategy is rather vague, since it is used simply to offer a more coherent coupling of defined assertions within the global macrostructure of development, and the topic fields they are directed to. Finally, if necessary, this step is complemented by the selection of the most relevant clusters of words that surround the search terms of the study.

Political asymmetry and the cognitive dimension of the norm of "modern development"

Following the contributions of Habermas, and the conception of the role of institutions as mediators of the public sphere, the analysis of text on this research enables the study of meaning that belongs to "theoretical constructions of discourse in (late modern) social life" (Fairclough & Chouliaraki, 1999, p. 16). Normative constructions carried by international organizations along these lines, are institutional devices capable of being criticized upon the explanatory potential of the theory of communicative action, which is embraced on assumptions hinged to practices of dialogical interaction. Since the first and second step of the methodology, carry the organization of the thematic representations and the context of the norm on "modern development", the third part embraces the analysis of the text corpus.

Following van Djik contributions on the operationalization of CDA, an adequate framework for discourse analysis is given summarily by the interrelation of discourse, cognition, and society (Djik, 1997, p. 67). In the study of normative interventions exerted at the level of the Bretton Woods Institutions, it is therefore our goal to interpret customary memory representations of "development", given by the thematization of the historical records –conducted in the first part of the methodology-, and further transformed into all-embracing discourses that interact permanently with social systems. This is why the analysis of the text corpus is divided within two fields, on the one hand, those given by the social dimensions of the thematization of "development" at the Bretton Woods Institutions. Each one of these thematizations is to be appraised separately, since they symbolize the cognitive boundaries in which the norm of "modern development" is customarily represented at the Bretton Woods Institutions. As such, thematization operate as an institutional device to represent semantically the "strategic construction" (Djik, 1997, p. 69) of content, that once put into circulation, define globally and normatively, what *development* means, and which life spheres, changes and direction social systems should embrace to "develop".

In the present research, the exploration of topical representations of discourse production on "modern development" is carried out by selecting two defined thematical fields of grey literature of the World Bank and the International Monetary Fund. This decision is taken due to the rather complex and wide-ranging systemic topics that the selected literature on the issue at the Bretton Woods institutions addresses[12]. On the other hand, the subject matters for the case study draws on the original three defined thematic spheres of the United Nations development goals (United Nations, 1983), which are summed up into three public policy and political fields: a) material goals (aka.Economic), b)Environmental goals (aka. Systemic) and c) political goals (aka. Individual liberties and rights). As such, the present case study draws the analysis of two defined topical fields of the first and the second goal as follows:

a) **Material goals:** For the case study the research addresses the implementation of discourse analysis and semantic macrostructures to depicts the role of corporations, and particularly, corporations within the global south along the progression of the global economy from the constitutions of the Bretton Woods Institutions
b) **Environmental** and (aka.) Systemic goals. For the case study, the research focuses on the role of Land acquisition and the semantic context of land within the normative construction of "modern development" within the same period, dating back from the end of the Second World War to the last decade.

Procedure

In order to establish how political asymmetry affects processes of construction of the cognition of norms, the procedure focuses in the analysis of discursive interventions produced by international institutions. The main assumption is that structures of governance tend to normalize cognitively asymmetric arrangements settled at the decision making process of institutions such as the World Bank and the International Monetary Fund. Discursive interventions of such institutions, which are fundamentally represented within the historical record of the organizations, are therefore devices of normalization of provisions that take place on environments characterized by the reproduction of advantaged, framed, or biased epistemological approaches to knowledge. Therefore, the goal to conduct research oriented to analyze the consequence of such institutional settings, is focused in disentangling both, the evolution and the semantic structure of normative interventions produced institutionally and reproduced within their customary operation.

On defining the procedure to analyze the cognitive dimension of a norm on modern development, the research on macrostructures adopts a method drawing upon contributions and previous studies on computational linguistics and discourse analysis. This decision is supported in the theoretical, ontological, and methodological section of the book. Our attempt in carrying out as a first step linguistics and semantic analysis, is given by the necessity of producing from the text corpus, data that serves to a variety of empirical purposes of reconstruction of meaning. In this task, our study will focus on three fundamental dimensions of discursive interventions; the thematization and semantic analysis of discourse, the definition of topical structures of linguistic interventions, and the ideological dimension of normative constructions such as the norm on "modern development". Finally, the goal of the study is also to use the outcomes of the present study as a conceptual map from which reconstruction of normative meaning can be later on conducted.

Part One. Text Corpus for Linguistic Interventions on "Modern Development"

Following the procedures and assumptions on how to carry research directed to reconstruct a norm on "modern development"[13], this section aims to describe the steps given in the selection of data that will conform our text corpus. Rather than attempting explicitly to conduct reconstruction of discursive interventions, the approach is focused in analyzing how at the level of international institutions normative interventions within the notion of "development" are semantically understood and produced on the *historical record*. For this reason, we prefer to frame original publications on "development" at the level of the Bretton Woods Institutions in four variables; time frame, extension, character and qualitative features of linguistic interventions.

Time frame is directed to define the chronological periods from which discourse is extracted. Following recommendations on previous studies on meaning reconstruction, institutional records frequently attempt to reproduce patterns that involve the repetition of performances, policies, norms and overall discursive practices. On contributions on the analysis of the sociology of institutions - particularly at the level of the World Bank-, this phenomenon has been considered as a customary mechanism to define and reproduce the "character and mission of institutions, the shaping of specific configurations through (…) interrelations, and their consequences on the future development of an institution" (Alacevich, 2008, p. 11). In our case, we consider this pattern a fundamental assumption to conduct the practices of both, the International Monetary Fund as well as the World Bank. In this regard, our analysis aims to carry out the *historical reconstruction of* modernity and development (Alacevich, 2008); two pivotal concepts on the foundational goals of both institutions.

In order to highlight the evolution of discourse within historical interventions, we define as a time frame three historical periods of the Bretton Woods Institutions; the foundational, the transitional and the contemporary period.

Table 1. Time frames for selection of the text corpus

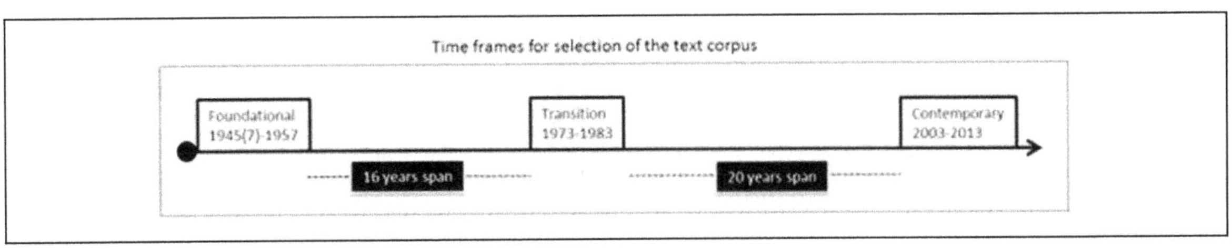

1. The foundational period is located within the decade 1945-1955. It covers the establishment of the institutions as well as the beginning of the implementation of their operational functions, such as the distribution of loans within a discourse on development (Alacevich, 2007) (Vetterlein and others, 2010). Since very early on the history of these institutions, customary publications describing the result, expectations and operational activities per year; established symbolic differentiations between "developed" and "underdeveloped" countries. The institutional material to cover the representation of development within the first decade of operation is given by the Agreement of the International Monetary Fund, and the articles of agreement for the International Bank for Reconstruction and Development (22 July 1944), the General Agreement on Trade and Tariffs (1947), and the "Development Prospects Reports" of the World Bank between 1953 and 1958. The decision of extending for three years the selection of the reports, is justified in the fact that public record on explicit literature on "development" at the Bretton Woods Institutions is exclusively represented on the World Bank reports, thus according to the official guidelines of the Bank, the only publicly available reports are dated since February 28, 1953. Given the limitations, we opt to take account of material that covers the decade after the definition of the GATT. In sum, the reports selected for the foundational period include the following selection;

Table 2. Doc name

Doc Name	Document Date	Report Number	Country
The position of the world economy on the eve of the outbreak of the Korean war; post-Korean developments and prospects (English)	FEB 28, 1953	EC8	United Kingdom/ Korea
Chile - Recent financial developments and economic prospects (English)	OCT 31, 1956	WH48	Chile
Japan - The development and prospects of Japan's economy (English)	JUL 31, 1957	FE2	Japan
Colombia - Recent economic developments and prospects (English)	JUL 31, 1958	WH75	Colombia
Mexico - Recent economic developments and prospects (English)	NOV 30, 1958	WH80	Mexico

2. The transitional period covers the decade after the end of the Bretton Woods Convertibility systems, which took place between the years 1971 till 1973. This period is characterized for three intertwined phenomena; first, the unilateral decision of the former US president Richard Nixon to declare publicly the unpegging of the dollar into gold, which enhanced the capacity of all nations to expand the money supply according to their own monetary policies. Second, the replacement of the "Development Prospects" of the World Bank by the "World Bank Development Report", issued every year since 1978. Third the United States -as the single most influential donor at the executive board of both the IMF and the World Bank- process of public indebtedness that reached a peak within the administrations of Ronald Reagan (1981-1989) and George H. W. Bush (1989-1993). Since those years, global monetary expansion of the United States was further linked with accumulation of reserves of the global economy on dollars. Without any linking value reference (such as the gold), this distinctiveness of the American economy boosted the development of global financial markets, increasing levels of leverage and indebtedness globally, as well as unusual trends on global inequality (Milanovic, 2007) (Milanovic, 2009) .

Bearing in mind this transitions, the discursive interventions to be analyzed within the decade 1973-1983, are formed upon the prospects of the period 1973-1976 (see Annex 01 and table 02), plus the following World Bank Reports.

Table 3. World development report

Number	World Development Report	Pages
1	WDR 1984: Population Change and Development	302
2	WDR 1983: Management in Development	228
3	WDR 1982: Agriculture and Economic Development	186
4	WDR 1981: National and International Adjustment	204
5	WDR 1980: Poverty and Human Development	178
6	WDR 1979: Structural Change and Development Policy	203
7	WDR 1978: Prospects for Growth and Alleviation of Poverty	135
	Average number of pages	**205**

Given the unbalanced representation between the yearly reports (7) and the prospects of the World Bank (65), a representative sample of the prospects is to be collected -rather than including in the corpus all the publications per year-. This sample is aimed to have the same extent of pages of the average World Development Report of the bank between 1978 and 1984. The sample is to be formed upon one or more of the less extent prospects analysis of each year that surpasses the average number of pages of the WDR reports for the decade of analysis. So for example, during the year 1973, the Bank issued the following prospects:

Table 4. Doc name

	Doc Name	Document Date	Report Number	Country	Pages
1	Zaire - Recent economic developments and prospects (Vol. 1 of 2): Rapport principal (French)	MAR 05, 1973	AE31	Congo, Democratic Republic of	83
2	Zaire - Recent economic developments and prospects (Vol. 2 of 2): Annexes et appendice statistique (French)	MAR 05, 1973	AE31	Congo, Democratic Republic of	FR
3	Malawi - Recent economic developments and prospects (English)	MAR 31, 1973	67	Malawi	111
4	Algeria - Economic development and prospects: Algerie - Evolutions et perspectives economiques (French)	MAY 29, 1973	155	Algeria	141
5	Malaysia - Development problems and prospects (Vol. 1 of 2): The main report (English)	AUG 14, 1973	217	Malaysia	81
6	Malaysia - Development problems and prospects (Vol. 2 of 2): Statistical appendix (English)	AUG 14, 1973	217	Malaysia	70
7	Guatemala - Recent economic development and prospects (English)	SEP 30, 1973	206	Guatemala	121
8	Netherlands Antilles - Development problems and prospects (Vol. 1 of 2): Main Report (English)	NOV 20, 1973	211	Netherlands Antilles	143
9	Netherlands Antilles - Development problems and prospects (Vol. 2 of 2): Statistical appendix (English)	NOV 20, 1973	211	Netherlands Antilles	116
10	Indonesia - Recent developments and prospects for 1974 / 75 (English)	NOV 30, 1973	286	Indonesia	152

Considering that the average extent of the reports has 205 pages, and that the less extent prospects (1,5 and 6) sum up a total of 275 folios, the sample for the year 1973 will be formed by prospects 1 (83 pages), 3 (111 pages) and 5 (81 pages) . Following this procedure, the complete list of prospects selected to analyze the discursive interventions on development at the level of the Bretton Woods institutions during the period 1973-1977, is included in Annex Number 2 of the present chapter.

3. The *contemporary* period is formed by the Development Reports of the World Bank for the years 2003-2013, and the Executive Reports of the International Monetary Fund for the same decade.

Considerations

Since the reports are customarily found in PDF format, conversion of the content in to Word, and later on text format, is carried for each document. This process can be carried out by text recognition software that may distort the content. This is why some cases require further manual edition (particularly in the case of the prospects that date in the period 1947-1980)

Bearing in mind that the material presented contain expressions that can be repeated within the formal format content -some of them derived from the inclusion of tables, institutional designs, appendix, catalogs, indexes and bibliography-, some reports can be amended manually to remove format subjects prone to bias outcomes of computational analysis.

Political Asymmetry and the Ideological Dimension of Discourse

Upon the explanatory character and the contributions on historical institutionalism and critical constructivism, the study proposes to set vector parameters directed to bring to the surface, the underlying meaning and overall evolution of ideological constructions that lay in the discursive interventions compiled within the text corpus. With this aim, the study opts to research on large organizational processes, macro historical and systemic features of the institutional biography of the World Bank and the International Monetary Fund, stressing the following properties.

a) Within the theoretical contributions of historical institutionalism, the reconstruction stresses the study of the following properties of the text:

The role of concrete temporal processes (Thelen, 1999). Clearly defined chronological events, rather than institutional foundational goals, easy up the adequate depiction of settings defined by concrete outcomes of political asymmetry. The fundamental assumption in the research of normative constructions at the Bretton Woods Institutions, is that historical contingencies, shaped upon the urgencies of the Second World War period, are the single fundamental case that enhance the call for legitimacy of the institutional arrangements settled at New Hampshire. From this fact, the research takes for granted a manifest deviation -at the global domain- of any attempt to produce normative arrangements endorsed by collective interests and symmetric agreement. Finally, the focus on concrete temporal processes at the level of the Bretton Woods institutions is directed to dig deeper on the consequences of intertextuality, and the biographical evolution of ideological constructions and power relations that nurtured upon unusual historical conjunctures, rather than symmetric interaction.

Control over the super-structures (Dijk, 1994). On the discursive interventions of the norm of modern development, the analysis of the text corpus is required to define which actors have the control over normative interventions, which of them determine the functional paths through which normative constructions on development are represented; who and under which conditions has access to determine how certain ideological constrains are to be nurtured discursively; or who has control over the functional categories in which actors are to direct their efforts to follow the settings of the institutions.

The role of institutional values and politics (Thompson, 1999, pp. 707-711). Following contributions on the field of institutional sociology, political science and history, the analysis of the text corpus aims to stress the relation between the reproduction of values nurtured institutionally and the interrelation of such values with the production of meaning and norms (Campbel, 2002) (Campbell, 1998). On international organizations, these properties are customarily found in the production of literature that engages in the interaction between politics and law, and that reproduce values nurtured on an institutional isolated environment over regulatory practices that are to be followed by countries.

b) Within the contributions of critical constructivism, discourse analysis directed to reconstruct meaning of normative constructions aims to highlight the following properties of the text corpus:

The historical influence of economic relations over ideological constructions. In embracing the task of exploring the underlying meaning of the text corpus, one has to assess the extent to which economic relations on contemporary social systems, affects normative constructions; further normalized upon regulatory, political and cognitive devices. Thus, the reconstruction of the norm of "modern development" requires a focus on how the transition of private economic relations of individuals to the public sphere, carried a disfiguration of normative arrangements that in previous stages of social organization were customarily settled by agreement, rather than money (tamed (Habermas, 1984, p. 33) (steered (Habermas, 1984, p. 342).

The relevance of subtle 'formal' structures (Wodak & Meyer, 2009, p. 72): Discourse production, whether if it is made at the macro or micro level is customarily controlled by the speaker. Within the arrangements given by thematization, topical structure, cognitive boundaries and overall confines excerpted over the language intervention, subtle formal structures reveals "less consciously" controlled facets of discourse. The performativity of discourse, holds unavoidably properties that just by analyzing the text corpus, can reveal peculiar features such as syntactic or propositional structures, rhetorical figures, nominalization (Baker, 2006, p. 155), use of metaphors (Campbell, 1998, p. 382), hyperborization (Dijk, 1994) or recurrence(Wodak & Krzyzynowski, 2008, p. 8), among others. Subtle formal structures reveal how the use of discourse in practice frequently articulates the acceptability (Wodak & Krzyzynowski, 2008, p. 9), normalization and selection of political features ordinarily hidden in the production of discourse, but tangible when inquiry is directed to reconstruct meaning of normative interventions.

The production of norms as a practice of symmetric interaction. In contemporary structures of governance, the presupposition that no actor is able to produce principles that favor his position over others is rooted in the condition of symmetric interaction. On regular contributions on critical constructivism, this value is settled by the assumption that dialogical interaction of societies, favors the reproduction of "norms that meet certain reciprocity"[14](Heath, 2009) (Habermas, 1984, p. 118). In this manner, constitutive traditions of social systems considered as symmetric are susceptible to be accepted as ethically constructed, and thus, to be transposed from an ethical entitlement into a binding claim via [modern] law (Habermas, 1996, p. 451). Thereby, in the analysis of discursive interventions at the level of international institutions, the analysis of the text corpus ought to be directed to distinguish to which extent such practices that belong to social systems are deterred or endorsed within the process of production of norms. In the research, the focus of the text corpus aims to contrast whether if discursive interventions on the norm of "modern development" favors or harm the practice of dialogical interaction, and how this property affects the process of production of meaning.

CONCLUSION

This chapter constitutes a methodological section to research directed to analyze how conditions of political asymmetry affect processes of construction of norms on institutions of governance. It makes part of an empirical section of inquiry focused in the case study of the norm on "modern development" at the Bretton Woods Institutions. It stresses the role of discourse analysis and defined features of historical institutionalism and critical constructivism for carrying out research about cognitive and semantic evolution of norms, as well as the ideological and historical meaning of discursive interventions within historical the record of publications issued by those same institutions.

In tracing the operationalization of discourse analysis, the chapter stresses the role of thematization and semantic macrostructures, providing an overview of theoretical strengths and weaknesses for exploring a defined text corpus. Paying attention of CDA as a problem oriented methodology, the approach embraced considers that analysis of linguistic interventions can be enhanced if a defined framework can improve the reconstruction of discourse. For solving this demand, two strategies of research are brought into account; first, the linguistic and cognitive dimension of discourse, and second, the ideological dimension of discourse.

For the cognitive dimension of discourse the method suggested is directed to analyze the text within fields extracted from the semantic macrostructures of the linguistic interventions. In this manner discourse analysis focuses in the thematization and the partial operationalization of strategies of exploration of the corpus linguistic such as the frequency of words, N-grams of linguistic sequences and concordance, and the analysis of the topical structures and the context dimension of the "norm of modern development".

For conducting inquiry over the ideological dimension of the norm, the methodology suggests to support reconstruction of features within a set of selected categories theoretically extracted from contributions on critical constructivism and historical institutionalism. In analyzing discourse, the method stresses the necessity to carry out reconstruction highlighting properties of the text such as the role of concrete temporal processes, the control over the super-structures, the role of institutional values and politics, the historical influence of economic relations over ideological constructions, the relevance of subtle 'formal' structures and the production of norms as a practice of symmetric interaction.

REFERENCES

Alacevich, M. (2007). *Early Development Economics Debates Revisited.* World Bank, Washington, DC. https://openknowledge.worldbank.org/handle/10986/7565

Alacevich, M. (2008). *The World Bank's Early Reflections on Development: A Development Institution or a Bank?* World Bank. https://openknowledge.worldbank.org/handle/10986/6840 doi:10.1596/1813-9450-4670

Andrus, J. (2012). Critical discourse analysis and rhetoric and composition. *College Composition and Communication*, 107–129.

Archer., D. A. W. P. R. (2002). *Introduction to the USAS category system.* UCREL. http://ucrel.lancs.ac.uk/usas/usas%20guide.pdf

Baker, P. (2006). Using Corpora in Discourse Analysis. Continuum. doi:10.5040/9781350933996

Barro, R. J. (2005). *IMF Programs: Who Is Chosen and What Are the Effects?* Department of Economics, Harvard University.

Blommaert, J. (2005). *Discourse: A Critical Introduction. Key topics in sociolinguistics.* Cambridge University Press. doi:10.1017/CBO9780511610295

Blommaert, J., & Bulcaen, C. (2000). Critical Discourse Analysis. Annual Review of Anthropology, *29*, 447–466.

Brown, V. (2011). *The Reflectivist Critique of Positivist IR Theory.* EIR. http://www.e-ir.info/2011/02/27/the-reflectivist-critique-of-positivist-ir-theory/

Campbel, J. L. (2002). Ideas, politics, and public policy. *Annual Review of Sociology*, *28*(1), 21–38. doi:10.1146/annurev.soc.28.110601.141111

Campbell, J. L. (1998). *No. 3 (Jun., 1998)* (Vol. 27). Institutional Analysis and the Role of Ideas in Political Economy. Theory and Society. Sprynger. https://www.jstor.org/stable/657900

Chimni, B. (2006). *A just world under law: A view from the south*. American Society of International Law.

Dijk, T. v. (1994). *Cuadernos. N°2, Año 2*. Octubre -Maestría en Lingüística. Escuela de Ciencia del Lenguaje y Literaturas.

Dijk, T. A. v. (1980). *MACROSTRUCTURES. An Interdisciplinary Study of Global Structures in Discourse*. Interaction, and Cognition.

Dijk, T. A. (2002). *Critical Discourse Studies: A Sociocognitive approach. Rewritten version of the author's contribution.*

Djik, T. (1994). Discurso, poder y cognicion social. Escuela de Ciencia del Lenguaje y Literaturas.

Djik, T. (1997). Handbook of Discourse Analysis (pp. 352-371). Oxford: Blackwell.

Djik, T. (1997). Discurso cognicion y sociedad. *Van Djik -En Signos 8*(22), 66-74.

Djik, T. A. (1993). Principles of critical discourse analysis. Discourse & Society, Sage.

Djik, T. A. v. (2008). Critical Discourse Analysis. In D. Schiffrin, D. Tannen, & H. E. Hamilton (Eds.), *The Handbook of Discourse Analysis*. Blackwell Publishers Ltd. doi:10.1002/9780470753460.ch19

Eichengreen, B. (2004). Global Imbalances And The Lessons Of Bretton Woods.National Bureau Of Economic Research. *Working Paper, 10497*, 2004. https://www.nber.org/papers/w10497

Eichengreen, B. (2004). *Global Imbalances and the Lessons from Bretton Woods*. National Bureau of Economic Research.

Eichengreen, B. (2008). *Globalizing Capital:A History of the International Monetary System* (2nd ed.). Princeton University Press. doi:10.2307/j.ctt7pfmc

Encyclopædia Britannica. (2013). *Encyclopædia Britannica Online Academic Edition*. Encyclopædia Britannica Inc.

Fairclough & Chouliaraki. (1999). Discourse in Late Modernity. Rethinking Critical Discourse Analysis. Edimburgh University Press.

Gialdino, I. V. (2009). Ontological and Epistemological Foundations of Qualitative Research. *Advances in Qualitative Research in Ibero America , 10*(2).

Habermas, J. (1984). The Theory of Communicative Action: Vol. 1. *Reason and the Rationalization of Society* (T. McCarthy, Trans.). Beacon Press.

Habermas, J. (1996). *Habermas Jürgen. Between Facts and Norms. Contributions to a Discourse Theory of Law and Democracy*. Massachusetts Institute of Technology. doi:10.7551/mitpress/1564.001.0001

Habermas, J. (2000). *The Postnational Constellation* (M. Pensky, Trans.). MIT Press.

Haig, E. (2001). A study of the application of Critical Discourse Analysis to ecolinguistics and the teaching of eco-theory. Studies in language and culture (Nagoya University).

Haig, E. (2006). *A Critical Discourse Analysis of News about Youth Crime in British Radio Programmes and Online Message Boards*. Lang. https://www.lang.nagoya-u.ac.jp/tagen/media/journal/200803/haig.pdf

Hansen, L. (2011). Theorizing the image for Security Studies: Visual securitization and the Muhammad Cartoon Crisis. *European Journal of International Relations*, *17*(1), 51–74. https://ejt.sagepub.com/cgi/doi/10.1177/1354066110388593. doi:10.1177/1354066110388593

Heath, J. (2009). Habermas and analytical Marxism. *Philosophy & Social Criticism, 35*(8). http://www.sagepub.co.uk/journalsPermissions.nav

Horvath, J. (n.d.) *Critical Discourse Analysis of Obama´s Political Discourse.*

Keller, R. (2006). Analysing discourse: An approach from the sociology of knowledge. *Historical Social Research (Köln), 31*, 2.

Khan Haider, Y. L. (2008). Globalization and the WTO Dispute Settlement Mechanism: Making a Rules-based Trading Regime Work. (MPRA Paper 7613). University Library of Munich, Germany.

Leech, D. (2004). Voting Power in the Bretton Woods Institutions. *Warwick Economic Research Paper*. Warwick Economic Research Group.

Leiteritz & Moschella. (2010). The IMF and capital account liberalization: a case of failed norm institutionalization. In S. Park & A. Vetterlein (eds.) Owning Development. Creating Policy Norms in the IMF and the WB. Cambridge University Press.

Lewis, N. (2011). 1971: Bretton Woods And The Four-Decade Trauma Of Its Collapse. *Forbes*. https://www.forbes.com/2011/07/07/bretton-woods-collapse.html. 2011.

Luke, A. (2008). Theory and Practice CDA. L. Saha (ed) *International Encyclopedia of the Sociology of Education*. Elsevier Science Ltd.

Maxwell, J. A. (1996). Applied Social Research Methods Series: Vol. 41. *Qualitative Research Design. An interactive Approach. Sage Publications, Inc.*

McCabe & Alonso. (2001). Theme, transitivity and cognitive representation in spanish and english written texts. *Circle of linguistics applied to communication*. Revista Canaria de Estudios Ingleses.

Milanovic, B. (2007). An even Higuer inequality than previously though: a note on global inequality calculations using the 2005 ICP results. *World Bank Policy Research Working Paper Series*. World Bank.

Milanovic, B. (2009). *Global inequality and global inequality extraction ratio: The story of the last two centuries*. World Bank, University of Maryland.

Park & Vetterlein. (2010). Do policy norms reconstitute global development? In S. Park & A. Vetterlein (eds.) Owning Development: Creating Policy Norms in the IMF and the WB. Cambridge University Press.

Pettenger, M. E. (2008). The Social Construction of Climate Change: Power, Knowledge, Norms, Discourses. *Journal of Environmental Law*, *20*(3), 486–489. doi:10.1093/jel/eqn016

Rayson, P. (2003). *Matrix: A statistical method and software tool for linguistic analysis through corpus comparison.* [Ph.D. thesis, Lancaster University].

Rayson, P. (2008). From key words to key semantic domains. *International Journal of Corpus Linguistics, 13*(4). . doi:10.1075/ijcl.13.4.06ray

Rodrik, D. (2001). *Trading in Illusions.* Washingtonpost.Newsweek Interactive, LLC. https://www.jstor.org/stable/3183155

Sheyholislami, J. (2001). Y*esterday's "separatists" are today's "resistance fighters": A critical discourse analysis of the representations of the Iraqi Kurds in the NY Times and the Globe and Mail.* [Thesis, Carleton University].

Stiglitz, J. (2004). Capital-market Liberalization, Globalization, and the IMF. *Oxford Review of Economic Policy, 20*(1), 57–71. doi:10.1093/oxrep/grh004

Sturm, A. D. (2006). Do IMF and World Bank Influence Voting in the UN General Assembly? (CESifo Working Paper Series 1724). CESifo Group Munich.

Thelen, K. (1999). Historical Institutionalism in Comparative Politics. *Annual Review of Political Science 2*(1), 369–404. https://www.annualreviews.org/doi/abs/10.1146/annurev.p

Thompson, A. (1999). Alexander Thompson and Duncan Snidal. The History of International Organizations. *University of Chicago., 9800*, 692–722.

United Nations. (1983). Process of preparation of the Environmental Perspective to the Year 2000 and Beyond. *Resolution 38*(161).

Van Dijk, T. (1980). *MACROSTRUCTURES - An Interdisciplinary Study of Global Structures in Discourse, Interaction, and Cognition.* Lawrence Erlbaum Associates, Publishers.

Van Dijk, T. (1993). Principles of Critical Discourse Analysis. *Discourse & Society, 4*(2), 249–283. https://das.sagepub.com/cgi/doi/10.1177/0957926593004002006. doi:10.1177/0957926593004002006

Van Dijk, T. (2014). Discourse & Knowledge - A sociocognitive approach. *Universitat Pompeu Fabra, Barcelona.*

Vetterlein, & Associates. P. (2010). Owning Development: Creating Policy Norms in the IMF and the World Bank. Cambridge: Cambridge University Press.

Wade, R. H. (2003). What strategies are viable for developing countries today? The World Trade Organization and the shrinking of 'development space.' *Review of International Political Economy, 10*(4), 621–644. http://www.in. doi:10.1080/09692290310001601902

Weaver, C. (2010). The strategic social construction of the World Bank's gender and development policy norm. In *Susan Park & Antje Vetterlein. Owning Development. Creating Policy Norms in the IMF and the WB.* Cambridge University Press. doi:10.1017/CBO9780511762710.005

Wodak, F. (1997). *Discourse Studies. CDA Discourse studies. A Multidisciplinary Introduction.* Teun A. van Djik - CDA.

Wodak & Koller. (2010). Handbook of communication in the public sphere. Walter de Gruyter.

Wodak & Krzyzynowski. (2008). Qualitative Discourse Analysis in the Social Sciences. Palgrave McMillan.

Wodak & Meyer. (2009). Methods of critical discourse analysis. (pp. 62-85). London Sage..

ENDNOTES

1 Commonly known as the "World Development Report".

2 Formally ratified in 1976

3 My position embraces a hard stand on cognition, as a pivotal component for a further framework for the analysis of institutional discourse. This focus on discourse analysis has been stressed on numerous contributions of van Djik. What substantially impacts and "control" discourse, is not the "social "objective" situation", but the "*subjective and mental constructions hold in the context models of language users*" (Djik, 1997, p. 70). *My translation.*

4 Ontological assumptions for normative meaning are discussed in a complementary section.

5 Chilton on (Tenorio, 2011, p. 196)

6 When we speak about the *components,* we do it by using a concept previously cited on methodology directed to the study of visual representations. The validity of the concept is given by the fact that visual man made products, such as the selection or creation of images for depicting events, are symbolic interventions able to be contextualized within a defined framework. In such cases, components include properties such as the image, the wider policy discourse and the text ascribing meaning to the image. See (Hansen, 2011)

7 "Language is based on human experience of the world and the way we perceive and conceptualize it". In (McCabe & Alonso, 2001). For a practical case, see (Haig, 2001).

8 For more information about the project, see https://ucrel.lancs.ac.uk/usas/

9 Though effective in Dec. 27th, 1945, they have been amended twice (1965-1989).

10 Since 1947, the International Monetary Fund has issued official yearly reports of the executive board. Such reports however cannot be lend, and nowadays access is restricted to visitors to the headquarters of the institution, at Washington, DC.

11 This assumption is taken following the guidance suggested by the World Bank Archive Department. Request number AI2551 of February, 2013.

12 As it has been noted, in the processes of analyzing broad range thematic representations of discourse, the use of macrostructures can clear up the way to focus in substantive semantic features of discourse. As such, "the second major function of macrostructures (is thus…) the reduction of complex information. Even if it would be possible to organize our plans, interpretations, or representations for complex information, we also need a way of effectively handling this organized information. For all cognitive operations this requires reduction of complex information."

13 See chapter 4.

14 Or symmetry condition (Heath, 2009). See also (Habermas, 1984, p. 118).

Chapter 5
Political Asymmetry and the Bretton Woods Institutions:
Introduction to a Case Study

ABSTRACT

This chapter carries out the operationalization of the concept of political asymmetry at the Bretton Woods Institutions. It conducts inquiry directed to analyze such property within their historical biography, institutional architecture, operational goals and their special features over the process of production of normative constructions at the global level. The aim in the present chapter is to set the ground for further explorations about how conditions of political asymmetry on international organizations have substantive consequences in the definition of the meaning of widely accepted norms. While this chapters focuses exclusively on the analysis of the Bretton Woods Institutions, its secondary goal is to enhance the debate about the implications of asymmetries on institutions for governance.

Economic progress, in short, is not the same thing as moral progress. Man does not come naturally by any of the attitudes and institutions necessary for economic growth; he must be driven-even to hard work-by need, or by the prospect of material gain, or somehow these attitudes must be made politically or religiously inspiring.

Eugene R. Black. (Black., 1960, p. 267)

Former World Bank President. 1949-1963

DOI: 10.4018/978-1-6684-9794-4.ch005

INTRODUCTION

The concept of political asymmetry on institutions of governance has been isolated from discussion on academic and political research in recent decades. A significant justification behind such shift lies in the fact that after the 90s, critical research has been highly influenced by the contribution of IR constructivism, which in turn redirected the study of world politics (Wendt, 1992) (Kratochwil, 1993) (Kratochwil, 2000). It is upon this shift that further contributions to IR, rather than offering disrupting alternatives, isolated the debate to the point of presenting realism and constructivism as a natural epistemological dichotomy (Wight, 2007) (Guilhot, 2008) (Niiniluoto, 1991). In this tension, research focused on the consequences of institutional or political imbalances has fallen short in offering credible alternatives without being labeled; isolating how asymmetries at international institutions have implications over processes of productions of norms and meaning. In recent decades, an endeavor to fill this gap has been embraced by the conjunction of cognitive sciences, psychology, behavioral decision theory (Goldgeier & Tetlock, 2001) (Herrmann, et al., 1997), linguistics (Blommaert, 2005) (Baker, 2006) (Dijk, 2002), anthropology (Blommaert & Bulcaen, 2000) and sociology (Haas, 1992) (Keller, 2006) (Pettenger, 2008), widening the scope of research directed to analyze how organizational imbalances at the level of international institutions affect processes of production of normative interventions.

This article is part of a wider research on the concept of "political asymmetry", and how normative arrangements at the level of institutions of governance distort, interfere, misrepresent or reduce the semantic horizon from which normative constructions nurture. On the other hand, it is an attempt to stress in the 21st century, the role that power relations have over the process of construction of normative meaning, and how rather than a coincidence, public policies and overall institutional practices, reproduce over time biased decisions within multi agents structures such as the World Bank of the IMF.

The following chapter is divided into four sections. Section one outlines the historical events in which the constitution of the Bretton Woods architecture took place, stressing successive features of unequal participation of actors, isolation of peripheral social systems interests, and the historical contingencies of the global economic architecture that pressed toward compliance of the participants with the conditions of the treaties. This section aims to highlight how with the end of the Second World War, and the overall reconstruction of the western territories, the conditions defined in the statements for the *Establishment of an International Monetary Fund* and an *International Clearing Union*, were made upon the economic structure and political provisions of the United States and Great Britain. Finally, the section also stresses, how such conjuncture isolated the interests of peripheral actors, some of whom adhered, being threatened by the consequences of being marginalized from the system.

The second part stresses how the discursive assumptions of the new regulatory architecture aimed to develop the productive capacity of societies, which in turn characterized the role of countries according to their radio of capital. The section stresses that such normative association[1] compelled capital scarce territories to meet under high vulnerability conditions the terms of the new normative constructions of the system. This in turn institutionalized asymmetric relations and unequal participation of countries.

In section three, I proceed by making a balance of the distribution of benefits of the new architecture, which relied fundamentally on trade relations between capital exporting and capital importing nodes. Finally, I transpose the features established on the previous sections over the framework of the concept of *political asymmetry*. Such concluding attempt aims to depict coherently how the configuration of the Bretton Woods organizations, presented concrete biographical unevenness at the cognitive, political and operational level. This in turn make them prone to reproduce such identical settings in their further upcoming discursive and normative interventions.

Historical Background

In 1913, the University of California Press, with the approval of the National Bureau of Economic Research, supported the publication of the book "Business Cycles and Unemployment" written by Clair Mitchel Wesley[2]. Although the relevance of the book was lately eclipsed by more recent studies that incorporated econometric techniques to the analysis of resource based problems, it served as the main scholarly contribution for clarifying the impact of economic cycles. The study highlighted measures to be taken on countries facing unexpected depression phases and the international urgency for setting conditions for long term stability for economies with different trade and monetary regimes. At this time, relevant differences divided the economic urgencies of national entities before and after the 20th century. As Eichengreen describes, currency stability became a national priority for administrations that started to feel the pressures of organized social actors that censored the monetary and political decisions of political elites.

In the beginning of the 20th century, high-income countries started processes of reallocation of their economic agendas, becoming increasingly concerned with the demands of trade unions and the impact of interest's rates on the income of workers. Besides, at the beginning of the century, "universal male suffrage and the rise of trade unionism and parliamentary labor parties politicized monetary and fiscal policy making" (Eichengreen, 2008). As a consequence, governments addressed the problem of unemployment as a priority, stressing the urgency for setting a long term-stable international monetary system. Moreover, this strategy also resolved complex political difficulties that were aroused by the maintenance of bimetallism until the decade of the 1870s[3], and the levels of fluctuations of the pre-wars gold standard[4].

The abovementioned circumstances outlined the agenda that anticipated the necessity for creating conditions for global monetary stability after the Second World War. In such historical context the meetings of New Hampshire took place. As a goal, they aimed to endeavor the agreement of the international community in two fundamental treaties of political and economic cooperation; 1) "The Atlantic Charter of 1941", and the 2)"Anglo American Mutual Aid Agreement of February 1942". Both agreements were highly influenced by the United States, and were negotiated in accordance with the interests of Great Britain as the main political European counterpart.

The United States and Great Britain acknowledged that the capacity of periphery economies for leading calls for participation on international conferences lacked real influential power. As such, further scenarios for negotiations directed to define common patterns for international monetary policies, were met plenty of hesitancy from the smaller countries, who were forced to comply with long-term sustainable international monetary agreements. Furthermore, the rise of the United States as the major political power in the world, and its historical relationship with Great Britain, increased the apprehensions of marginalized countries, who doubt about the capacity of the new monetary system to reach their concerns.

Once the conference was settled, the expected suspicions were clearly exemplified by the broad influence of the two main ideological proposals, the "White" (USA) and the "Keynes" (Great Britain) plan, created by the two most influential countries of the conference (Mikesell, 1994) (Eichengreen, 2004) (Boughton, 2002). As a consequence of the weak participation of the rest of the countries that assisted at the Bretton Woods conference, the first "*Joint Statement by Experts on the Establishment of an International Monetary Fund*" overrepresented the influence of selected wealthy nations. This foundational document of the IMF, based upon the "*United States Proposal for a United and associated nations stabilization Fund*" and the -British- "*Proposal for an International Clearing Union*", of April 7th and 8th of 1943, traced the interests of the two main political powers of the world at the time, highlighted the relationship between a newly created political and economic core and a periphery for the upcoming decades (Eichengreen, 2004).

Since Europe was incurring in large amounts of debt as a necessary step for reaching postwar reconstruction, the United States saw the possibility of financing the process by running account deficits under the new scheme, pegging the rest of the currencies to the dollar rather than to the gold. This arrangement, was related to a "compromise (…) between the U.S. desire for pegged exchange rates to promote the recovery of international trade, and the British desire for exchange rate adjustments to accommodate the policies necessary for the maintenance of internal balance" (Eichengreen, 2004). In such historical framework, the interests of the nation's taking part at the conference, remained bounded to the economic and political agendas of Great Britain and the United States. As a consequence, the events were outlined by the lack of participation, discussion, and veto[5] conditions established for the participants at the conference. Finally, on July 22th 1944, the meeting´s final act was signed by 44 countries, settling the foundation of the International Monetary Fund and the World Bank[6].

The Discursive Normalization of Asymmetries

Although the operative nature of the Bretton Woods Institutions focused on the regulation of economic and monetary policies, a broad part of their foundational purposes addressed their outstanding position in shaping, approaching, assisting, financing, and leading "institutional" policies for "global development". On the global political arquitecture, they represented the "International Institutionalized Commerce System"[7] (Arenal, 1984), a fundamental support for the exercise of global governance. The composition and distribution of their internal political practices, and the outcomes of the policies shaped for addressing development, defined to which extent certain political relations between core and peripheral actors were continually reproduced or transformed on the exercise of governance. Their normative narrative settled fundamental conceptions for the understanding of the concept of development by the World Bank[8], the IMF and the WTO. In the case of the International Monetary Fund, Article first (Purposes) of the foundational document explicitly stated that the organization was conceived to:

"…facilitate the expansion and balanced growth of international trade[9], and to contribute thereby to the promotion and maintenance of high levels of employment and real income and to the development of the productive resources of all members as primary objectives of economic policy" (IMF, 1944).

Consequently, the third numeral (Article 1st. "Purposes") of the foundational articles of agreement of the International Bank for reconstruction and development quoted:

"To promote the long-range balanced growth of international trade and the maintenance of equilibrium in balances of payments by encouraging international investment for the development of the productive resources of members, thereby assisting in raising productivity, the standard of living and conditions of labor in their territories" (World Bank - AA, 1945).

This condition, eased the normalization of systemic institutional patterns of unequal distribution of economic burdens and benefits along the 20th and 21th century. By now at the IMF, for instance, loans (Lombardi, 2006) (Barro, 2005) tend to be "larger and more frequent when a country has a bigger quota and more professional staff (…) and when a country is more connected politically and economically to the United States and major European countries". Both the political as well as the economic result of the situation reinforced processes of normative and institutional exploitation of underweighted countries. In addition, the voting dynamic not only implied processes of asymmetric concentration of power by single players at the board of the IMF or the World Bank but also at the United Nations (Dreher et. al., 2010). In such cases, bargaining power from influential countries eased support from small territories looking for retributions by voting in accordance with the average G7 country. Indeed, during the recent decades, the quotas mechanisms, and the level of influence of dominant shareholders created a differentiation not only in terms of voting power, but also in the representation of each country in the staff of the organisms. As it has been recently evaluated, this situation "eroded the original credit union nature of the IMF" producing a differentiation between lenders and borrower's countries (Rowlands & Bird, 2006).

Historically[10] (Mikesell, 1994)., the conditions for participation at the Board of Governors[11] and the executive Board of the IMF and the WB, defined the level of influence of the countries, some of them affected by highly unequal levels of "voting power"[12] (Dennis Leech, 2004). Furthermore, this settings, outweighed the capacity of influential countries to be crucial in decision-making procedures taken by votes. For example, considering that the United States in both corporations has a percentage of voting weight between 16% and 17%, its level of voting power is superior in cases in which supermajority rule of 85% is mandatory. In these situations, the United States and the three major western European countries, not only have a normative foundational power weight, but also exceptional veto power. For the case of the Board of Directors, the study concludes that the "voting power of the United States, is considerable more than its weight in both institutions", in contrast with all other members that have "less power than their weight". Finally, in the case of the Executive Board, the results show "strong tendency for weighted voting to enhance the voting power of the United States at the expense of the other directors".

Global inequalities, historical maintenance of bargaining power[13] and the difficulties in grasping and controlling the exercise of global governance, reveal conflicting interactions between power, norms, institutions and meaning (Mikesell, 1994). They underscore inner relations of discursive hegemonies that unequally distribute the burdens of normative interventions that presented symptoms of crisis beyond national boundaries. Although the centralization of international monetary policies eased up the avoidance of pre-Bretton Woods financial crisis, international integration by means of the enforcement of fair economic relations and structural long term institutional strategies for economic stabilization remained marginal. On the other hand, while the policies established at New Hampshire enhanced the implementation of **a)** pegged exchange rates, **b)**IMF reserves for urgent measures for small economies in the face of market pressures, and **c)**fund surveillance; later studies revealed that "the adjustable peg proved to be an oxymoron… IMF surveillance turned out to have blunt teeth", and "the fund´s resources were quickly dwarfed by the postwar payments problem and the scarce-currency clause that was supposed to sanction countries whose policies threatened the stability of the system was never invoked" (Eichengreen, 2004, p. 92). The consequences that aroused from the lack of "implementation effectiveness" of foundational goals, made possible the deinstitutionalization of political relations, increasing the difficulties of isolated actors to set positions and agendas in circumstances of irregular negotiation. This explain how the pitfalls described by Eichengreen, later on became the historical background for the erosion of the pegged exchange rate system and the input for increasing "free riding" behavior of core countries. As a fact, the collapse of the gold peg in November 1968, the Nixon shock[14] (Nixon, 1971) in the midst of the Vietnam War and the 1971 unilateral termination of the United States of the convertibility epitomized the imbalances of the system.

Despite the circumstances, United States continued to be the main global provider of liquidity in the world, flaunting the exorbitant privilege of running large direct investment surpluses by issuing dollars held by foreign banks. In fact, the collapse of the fixed exchange rate, increased US capacity, for "issuing short term and fixed income liabilities and investing primarily in equity and direct investment abroad", enjoying a globally unique "higher premium on its gross assets" relative to its obligations (Gourinchas & Rey, 2005, p. 12).

Trade as a Power Dimension Between Capital Exporting and Capital Importing Nodes

The agenda settled with the constitution of the World Bank and the International Monetary Fund boosted up global economic interdependency. This shift implies not only a reconsideration of the state as a single multifaceted global agent but furthermore the role both civil society and private corporations had in defining transnational relations (Buzan, 2004). On the other hand, this new feature of interactions beyond the state found its way by stressing at the level of international institutions the enlargement and entrenchment of trade, and the incorporation of the normative construction of development via global economic liberalization (Leiteritz & Moschella, 2010) (Spanu, 2003).

The theoretical assumptions of the newly created economic architecture aimed international economic growth in accordance with the contributions of classical liberal economy. On the other hand, amidst the Bretton Woods conference, diverse participants asked for the necessity of founding at the same time an International Trade Organization. This demand pointed to match the role that the new global monetary and financial architecture -represented on the World Bank and the IMF-, was expected to fulfill. The time constraints of the agenda and the impossibility of advancing negotiation on issues of trade[15] however, postponed the initiative. Finally, by the time of the Bretton Woods conference, it was commonly acknowledge the reluctance of the American congress to allow the establishment of an international institution on trade. This was because after the Second World War, the United States remained with the single most advanced industrial and commercial infrastructure of the world, which allowed them to hold numerous trade advantages in absence of global trade regulation. One year a half later however, this goal was finally embraced by the former US president Harry Truman, calling for an international conference for the creation of the organization. In 1947, with the signatures of 23 countries[16], the General Agreement on Tariffs and Trade was established (GAAT, 1947, p. 1).

The main goal of the agreement consisted in offering a juridical frame for promoting and securing the liberalization of trade. Until 1994, when the World Trade Organization was finally set up, the GATT ensured the enhancing of global trade through numerous rounds of trade negotiations among the signatories of the agreement. Broadly, three main principles characterized the new rules for international trade; the general most favored nation treatment, non-discrimination, and the general elimination of qualitative or quantitative restrictions[17] to commerce (GAAT, 1947, p. 17). Between 1947 to 1995, the world experienced the major sustained growth on international trade alongside with the most rapid growth of global inequality on history[18] (Sutcliffe., 2004). Within such circumstances, the development of both trade and political relations between capital core and periphery countries between the years 1950 to 2000, were characterized by two patterns:

1) "Both wealth and trade volumes were unevenly distributed, and the richer countries were found to be more likely to have positive trade surplus"[19] (Piketty, 2014).
2) "An individual trade value depended on the wealth of the trading countries asymmetrically: A richer country tended to attract more money from a poorer country… the wealth distribution took a power-law form under an asymmetric money exchange and that the wealth condensed on a few agents… was consistent with the global wealth distribution" (Cha & Lee, 2010 B).

In recent decades, trade relations have consistently acquired a fundamental dimension in how profit distribution around the world allocated historically (Cha & Lee, 2010 A) . In this regard, economic research has found similar patterns in terms of increasing processes of inequality[20] in almost all methods implemented (Milanovic, 2009) (Sutcliffe, 2004). Although the studies differ in methodological approaches (Duangkamon Chotikapanich, 1997) (Milanovic, 2006) they reveal a consistent tendency that expose a process of gap-increasing (Harjes, 2007) (Milanovic, 2007) (David Rueda, 2000) in the distribution of income and wealth both globally and locally[21]. The results frequently point out the decade of the 1980´s, as a global turning point that boosted worldwide economic inequalities. Indeed, despite the recent economic growth of the Asian Tigers, South America, and specially India and China, the phenomena has been depicted as a relation of have and have-not between countries, to a relation more notably between individuals in the world.

At the level of the Bretton Woods Institutions, the reasons by which trade liberalization was promoted, lay primarily in the historical approach of classical economy, based on the enhancement of productivity upon the driving forces of specialization and comparative advantage. In such setting, liberalization of trade pushes the development of competition and economic relations on the market, increasing the movement of goods, capital and labor. It is therefore expected, that even the nations with the lowest profile benefit if conditions of perfect competition are fulfilled. Pressures of trade liberalization however, often increase the risks of small countries to bear the decay of national industries under the burdens of foreign capital backed corporations. On the other hand, while the regulations and aims established at the World Trade Organization promoted the establishment of free trade, historically the most robust structures of national protectionism remained always at the head of the most industrialized countries of the world, weakening extensively the competition conditions of non-industrialized nodes (Aggarwal, et al., 1987) (Chorev, 2007) (Kahler, 1985). Finally, while these imbalances are commonly acknowledged, they continuously reproduce on the regulation of the World Trade Organization, inspired in the original General Agreement on Tariffs and Trade.

A major step forward in easing the tensions of the system, was held in 1995 with the creation of the Dispute Settlements Understanding (DSU) in the Uruguay round. Such new legal device was inspired by demands of periphery economies, aiming to set a new important regulatory agreement for improving the fragility of peripheral countries amidst influential trade actors. In recent studies however, four mayor pitfalls have been highlighted under the new settlement. 1) Lack of legal expertise of small countries during the process of protecting their interests in accordance with the regulation of the DSU mechanisms. 2) Strongly constrained financial resources that result in the lack of capacity of representation. 3) Political and economic pressures over small countries by big donors of financial aid. 4) Strong differences in bargaining power (Khan Haider, 2008, p. 4) .

Moreover, after the implementation of the DSU, trends in unequal relations of power increased rather than being reduced. Up to now, the number of complaints of developed countries against developing countries escalated from 9,5% to 28,1%. Indeed, nowadays "developing countries are one third less likely to file complaints against developed states under the WTO than they were under the post-1989 GATT regime"[22] (Khan Haider, 2008, p. 23). According to this tendency, it is expected in the long run a systematic increase in the influence of developed members over the WTO legal system. Indeed, the handicaps of developing countries lead to conclude the existence of an informal bias against them, due to their structural disadvantages for making use of the DSU provisions.

While the disastrous consequences of the DSU can be accounted as an unexpected contingency of the regulations, the described anomalies have not aroused under the new mechanism, but have arguably represented the common denominator of the negotiations between core and periphery countries. Since 1947, such mechanisms operated not only as devices for solution of commercial disagreements, but also as institutional mechanisms of legitimation of extensively unbalanced trade profits distributions. In theory, trade liberalization rests on the hypothesis of perfect competition conditions in which the existence of monopolies, oligopolies and politics is widely ignored. By now, however, the unequal power relations between countries and the extensive measures for distorting conditions of competition erode the application of the fundamentals of the economic approach. This is how strong pressures in weak economies with fragile institutions and abundant natural resources, often lead to situations of broad deinstitutionalization and growth of inequality (World Bank - EDP.Ph, 1976) (Cotula, 2014) (Cotula, 2009).

So far, the present normative structure of the WTO favors widely the interests of developed economies with the ability to fund national industries and processes of outward oriented development. This situation epitomizes in the phenomena of strong protectionist trade policies of industrialized countries; a customary practice that has pushed economic growth on most of the "first world" (Spanu, 2003, p. 7). The structural adjustment policies, commonly stressed by the IMF with the aim of "grounding" the institutional capabilities for free trade -developed over time on the effort of exporting an Anglo American concept of governance-, often misguided or forced local authorities to follow paths in accordance with private agendas, overwhelming them by the retaliation of the market. Conversely, successful cases of liberalization, like those of East Asian countries, China, India or Chile, are often taken into account as models of independence and autonomy[23] (Spanu, 2003, p. 13)..

Although historically, the World Trade Organization and the World Bank have acknowledged the existence of asymmetries between relations of free trade, up to now serious compensatory measures are out of discussion. Although the current guideline on liberalization has been pushed especially by industrialized territories and exercised politically in "developing" areas, official estimations of the World Bank indicate that only in agricultural subsidies, barriers to trade imposed by "developed" countries sum U$ 1 Billion a day. This single amount is indeed, "six time bigger than the aid to *developing* countries". According to the same estimation, protectionist measures on industrial economies develop sharply, as such, "the average European cow receives around $2.5 a day in subsidy, … the average Japanese cow receives around $7 a day, …while seventy-five percent of the people in Sub-Saharan Africa live on less than $2 a day" (Spanu, 2003, p. 14). Indeed, previous IMF economic reports have suggested that, for the year 2012, the profits that "developing" countries may earn by the elimination of protectionism on industrialized territories, more than tenfold the current amount of aid transfers. In solely the cotton sector, the elimination of US subsidies would bring to Western Africa about "$250 million in revenues per year, a larger amount than the budget for the Highly-Indebted Country Initiative debt relief[24] (HIPC). to these same countries"[25] (Spanu, 2003, p. 15).

Under the current normative scheme, trade relations between countries facilitate the process of reinforcement of structural differences in terms of power between core and periphery participants. With such background, the Dispute Settlement Mechanism at the World Trade Organization has often generated heated discussions due to the lack of regulation for addressing distorted power relations. These stings, as expected, worsen the process of global inequality between influential and non-influential arenas, enhancing political distortions. Up to now, it seems economic and financial globalization has not been a history shaped by winners and losers of the process itself, but between capital abundant nodes and a diminishing resistance from scarce capital social groups or communities. In the arena of governance, the rationality of profitability led to the oblivion of periphery political demands and perspectives. At the end, the exercise of governance blurs, isolating fundamental information that potentially led to the violation of fundamental constitutional or political principles from which the system originally nurtured.

The extent of asymmetry in ideological or politicized agendas expose incompatible situations that commonly affect peripheral actors, distorting both, local as well as global processes of governance. At the level of the Bretton Woods Institutions, this pathology is enforced by the normalization of biased regulation about "technically aseptic" approaches to a defined set of monetary, cultural, social and political practices (Wray, 2001) . Indeed, politization of technical guidelines can be found in numerous policies that avoid the implementation of principles of neutrality. Swedberg indicates three historical patterns of non-neutral actions; 1) internal normative and institutional adjustment for maintaining agendas of major western countries, 2) external pressure for these same countries, 3) political pressure from the institutions -favoring highly influential actors- exercised in third world territories (Swedberg, 1986). The pressures, he added, increase the implementation of "openly political" private foreign agendas. This is why, IMF lending has been depicted as *politicized,* aligning periphery countries with U.S. decisions by optimizing their chances of receiving loans. Indeed, this explains why recently it has been portrayed as an international tool for "specific, identifiable, political goals on the output side, such as realignment within the international system" (Thacker, 1999).

Normative Constructions and Asymmetry

The historical policies on trade liberalization and it´s constant unequal distribution of profits and burdens make impossible any attempt to conceive a balanced development of the global economy. Consistent and increasing inequality is perhaps the single most fundamental phenomenon behind the legitimation of free trade policies. Normatively, the power relations confronted in a global arena of unequal bargaining levels legitimizes subjective discourses customarily addressed by highly influential actors. This background brings up cyclical effects that reproduce global imbalances, institutionalizing normativity prone to be labeled as fair, yet taking place on competition under conditions of asymmetric circulation of power (Rodrik, 2001) (Rodrick, 2002). At the policy making level, such arrangements frequently green-wash long term sustainable policies, branding as "impossible" global claims for regulation of sensible operational spheres of today's political systems, such as the environment[26]. In these cases, the institutions accept tacitly the misbehavior and even the violation of fundamental principles of international law that conflict agendas of influential players. This explains why solutions remain bordered by their own subjective discursive constructions on justice and legality.

Upon conditions of asymmetry, the notion of economic growth tends to acquire a normative category that isolates marginalized views about how social systems should develop in the global arena. This pattern has ostracized demands for change in the global regulation, and isolated voices of actors that look to transpose the distributive character of the nation state, to the global level, so local budgets are able to handle their priorities adequately. In Rodrik´s conclusion, "the main strike against existing trade rules is not that they over-emphasize trade and growth at the expense of poverty alleviation, but that they over-emphasize trade at the expense of poverty reduction and growth" (Rodrik, 2001).

Structural imbalances make unreachable stable normative outcomes, under those circumstances, inequality is internalized as a customary praxis. It builds up in between subjective cultural practices, institutional and power relations, and is formally regularized in the process of creation of international regulation. This carries out the evolution of highly problematic normative constructions embraced at the global level. In fact, imbalanced distribution of economic power has direct consequences over the development of global and local economic and political structures (Sachs., 2006) (Galbraith, 2008). As it was stressed by Galbraith[27] "…the issue of economic inequality, both within and between countries, [configures] an issue of global economic governance, strongly influenced by structures of regulation of financial and commodity markets and by the conduct of monetary and financial policy in the rich and powerful countries".

A fundamental normative construction that legitimate institutional guidelines on the issue has been the idea of modern "development", excerpted at the institutional record of highly influential organizations such as the World Bank and the IMF. The discursive interventions on development are made by articulating two main functional features. First, an institutional that builds up from the fact that the current Bretton Woods institutional architecture, makes no distinction between the subjective roles and interests of isolated actors for defining the norm. While the Stockholm conference of 1972, was the first attempt to bring into the public debate the necessity of building a world with an environment not separated from "human ambitions", by now changes in the regulatory efforts of the institutions are practically absent. Indeed, whereas the declaration stressed the fundamental material gaps between rich and poor countries, and the effects of industrialization over the environment; by now, global gaps between rich and poor people have increased, and the world is experiencing the single most critical situation on climate change provoked specifically by 40 years of uninterrupted CO_2 emission of industrialized countries (McCright & Dunlap, 2011) (Paterson, 1996). At the moment, the discursive transition has not only normalized previously highly criticized arrangements, but has converted them in a customary rhetoric absent from sanctions, definition of responsibilities, or modification of institutional settings -such as with the case of the failed 2000 World Bank and the United Nations Millennium Declaration-[28].

The second reason has to do with the rather absent research on alternative approaches to development besides those given by the boundaries of the current free market system (Escobar, 1995) (Escobar, 2008). This task, indeed, can imply for international organizations an institutional withdrawal from their customary understanding of fundamental principles on Global Constitutionalism, Global Governance and Justice. In their role, the implementation of regulation directed to conceive processes of development as a productive enterprise of nation states, legitimized relations of exploitation with social systems historically isolated from the global chain of economic production. Indeed, cultural and social structures of organization of non-western signatories, instead of promoting trade, relied almost exclusively in social traditions unfamiliar to the global chain of production. Even previous decades before the outbreak of the war, the cultural differences were stressed mainly in how now western areas located social values and moral responsibilities in the "family, tribe, or some other social unit" besides private associations (Frith, 1988) (Hurtado, 2008).

Within the epistemology of the Bretton Woods Institutions, capitalist relations were enhanced through the disintegration of tribal ties, and the expansion of "individual legal rights" into the collective idiosyncrasy (Finnemore, 1996, p. 333). Indeed, cultural differences were given mainly by the shocking evolution of the industrial revolution in Europe, carried out during the great extent of the 19th and 20th century with the destruction of the "family life, the devastation of neighborhoods, the denudation of forests (…) and of private and public [forms of] life that do not affect profit" (Polanyi, 2001, p. 115). Within such arrangements, western and non-western territories embraced different patterns of political organization that ease in Europe the implementation of measures directed to set political provisions in compliance with a global structure of capital. This is why at the normative construction on development at the level of the Bretton Woods Institutions; they found their way in the form of the *capitalist enterprise*, which aimed to reconfigure social systems threatened by the effects of flows of investment, and their acceptance of trade relations within schemes of asymmetric distribution of profits[29] (Mc. Carthy, 1984, p. XXX) (Campbel, 2002).

In western countries, such biographical background implied the systematic rationalization of life spheres along the regulation of private household relations, the institutionalization of entrepreneurial activity, consistent trends in oppression of labor workers, "investment decisions oriented to the opportunities of the market, rational organization of labor, technical exploitation of scientific knowledge, and so forth" (Habermas, 1984, p. 360) (Sachs, 1993) (Weber, 2001). The implications of these patterns over social demands outlined important governance malfunctions further replicated to social systems that aimed to steered structural problems by governance strategies, public policies, and "norms construction". Finally, besides market oriented provisions, global political asymmetries and uneven outcomes of economic relations between nodes of consumption and production, revealed indeed problematic underlying dynamics that threatened any attempt to interact at the global level dialogically.

Table 1, sums up asymmetric properties of the Bretton Woods Architecture. Column A, lists structural fields in which defined actors were privileged to formalize normative constructions into the institutions. Column B, notes cultural distinctions between social systems part of the agreements at New Hampshire, as well as their role in easing cognitive operation of influential actors. The third column lists the distribution of leverage (power) of the regulatory arrangements of the institutions in a global structure of capital.

Table 1. Asymmetric properties of the Bretton Woods Architecture

Formalization of normative constructions into systemic structures	**Cognitive operation into the system**	**Operation within an institutional power field**
A	**B**	**C**
Quotas define the voting leverage of participants for the decades to come	Normalization of systemic patterns of global unequal distribution of economic burdens and benefits along the 20th and 21th century.	A. Both wealth and trade volumes where unevenly distributed... Richer countries were more likely to have positive trade surpluses b2
Decision making procedures taking by votes	Rationalization of life spheres upon the regulation of private household relations,	B. Richer countries tended to attract more money from poorer ones
The United States and the three major western European countries not only hold a normative foundational power weight, but also exceptional veto power.	Informal bias against "developing" countries while making use of the Dispute Settlement Mechanism	Constrained financial resources for carrying suing processes
Veto power	Institutionalization of entrepreneurial activity, consistent trends in oppression of labor of capital scarce nodes	1)internal normative and institutional adjustment for maintaining agendas of major western countries
Bargaining capacity	Implementation of "openly political" private foreign agendas	3) political pressure from the institutions, favoring highly influential actors, exercised in third world countries
Operationalization of the most influential regulatory proposals. The "United States Proposal for a United and associated nations stabilization Fund" and the -British- "Proposal for an International Clearing Union"	Cultural and social structures of organization of non-western signatories, instead of promoting trade, relied almost exclusively in social traditions unfamiliar to the global chain of production	US keeps the privilege of running large direct investment surpluses by issuing dollars held by foreign banks
Voting dynamics not only imply processes of asymmetric concentration of power by single players at the board of the IMF or the World Bank but also at the United Nations	Patterns of political organization that ease the implementation of measures directed to set social provisions in compliance with a global structure of capital	Loans tend to be larger and more frequent when a country has a bigger quota and more professional staff
	Investment decisions oriented to the opportunities of the market, rational organization of labor, technical exploitation of scientific knowledge	Lack of serious compensatory measures in the distribution of trade profits
	Normalization of processes of global liberalization within policies such as the general most favored nation treatment, non-discrimination, and the general elimination of qualitative or quantitative restrictions to commerce	Double standards in resolutions and political pressures against practices tending towards the creation of a monopoly, industrialized countries protectionism or the undue restraint of trade
	Biased regulation about "technically aseptic" approaches to a defined set of monetary, cultural, social and political practices. Politization of technical guidelines	Smaller countries; forced to comply with long term sustainable international monetary agreements
	Lack of legal expertise of small countries (DSU).	

CONCLUSION

In the operationalization for further research of a concept of political asymmetry at the level of international organizations, we have carried out the study of the relationship of actors and structures at the Bretton Woods Institutions. This task has studied the two defining patterns of political asymmetry; 1) The generation of unequal capacities of actors to formalize normative constructions on systemic structures, and 2) the administration of power along two functional dimensions, social (institutional and cultural patterns of societies part of the agreement) and the asymmetric distribution of profits in a global structure of production. This chapter stresses that both circumstances have historically colluded within the regulatory framework of the Bretton Institutions. It is the aim of this chapter to suggest further research concerning the consequences of such institutional arrangements, both from the governance perspective, as well as for inquiry directed to contextualize and to depict adequately the meaning of normative interventions on asymmetric institutions.

While the mere notion of political asymmetry is not capable to give details about underlying facts related to the existence of governance crisis, it represents a measurable standard to deduce how discourses and normative outcomes of asymmetric institutions, define terms of the global distribution of power, and the asynchronisms between global structures of governance, policies and goals[30]. The present chapter also stresses the relevance to study from a critical perspective, how discourses at the level of asymmetric organizations, are lately institutionalized in the process of construction of meaning and norms, beyond domestic cultural environments (Wiener, 2007). Our assumption is that the theoretical contributions of this chapter raise awareness about how contemporary processes of creation of norms pretend to present as aseptic narratives that belong to actors that intervene on asymmetric bargaining scenarios.

Frequent discussions on international relations and international law have addressed critically the study of the unevenness of the foundational settings of the contemporary global economic architecture, yet inquiry of the construction of normative outcomes of asymmetric international organizations is frequently avoided. By now it is recurrent in customary analysis to consider that normative interventions represent outcomes of dialogical interaction. At the level of the Bretton Woods Institutions, with the operationalization of the concept of political asymmetry, such assumption is revealed as highly problematic or rather false. This chapter draws attention to the cognitive sphere of institutional practices, and the implication of conflicting settings in framing the language, goals, interests, discourses and the overall functional practices of the policy-making process.

REFERENCES

Aggarwal, V., Keohane, R., & Yoffie, D. (1987, June). The Dynamics of Negotiated Protectionism. *The American Political Science Review*, *81*(2), 345–366. doi:10.2307/1961956

Arenal, C. d. (1984). *Introducción a las relaciones Internacionales. Introductions to the International Relations*. Tecnos.

Baker, P. (2006). Using Corpora in Discourse Analysis. Continuum. doi:10.5040/9781350933996

Barro, R. J. (2005). *IMF Programs: Who Is Chosen and What Are the Effects?* Department of Economics, Korea University.

Bird, G., & Rowlands, D. (2006). IMF quotas: Constructin an international organization using inferior building blocks. *The Review of International Organizations*, *1*(2), 153–171. doi:10.100711558-006-8342-x

Black, E. R. (1960, June). The age of economic development. *Economic Journal (London)*, *70*(278), 266–276. doi:10.2307/2228727

Blommaert, J. (2005). *Discourse: A Critical Introduction. Key topics in sociolinguistics*. Cambridge University Press. doi:10.1017/CBO9780511610295

Blommaert, J., & Bulcaen, C. (2000). Critical Discourse Analysis. *Annual Review of Anthropology*, *29*, 447–466.

Boughton, J. M. (2002). *Why White, Not Keynes? Inventing the Postwar International Monetary System.* (IMF Working Paper). IMF.

Buzan, B. (2004). *From International to World Society.* Cambridge Studies in International Relations.

Campbel, J. L. (2002). Ideas, politics, and public policy. *Annual Review of Sociology*, *28*(1), 21–38. doi:10.1146/annurev.soc.28.110601.141111

Carthy, M. (1984). Introduction. The theory of communicative action. Boston: Beacon Press.

Cha, M.-Y. & Lee, J. W. (2010). *Wealth dinamics in world trade (Moon-Yong Cha a, Jae Woo Leea – Patterns of International Trade and a Nation's Wealth.*. Cornell University Press.

Cha & Lee. (20100. Patterns of International Trade and a Nation's Wealth. Department of Physics, Inha University, Incheon, 402-751.

Cotula, L. (2014). *Foreign Investmente, law and sustainable development. IIED Natural Resources Issues.* International Institute for Environment and Development.

Cotula, L. V. S. L. R. K. J. (2009). *Land grab or development opportunity? Agricultural investmente and international land deals in Africa.* IIED/FAO/IFAD, London/Rome.

David Rueda, J. P. (2000). *Wage Inequality and varieties of capitalism.* Cambridge University Press.

Dennis Leech, R. L. (2004). *Voting Power in the Bretton Woods Institutions.* (Warwick Economic Research Papers). Warwick Economic.

Dreher, A. &. J.-E. S. (2010). *Do the IMF and theWorld Bank influence voting in the UN General Assembly.* Springer. .. s.l.:s.n. doi:10.1007/s11127-010-9750-2

Duangkamon Chotikapanich, R. V. D. R. (1997). Global and Regional Inequality in the Distribution of Income: Estimation with Limited and Incomplete Data. *Empirical Economics*, *22*(4), 533–546. doi:10.1007/BF01205778

Eichengreen, B. (2004). *Global Imbalances and the Lessons from Bretton Woods.* National Bureau of Economic Research.

Eichengreen, B. (2008). *Globalizing Capital:A History of the International Monetary System* (2nd ed.). Princeton University Press. doi:10.2307/j.ctt7pfmc

Escobar, A. (1995). *Encountering Development. The making and unmaking of the third world.* Princeton University Press.

Escobar, A. (2008). The Problematization of Poverty; the tale of three worlds and development. In *The development reader* (pp. 131–140). MPG, Books Ltd. Bodmin.

Finnemore, M. (1996). Norms,culture, and world politics: insights from sociology's institutionalism. *Intemational Organization 50*(2).

Frith, K. (1988). *More than we bargained for: The impact of consumer culture in South East Asia. Department of Journalism and Mass comunication.* Iowa State University.

GAAT. (1947). *The general agreement on tariffs and trade ("GATT 1947").* World Trade Organization.

Galbraith, J. K. (2008). *Inequality and Economic and Political Change.* UTIP Working Paper No. 51). UTIP.

Goldgeier, J. M., & Tetlock, P. E. (2001). Psycology and International Relations Theory. [Annual Reviews.]. *Annual Review of Political Science, 4*(1), 67–92. doi:10.1146/annurev.polisci.4.1.67

Gourinchas, P.-O., & Rey, H. (2005). *From world banker to world venture capitalist: us external adjustment and the exorbitant privilege.* National bureau of economic research.

Guilhot, N. (2008). The realist Gambit: Postwar American Political Science and the Birth of IR Theory. International Studies Association. *International Political Sociology, 2*(4), 281–304. doi:10.1111/j.1749-5687.2008.00052.x

Haas, P. (1992). Introduction: Epistemic Communities and International Policy Coordination. *International Organization, 46*(1), 1-35.

Habermas, J. (1984). The Theory of Communicative Action, Volume 1: Reason and the Rationalization of Society. Translated by Thomas McCarthy. Boston: Beacon Press.

Harjes, T. (2007). Globalization and Income Inequality: A European Perspective. International Monetary Fund.

Herrmann, V., Voss, J. F., Schooler, T. Y. E., & Ciarrochi, J. (1997). Images in International Relations: An Experimental Test of Cognitive Schemata. [September.]. *International Studies Quarterly, 41*(3), 403–433. doi:10.1111/0020-8833.00050

Hurtado, S. (2008). *Ecología, agricultura, comunidad.* Universidad Central de Venezuela.

IMF. (1944). Articles of Agreement of the International Monetary Fund. International Monetary Fund.

Kahler, M. (1985, July). European Protectionism in Theory and Practice. [Cambridge University Press.]. *World Politics, 37*(4), 475–502. doi:10.2307/2010341

Keller, R. (2006). Analysing discourse: An approach from the sociology of knowledge. *Historical Social Research (Köln), 31*, 2.

Khan Haider, Y. L. (2008). Globalization and the WTO Dispute Settlement Mechanism: Making a Rules-based Trading Regime Work. University Library of Munich, Germany.

Kratochwil, D. (2000). Constructing a New Orthodoxy? Wendst's Social Theory of International Politics and the Constructivist Challenge. Milennium. *Journal of International Students*, *29*, 73.

Kratochwil, F. (1993). The embarrassment of changes: Neorealism as the science of Realpolitik without politics. *Review of International Studies*, *19*(1), 63–80. doi:10.1017/S0260210500117346

Leiteritz & Moschella. (2010). The IMF and capital account liberalization: a case of failed norm institutionalization. In S. Park & A. Vetterlein (eds.) Owning Development: Creating Policy Norms in the IMF and the WB. Cambridge University Press.

Lombardi, N. W. &. D. (2006). Uneven patterns of governance: how developing countries are represented in the IMF. *Review of International Political Economy, 13*(3), pp. 480-515.

McCright, A., & Dunlap, R. (2011). The politicization of climate change and polarization in the american public's views of global warming, 2001–2010. The Sociological Quarterly, 52(2).

Mikesell, R. F. (1994). The Bretton Woods debates. A memoir. Essays in International Finance, 192.

Milanovic, B. (2006). *Global income inequality: What it is and why it matters.* Washington: (World Bank Policy Research Working Paper 3865). World Bank.

Milanovic, B. (2007). *An even Higuer inequality than previously though: a note on global inequality calculations using the 2005 ICP results.* (World Bank Policy Research Working Paper Series). World Bank.

Milanovic, B. (2009). *Global inequality and global inequality extraction ratio: The story of the last two centuries.* World Bank, University of Maryland.

Niiniluoto, I. (1991). *No. 1. Scientific knowledge and Scientific Practice (Oct., 1991)* (Vol. 89). Realism, relativism and constructivism. Synthese. Springer.

Nixon, R. (1971). Address to the Nation Outlining a New Economic Policy: 'The Challenge of Peace.' *Public Papers of the Presidents, Richard Nixon, Containing the Public Messages, Speeches, and Statements of the President.*

Paterson, M. (1996). *Global warming and Global Politics.* Taylor & Francis Group.

Pettenger, M. E. (2008). The Social Construction of Climate Change: Power, Knowledge, Norms, Discourses. *Journal of Environmental Law*, *20*(3), 486–489. doi:10.1093/jel/eqn016

Piketty, T. (2014). Capital in the Twenty-First Century. *The Belknap Press.*

Polanyi, K. (2001). *The Great Transformation. Beacon Press Books. 1944 - 2001.* Foreword by Joseph E. Stiglitz.

Rodrick, D. (2002). Feasible Globalizations. *(NBER Working Paper No. 9129).* NBER.

Rodrik, D. (2001). *The Global governance of Trade. As if development really mattered.* Bureau for Development Policy.

Rodrik, D. (2001). *Trading in Illusions.* Foreign Policy. No. 123 (Mar. – Apr), pp. 54-62. Washingtonpost. Newsweek Interactive, LLC. https://www.jstor.org/stable/3183155

Sachs, J. D. (2006). The End of Poverty: Economic Possibilities for Our Time. London: Penguin (Non-Classics).

Sachs, W. (1993). Global Ecology and the Shadow of Development in Global Ecology: A New Arena of Political Conflict. Zed Books.

Spanu, V. (2003). Liberalization of the international trade and economic growth: implications for both developed and developing countries. John F. Kennedy School of Government, Harvard University.

Spanu, V. (2003). *Liberalization of the international trade and economic growth: implications for both developed and developing countries.* Harvard University

Sutcliffe, B. (2004). World Inequality and Globalization. Oxford Review of Economic Policy Limited. Oxford Press. . doi:10.1093/oxrep/grh002

Sutcliffe, B. (2004). World Inequality and Globalization. Oxford University Press and the Oxford Review of Economic Policy Limited. Oxford Press. . doi:10.1093/oxrep/grh002

Swedberg, R. (1986). The Doctrine of Economic Neutrality of the IMF and the World Bank. *Journal of Peace Research, 23*(4), pp. 377-390.

Thacker, S. C. (1999). The High Politics of IMF Lending. *World Politics*, *52*(1), 38–75. doi:10.1017/S0043887100020025

Weber, M. (2001). *The Protestant Ethic and the Spirit of Capitalism.* [T. Parsons, trans.] Routledge Classics.

Wendt, A. (1992). Anarchy is what states make of it: The social construction of power politics. *International Organization, 46, 391-425..*

Wiener, A. (2007). The Dual Quality of Norms and Governance beyond the State: Sociological and Normative Approaches to 'Interaction'. *Critical Review of International Social and Political Philosophy, 10*(1), pp. 47-69.

Wight, C. (2007, March). A Manifesto for Scientific Realism in IR: Assuming the Can-Opener Won't Work! *Millennium*, *35*(2), 379–398. doi:10.1177/03058298070350021601

Wray, B. (2001). *Science, Biases, and the Threat of Global Pessimism.* University of British Columbia.

ENDNOTES

1 Contained in the formal agreements of constitution of the International Monetary Fund and the World Bank and the articles of the General Agreement on Tariffs and Trade

2 A recognized American economist known for his detailed and well documented contributions on business cycles.

3 At the end of the decade, the majority of the nations initiated a process of pegging their currencies and silver coins to the gold standard previously established by the United States, and the British economies. There are currently diverse discussions that try to justify the reasons by which bimetal-

lism was sustained for so long, despite the extreme difficulties that aroused by the participation of arbitragers and the national overvaluations and undervaluation's of both, gold and silver. Among the different explanations, the reason may layin the difficulty for different governments for arranging different standardized monetary agreements, and the relation between the benefits of bimetallism against it´s externalities. To a certain extent, the widespread tacit acceptance of bimetallism among the main economies of the world simplified trade to a profitable extent.

4 At the beginning of the 19th century, destabilizing flows represented a secondary point of interest in the agenda of central banks. Since societies lack the level of organization achieved during the first half of the 20th century, currency depreciation was considered as a common alternative for arranging monetary imbalances. The interlude between the first and the second world war, increased the levels of tension between economies, that by forcing the pressure over certain social sectors, made use of monetary policies to reach national economic interests.

5 The arrangement of the participation of the countries was settled in according of the level of political influence of the participant, and the political proximity with the United States. Diverse committees where created as an "operational" strategy for approach different topics, during the creation of the institutions. The main two committees, where leaded respectively by Harry Dexter White (US), and John Maynard Keynes (Great Britain). These committees defined the structure, normative outcome, and shares of participation of the representatives, signatories of the final agreements. The rest of the committees were mainly concerned for logistic and operational subjects.

6 For a term of 3 years, the initiative for creating a free trade international organization was diluted.

7 In the definition of (Arenal, 1984)

8 Originally conceived as the "International Bank for Reconstruction and Development".

9 Cursives by the author of this chapter.

10 The Foundational participation at the International Monetary Fund for example, was settled by a distribution of "voting weight" in accordance with a mixture of a standardized fixed component, and a defined quota. The original quotas established in 1946 for the inaugural aimed the maintenance of the political and economic influence of England, United States, URSS and France. The calculus -conducted by the technician Raymond Mikesell-, was suggested in a formula in which the quota of the United States explicitly two folded UK. Later on, when the technician in charge was submitted to reveal the calculation, he pointed out:

I tried to make the process appear as scientific as possible, but the delegates were intelligent enough to know that the process was more political than scientific. Following my explanation, there was a long silence, during which I waited for a harsh cross-examination. The silence was broken by Rasminsky of Canada (later head of the Canadian Central Bank), who said he was well satisfied with my explanation and moved to accept the list. Rasminsky had discussed the quota recommendations with the U.S. delegation earlier and had agreed to support them. (Mikesell, 1994).

11 Highest level of representation, in which each government has direct participation. The management of both institutions –IMF and WB-, is done in the respective Executive Board. This last organism is composed by elected or appointed representatives.

12 (Dennis Leech, 2004)

13 "With forty-four delegations coming together for three weeks, the Bretton Woods conference could not have been expected to reach a consensus on dozens of technical questions and then negotiate a report…" Although delegates from other countries made numerous proposals that conflicted with the basic preconference positions and agenda, the technicians were positioned to prevent their

introduction into the charters. The commissions and committees at Bretton Woods presented a façade of democratic procedure, but the outcome had been largely predetermined by the U.S. and U.K. delegations". (Mikesell, 1994)

14 In 1972, in a national broadcast transmission, former president of the United States Richard Nixon, reported to the citizens, the unilateral decision of ending "temporally" the convertibility of the dollar into gold. The ulterior attempts to restate the convertibility failed, leading to the end of the Bretton Woods system in 1973. The reasons mentioned by Nixon were that the United States, in the path of ending a war, must face the "challenges of peace", namely;
To bring about a new generation for peace, and to create a new prosperity without war... it calls for the greatness, and a great people... prosperity without war require action on three fronts, we must create more and better jobs, we must stop the rise in the cost of living, *we must protect the dollar from the attack of international money speculators*" (Nixon, 1971).
Although Nixon didn't described underlying reason behind the decision, it is well know that the levels of debt acquired by the government, for maintaining the War of Vietnam harmed seriously the credibility of the dollar. The necessity of producing more money became and imperative for the United States, in this regard, the unpegging of the dollar, facilitated the lack of control over the capacity of the American Government to increase their level of indebtedness and to print money. The war ended two years later.

15 Due to the absence of official trade representatives of the leading nations

16 United States of Brazil, Burma, Canada, Ceylon, the Republic of Chile, the Republic of China, the Republic of Cuba, the Czechoslovak Republic, the French Republic, India, Lebanon, the Grand-Duchy of Luxemburg, the Kingdom of the Netherlands, New Zealand, the Kingdom of Norway, Pakistan, Southern Rhodesia, Syria, the Union of South Africa, the United Kingdom of Great Britain and Northern Ireland, and the United States of America. (GAAT, 1947, p. 1)

17 *"No prohibitions or restrictions other than duties, taxes or other charges, whether made effective through quotas, import or export licences or other measures, shall be instituted or maintained by any contracting party on the importation of any product of the territory of any other contracting party or on the exportation or sale for export of any product destined for the territory of any other contracting party"*. (GAAT, 1947, p. 17).

18 Between 1950 and 1980 (Sutcliffe., 2004).

19 This phenomena can be much more broadly explained by the historical studies on the profits relation between capital and other assets by Thomas Piketty (Piketty, 2014).

20 Nowadays, the level of research of Branko Milanovik on this topic is arguably unbeatable. His contributions have clarified debates about diverse conflicting methodologies that created confusion about the trends of inequality in the world. Two academic insights are of main importance on this issue. On the first place the analysis of periods of time before the decade of the 80`s, the most relevant tipping point for signaling the boosting of globalization as a recognized phenomenon (Milanovic, 2009), on the second hand, the academic consensus in regards of the translation of inequalities from the local to the global level, that is the process of reinforcement of divergent economic strata's, regardless of the methodology (Sutcliffe, 2004).

21 Seldom exceptions at the European Union.

22 Bush and Reinhardt. Cited in (Khan Haider, 2008, p. 23)

23 The pathology of the asymmetry of treatment of the conditions established at the WTO is represented in the outstanding absence of means for developing countries to countermeasure first world

protectionism. According to institutional research "the welfare gains from eliminating barriers to merchandise trade range from \$250 billion to \$650 billion annually, with about one-third to one-half accruing to developing countries. The World Bank estimates that by reducing protection", especially in the US, European Union Countries and Japan, "the number of people living in poverty could be reduced by 14 percent in 2015" (Spanu, 2003, p. 13).

24 Debt Relief Under the Heavily Indebted Poor Countries (HIPC).

25 "US subsides to cotton farms was \$3.9 billion in 2002, that is three times US foreign aid to Africa". (Spanu, 2003, p. 15).

26 This situation can be found clearly on the reluctant conduct of the United States when pushed internationally to decrease CO2 emission.

27 Head of the University of Texas Inequality Project.

28 Resolution -A/55/L.2- adopted by the General Assembly. 55/2. United Nations Millennium Declaration. For more information see: https://www.un.org/millennium/declaration/ares552e.htm.

29 This assumption is part of the most widely acknowledged sociological analysis on the evolution of modern societies. From recent contributions on critical constructivism read (Mc. Carthy, 1984, p. XXX). Criticism can be found in (Campbel, 2002)

30 As they have been established in the 2001 United Nations millennium summit.

Chapter 6
The Normative Construction of Modern Development at the Bretton Woods Institutions

ABSTRACT

This chapter depicts the operational stages through which a norm on modern development evolved institutionally at the level of the World Bank and the International Monetary Fund. It describes such historical evolution within two biographical periods of both institutions, the first one between their foundation in 1945 until the 70s decade. The second one, from that decade until today. In recent decades, the influence of the regulatory scope of the Bretton Woods Institutions extensively shaped domestic and international identities and norms. In essence, for the last 70 years, settings of the global economy were transposed along the cultural, social, industrial, and overall political architecture of each one of the nation-states part of the World Bank or the IMF.

INTRODUCTION

In recent decades, the influence of the regulatory scope of the Bretton Woods Institutions extensively shaped domestic and international identities and norms. In essence, for the last 70 years, settings of the global economy were transposed along the cultural, social, industrial and overall political architecture of each one of the nation-states part of the World Bank or the IMF. On the other hand, since these customary political transitions have affected dissimilarly the conditions within which nation-states have endured over time the transnational economic arena, little can be said about the role of global organizations in affecting such domestic institutional biographies. Aiming to disentangle this historical constellation, the goal of the present chapter is twofold. On the one hand, it explains how the Bretton Woods Institutions managed to create a norm of "modern development" that evolved globally, discursively and normatively along diverse spheres of social systems. This process was carried out through two operational stages. The first one was in between the end of the Second World War and the 70´s decade, when following harsh volatilities, the Bretton Woods convertibility system developed amidst international actors eager

DOI: 10.4018/978-1-6684-9794-4.ch006

to increase their influence in a highly unstable international realm. The second one, is framed between the end of the 70´s decade and today. This period is characterized by the institutional attempts of the Bretton Woods Institutions to broaden the influence of its normative construction to spheres of social systems beyond the economy, such as the family structure, the forms, dimensions and shapes of urban settlements, the structure of income and knowledge based societies, the institutions of governance at the national level, the architecture and role on social spheres of highly sophisticate financial systems, the ideological boundaries of deontological practices of the organizations, and the principles of global trade, among others.

For conducting the depiction of such historical transitions, the present chapter adheres to the contributions of historical institutionalism and critical constructivism. On the one hand, historical institutionalism conceives institutions not only as systemic and deterministic arrangements of social systems, but also as political construction that arouse within singular historical events. Moreover, they operate not only as appendices of nation state entities, but create and reproduce their own cultural, political, ideological and overall normative practices. This process takes place through interaction of representatives of the institutions (bureaucrats), but also through power structures, institutional arrangements and tradeoffs of information, practices and interests within the organization. On the other hand, institutional analysis frequently adheres to the practice of not questioning how normative constructions of highly influential international organizations evolve through processes of asymmetric interaction. In this matter, the role of critical constructivism aims to offer a defined theoretical framework able to contextualize the role of the ideology and the economy in the formation of late modern social systems. As such, in an attempt to cover the limitations of alternative theoretical standpoint, the present chapter aims to validate the use of historical institutionalism and critical constructivism as an empirical research framework to contextualize international discursive interventions and normative constructions, such as the norm of "modern development".

PART ONE

Historical Background

After the end of the Bretton Woods convertibility system, the increase of global economic flows of capital was triggered by two causes. On the one hand, the demand of the global economy to boost financial markets eager to take advance of a more interconnected world in which traceability of investment was possible due to relatively new technological improvements. Since the agents carrying out this process were also aware of the limitations of and exchange rate tied to gold reserves, the increasing demands of capital generated distrust over the amount of *gold-backed dollars* into the global economy. On the second hand, global economic growth was accompanied with the expansion of liberal democracies in which education systems increased the cognitive capacities of populations to play a role into vacancies of technical or scientific labor. Likewise, social nets built sectors increasingly coordinated between each other to attend demands on health or household utilities. This phenomenon was boosted by the immense mobilization of populations between rural to urban areas, generating strong social and economic differences between workers engaged into agricultural production, and population keen to participate in sectors like manufacture or services at the level of highly dense urban settlements (Habermas, 2000, p. Ch 3).

In the second half of the century, the influence of the Bretton Woods Institution in exerting pressure over broad social systems formerly excluded from the global structure of production, transformed the way domestic politics were customarily addressed. Moreover, the effects of flows of money over capital scarce economies, transformed the direction towards which national institutions defined how to prioritize investment with the influence of international organizations. In the Bretton Woods Institutions, these practices were normalized within a single customary narrative, constructed discursively according to their foundational goals back in 1945. With this framework, the social changes experienced in the world at the end of the Second World War led to diverse diagnosis that frequently oscillated between measuring the role of the markets in shaping global modern societies, and the cultural changes experienced in liberal economies in contrast with the countries of the iron curtain. From an institutional perspective, this analysis was frequently carried out by mainstream media interventions on "development", upon which social, economic, cultural and overall political events were interpreted and thus conducted along the foundational/ideological and operational settings of the international architecture. The historical record of the institutions such as the World Bank, and the International Monetary Fund however, were frequently kept private from the public opinion, and thus apart from the access of customary criticism, or simply isolated from the public discourse. Modernity and development within the global economy, however, represented a fundamental sociological category interpreted along the scope of nation states, bounded and interdependent from transnational structures of organization. While in many cases, these categories embraced differentiations among social systems, in the public record of the Bretton Woods Institutions they were embedded homogeneously, in a discursive construction that standardized policies within signatories, and has remained unchanged over decades.

While for the most part of the 20th century, the relation of international organizations - such as the World Bank and the IMF- with societies and national institutions were tied along their executive operative functions, in recent decades this practice has changed profoundly. With the increasing levels of influence of the organizations, official publications copped the gap left by their customary internal operation, becoming a public voice for international actors. This is how, modern development at the Bretton Woods Institutions, became not only a concept rooted into the customary analysis of the staff inside the organization, but, a normative construction built upon the interaction of this structures with social systems through official binding guidelines and publications.

At the level of the World Bank, and the International Monetary Fund, two structural forms of institutional publications concerning the concept of "development" were carried out. A) In the case of the World Bank, these were exemplified in the "Development and Prospects" reports, conducted by the economic department. The distribution of these reports, was directed exclusively to the private or temporary staff of both organizations, therefore it was frequently used for internal purposes, or by recipients only in the performance of their "official duties". Moreover, the information contained in the reports was frequently classified, thus attempts of disclosure were to be carried according to the guidance of the World Bank. B) Later on, in 1978, while the bank continued issuing the "Development and Prospects" report, it shifted to issue a partially public material with the official publication of the "World Development Report". In contrast, this publication has been, during recent years, the institutional most influential public material of the World Bank on the concept of "development". It contains a customary overview of the development of the world economy, as well as an institutional analysis of social and economic indicators upon which the bank addresses normative issues on the concept of "development".

In the case of the International Monetary Fund, institutional publications are led by the Annual Report of the Executive Board -made public since 1996-. The report is presented by the Chairman of the executive board to the Board of Governors, Executive Board, Interim Committee and the Development Committee of the institution. This document is also a complementary account of prospects of the Fund that aims to stress the relevance of the foundational Articles of Agreement of the organization. Issued every mid-year, it contains the financial statements of the fund for the immediate previous period -which ends every April 30th-. While in the beginning, the report frequently contained information concerning interactions in the global economy, and thus of the health and prognosis of loans given to borrower countries, during the recent decades, it has focused fundamentally on the forecast and analysis of global economic and financial growth. As a consequence, this entirely financial approach issued for the first time in 2000, has considerably placed the role of the institution as a kernel for the promotion of the process of global production, while reducing the accountability of their practices with each one of their borrowers.

The Origins of the Discourse on Development After the End of the Second World War

The demands for the reconstruction of Europe, enhanced on international politics the debates on how to adopt strategies for the recovery of their industrial capacity, cultural legacy, political influence and economic role in the world. In such scenario, calls for capital became a primary concern of territories affected by the consequences of the Second World War. In fact, these regions not only experienced physical devastation but the disappearance of financial means to leverage post war investments under safe circumstances. Meanwhile, the productive capacities of these countries faced a mixture of depreciation of productive equipment and technical impairment of machinery. This situation barely allows to some of their populations to meet the survival necessities. Upon such circumstances, the constitution of the Bretton Woods Institutions provided not only an international regulatory framework for foreign investment, but also an alternative source of capital for post war reconstruction of Europe and Japan, primarily. This necessity was warranted, because, after the war -besides the countries belonging to the iron curtain-, amounts of capital concentrated acutely in the United States. In fact, during the period of July 1st of 1945 and June 30th 1948, post war aid of the United States to foreign countries in relative value to 2011 GDP, amounted $1,2 trillion dollars[1] (Dickens et al, 1949). Among them, about $191.000 million were directed to a paid on capital contribution to the International Monetary Fund, while, a subscription of capital with the International Bank for Reconstruction and Development amounted to $143.000[2] million.

During the second half of the 20th century, nongovernmental sources for financial leverage became a necessity for countries that required investment for the development of their productive capacity. This is why the role of private foreign investment, frequently pushed for establishing regulatory boundaries for profitability beyond the nation state boundaries. While many of the limitations of the majority of the countries of the world lay in the difficulties of establishing financial and commercial relations on a safe international environment, the constitution of the Bretton Woods Institutions took the lead in offering such international setting with private capital located fundamentally in the United States.

In such scenario, the possibility of boosting the productive capacity of capital importing nodes, became a priority for actors eager to exploit the advantages of isolated areas socially, politically and economically organized, but without currency. In turn, this situation made highly profitable any foreign investment focused in resource extraction for the decades to come. In fact, in 1947, the investment pattern of the United States as the only country with reserves to boost the global economy is emblematic. As it has been depicted:

Direct (Dickens et al, 1949, p. 215) [US] investments abroad amounted (net) to $666 million, although a special type of investment, the purchase of ships for the use of American-owned foreign-flag operators, accounted for $124 million of that total. Investments in the petroleum industry, exclusive of additions to tanker fleets, totaled $353 million. More than two thirds of the petroleum investments were made in Venezuela and the Middle East. Of the investments other than those in the petroleum and shipping fields, 40 per cent were made in Brazil and Argentina[3].

In such scenario, the Bretton Woods Institutions became the organizations for economic development of regions in capacity to pay back loans. In fact, it turned out to be the single most profitable alternative for guiding direct foreign investment in such a way, that interests of capital exporting countries prevail. The robust structure of the former western industry, allowed levels of concentration of capital in the western world hardly comparable to any other areas around the world. Even after the wars, international finance continued playing a key role. This process of institutional modernization of the international realm, was initiated at the end of the 19th century. While at the domestic level, nations developed with the separation of the social life into modern functional spheres of production and organization[4] (Escobar, 1995, p. 60). On an international scale, the influence of the economy and the complex interests of countries and actors operating upon different regulations, currencies and levels of information, made impossible any attempt to implement serious regulation.

As such, the division of the modern society into functional spheres of production, and the role of this spheres in the process of capital accumulation, made possible the construction of a concept of development structurally tied with the language of the market and the economy. Whereas at the end of the Second World War, the majority of the economies of the peripheries kept average levels of organization upon interactions not entirely determined by the role of production, highly industrialized economies frequently presented tensions between a reduced number of inhabitants with economic means, and broad levels of population under the stresses of large scale physical labor. This phenomenon further boosted political uprisings, whose consequences remained until the fall of the Berlin Wall and the dismantling of the "communist" world.

The Reconstruction Period and the Development of a Global Free Trade Market Environment

In the earliest discussions concerning the role of an international monetary system as a mean to replace the gold standard, the concept of development was frequently addressed as an entirely economic category. In this fashion, social relations rather than disappearing as the main behavioral vector of complex societies, were mediated by structures of institutional justice, and a free market environment that simplified coordination in the process of production[5]. On a global level, this goal were to be achieved by the implementation of an alternative system of currency stabilization, which was from the beginning focused in the contributions of Harry D. White[6], and Lord Keynes[7]. The goal of the architecture was reconstructing a "functioning international economic system; and its potential usefulness (…) on cognate problems such as commercial policy and international long term investment". This goal was tied to the fact, that any effort to increase a future stable international environment, was to safeguard the capacity of core economies to foster production processes of their common leading industries

In 1944, an article written by the former Chairman of the Canadian Foreign Exchange Control Board[8], pointed out that "tolerable international economic arrangements will not endure, and competitive currency depreciation, excessive trade restrictions, barter trade deals, rigid and stultifying exchange controls will not be avoided, unless the great industrial nations are successful in maintaining a high and reasonably stable level of domestic economic activity" (Rasminsky, 1944). In essence, the conception of development, revealed itself as an economic category. In this perspective, international institutional arrangements, were to be conceived to benefit extensively capital exporting nodes, replacing previous agreements based on political coordination between equal administrative entities. As such, international commerce and global productivity demands, rather than politics, filled the gaps left by the limitations of the nation state on an international system. As such, the speed of interactions mediated by relations of capital, outpaced the capacity of the institutional architecture to steer relations of power. At the global level, the institutional goal was characterized by the urgency to achieve in the short term, higher levels of economic growth. Finally, it was upon such category that the entire efforts of the newly conceived international architecture pointed to.

The discursive interventions of the Bretton Woods Institutions, addressed permanently the necessity to increase the "stability and expansion" of the global economy (Hansen, 1944). The idea of development as a cost-effective category, was basically nurtured as a technical approach to increase the standards of living of the population of the western World, even at the back of a highly exploited periphery. On a global level, this goal draw upon the assumption that increases in levels of production of societies, inevitably lead to increases in the overall quality of life of the population. Following this objective, the prognosis of technical journals during the years after the conference, repeatedly pointed out, that the mayor negligence of the western world in the prewar periods, lay in the *miserable* (Hansen, 1944) failure of coordinating stability, full employment and increasing's in real income standards[9]. Therefore, the new political architecture of capital scarce territories, was to avoid such early pitfalls in the process of development of the global economy.

This line of thought was transposed on an international level, in which market expectations of low industrialized countries, were to be coped with the constitution of an International Institution for foreign investment of private capital such as the World Bank. This forecast however, was not a guarantee of the operability of the system, since many projects which deserved to be developed in low industrialized countries were not capable of earning returns in the short, nor in the medium term[10] (Hansen, 1944). On the other hand, the limitations of the economic approach on a global level, were consistent with the fact that they tended to create a world divided[11] (Williams, 1944) into debtor countries against one former single creditor, the United States[12]. Indeed, this situation, was acknowledged even by core economies that openly embraced the idea, that further projects for expansion of capital, were to be coordinated with the interests of core economies, to continue a trend of high capital concentration allocation at the global level.

At this point, every discursive construction about the notion of a future development, was linked upon the structure of a profit market global environment, therefore, development implied basically *development of capital*. This approach was indeed, customarily discussed within the period of the Second World War, serving as an ideological foothold for actors interested in boosting processes of economic liberalism globally. Indeed, the classified war cabinet documents[13] on the negotiations, which stored the expectations of UK concerning the foundation of an international commercial and financial system, made clear the *terms* upon which negotiations on "development" were settled. In this regard, the 1944 report (World War Cabinet file) in relation with the proposal for the constitution of a United Nations Bank for Reconstruction and Development, pointed out explicitly that:

It is most important, both from the point of view of the countries whose economies have been dislocated by the war and from our own point of view, that a Reconstruction Bank should be organized at as early a date as possible. (…) We cannot look to U.N.R.R.A to provide finance for reconstruction, for the present tendency of the UNRRA[14]. (…) Looking further ahead, it is important for the world that a Bank should be set up which will enable American money to be adequately and wisely investment in ***capital development*** *schemes in those countries where* ***capital development*** *is most needed (UK War Cabinet 338, 1944).*

Surrounded by such context, development, rather than being secured as a political category, was embedded within the boundaries of economic growth, and particularly within the conditions of expansion of capital accumulation for further venture resources according to settings necessary to reproduce *wise investment.* As such, the Bank endorsed to the necessities of restarting the "economic life" of the world, by putting into the economy the amount of money necessary to "finance the purchase of raw material and other overseas expenditure needed" to boost production. Thereby, development of capital was to conform the fundamental function of the Bank, determining the prioritization of investment in according to "the prospects of the recipient country being in a position to service it in *free exchange*" (UK War Cabinet 338, 1944).

The assumption of a global environment of "free exchange" upon asymmetric global conditions, and the existence of one international currency creditor as a savior for scenarios of structural scarcity of capital of periphery economies, was less than a fallacy. Any decision concerning the possibility of constituting an international bank for development, was bounded to the necessity of maintaining a permanent international "flow of international investments", thus to the capacity of any debtor to prove in the short or medium term the returns of capital ventures taking place on a highly unequal global market. This principle of free market exchange, was further stressed for two reasons; on the one hand, a big part of the expected capital to boost the bank was likely to be received by private investors. Second, loans were estimated to be completely untied from a defined nation state, therefore "available for purchase not only in the country in which they were issued, but in any member country" (UK War Cabinet 83, 1944, p. 139).

With the isolation of the political demands of peripheral actors, the norm of development to be established at the international level, "made no provisions" to protect nascent industries among the periphery. In contrast, these industries required rather than trade liberalization, the capacity of being boosted by protectionist measures, before being placed into a global environment of highly unequal competition. Indeed, this remarkable demand was consistently highlighted even by Great Britain, who saw into the conditions of the United States, an unavoidable threat to their colonial infant industries, some of them in territories highly problematic to be managed from abroad[15]. Up to 1944, amidst the negotiations between the representatives of commerce and industry of the United States, and the Chancellor of the Exchequer of Great Britain, these worries continued to be raised as a sensitive point of the agenda. According to Great Britain, "if a satisfactory solution [for special assistance to infant industries] were to be achieved, it would be necessary to consider ways of permitting some measure of additional tariff protection, subject to certain general rules" (UK War Cabinet 83, 1944, p. 5). At the beginning of 1945, six months after the signing of the Bretton Woods Agreement, the interests of Great Britain were made possible by a political exception granted by the United States, directed exclusively to Great Britain. The exception warranted a 5 years transitional period in which the rusted empire was able exclusively to adopt "any policy" regarded as in their own interest, "however *discriminatory* that policy might be" (UK War Cabinet 45, 1945).

Whereas with the foundation of the IMF and the World Bank in 1944, the idea of development was embedded symbolically within relations of global capital expansion, with the constitution of an International Institution for Trade and Employment, it acquired an institutional category. As such, the new functional quality of the global architecture, were to set *free* trade as the guiding path towards which any country eager to develop was supposed to transit. This operational condition, kept a functional relation with the interests of former or industrial economies, isolating demands of capital importing nodes to be treated fairly according to the distribution of profits, and the protection of infant industries in a global chain of production and capital. Indeed, the formal endorsement of the General Agreement on Trade and Tariffs, normalized symbolically and functionally, trade relations with so far no considerations concerning interests and political rights for equality of treatment of periphery political actors.

The proposals for deliberation for an international conference on trade written by a technical staff of the government of the United States, summarizes the instrumental boundaries of the norm into four economic working principles; a)the promotion of international commercial cooperation, b)the prohibition of measures to reduce commerce, c)the expansion of global production, and d)the boosting of "*all members on "equal" terms*[16] *to trade and raw materials*[17] (US State Department, 1945) *of the world* which are needed for their economic prosperity"[18] (US State Department, 1945).

The proposal, rather than a treaty of international liberalization of commerce, was formerly presented for consideration by the "peoples of the world" as the "Proposals for the expansion of world trade and employment". Raw materials however, just like money, are assets. Nonetheless, the capacity of peripheral actors to set conditions upon which raw materials were to be commercialized, were extensively diminished by their lack of coordination and the contingencies of their own cultural and political environments. With the stresses exerted upon nations to liberalize trade relations according to the prospects of capital exporting nodes, increasing levels of inequality were to become customary settings of the process of modernity. With the instrumentalization of economic interests upon formal institutional arrangements, development became increasingly a synonym of unequal power relations. Hence, the regulation rather than enhance overall conditions of living, favored populations of high income countries, along a globe with no commerce redistributive measures[19]. As such, the demands to a permanent state of high economic production tied to the principle of plenty employment, rather than including political or legal values, claimed the necessity of capital exporting nodes to spread manufactured goods and to achieve a positive balance of payments, while importing basic basket products plus raw materials from debtor countries.

Since during the preliminary negotiations of the final agreements, the voice of low capital signatories was widely ignored, calls for enhancing the political role of the United States were openly raised in the schedule of the delegations that took part on the preparatory meetings. This practice, hardly refuted in the upcoming decades, was embraced primarily with the support of England[20]. Indeed, the official statements of the American delegation, led by the former Head of the Commercial Relations Division of the State Department and Economic Council of the American Delegation in London, confirmed the degree of asymmetry and the extent of the influence of core economies within the negotiation. As it was declared in a confidential report dated on February of 1945:

"The United States can validate the (…) contemplated exportation of its capital for purposes of reconstruction and development only by attaining an eventual excess of imports over exports. The American Delegation recognizes the urgent need for a general reduction of tariffs throughout the world and the elimination of other barriers to international trade. We feel that the United States should assume a position of aggressive leadership in this movement, and, to the extent that revisions in tariff may be

necessary to reverse our previous American trade balances, such tariff reductions should be made"[21] [1] *(UK War Cabinet 45b, 1945, p. 2).*

With the blatant unequal distribution of power during the preliminary meetings for the constitution of an international architecture for reconstruction and development, the role of commerce to steer political relations between actors replaced requests for shaping a system able to balance the global outstanding asymmetries. While, "for the workability of an international monetary system"[22] (Beyen, 1944, p. 535) (Royal Institute of International Affairs 1944), the goal of reconstruction was narrowed within the geographical boundaries of Europe and Japan, "development" besides those regions was left to the forces of global markets.

From the Second World War to the 70´s Decade

Whereas the role of international organizations in shaping a postwar institutional structure for global development was left to the market, the project of reconstruction endorsed not only economic, but political measures. Indeed, the World Bank, formerly known as the "Bank for reconstruction and development", defined clear categories of policies to be implemented within signatories. These categories were stressed by the former 1944 vice-president of the Federal Reserve Bank of New York. For him, it was necessary to set the discussion between the plan for a reconstruction and the development of an international architecture upon provisions that a)embrace the demands on "relief and reconstruction, war balances, and all other requirements of the transition from war to peace" and b) attend the implementation of mechanisms for "currency stabilization"[23] (Williams, 1944) . In essence, the division between reconstruction and development appeared necessary as to safeguard the historical and political relations that tied the United States with Europe, and to deter the increasing influence of the Soviet Union on international politics. Bearing in mind this goal, the clearest attempt to articulate in a single international organization the process of economic expansion and finance within an international corporation for financial reconstruction, was made by Alvin H. Hansenm -special economic advisor of the Board of Governors of the Federal Reserve System-. In his view, the limitations of monetary arrangement in achieving the "economic goals that the public want", highlighted the necessity to create an International Development and Investment Bank, which ensured expansion of capital raised primarily "in the various private capital markets of the world". In his opinion such initiative:

"...Could act in a powerful manner to offset declines in private capital outlays in the leading industrial countries. At the onset of such a decline, the Bank should enter vigorously with development projects. It is especially in such periods that the Bank could afford to assume larger risks and, indeed, face the prospect of some direct loss, rather than permit large-scale unemployment of the capital goods industries in the leading industrial countries"[24] *(Hansen, 1944)*

Within his analysis, any strategy directed to boost the expansion of the economy of capital exporting countries was to be articulated with the constitution of an *International Commodity Corporation*, "designed to buy, store and sell international raw materials and to act as a *buffer* in the raw materials market".

The double standards of the western world in differentiating policies for Europe and Japan, at the back of raw material exportation nodes, was predominantly carried out through the conditions settled in the "Marshal Plan". As such, with the increasing threat of communism, the single most important policy besides the market to develop the productive capacity, and to better off living conditions of the people of Europe, was tackled by the economic assistance of the United States under the European Recovery Program (Marshall Plan). As a relative share of 2012 US GDP, the total amount of money granted to European reconstruction in this program, amounted $497,.7 billion.

Table 1. Marshall Plan, April 3, 1948-June 30, 1952 as a relative share of US 2011 GDP, millions of dollars

TOTAL OBLIGATIONS FOR MARSHAL PLAN COUNTRIES	Total	Year 1952		2011 Values		Total
		Grants	Loans	Grants	Loans	Year. 2012
	13.325,8	**11.820,7**	**1.505,1**	**497.637,1**	**63.362,9**	**561.000**
Austria	677,8	677,8	-	28.534,6	-	28.535
Belgium-Luxembourg	559,3	491,3	68,0	20.683,1	2.862,7	23.546
Denmark	273,0	239,7	33,3	10.091,1	1.401,9	11.493
France	2.713,6	2.488,0	225,6	104.741,8	9.497,5	114.239
Germany, Federal Republic	1.390,6	1.173,7	216,9	49.411,3	9.131,2	58.543
Greece	706,7	706,7	-	29.751,2	-	29.751
Iceland	29,3	24,0	5,3	1.010,4	223,1	1.233
Ireland	147,5	19,3	128,2	812,5	5.397,1	6.210
Italy	1.508,8	1.413,2	95,6	59.494,0	4.024,6	63.519
Netherlands	1.083,5	916,8	166,7	38.596,2	7.017,9	45.614
Norway	255,3	216,1	39,2	9.097,5	1.650,3	10.748
Portugal	51,2	15,1	36,1	635,7	1.519,8	2.155
Sweden	107,3	86,9	20,4	3.658,4	858,8	4.517
Turkey	225,1	140,1	85,0	5.898,0	3.578,4	9.476
United Kingdom	3.189,8	2.805,0	384,8	118.087,1	16.199,6	134.287

Source. U.S. Economic assistance under the European recovery program. USAID.
https://pdf.usaid.gov/pdf_docs/PDACS197.pdf

In such situation, social systems isolated from the central structure of capital, became increasingly threatened by the scope of influence of actors with spending capacity in need of resources, labor, or other productive assets. Indeed, countries like the United States, hold the advantage of operating in an international financial architecture in which his currency were redeemed globally; and therefore, with a more liquid asset on a global capital environment; the dollar.

In sum, after the Second World War, with the constitution of the Bretton Woods Institutions, the only structural agreement for economic development was made upon the implementation of the "Plan". Hence, the cultural heritage shared of the countries that took part on the war, pointed to a political interaction not only focused on international profitability, but also in schemes of social and institutional organization of nations devastated by the confrontation with a common cultural heritage. The former president of the World Bank, Eugene R. Black; epitomized this feature of the Marshall Plan, as the strategy that allows them to get again "banded together [and] to restore to themselves the economic strength and financial independence which had been lost in war" (Black., 1960, p. 266).

Rather than an isolated event, the plan constituted a fractural division of the idea of modern development. While in capital exporting economies, the concept was related to the construction of political institutions for economic and social advancement, on capital importing countries, it was bounded to profitability and interests of the capital exporting nodes, therefore tied to control their influence and investments on not yet industrialized social systems. This endeavor constituted not only the implementation of global conditions for increasing levels of economic production of core economies, but, essentially, managing the international acceptance of social and political structures prone to take advantage of capital scarce territories. From an institutional perspective, this shift was described as a necessary "transform[ation of] societies[,] and [the] creat[ion of] new traditions, to replace traditions which have been rendered tragically inadequate by the passing of time" (Black., 1960, p. 266); as well as the social configurations to achieve global growth by "hard work (…) by *need*, or by the prospects of material gain" (Black., 1960, p. 267).

The necessity of increasing levels of global production, embraced the implementation of relations of political asymmetry upon which prospects of material gain of capital exporting nodes, and the exploitation of capital scarce nodes, raised overall levels of efficiency of the system. This implied also the elimination of social structures prone to adopt patterns of interaction based on equal conditions of competition, or the implementation of "labor amenities (…) so that [factory] laborers shall have a better life"[25] (Black., 1960, p. 271). The constant erosion of traditional arrangements at the social level, was carried discursively through economic theory, which in turn privileged the elimination of equality, greater regional (global) fairness, or "possibly fewer revolutions". At the Bretton Woods Institutions, it was clearly acknowledged that social uncertainty derived from calls to global justice in terms of profit distribution, were at certain point to realize the inexistence of institutional or political structures to support them. As such, in the beginning of the second half of the 20th century, the former World Bank president recognized that there was "hardly a human society left on earth which has not been thrown off its traditional balance by the expansion of *modern* economic life" (Black., 1960, p. 268).

While at the level of core economies, productivity of investment was partially granted by the commercial relations between the United States and an increasingly strengthened Europe, in a global perspective it was based in the role and geographical allocation of loans of the World Bank and some still infant flows of global direct investment. It was just in 1958, when this trend experienced a slightly variation with the increasing levels of postwar private outflows, which moderately replaced the role of the World Bank as an engine of economic development in economies at the periphery. These new settings however, didn't include the duplication of public redistributive schemes of wealth, such as those experienced after the Second World War with the Marshall plan, but the transposition of the institutional functions of the Bretton Woods Institutions into the private sector. Adopting transfers of capital according to the levels of viability of investments. While since the beginning of the 1960´s rates of economic growth[26] of low and medium income countries remained similar with high income OECD countries, flows and concentration of capital represented in the GDP of each one of the countries of the groups acutely mounted up in high income OECD territories[27]. It was just a few years after the 2000 decade, with the increasing role of former periphery economies such as China and India -boosted by capital flows from western economies-, that the trends from the outburst of the development of world capital markets since 1958, acquired a different direction[28]. Indeed, the transfer of capital from the western territories to China and India, taking advantage of the availability of hundreds of millions of people in necessity to participate in the global cheap labor market, represented for the first time in half a century a reduction in the accumulation of capital between high income territories and the rest of the world.

Figure 1. GDP growth

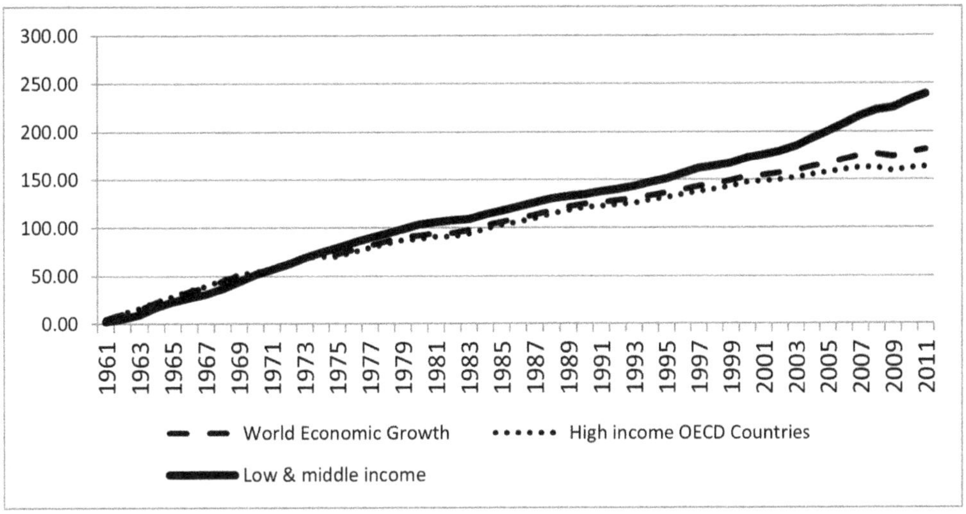

"Annual percentage growth rate of GDP at market prices based on constant local currency. Aggregates are based on constant 2000 U.S. dollars. GDP is the sum of gross value added by all resident producers in the economy plus any product taxes and minus any subsidies not included in the value of the products. It is calculated without making deductions for depreciation of fabricated assets or for depletion and degradation of natural resources". *Source. World Bank national accounts data, and OECD National Accounts data files.*

Figure 2. GDP

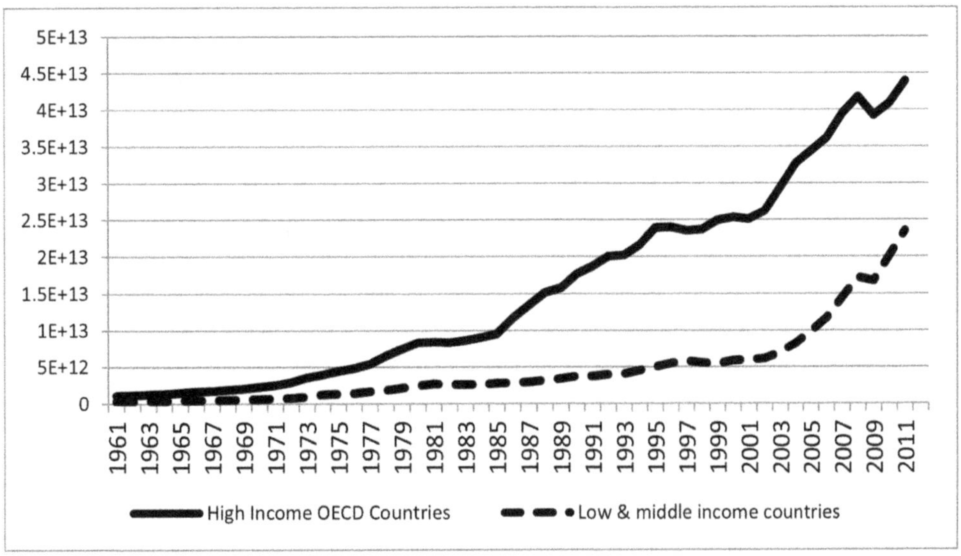

Figure 3. GDP gap between OECD high income; low and middle income economies with and without China and India

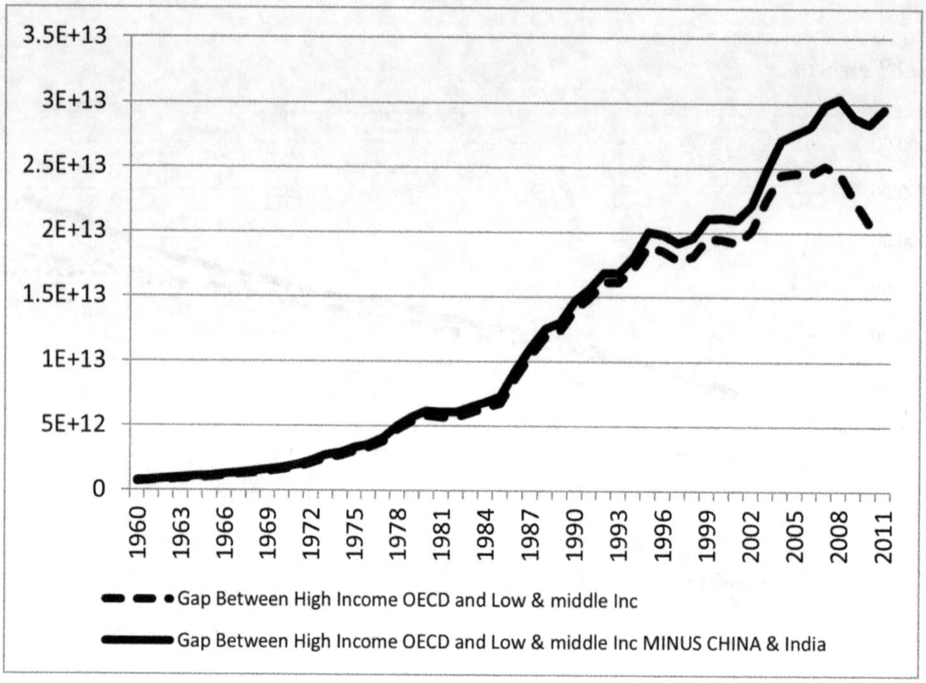

In essence, by adopting a different strategy than that implemented after the Second World War, the Bretton Woods Institutions were capable of establishing a path of industrial expansion where private investment replaced any public non-profit institutional intervention such as the one that boosted the reconstruction of Europe after the war.

In a global market system, allocation of capital in foreign territories, rather than being directed to develop political autonomy of populations, was focused in generating conditions of dependency that ensured short and medium term returns. In this context, the bank focused on increasing levels of economic rivalry of peripheral populations, that lagged from the central structures of capital and production. In a global environment of competitiveness, this assumption failed to grasp the increasing fissures leaved by the asymmetric distribution of profits. Thus, the contradictions between demands for global productivity and real labor wages, decreased relative living standards. This phenomena appeared both in low industrialized as well as in highly industrialized countries. At the same time, it was represented in the increasing disparities of allocation of wealth globally[29] (Rueda C, 2013) (World Bank - EDP, 1969) (World Bank - EDP.Tz, 1970)(EDP.Mal, 1973) (World Bank - EDP.Ph, 1976), and the maintenance and increasing of population living under poverty, both in high income as well as in low income territories (See annex number 1).

Figure 4. GDP: OECD vs. NON OECD USD dollar million 2015

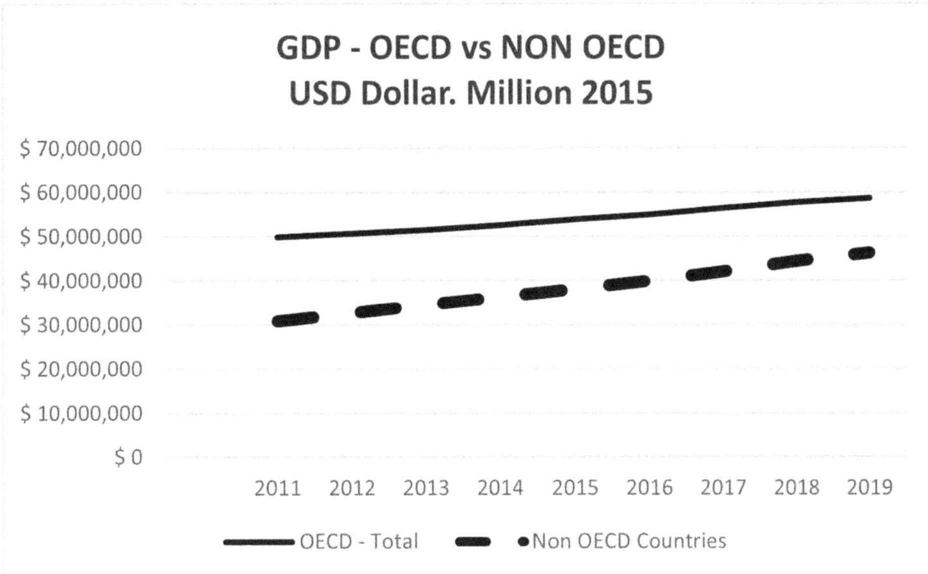

As it will be explained in the following section of the present chapter, these conditions cannot be sustained indefinitely, due to the fact, that capital exporting countries cannot maintain permanent accumulation of reserves without falling into a situation of acute speculation, and therefore economic crisis. This event exemplifies the limitations in productivity of flows of direct investment between high income territories, and thus, their negative effects over the confidence of the global markets. Finally, the relation between capital importing and exporting nodes became fundamental for the reproduction of the idea of development established at the level of the World Bank, as far as it doesn't represent a threat to industrialized-economies[30] (Olmstead, 1964) (Diamond, 1956).

PART TWO

The End of the Gold Convertibility System and the Official Publications on "Development" at the Bretton Woods Institutions

The construction of a process of development embedded in the notion of the modern economy, became for the Bretton Woods Institutions a fundamental assumption of contemporary social systems. Modernity, rather than a political category, was established upon the existence of structures of productive nodes of social organization. For the World Bank, the idea of modernity doesn't embrace the conjecture of the nation state as a total political category, but rather as a divided structure. This is why poverty or exclusion is not seen as a structural problem of social systems, but rather as an externality that coexist with modernity. Three major operational definitions of this approach can be extracted from the World Trade Development report. On the one hand, the normalization of A) the concomitance -in countries that transit towards economic development- of social systems that are fragmented in islands of "high income "modernity" in *coexist[ence]* with shanty towns and slums" (World Bank, 1978, p. 5). B) The discursive representation of the sophistication of societies as a singularity that doesn't belong to the political but rather to the economic analysis. C) And the institutional isolation of structural inconsistencies of the economic architecture, dealing with segregation phenomena that derive from the progression of the contemporary global chain of production.

While it is clear that processes of liberalization are endorsed to the competitive capacities of nations to participate in a global scheme of production, this process lacks any structure of redistribution of wealth for economic development, such as the one that take place at the national level –modern welfare state-. In this case, modernity doesn't refer to the capacity of the economic system to enhance global competitiveness, but rather to ease relations of dominant position of capital exporting nodes which frequently adhere to monopolistic or protectionist practices. While on the one hand, customary economic theory demonstrates the lack of competitiveness that arise from monopolistic or dominant position practices, at the level of the Bretton Woods Institutions, this practices are not addressed as a fundamental problem. Therefore, development at the level of international politics, under highly clear conditions of political and economic asymmetry, differentiate between economic theory and politics. As such, the institutions describe continually the effects of such practices, but employ, empower, keep and reproduce at the top of their institutions, the representatives of countries that incur in such activities.

To address the concept of development, the institutional practice often avoids to create indicators, or to track harmful behavior of influential actors analyzed within the grey literature of the IMF or the World Bank. Therefore, compliance with norms on trade liberalization, is not represented along the diagnosis on the behavior of the influential signatories -though it has profound consequences in the process of global production-. During the recent decades, and especially since the official publications of the "World Bank Development Report" (WBDR), the effects of this situation have been slightly included into the descriptive situation of the global economy. Indeed, the development of such systemic anomalies, is described as a functional pattern of a "modern economy", which enhanced the transformation of populations into highly uneven environments at a higher level. In early reports, very indicative cases of this situation were recurrently described by the Bank in Africa and parts of South Asia, where integration of social systems with the global economy intensified rather than decrease social exclusion. This phenomena, in turn, generated displacement of labor and poverty for a long period of the 20th century. According to the World bank, in such social systems, the poorest members of the population are "unlikely to share economic growth" (…) therefore, by 1978, "the incomes and consumption levels of the poorer half of the population (…)stagnated, [and], in countries where agriculture has expanded more slowly than population (…) the incomes of some of the rural population (…) declined" (World Bank, 1978, p. 7).

While these social and economic impacts in peripheral economies are extensively documented in the institutional record of the Bank, at the level of highly industrialized countries, increasing levels of inequality and exclusion are customarily taken apart from the political analysis of the reports[31]. This is because according to the institutional guidelines, the analysis of "development" of highly industrialized economies, is conducting by taking their own context as agents. In addition, the methodology of the Bank doesn´t include such features in terms of exclusion or asymmetry that take place in industrial economies, since "modern development", in such cases, embrace those phenomena as externalities of a modern economy. Indeed, since the first report of the Bank, this trend is forecasted as the "historical experience" (World Bank, 1978, p. 7). This means that in the current political structure, the report moves to offer a slight depiction of political consequences of processes of economic development, on behalf of the relevance of the "expansion and diversification of the economy productive capacity" (World Bank, 1978, p. 2).

The increasing inequality of social systems that arise within the process of "development", is seen at the institutional level as a necessary stage of the path to modernization of the contemporary structures of human settlements. The perspective adopted by the Bank, embraces the permanent replacement of activities that belong to the "traditional line", which in turn carries the impoverishment of large sectors of populations, and the concentration of opportunities in modern sectors of "industry, commerce and agriculture" (World Bank, 1980, p. 41), often located in urban areas and characterized by high levels of concentration of capital-.

The disjointment between the economic sphere of social systems and the political sphere, is given by the fact that even from the early 80´s, the institutional report acknowledged that at the level of the nation state, the relation between economic growth and inequality doesn´t necessarily adopt the trend defined by the Kuznets curve[32]. Hence, exclusion from the political and economic activities of social systems arises from increasing trends on inequalities that could have been tackled by public sectors. As it has been also depicted by the World Bank:

(inequalities) "...depends on government policy, which can reduce the unevenness of the modernization process and accelerate growth by promoting productivity gains in traditional small-scale agriculture, increasing the rate at which labor is absorbed into the modern industrial sector, and not concentrating public investment and services on a few places and social groups" (World Bank, 1980, p. 41).

In practice, however, such policies are not taking into account in the everyday practice of the institution, which has turned a blind eye upon the increasing levels of inequality globally and locally (both in highly industrial as well as in low industrial countries) (Rueda C, 2013). It was just in 2006, that the issue of inequality was addressed as a thematic category. Indeed, the publication of that year -called "Equity and Development"-, tended to raise awareness of the relation between those two concepts. Following the historical record of the Bank, the report admitted the existence of "persuasive evidence that a broad sharing of economic and political opportunities is also instrumental for economic growth and development", which again meant turning away from the political consequences of such social arrangements. Later on however, the former president of the bank stressed that:

"Excessive inequalities in power and influence can lead to political, social and economic institutions that are less conducive to long-term growth"[33] (World Bank, 2006, p. XI).

Such final depiction stressed that the political consequences of inequalities in terms of exclusion, operation of democratic structures, or overall practices on governance of nation states were necessary to be secluded from the productive capacity of societies. In this manner, both, global and local inequalities derived from the conditions imposed by a free market environment were tamed, appealing through institutional literature to the normative imperative of growth. Over the most recent decade however, capital reallocation has dramatically change the direction to set ground on territories formerly isolated from the global financial center. This explains why, selected non OECD countries are increasingly having a role in the global production of good and services.

CONCLUSION

The present chapter depicts concrete historical events that defined the institutional landscape through which the normative construction of a norm on "modern development" at the Bretton Woods Institutions fostered. Drawing on historical institutionalism, and following the theoretical consideration to study *concrete historical processes* (chapter three), and the influence of economic subtle structure to explain cornerstones through which these institutions evolved, and determined norms, reproducing their own internal discourse on the idea of *development*. Furthermore, the chapter stresses the historical influence of economic relations over political decisions taken both in industrialized and non-industrial territories, the relevance of the structure within decision making processes at the executive board of the IMF and the World Bank, and the strong historical absence of normative constructions derived as a practice of symmetric interaction. In concrete, normative production of a norm on "modern development", took place within defined biographical periods of these institutions, as such, the chapter highlights and depicts through grey literature how this process took place globally.

This events, replicated over decades through the production of the normative meaning on the idea of *development*. Furthermore, they were to be made possible by applying direct pressure to weak members of the institutions, as well as through processes of reconstruction of countries through global free trade market agreements, further carried out with full control by highly influential players of both the IMF and the World Bank.

REFERENCES

Beyen, J. W. (1948). The International Bank for Reconstruction and Development. *International Affairs*, 24.

Black, E. R. (1960, June). The age of economic development. *Economic Journal (London)*, *70*(278), 266–276. doi:10.2307/2228727

Diamond, W. (1956). Economic Problems of Foreign Trade and Investment in Underdeveloped Countries. *Ohio State Law Journal*, *17*, 254.

Dickens. (1949, June). Private Foreign Investments: A Means of World Economic Development. [Jun.]. *Political Science Quarterly*, *64*(2), 211–244.

Escobar, A. (1995). *Encountering Development. The making and unmaking of the third world*. Princeton University Press.

Habermas, J. (2000). *The Postnational Constellation* (M. Pensky, Trans.). MIT Press.

Hansen, A. H. (1944). World Institutions for Stability and Expansion. *Foreign Affairs*, *22*, 248–255. .. doi:10.2307/20029821

Olmstead, C. J. (1964). *Foreign aid as an effective means of persuasion*. American Society of International Law.

Rasminsky, L. (1944, July). International Credit and Currency Plans. *Foreign Affairs*, *1*. https://www.foreignaffairs.com/articles/70355/louis-rasminsky/international-credit-and-currency-plans

Rueda, C. R. (2013). Global Crisis and History Repeating: Three Historical Stages of the Norm of "Modern Development" within the Regulatory Framework of the Bretton Woods Institutions. SSRN Scholarly Paper.

UK War Cabinet 338, I., 1944. Memorandum by the Chancellor of the Exchequer. The Proposed United Nations Bank for Reconstruction and Development. Secret. W.P. (44) 338. 20th June, 1944. S, 27679.

UK War Cabinet 45, I., 1945. War Cabinet Document. Confidential Annex. W.M. (45) 9th conclusions. Minute 4. International Monetary Fund. 25th January, 1945 – 5,30 p.m. S,1 (35). Copy No. 10..

UK War Cabinet 45b, I., 1945. W.P. (45) 96. Commercial Policy; Article VII. Memorandum by the Chancelor of the Exchequer. 24th February, 1945. S, 2.

UK War Cabinet 83, I., 1944. War Cabinet 83 (44). Conclusions of a Meeting of the War Cabinet held in the Cabinet War Room on Wednesday, 28th June, 1944, at 6 pm.

US State Department. (1945). *Proposals for Expansion of World Trade and Employment.* Federal Reserve Bank.

Williams, J. H. (1944). Currency Stabilization: American and British Attitudes. *Foreign Affairs, 22*, 2. .. doi:10.2307/20029820

World Bank. (1978). *World Development Report.* World Bank.

World Bank. (1980). *World Development Report.* World Bank.

World Bank. (2006). *World Development Report.* World Bank.

World Bank - EDP (1969). Ke*nya - Economic development prospects (Vol. 1 of 2): Main report (English).* World Baannk.

World Bank - EDP. (1970). *Tanzania - Economic development and prospects (Vol. 1 of 2): Main report (English).* World Bank.

World Bank - EDP. (1976). *Philippines - Priorities and prospects for development: basic economic report (Vol. 3 of 3): Investments & resource management (English).* World Bank.

ENDNOTES

1 "$21,219 [b]million of which about $3,592 million, or roughly 17 per cent, was supplied from private sources". In (Dickens et al, 1949)

2 Relative shares of 2011 GDP. „In addition, the United States government has contributed $3,385 million to the paid-in capital of the International Monetary Fund and the International Bank for Reconstruction and Development and has subscribed a further $2,540 million to the capital of the latter institution, which is su(bject to call under certain conditions".

3 The world's largest agricultural export economy after the Second World War.

4 "It is well known that one of the quintessential aspects of modernity is the separation of social life into functional spheres (the economy, the polity, society, cul ture, and the like), each with laws of

its own. This is, strictly speaking, a modern development. As a separate domain, the economy had to be given expression by a proper science; this science, which emerged at the end of the eighteenth century, was called political economy. In its classical formulation by Smith, Ricardo, and Marx, political economy was structured around the notions of production and labor". See (Escobar, 1995, p. 60).

5 Yet money steered

6 Director of the Division of Monetary Research of the Treasury Department of the United States

7 Former adviser of the British Treasury.

8 Who tended to present an alternative proposal than those determined by Great Britain and the United States, describing the mood of the environment during the Bretton Conference.

9 It is of main importance to consider that both on the United States and Great Britain, since the period of the foundation of the Bretton Woods Institutions, levels of unemployment and structural have increased over time See Annex 01. On the other hand, historical increasing of global and local production has overall augmented real income of the population. This phenomena however in the two main countries taking part in the negotiations, have been accompanied by increasing levels of economic inequality, and indeed, in and increasing in the number of people living in poverty, both in the United States and in Great Britain. On a global level, the trends maintain the same tendency. Since 1948, levels of inequality in the world have increased steadily, while number of people living on poverty has increased. See Annex 02.

10 "If we are really going to achieve an expanding economy and provide full employment and higher income standards, I am convinced of the necessity of searching out development projects which, from the standpoint of a private business, would not yield satisfactory returns and hence could not be undertaken by private investment, but which nonetheless are profitable and sound from the standpoint of the economy as a whole. For such projects only public funds can be found". (Hansen, 1944).

11 These observations were clearly mentioned by the former vice-resident of the Federal Reserve of the Bank of New York. See. (Williams, 1944).

12 Which with the fall of the convertibility systems of the Bretton Woods Institutions in 1974, was able to run large accounts deficits because emerging market were eager to continue accumulating dollars.

13 Released 30 years after the events of the Second World War,

14 United Nations Relief and Rehabilitation Administration, operating between 1943 and 1947.

15 Especially India.

16 Emphasis added.

17 Chapter IV of the proposal is clear concerning the compulsory prohibition of any measures to trade with raw material under open market conditions. It clearly states that the organization look "to promote expansion of production and trade, equal access to markets and raw materials, and the maintenance in all countries of high levels of employment and real income". Needless to say that in recent decades, increasing levels of inequality in developed societies have been followed by a steady decreasing in wage of employees in relation with productivity, thus a decrease in living standards of populations in comparison with economic growth. In ependency of capital exporting nodes of peripherycal raw materials, refer also to Annex A. Draft statement for use in parliament on the United States commercial policy proposals. S,3. In (US State Department, 1945) "Proposals

for Expansion of World Trade and Employment. November 1945. Federal Reserve Bank. Publication 2411".

18 In Chapter I. Purposes. (US State Department, 1945) On Proposals for Expansion of World Trade and Employment. November 1945. Federal Reserve Bank. Publication 2411.

19 Or to broad the spectrum of democratic or sustainable practices on modern social systems.

20 Presumably considering a medium term global arena in which the influence of the Soviet Union gained ascendancy.

21 (UK War Cabinet 45b, 1945, p. 2) War Cabinet.W.P. (45) 96. Commercial Policy; Article VII. Memorandum by the Chancelor of the Exchequer. 24th February, 1945. S. 2.

22 (Beyen, 1944, p. 535) J. W. Beyen. The International Bank for Reconstruction and Development. International Affairs (Royal Institute of International Affairs 1944), Vol. 24, No. 4. S,535.

23 (Williams, 1944) John H. Williams. Currency Stabilization: American and British Attitudes.

24 (Hansen, 1944) World Institutions for Stability and Expansion. By Alvin H. Hansen. January 1944.

25 Zinkin Maurice. Development for Free Asia. In (Black., 1960, p. 271)

26 See Graph 1.

27 See Graph 2.

28 See Graph 3.

29 On inequality at high income countries see (Rueda C, 2013). At the level of low income territories, inequality as a phenomena bounded to the process of economic growth, has been extensively documented in the official "development prospects of the World Bank". See (World Bank - EDP, 1969) Kenya - Economic development prospects (Vol. 1 of 2): Main report (English). OCT 22, 1969 AE6; (World Bank - EDP.Tz, 1970)Tanzania - Economic development and prospects (Vol. 1 of 2): Main report (English) MAR 17, 1970. AE7; (EDP.Mal, 1973) Malaysia - Development problems and prospects (Vol. 1 of 2): The main report (English) AUG 14, 1973. 217; (World Bank - EDP. Ph, 1976)Philippines - Priorities and prospects for development: basic economic report (Vol. 3 of 3): Investments & resource management (English) MAY 05, 1976, 1095; among others.

30 "Nationals and their capital when they are engaged in the building of a truly interdependent international economy". On (Olmstead, 1964). See also (Diamond, 1956).

31 See. Rueda. Social Crisis and global repricing of financial instruments.

32 The theory suggests that as an economy develops, market forces first increase and then decrease economic inequality.

33 In Foreword by Paul D. Wolfowittz (World Bank, 2006, p. XI).

Chapter 7
Social Crisis Within the Historical Progression of the Norm of Modern Development at the Bretton Woods Institutions

ABSTRACT

In the ongoing political debates over how Greece should overcome the consequences of the burden of its debt, a major phenomenon of the current global financial and economic structure is commonly avoided; namely, a process of global structural adjustment of social systems, dramatically known by peripheral economies in the past decades. In an attempt to explain the process, the following chapter draws on contributions from the international economy, historical, and institutional sociology. It traces how with the increasing influence of deregulation of financial capital, former isolated countries are now capable of tightening up the strings of the global economic system over the social system. The distrust of global debt rating agencies over the credit of the United States, Spain, Greece or Italy, represents an upcoming reality of core western territories on an historical process of "modern development".

INTRODUCTION

From the outburst of the financial bubble of the US housing market, to the difficulties some European countries are facing repaying or refinancing their debt, the concept of economic and systemic crisis has filled tabloids and research agendas at unusual levels. The attention paid to the "unpredictability" of the events has consistently ignored their similarity with previous cases of speculation of financial instruments or failed fiscal policy choices that occurred repeatedly during the recent decades. The economic measures that seek to deter the course of the devaluation of debt instruments in some of the most developed economies in the world, frequently appear problematic and socially conflicting. Yet, at the moment of

DOI: 10.4018/978-1-6684-9794-4.ch007

the elaboration of this chapter, the aftermath of the events has not ceased, and the debt levels of countries like Spain, Italy or Greece have increased to historical peaks[1] (País, 2013) (The Economist., 2013). Meanwhile, the economic projections of the US Federal Reserve forecast high levels of unemployment up to the year 2015[2], and a difficult recovery from the depression that began in 2007 (Krugman, 2012b).

While a glimpse at the diverse diagnoses reveals multiple causes for the deviation from the normal stability, of some of the countries currently implementing shock measures, a more structural element has been consistently set aside from the political debate. This is; in a global economic system based on competitiveness, political asymmetries, exponential debt growth, and legal and normative structures of financial capital and trade liberalization, the ability of national political entities to halt the pressure of economic actors over national policies is smoothly eroded until symptoms of systemic disability arise. The events experienced since 2008, entail a de facto reconfiguration of the geographical boundaries of an economic system that, in previous decades, had tightened both the discretionary margins and the living conditions of numerous peripheral economies and societies. With the inclusion of new players in the global economy, the system is gradually beginning to exert pressure on social and political orders that had experienced relative advantage over most of the previous century.

While such events are customarily described as signs of a weakening or breakdown of the current economic system, this chapter argues that they are quite the opposite. Re-pricing of financial instruments owned by core economies, such as mortgage securities, public and private debt or subprime bonds; are indeed clear signs of the contemporary robustness of the economic system over the boundaries of the political sovereignty of the nation state. They represent a wider transition to "modern development": a normative construction inherited from the end of the Second World War with the constitution of the Bretton Woods organizations.

In an attempt to explain this process, this chapter draws on contributions from international political economy, historical institutionalism and institutional sociology. It adopts a twofold structure. First, it describes in historical terms how the Bretton Woods Institutions embraced the task of shaping a norm of "modern development", carried out via political or economic measures, to affect systems isolated from the central structures of technology and capital. This process is founded in three articulated phenomena: a) the erosion of sovereignty, b)global financial deregulation and the shift of national entities from social to productive structures, and a c)weakening of wage and labour conditions. Secondly, it describes how, from the 1960s (currencies pegged to the dollar), these political settings began a geographical reallocation from peripheral to core economies. This transition can be traced over three major historical peaks: first, the international debt crisis and the lost decade experienced by low income countries between 1970s and 1980s; second, the structural reforms undertaken by the United States and United Kingdom during the late 1980s; and, finally, the 2008 U.S. subprime mortgage crisis and its international repercussions. This last events included the necessity of influential countries to initiate processes of adjustment of their productive capability, while enduring a cycle of global re-pricing of financial instruments. Finally, it addresses the future of this normative construction in scenarios in which emerging influential economic "nodes", gain momentum against increasingly eroded structures of governance within the nation state.

1) The construction of modern development and the Bretton Woods Institutions.

Against the backdrop of the final stages of the Second World War, the 1944 Bretton Woods conference set the ground for the constitution of an international system of institutionalized commerce for global "development". The foundational agreements, highly influenced by the interests of the representatives of the United States and Great Britain, determined the normative relations through which a newly institutional core and periphery (Eichengreen, 2004) (Eichengreen, 2008) (Spanu, 2003) should relate in the decades to come. From that historical event, the institutionalization of asymmetric relations in terms of representation (Lombardi, 2006), influence (Swedberg, 1986) (Mikesell, 1994), voting power (Dennis Leech, 2004), distribution of loans (Dreher et. al., 2010) (Thacker, 1999) (Rowlands & Bird, 2006), trade (Cha & Lee, 2010) (Barro, 2005) (Cha & Lee, 2010 A) (Barro, 2005) (Cha & Lee, 2010 B) and global wealth (Harjes, 2007) (Milanovic, 2007), have shaped the political interaction of the representatives of these institutions for almost seven decades.

The notion of development related to the role of economic growth as the cornerstone for satisfying the material needs of societies, led to the acceptance of the increasing influence of economics over politics. The urgency of the post-war recovery for the affected countries, enhanced the implementation of policies that would otherwise have been deemed unacceptable by peripheral nations or marginal populations in Europe and the United States. After the war, among the provisions established during the conference at Bretton Woods[3], the notion of modern development unbounded from the domestic capabilities of societies and bounded rather to their role in a global economic system; appeared as a construction unfamiliar even to the citizens of the western world. As such, what appeared to be a perfect scenario for the former most-industrialized economies to improve their social and economic structures (while boosting other countries to follow the same path), has in recent decades become a conflicting construction in which both "developed" and "not developed" countries face permanent risks of systemic failure.

In the global structure of capital, this process was embedded in the promise of modernity[4] (Escobar, 1995, p. 60), a discursive construction of social "development" rooted in an economic rationality. Such conception measured the development of social systems by quantifying the productive and economic capabilities of their domestic productive apparatus. This shift was carried along through the progression of three operational events; 1) the increasing erosion of nation-state sovereignty and the reinforcement of conditions of trade and capital deregulation measures upon asymmetric relations, 2) the shift from social structures to economic productive structures, and 3) the degradation of human and labour conditions as a means to attract investment from capital exporting nodes.

a) The development of deregulation and the asymmetric relationship of capital over nation-state sovereignty.

The process of modern development implies an increasing flexibility about the role of the state over the demands of the economy. The Bretton Woods system acknowledged that peripheral economies are dependent on capital flows to strengthen their own systems of economic organization within the global structure of production. Furthermore, in a competitive environment, dependency implies the systemic erosion of the nation-state's capacity to set domestic political agendas when these differ from global market imperatives, which simultaneously increases the power of capital exporting countries.[5] (World Bank, 1978).

Two regulatory official agreements reveal the relevance of capital flow profitability as an institutional provision for defining the extent and pace of "developmental" processes in peripheral economies. The foundational purposes of the Articles of Agreement of the World Bank, effective since 1945, and the Articles of Agreement of the International Monetary Fund. In the case of the first one, it establishes that processes of "development of territories of members", are to be carried out via "investment of capital for productive purposes" [6] (World Bank - AA, 1945) . Thus, promotion of capital exporting is linked to the insurability of private money to be invested abroad, as far as it is backed by credible forecasts predicting high profitability. The second paragraph of the same article stresses such measures upon loans:

"To promote private foreign investment by means of guarantees or participations in loans and other investments made by private investors; and when private capital is not available on reasonable terms, to supplement private investment by providing, on suitable conditions, finance for productive purposes out of its own capital, funds raised by it and its other resources".

From an economic approach, this assertion is supported by the relevance of economic growth and competitiveness, rather than by political redistributive measures in an environment of global asymmetry. On the other hand, it isolates alternative theoretical approaches to the conditions that should guide trade relations, as well as any attempt to implement further redistributive measures to steer the effects of highly unequal economic relations within independent jurisdictions. Consequently, capital exporting nodes benefitted extensively from the settings of the system.

While mechanisms of redistributive justice seek to ensure the regulation of profits and loss through fiscal measures and public investment in the nation-state setting, this process cannot be institutionally warranted at the global level. On a global level, development was thus determined by the structures and flows of different forms capital within the market. In this manner, countries are frequently forced to adopt defined policies if they want to be eligible to receive such capital inflows in accordance with market conditions[7], cutting into the sovereignty of the nation-state.

In the case of the Articles of Agreement of the International Monetary Fund, its content stresses how asymmetric relations of capabilities, capital and power (Barro, 2005) (Dennis Leech, 2004) (Eichengreen, 2004) (Lombardi, 2006). on a global level, are to be balanced without interventionist measures taken by supranational organizations:

"...facilitat[ing] the expansion and balanced growth of international trade, and to contribute thereby to the promotion and maintenance of high levels of employment and real income and to the development of the productive resources of all members as primary objectives of economic policy..."

Contrary to expectations, since the first half of the 20th century inequality between nations has increased as never before; relations of trade between highly industrial and less developed countries deprived and affected domestic industries, while flows of capital have increasingly accumulated in highly industrialized economies (Easterly, 2000) (Dowrick, 2005) (Cha & Lee, 2010) (Milanovic, 2007).

The reconfiguration of national institutions by market relations represents an idea of development that functions via the elimination of the principle of sovereignty. This reveals a transition from countries recognizing each other as actors with a similar political autonomy, to one in which they view each other as components of a global market within which mutual predation becomes increasingly necessary, lest national economies face setbacks in increasing their competitive capacities. The necessities of competition and the increasing pre-eminence of financial capital over sovereign will, implies a mutual use market-based, political or economic advantages to increase profit margins, ensuring the adjustment of social structures by global institutions.

Together with the erosion of the capacity of the state to implement policies independent of global market concerns, the modernization of social systems implies a reconfiguration of the definition and role of the citizen as an actor with political rights. Hence, noticeable rights, must be addressed within the background restrictions inherent to global economic relations. The progression through developmental stages for societies is predicated upon increasing levels of sophistication of the "productive resources of all members as primary objectives of economic policy" (World Bank - AA, 1945, p. Art.1). This transition takes place under conditions of free market competition which, rather than being a rhetorical construction of the IMF, represents the pivotal goal of the international institutionalized economic system, as well as the main characteristic of the concept of "modern development" as an economic category.

The necessity of each country to ensure competiveness while increasing capital reserves, dislocated the social redistributive role of national governance structures that predominated after the end of the Second World War. This shift was characterized by transitions covering three institutional ranges of sovereignty erosion: First, the increasing necessity of nation-states to attract private capital, while either preventing capital flight in high income centres, or brain drain in low income territories. This stage is based upon institutional advice stressing that such measures, "have a host of other attributes that make them both more attractive for investors and better able to absorb the shocks and instability associated with short-term capital flows" (Stiglitzt, 2004, p. 60). Second, the necessity of the state to set life projects within the boundaries given by the levels of efficiency of their productive structures (Frericks et. al., 2010) (Frericks et. al., 2010.). Third, the adoption of policies designed in international institutions which ensure the reproduction and expansion of the global economy, rather than the domestic social interests of the inhabitants of both high and low income territories.

In conditions of constant rivalry for the attainment and retaining of capital and productive forces, modern development becomes an unattainable political category, always endangered by slips in competitiveness. On the other hand, the enduring role of the Bretton Woods Institutions to reproduce this same formal construction, operates as a discursive device destabilizing the faculty of nation states to collectively agree new regulations to safeguard domestic economic structures from the stresses exerted by the global economy. Formal institutional publications of the World Bank, such as the World Development Report (made public for the first time in 1978), or the IMF annual report (issued since 2007), ensure the legitimation and preservation of highly asymmetric global relations between regions in the name of growing the economy. The institutional literature avoids theoretical or technical content regarding the unequal distribution of profits, and the institutional inability of marginal countries to change the conditions established by key shareholders of the World Bank (Dreher et. al., 2010) (Swedberg, 1986), the International Monetary Fund (Woods & Lombardi, 2006) (Cooper & Truman, 2007) (Barro, 2005), and major economies at the WTO (Khan, 2008) (Subramanian et. al, 2007).

Within the IMF, for instance, this situation has greatly limited the voting power and influence of less competitive economies. In this regard, research oriented to the study of voting power outcomes between capital importing and capital exporting territories points out that:

> *[At] the IMF's Board of Governors (…) directors are appointed by the largest eight shareholders*[8]*. (…) The major shareholders have strong influences on the IMF's decisions. (…) [H]ence, the United States alone and a group of three major Western European countries have veto power (…) sometimes openly wielded this power to influence decisions (Barro, 2005, p. 4).*

Given such circumstances, sovereignty as a political construction seeking to ensure autonomy, self-sufficiency and independence of a nation state from the influences of the environment; dilutes into institutional constraints that prevent members from isolating domestic politics from the international economic system. This is how the Bretton Woods Institutions, foster the pre-eminence of economic relations between nations, instead of recognizing the limitations and asymmetries upon which national entities weather the construction of their own productive apparatuses. Consequently, countries' roles are globally reconfigured as multidimensional spaces characterized by technological or knowledge clusters, financial centres, sweatshop labour zones (*maquilas*), geostrategic resource extraction areas, or low-employment reserve labour territories.

a) Liberalization and the shift from social structures to economic productive structures.

Increasing stages of financial integration drive economic actors to set conditions and promote the role of trade relations as a mandatory necessity for global economic growth. With the elimination of the role of the state, as a retaining wall against market pressures, processes of trade liberalization are adhered to as inherent to a discursive category of development. This process is achieved via the gradual elimination of obstructions to commerce for each one of the contractual areas of the WTO. This can be observed in international agreements for dismantling customs and trade barriers, in accordance with the bargaining capacities of states in bilateral or multilateral negotiations. Meanwhile, the normative construction of such approach, is supported by deepening commercial interdependence, a process that is gradually fulfilled by the selective implementation of postulates of economic liberalism by capital exporting signatories[9] (Chang, 2002).

While global wealth rises with the sophistication of production, and the inclusion of new labour capital in the process, uneven allocation of capital between core and periphery nodes increases. In fact, the elimination of subsidies frequently expected of industries in peripheral economies, such as agriculture or manufacturing, are systemically avoided by wealthy economies, protecting them from competition from low-income regions. The 2009 report of the Organization for Economic Co-operation and Development (OECD) was in fact one of the first official publications issued by the Bank that stressed this trend. As it accounts, "While in recent decades distribution of capital around the globe has permitted more countries to participate in agriculture, (…) a small number of countries continue [to] capture most of it" (Frericks et.al., 2009, p. 41).

In recent decades, the global distribution of wealth present higher levels of correlation with the allocation of wealth within regions. A 2010 estimate of wealth distribution among 190 countries engaged in trade demonstrates how, in the period of 1950 to 2000, flows of wealth benefited extensively rich countries, harming the wealth accumulation capacity of poorer countries. Although this distribution can also be related to economic performance, instead, the relevance of interaction between territories reveals how in given conditions of political asymmetry; patterns of wealth inequality between regions deepen rather than diminish. In conclusion,

"[b]oth wealth and trade volumes were unevenly distributed, and the richer countries were found to be more likely to have positive trade surplus. (…)A richer country tend[ed] to attract more money from a poorer country.(…) the wealth distribution [takes] a power-law form under an asymmetric money exchange and that the wealth condensed on a few agents, which was consistent with the global wealth distribution" (Cha & Lee, 2010 B).

International economic inequality in a system *normatively* seeking to ensure economic growth, suggests an ethical transformation of the global realm from being a political construction to an economic one. In this normative assumption, the pivotal behaviour vector between countries, is given by the necessity of each region to increase a dominant position within unfair regulatory settings. Such strategy facilitates increasing returns on foreign investment of actors interested in participating in the commercial system, isolating the political consequences of decisions taken abroad. The liberalization of international trade thus represents not only the constitutionalization (Peters, 2011) of increasingly unequal regulation, promoted by institutions such as the WTO or the IMF, but also, and primarily, the tacit acceptance of the erosion of the political sphere on a global scale.

Indeed, while during recent decades GDP distribution present slight variations, "global wealth condensation is ongoing". In fact, during the second half of the 20th century, the wealth of the top 20% richest countries increased from 0.8 to 0.9, whereas the wealth of the bottom 20% (poorest countries) decreased from 0,005 to 0,001. While "numerous factors affect (...) wealth and (...) living standards of a country, [the] results suggest that the underlying dynamics governing a nation's wealth does not reach a stationary state and is characterized by richer countries getting richer" (Cha & Lee, 2010 B, p. 3) (Cha & Lee, 2010 A) .

With the aforementioned events, the capacity of the peripheral production nodes such as small economic nation-states, to address sovereign decisions within a global economic system, fade in the face of unequal power relations. Given such tensions, even recent critical analyses (Rodrik, 2001) fall short in explaining the phenomena as economic, since the events are also of a social and political nature. On the other hand, the inability of the nation state to assure conditions of organization beyond market pressures, leads to an economic sophistication of life spheres in both core, as well as in peripheral economies. This shift in the goals of nation-states is followed by cultural, political and economic changes that look to orient social structures toward economic productivity; a transition with critical consequences for populations unprotected by social safety nets or adaptation measures within the new scheme. Given these new conditions, countries vulnerable to the regulation of the Bretton Woods Institutions, tend to unfavourably experience the effects of market liberalization and capital flows that increase global volatility[10] (Stiglitz, 2004). Domestic measures to increase productivity thus requires social shocks, all for the sake of maintaining market dominance.

The project of sustaining structures of production to keep pace with national and international economic demands, is frequently associated with decreasing ranges of autonomy individuals have in defining social life projects besides the market. This phenomenon is related to changes in three fundamental aspects of the lives of the citizenry: an increase in the age of retirement of populations[11] (Jackson, 2002) (International Monetary Fund, 2012), increasing time and intensity dedicated to formal education, and an increasing gap between yearly real wage growth and labour productivity (Stiglitz, 2006, p. Ch.8) (Frericks et. al, 2010). This last feature means that there is a relative decrease in the living standards of the majority of the inhabitants in comparison to economic growth[12]. To address these phenomena, governments must create policies aimed at balancing accumulative amounts of time spent in education with the necessities of production and economic growth. This goal is also accomplished through public investment focused on strategic areas that ensure stability within international competition[13] (Frericks et. al., 2010).

Finally, the role of the government is transposed from being an intervening actor, to be a *subject* of intervention. In highly industrial countries[14] (Campbell, 1998), this phenomenon is followed by increasing levels of ideological polarization on how best to maintain effectively high levels of productivity without endangering constitutionally ensured rights[15].

b) The transformation of labour conditions, wages, and inequality as lures for financial investment.

In accordance with the conditions established by an institutionalized system of commerce, national efforts to attract capital lead to set policies that increase countries likelihood of becoming nodes of financial investment. These provisions are frequently inspired by the structural reform policies advocated by the International Monetary Fund, which for the most part of the second half of the 20th century, found their way in peripheral economies eager to attract investment within the fund settings.

In the shift from social life projects to economic systemic projects, populations experience a market depreciation of years spent in formal academic formation. With the oversupply of highly skilled workers, investment on medium levels of high education develops a decreasing return rate (Frericks et. al, 2010). This adjustment is intensified by policies directed to set wages that are able to meet labour market demands. .Therefore, schemes of remuneration based on salary, increasingly replace long-term contracts and their relatively more stable structures of pay and other benefits[16] (OECD, 2013). Such measures, ensure a necessary reduction of moral hazard for capital, that seeks to safeguard profitability in foreign territories. This strategic policy avoids further economic crises that arise from lags in productivity due to high wages (Read, 2009), enhancing the risk of rising structural unemployment (OECD, 2013, p. 29).

While structural adjustment policies recommended by the IMF seek to maintain profitability of investment deployed in capital-importing countries, the World Bank warns against wage increases, making less industrialised countries more cost efficient in their productive processes[17] (Groom, 2013). In this transition, *development,* as a normative construction of the Bretton Woods Institutions, is linked to the necessity of improving condition for investment rather than to tackle consistent nodes of "underdevelopment" and poverty in high and low income territories.

Whereas levels of global inequality have increased unprecedentedly in recent decades, they have not affected the discursive interventions of the World Bank's Development Report. In 1978, when the Bank first authorized the publication of the report, the rationalization of wage flexibility and the unequal distribution of corporate profits (Palley, 2007, pp., 2007), was discursively internalized and institutionally endorsed. Though the publication acknowledged the difficulties faced by peripheral economies and former colonies to compete with core countries, it insisted that failures of economic policy in most of them, derived from the "difficulty of making drastic changes in the colonial salary structures[18], (which) led to severe rigidities and distortions in urban labour markets and excessive growth in bureaucratic employment" (WDR, 1978, p. 48). Post-colonial territories, however, faced both a degradation of the standards of public administration and a deterioration of labour conditions.

"Modern development" processes, rather than tackling the causes of economic and political deprivation of peripheral economies in relation to a global architecture, conditioned their political role to an economic performance, enhancing the attractiveness of investment in their low wage labour intensive sectors. Indeed, the subsection "Government Support for Industrialization" of the 1979 World Bank Development report clearly insisted that:

"Most public undertakings in developing countries operate in monopolistic domestic markets protected from international competition by tariffs and quotas, and receive significant benefits from tax exemptions and priority allocations of scarce foreign exchange and domestic credit. (...). The (...) history of poor profitability stems partly from their pursuit of (...) social objectives, such as employment and the development of backward regions" (World Bank, 1979, p. 64).

The transformation of labour from a social asset to a pivotal variable of investment maximization, embraces the conception of local development as a construction reliant on global economic forces. This is why, permanent levels of unemployment are increasingly necessary to ensure marginal productivity in labour intensive industries. Indeed, permanent surplus labour ensures the capacity of governance structures to maintain workforce flexibility and thus wage competitiveness [19] (Escobar, 1995, p. 79) (OECD, 2013, p. 29) (Escobar, 1995).

The cumulative gap between wages and productivity becomes a lure for foreign investment. Cheap labour, represents the main competitive that advantage the majority of peripheral economies have for ensuring profitability and economic growth in an environment of capital scarcity. Meanwhile, redistributive mechanisms warrant the subsistence of the unemployed population by ensuring the distribution of food and vital needs. In low-income countries, these can customarily be met by maintaining low prices of the basic family basket. In high income territories such policies are embraced upon the distribution of bonuses, supplemental nutrition programs such as food stamps[20] or unemployment benefits.

The decreasing space for national politics to adopt policies that contravene the market conditions established by the regulation of the World Bank, the WTO and the International Monetary Fund, generates a narrative that pretends to justify the increasing gaps between levels of productivity and salary. Yet, with the free movement of capital, and the increasing international competition, maintaining economic inequality acquires a normative dimension that is further entrenched within the idea of development as a rational imperative. The hypothesis reads as follows: any country interested in maintaining increasing levels of material prosperity in a global economic environment, should keep pace with levels of competitiveness of other countries, even if it means dismantling previous social arrangements or safety nets. As such, concentration of corporate profits in capital exporting nodes, deterioration of labour conditions for the sake of productivity, permanent levels of unemployment and complicated schemes for unequal wage remuneration under market pressures are to be discursively vindicated as an outcome of a globalised modernity.

In 1995, Krugman described how the process of trade growth, operates in coordination with the progression of influence of the customary regulation. In his view modern world trade entails four aspects: "(a) the rise of intra-industry trade, *(b) [the] ability of producers to break production geographically, (c) [the] emergence of countries with high trade-GDP ratios, and (d) [the] large exports of manufactured goods from low- to high- wage countries.*"[21] (Michael D. Bordo, 1999, p. 14) (Wade, 2003) (Wade, 2004). In this manner, the institutional construction of "modern development" at the Bretton Woods institutions, has been able to evolve within the boundaries of the last three phenomena. On the one hand, the geographical flexibility of corporations, increases their ability to reallocate investment between capital and labour intensive countries. Secondly, the emergence of countries with high trade to GDP ratios, is explained by the historical asymmetric structures of profits between labour and capital/technology intensive industries. This aspect is defined on the one hand, by the location of labour intensive industries in countries capable of attracting investment focused on manufacturing. In opposition, technological industries are located in capital-intensive countries, in which the regulation of intellectual property and highly trained labour, safeguard their position as nodes of exportation of highly profitable technology-based products[22]. Finally, the distribution of manufactured goods from low to high wage countries is a consequence of the relations that arise under conditions of international trade. This last transitions was clearly defined in the classical Heckscher–Ohlin model, complemented by the contributions of Wassily Leontief in cases such as the United States, in which higher export rates of labour intensive goods were explained by labour's division between skilled and unskilled[23] (Michael D. Bordo, 1999, p. 15). categories. In both cases however, wealth distribution remained asymmetric.

In theory, it was supposed, that the burdens of the global economy were not to harm sovereign projects isolated from the structure of trade and capital; in practice, however, the increasing levels of influence of economic relations eroded any idea of development isolated from the exigencies of the global market. After all, the space for "development" beyond market demands was gradually diminished due to constraints imposed by an institutionalised international system of commerce, which made no distinctions between highly and less industrialized countries. As Wade describes:

"Countries (...) are being more tightly constrained in their national development strategies by proliferating regulations formulated and enforced by international organizations. These regulations are not about limiting companies' options, as 'regulation' normally connotes. Rather, they are about limiting the options of developing country governments to constrain the options of companies operating or hoping to operate within their borders" (Wade, 2003).

Given the impossible task for many peripheral economies to ensure levels of capital inflows, the adoption of debt from financial institutions such as the World Bank or the International Monetary Fund, became a standard measure to avoid competitive lags. Such calls for capital, increased the national dependency of debtor economies, while at the same time ensured an unvarying conception of development according to structural adjustment policies, and the fiscal policy measures intended to prevent defaulting on debt repayment.

GREECE: GLOBAL REPRICING OF FINANCIAL INSTRUMENTS AND HISTORY REPEATING

The International Debt Crisis and the Lost Decade Experienced by Low-Income Countries Between the 1970's and 1980's

In current structures of production, all securities represent relations between borrowers and lenders in a global scheme of debt that ensures investment while aiming to safeguard increasing levels of profitability of capital ventures. Money supply however, experienced an important variation at the beginning of the 1970's. This is because levels of international capital increased dramatically after the collapse of the Bretton Woods currency conversion system[24] (Eichengreen, 2004) (Eichengreen, 2012).

In the case of the United States, this shift happened due to the state's capacity to issue dollars as a customary global reserve currency. This policy enabled the country to get the necessary flexibility to adopt contra-cyclical measures, and to accumulate structural current account deficits (Eichengreen, 2004) (Eichengreen, 2012). Meanwhile, peripheral economies began to accumulate structural current account surpluses.[25] The explosion of lending capital, "led to an unprecedented rise in lending, especially the lending of private bank capital to third world governments. From 1970 to 1984 the total external indebtedness of developing countries rose from $64 billion to $686 billion, and the proportion of that debt held by private banks rose from on third to over one half" (Walton& Ragin, 1990).

While the burden of debt repayments didn't clearly create stresses on the debtor countries for most of the decade, things changed in 1982, when Mexico's finance minister, Jesus Silva Herzog, announced the country's inability to meet their obligations. Markets identified the situation as critical, leading to a chain reaction of numerous economies, declaring the inability to pay the interest on debt, which was acquired mainly during the 1970's. Since 1982, as a category of the global pathology of the decade, "more than 40 developing countries [were] forced to reschedule their debts with commercial bank creditors, and to seek additional lending and other forms of relief from the international financial community" (Sachs & Huizinga, 1987).

After the collapse of the Bretton Woods currency convertibility system, pressure for increased surpluses of *fiat* currency changed levels of available money globally. The increasing ease of governments to produce money not backed in fixed assets, unleashed an acute boost of currency into the market, corresponding expectations of both peripheral and core economies during the 1970's. This shift acquired unexpected dimensions when by October 1973, OPEC countries declared an oil embargo that worsened tensions in the Middle East while increased fears about slowing economic growth in the coming years.

The reaching of oil peak production of many industrialized countries[26], substantially increased the price of crude globally, expanding OPEC current account surpluses. With the overflow of capital and within market pressures to escalate levels of debt, non-industrialized countries turned to boost public spending. The event was further encouraged by the lending expectations of industrialized economies, leading to massive inflation events (particularly in Latin America), and to the proliferation of current account derived from the policies adopted during the surplus period.

Many western European countries adopted the same unsustainable policies during the 1970's and the 1980's. By 1982, forecasts of the Organization for Economic Cooperation and Development, estimated that:

"bank medium- and long-term loans to non-OPEC developing countries increased from $69 billion at year-end 1977 to $182 billion at year-end 1982, an increase of $113 billion. Other private lending to borrowers in these countries increased from $20 billion to $46 billion. These loans do not include credits to finance exports to these countries, which jumped from $45 billion to $105 billion during the same period.[...] By the second half of 1982, it was clear that there were problems" (Weintraub, 1984, p. 25).

The difficulties of peripheral economies to keep up their former pace of public investment, generated distrust about their debt instruments. This is why, between 1981 and 1982, only interest rate variations, represented debt increases of $593, $455 and $205 million for countries like Mexico, Brazil, and, Argentina, respectively. These, in turn, "greatly strained the abilities of these nations to meet their debt service obligations" (Weintraub, 1984, p. 28). With the need for borrower countries to meet their debts, schemes of rescheduling of obligations become the primary solution for international debtors. Finally, in order to meet obligations debtors opted to accept new loans endorsed by the International Monetary Fund.

Following the inability of many periphery economies to service their payments, the following months saw new private and IMF long term credits to those countries in danger of default. All of them rested upon the same structural adjustment conditions, that tended to pull social safety nets policies into a market oriented environment.

During the 1980s, despite growth difficulties for numerous countries who adopted IMF conditionality policies, their process of development was guided by the scheme suggested by the Fund. It embraced the acceptance of a decrease in public spending. Thereby, in an attempt to schematize the adoption of the "developmental" stage, countries were to follow structural adjustment policies which sought to ensure repayment of loans owed to the World Bank and the International Monetary Fund. This included overall austerity measures that increased the stability of investments, balancing the deficit acquired from borrower economies during the beginning of the fiscal crisis, privatization, the removal of price controls and trade liberalization among others. The impact of these measures in economies highly affected by the decisions made during the 1970's, led to the "Lost Decade" in Latin America; a period characterized by currency volatility, inflation and low economic growth.

Rather than being a symptom of systemic failure, the financial crisis of the 1980´s, made explicit the robustness of the global economic system over the autonomy of countries playing a role in a global environment. The implementation of fiscal policies to ensure profitability for foreign capital, characterized the increasing influence of economic actors, who were keen to find new frontiers for economic productivity in countries highly vulnerable to market pressures. The financial difficulties endured in such countries, provided the perfect scenario for international capital to penetrate, influencing the decisions of local governments to adopt policies in clear opposition to the will of large portions of the population. Development, as a by-product of economic growth, gradually overcame local agendas, which amidst the lack of competitiveness of countries with surpluses of labour and raw materials, fitted in the demands of highly influential actors.

United States and the United Kingdom at the End of the 80s, and the Fall of the Berlin Wall

After the social crisis experienced by Latin America and most of the less industrialized world, western leaders became primary advocates of trade liberalization. The symptoms of fatigue of the USSR project, and the tensions of the Cold War, boosted the appearance of political figures who took economic liberalism to a new level. In such a scenario, industrialised societies adopted processes of deregulation and privatization. These included for the most part the United States and Great Britain, in which the liberal agendas of Ronald Reagan and Margaret Thatcher took the lead in aligning their own political projects with the postulates demanded by the market. In this approach, the norm of "development", was to be accomplished by replacing the role of state politics with market forces; a shift within the consistent guidelines of the economic international architecture[27] (Escobar, 1995, p. 93) .

The policies implemented in the late 1970s and 1980s, kept pace with the influence of financial capital and international competition. Asymmetric distribution of corporate profits, and the sophistication of financial and debt instruments, generated a social rupture, experienced in the decreasing influence and number of trade unions, and the reduction of corporate taxes that privileged reduced segments of the population. This explains in part, why levels of inequality, measured as the distribution of concentration of wealth, increased acutely in the 70´s[28].

In the case of the United States, this shift took place starting with isolated deregulatory measures, implemented during the Carter administration[29], and vastly accelerated under the political agenda of Ronald Reagan. Such "hard" stances on privatization and liberalization were further deepened by the capacity of the government to incur ever greater levels of debt. The capacity of the US to adopt contra-cyclical measures after the collapse of the convertibility system was used to increase the rate flexibility of the dollar globally. Policies cutting personal income tax were accompanied by containing military expending and inflation. However, government deficit widened steadily. In the meantime, during the first part of the 1980's, the administration was capable of containing inflation by maintaining high interest rates (Eichengreen, 2008, p. 143), moreover, this goal was achieved even facing flows of capital from Germany and Japan to the United States.

So-called shock policies, cut social spending to attract investment, satisfying rating agencies, and aiming to increase growth in the industrialized territories. This shift however, rather than heralding an overall increase in the standard of living, gradually turned into an unequal distribution of benefits and burdens among the population. This is how core economies experienced sustained growth since the implementation of structural adjustment policies during the 1970's and 1980's; yet social ills such as poverty[30] or incarceration rates[31] went up.

Margaret Thatcher's ascendance as Prime Minister, opened with fiscal austerity policies suggested by conservative British think tanks, which promoted cuts in income taxes, massive privatization, measures against trade unions, and a significant reduction in public expenditure. Her administration found acceptance for these measures, due to the concerns of a population eager to avoid the stagnation experienced between 1973 and 1975[32]. Moreover, her role as the leader of the opposition, between 1975 and 1979, catapulted her image as a figure capable of boosting market confidence, while introducing Great Britain into a global market economy within which the country maintained international attraction. In the two first years of her government, however, the British economy experienced the deepest recession since the Second World War.

During this period, privatization policies accelerated as never before in the UK, while state contraction became a priority. Gas, water and electricity utilities were privatized following core principles of global institutions, but also guidelines of organisms such as the Federal Reserve Bank of the United States, which suggested deeper measures "to cut down on very high rates of inflation and budget deficits; [enhancing] greater economic efficiency and substantial reduction in [...] current account deficits" (Weintraub, 1984, p. 52).

The role performed by the United States and Great Britain, in reviving the ideology lately known as neo-liberal, even in the face of strong popular opposition, legitimated their roles as main actors in a global system in which citizens were bounded by state apparatuses, but capital could move freely as to threaten the stability of even these two economies. In both the United States and Great Britain, the adoption of selected shock measures, that tended to eliminate forms of redistributive justice within the limits of the nation state, were implemented in an effort to keep pace with a global environment in which economic power increased across diverse commercial nodes. In these cases, rising inequalities between citizens were further addressed as a necessary arrangement, in which low salaries ensured continued growth in profits, while an ethic of sacrifice reduced class conflicts in social sectors not helped by redistributive justice measures (Crocier & Huntington et. al, 1973, p.:1975).

From the Global Financial "Crisis" to Greece

At the level of the IMF, the Greek financial crisis is reconstructed as an event originated in the nation state, implying the isolation of the systemic nature of the phenomenon. Such narrative is based on a vision of Greece as detached from the global context, fitting the interests of lenders, and creating a misrepresentation offered to a public eager to grasp the reasons behind the crisis.

The economic narrative frequently dates back to mid-2007, when the US credit suffered a fast paced contraction, generating market concerns about the price of subprime mortgage securities, and the overall process of deregulation for loans that banks had given out over the past years. Despite the efforts of the government to dissipate distrust, the aftermath of the events triggered a fall in consumer confidence generating a strong perception of market volatility. Amidst increasing suspicion over the price of housing and financial assets, and the aftermath of the 2006 housing bubble peak, US measures were limited to an economic stimulus package[33] to bail out financial institutions that borrowed money from the government. This helped to finance a scheme of low value mortgage backed securities that spread globally.

The turmoil of the events experienced in the United States (Elliott, 2009), manifested in a liquidity crisis, re-pricing of value securities tied to the US, increasing levels of distrust over financial institutions, and a downturn in overall global economic activity between 2008 and 2012. In Europe; the aftermath of the episode generated incredulity about the capacity of some European countries to meet their financial obligations. In 2010, the US situation reached an international peak, when fears over the sovereign debt of some countries of the Euro zone led to a wave of credit rating downgrades[34] that affected Greece, Ireland, Italy, Portugal, Spain, Slovenia and Slovakia, among others.

In 2010, threatened by market retaliations, Greece was found to be in need of implementing deep austerity measures, with a view to restoring the fiscal and current account balance, privatizing government assets in order to improve growth prospect.

The implementation of the structural adjustment policies to boost market confidence in Greece, brought back into the narrative the image of economic growth as the fundamental category for understanding development. Meanwhile, the impact of the measures recommended by the Fund generated a social crisis, with the main brunt beared by those of the middle and lower classes[35] (Records kept since 1946) (Treanor, 2011) (Garofaldo, 2012). In an effort to justify measures that contradicted the interests of vulnerable segments of the population, the institutional storyline stressed the inevitability of the measures. This strategy acknowledges the undemocratic nature of specific bailouts, underwritten by taxpayers, or the consequences of policies directed to increase financial volatility. Indeed, ignoring the dimension of the upcoming crisis, as a customary discursive intervention at the level of the Bretton Woods Institutions, the 2009 World Bank executive report -called "Putting development in place"- reads:

"The challenge for governments is to allow—even encourage—"unbalanced" economic growth, and yet ensure inclusive development. (…) This integration can best be done by unleashing the market forces of agglomeration, migration, and specialization, not by fighting or opposing them" (World Bank, 2009, p. 21).

In the isolation of alternative political categories; unbalanced growth plays a core role that is established by two explanations. On the one hand, it eases processes of labour replacement. In such circumstances, inequality becomes a goal that ensures potential profitability, rather than being presented as a loss of sovereignty of the individual, or the state, in an effort to establish economic relations on balanced conditions. Additionally, it safeguards the discursive legitimation of the economic relations as a superior category for steering political, or social problems (Sachs., 1993). Thereby, global repricing of financial instruments, such as those that take place along financial crisis, rather than symptoms of systemic stress, become necessary adjustments to refine economic expansion. These events are wrongly presented as structural failures, though indeed being failures of performance, are successes insofar as they represent the ability of financial and economic actors to tune social arrangements in order to meet market demands.

From an economic perspective, "financial crisis", can be regularly considered as cases of inattention about potential stages of disequilibrium that built up within periods of global or local economic expansion (Wihlborg et, 2010). In the case of Greece, these cases are further reinforced by governance shortcomings that overlook early market inconsistencies. In face of fundamental weaknesses of the governance praxis, the economy operates as an instrument for steering social relations, redistributing the burdens of structural policies "efficiently".

Institutionally, the annual report of the International Monetary Fund, makes use of a standard discursive construction to justify these problems (IMF, 2012, p. 21/76). In their approach, the necessity to implement market condition on social systems, is derived from trends in losses of productivity and competitiveness that may arise in presence of alternative policies. Such prognoses however, fail to account the international character of the problems, which in the case of Greece is bounded with the terms of the technological and economic asymmetries between the country and some of their neighbours in the Euro zone, increasing domestic trade deficits in absence of a fiscal union[36].

With the Eurozone, "modern development" manifests as the enlargement of structures of industrial production, that by a progressive loss of state sovereignty take shape by market imperatives. The cornering of the population by fiscal policy measures, led to highly aggressive social shocks, which were presented as a profitable imperative to achieve higher efficiency standards in an unending cycle. Meanwhile, an unbalanced distribution of corporate profits, regulated impacts across different social strata. In such settings, the reallocation of labour, and the process of wage stagnation, were accompanied by a decrease in public spending and increasing unemployment for the active labour force. In the meantime, forecasts of the Bretton Woods institutions falsely ascribe the origin of the financial collapse, while public officials justify shock measures. In the case of Greece, this notable role of the public opinion is highlighted with a 2010 declaration of the president of the European Central Bank. In his assertion; "The idea that austerity measures could trigger stagnation is incorrect" (Krugman, 2012), yet two years later Greece youth unemployment reached an historic peak of 50% (Nick Malkoutzis - Friedrich Ebert Stiftung, 2011).

CONCLUSION

Trends of Global Asymmetry and the Unreachable Project of Development

The increasing influence of economic imperatives over national political projects, exposes the imbalances of an international system based upon mixtures of overrepresentation and underrepresentation. The influence of flows of capital within autonomous domestic political projects, led to a deepening of global inequalities that in recent decades reduced the remit of practices of domestic governance. Alternatively, national regimes, seek to remediate social tensions by pursuing more growth. On a global level, this phenomenon has acquired an unprecedented dimension, due to the stresses that economic dynamics impose upon peripheral actors. Wealth and the overall welfare of populations, while conditioned by features of national institutions, are increasingly affected by "a country's [relationship] to others, in various fields such as politics, trade, geography, and culture, implicitly as well as explicitly, affect[ing] its economic performance and wealth". On an international irregular environment, however, both wealth and trade are "unevenly distributed" (Cha & Lee, 2010 A) (Cha & Lee, 2010 A), increasing the scope of burdens over actors marginalized from the policy making process.

With the constitution of a global political architecture such as the Bretton Woods Organizations, the settings of the system granted the institutionalization of power and economic relations in accordance with market conditions. These settings carried out the avoidance of alternative agendas that searched for the origins of social problems besides the economy. In such settings, the system led to the formalization of regulation biased by the same imbalances that aroused in the economic sphere, benefiting overrepresented actors or those with influence on executive bodies of international institutions (Barro, 2005) (Dreher et. al., 2010) . Moreover, in recent decades, processes of liberalization reveal clear trends on overall instability of the global economy, which in turn opposes even more the conflictive idea of relying in global "market forces" as long term solutions for domestic social demands (Rodrik, 2001) (Spanu, 2003) (Stiglitzt, 2004).

The increasing influence of the liberalization of commerce, and the restrictions of national entities to regulate pressures of the global economy on domestic political projects, has led to the construction of an idea of development in which the Bretton Woods Institutions have played a dominant role. These settings have their empirical roots in the 1970's, during the shocks then suffered by peripheral economies. These countries, acknowledging the burdens of the measures, were forced to embrace them, avoiding harsher consequences of isolationist strategies. In recent years, however, the view of liberalization and growth as a synonym of development has been increasingly contested (Frericks et. al., 2010.) (Sachs., 1993) (Chang, 2002). Despite the fact, financial institutions and capital flows have acquired acutely real political influence and control over social systems.

The events taking place in Greece, Spain and other countries of the Euro zone, are indicative of a normative construction that intends to expand the same ideological settings, over social and political systems formerly in privileged positions in the global economy. In such circumstances, the project of "development" can never be fully attained, if market burdens threaten social systems that are temporarily lagging within the structure of global competition.

In the present chapter, we have seen that the normative construction of "modern development", rather than being a product of a global democratic arena, has been a normative construction influenced by the way international institutions settled the regulatory boundaries of economics and politics for almost 70 years. By making use of contributions on international political economy, historical institutionalism and sociological institutionalism, the present chapter stresses how political asymmetries at the Bretton Woods Institutions, continue mapping the reality of nationwide political projects. The rationalization of development as an economic category, carried within, the reproduction of patterns that through three historical periods since the end of the Second World War, reproduced in non-industrialized and industrialized territories. Within such circumstances, social shock measures previously reserved to capital importing nodes, shifted to high and medium income countries.

While in recent years, the view of liberalization and growth as a synonym of development has been increasingly contested, financial institutions and capital flows continue acquiring real political influence and control over social systems. In current circumstances however, the project of "development" can never be fully attained if market burdens threaten social systems temporarily lagging within the structure of global competition.

The present chapter stresses how political asymmetries at the Bretton Woods Institutions, continue mapping the reality of nationwide political projects in non-industrialized and industrialized territories. In such transition, social shock measures, previously reserved to capital importing nodes, shifted normatively and in the policy praxis to high and medium income countries. Since our paper was written with the aim of analysing how political asymmetries at international organizations have a direct effect over normative constructions, our conclusions points to the fact that the idea "modern development", is indeed the representation of conflicting normative interventions that erode attempts to construct social projects isolated from global flows of capital. Cyclical processes of re-pricing of financial instruments, characterized customarily as financial crisis, have determined the institutional operationalization of such arrangements. Under most of our expectations, given increasing conditions of global asymmetry, this discursive construction appears to be not an unforeseen phenomenon but as it has been pointed out, rather a permanent "conscious political action" (Habermas, 2001) in which the role of the state diminishes inevitably under the influence of global economic actors.

Figure 1. UK GINI index period 1968-2019

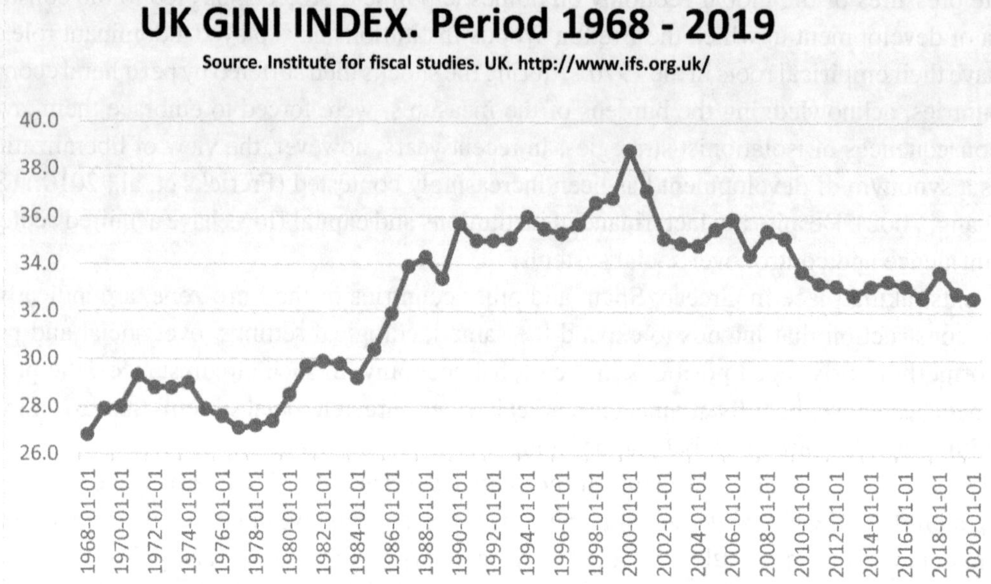

Figure 2. USA GINI indez 1963-2008[37]

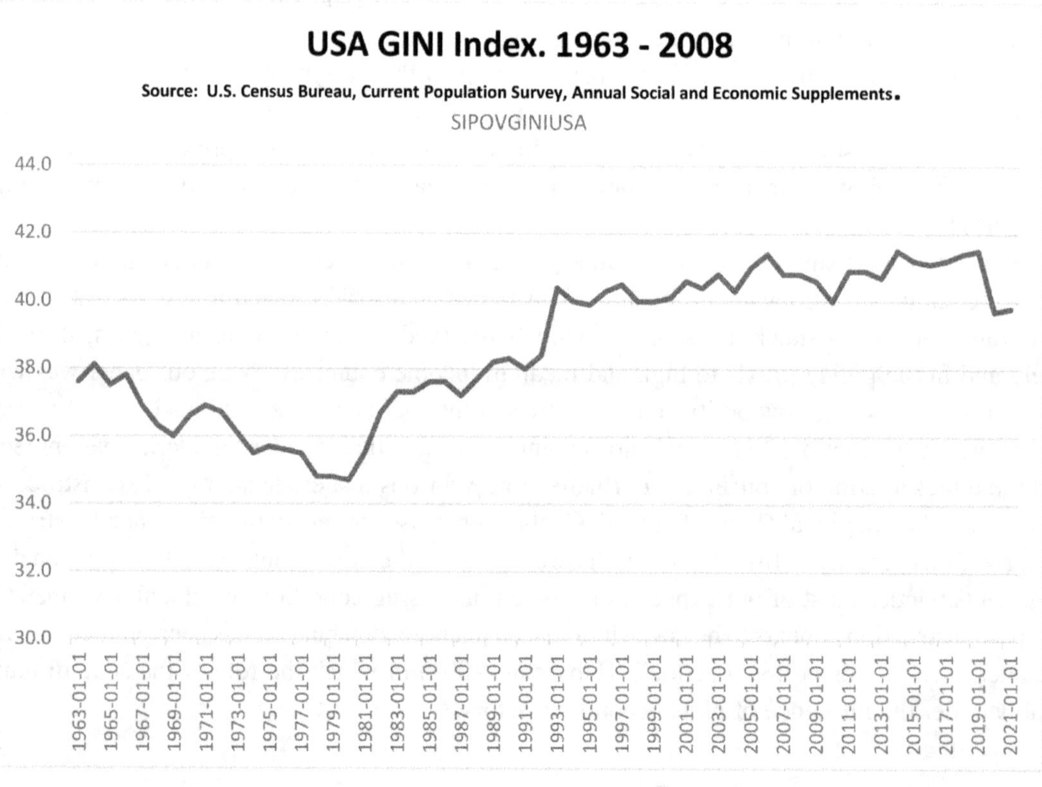

Figure 3. UK poverty index 1974

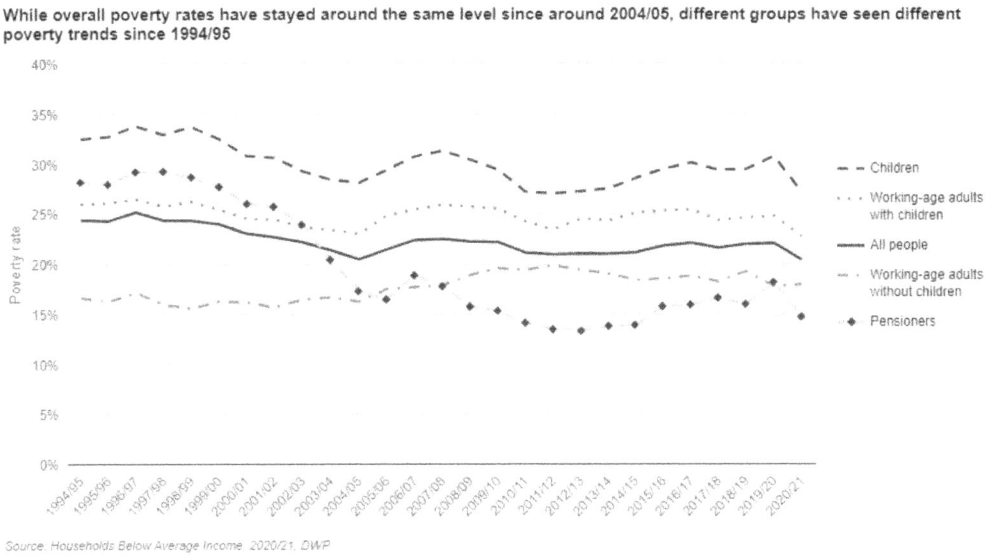

Table 1. UK poverty index 1974

YEAR	POVERTY INDEX	YEAR	POVERTY INDEX
1961	103,95	**1984**	107,5
1962	98,88	**1985**	112,32
1963	107,94	**1986**	115,86
1964	105,18	**1987**	121,46
1965	100,03	**1988**	128,45
1966	103,8	**1989**	130,14
1967	99,94	**1990**	135,05
1968	99,37	**1991**	135,72
1969	102,19	**1992**	135,42
1970	103,19	**1993**	135,27
1971	106,05	**1994**	132,47
1972	107,23	**1995**	132,68
1973	102,98	**1996**	132,74
1974	100	**1997**	135,62
1975	96,76	**1998**	138,72
1976	96,62	**1999**	137,84
1977	95,37	**2000**	140,54
1978	95,38	**2001**	138,81
1979	100,78	**2002**	137,22
1980	102,54	**2003**	135,5
1981	104,84	**2004**	135,59
1982	104,01	**2005**	137,77
1983	106,66		

Source. Institute for fiscal studies. UK. https://www.ifs.org.uk/

Figure 4. US poverty

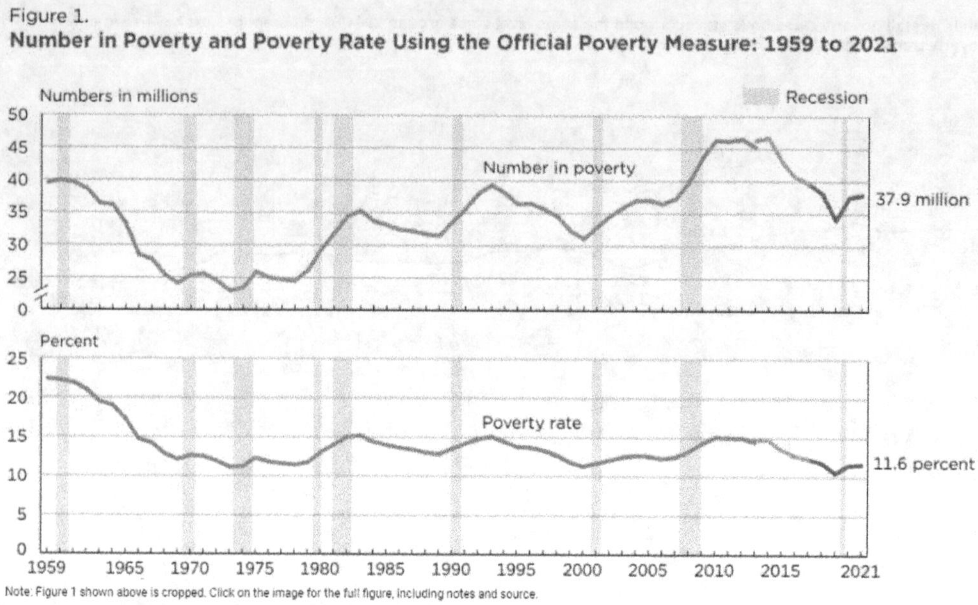

Table 2. US poverty

Year	GDP Growth	Population below poverty levels. Millions.
1980	5834	29,3
1981	5982,1	31,8
1982	5865,9	34,4
1983	6130,9	35,3
1984	6571,5	33,7
1985	6843,4	33,1
1986	7080,5	32,4
1987	7307	32,2
1988	7607,4	31,7
1989	7879,2	31,5
1990	8027,1	33,6
1991	8008,3	35,7
1992	8280	38,0
1993	8516,2	39,3
1994	8863,1	38,1
1995	9086	36,4
1996	9425,8	36,5
1997	9845,9	35,6
1998	10274,7	34,5
1999	10770,7	32,8
2000	11216,4	31,6
2001	11337,5	32,9
2002	11543,1	34,6
2003	11836,4	35,9
2004	12246,9	37,0
2005	12623	37,0
2006	12958,5	36,5
2007	13206,4	37,3
2008	13161,9	39,8
2009	12757,9	43,6

Source. US Census Bureau.

REFERENCES

Barro, R. J. (2005). *IMF Programs: Who Is Chosen and What Are the Effects?* Department of Economics, Harvard University. Department of Economics, Korea University. April.

Barro, R. J. a. J.-W. L. (2005). IMF Programs: Who Is Chosen And What Are The Effects?. *Journal of Monetary Economics, 7*(52), 1245-1269.

Bird, G., & Rowlands, D. (2006). IMF quotas: Constructin an international organization using inferior building blocks. *The Review of International Organizations, 1*(2), 153–171. doi:10.100711558-006-8342-x

Campbell, J. L. (1998). *No. 3 (Jun., 1998)* (Vol. 27). Institutional Analysis and the Role of Ideas in Political Economy. Theory and Society. Sprynger. https://www.jstor.org/stable/657900

Cha, M.-Y. & Lee, J. W. (2010). Wealth dinamics in world trade (Moon-Yong Cha a, Jae Woo Leea – Patterns of International Trade and a Nation's Wealth.. *Journal of the Korean Phys ical Society, 56*(3), p. 998 - 1002.

Cha & Lee. (2010). Patterns of International Trade and a Nation's Wealth. Department of Physics, Inha University, Incheon.

Chang, H.-J. (2002). *Kicking Away the Ladder. Development Strategy in Historical Perspective*. Anthem Press.

Chang, H.-J. (2002). Kicking Away the Ladder. Development Strategy in Historical Perspective. Anthem Press.

Cooper & Truman. (2007). *The IMF Quota Formula: Linchpin of Fund Reform. Harvard University.* Peterson Institute for International Economics.

Crocier & Huntington. (1973). The crisis on democracy. The trilateral comission. New York University Press.

Dennis Leech, R. L. (2004). Voting Power in the Bretton Woods Institutions. (*Warwick Economic Research Papers).*

Dowrick, S. (2005). CONTRADICTORY TRENDS IN GLOBAL INCOME INEQUALITY: A TALE OF TWO BIASES. *Review of Income and Wealth, 51*(2), 201 - 229.

Dreher. (2010). *Do the IMF and theWorld Bank influence voting in the UN General Assembly.* Springer. . doi:10.1007/s11127-010-9750-2

Easterly, W. (2000). The effect of IMF and World Bank programs on poverty. *Social Science Research Network Electronic Paper Collection*, (December), 31.

Eichengreen, B. (2004). Global Imbalances and the Lessons from Bretton Woods. *National Bureau of Economic Research.*

Eichengreen, B. (2008). *Globalizing Capital:A History of the International Monetary System* (2nd ed.). Princeton University Press. doi:10.2307/j.ctt7pfmc

Eichengreen, B. (2012). *Exorbitant Privilege: The Rise and Fall of the Dollar and the Future of the International Monetary System*. Oxford University Press.

Elliott, M. N. (2009). *The US Financial and Economic Crisis: Where Does It Stand and Where Do We Go From Here?*

Escobar, A. (1995). *Encountering Development. The making and unmaking of the third world.* Princeton University Press.

Frericks et.al., P. (2009). Toward a Neoliberal Europe?: Pension Reforms and Transformed. *Administration & Society, 41*(135). doi:10.1177/0095399708328874

Frericks. (2010). Capitalist Welfare Societies' Trade-Off Between Economic Efficiency And Social Solidarity. *European Societies, 12*(5), 719–741. doi:10.1080/14616696.2010.483010

Frericks, Harvey, M., & Maier, R. (2010). P. M. H. a. R. M., 2010. The 'paradox of the shrinking middle': The central dilemma of European social policy. *Critical Social Policy, 30*(3), 315–336. doi:10.1177/0261018310367671

Frericks, P. (2010). *Patricia Frericks, Mark Harvey and Robert Maier The 'paradox of the shrinking middle': The central dilemma of European social policy.* Sage.. https://csp.sagepub.com/content/30/3/315. s.l.:s.n. doi:10.1177/0261018310367671

Garofaldo, P. (2012). *Corporate Profits Hit Record High While Worker Wages Hit Record Low. December 3th. Think progress.* Think Progress. https://thinkprogress.org/economy/2012/12/03/1270541/corporate-profits-wages-record/?mobile=nc

Groom, B. (2013). OECD jobless rates forecast to remain stubbornly high. *Financial Times, 16.* http://www.ft.com/cms/s/0/5d7c8300-ede4-11e2-816e-00144feabdc0.html#axzz2dl8t6Nz2..

Habermas, J. (2001). Why Europe Need a Constitution. *New Left Review, 11.*

Harjes, T. (2007). Globalization and Income Inequality: A European Perspective. International Monetary Fund.

IMF. (2012). International Monetary Fund. *Executive Board Report.* International Money Fund.

International Monetary Fund. (2012). *Global Financial Stability Report. A Report by the Monetary and Capital Markets Department on Market Developments and Issues.* IMF.

Jackson, R. (2002). *The Global Retirement Crisis.* The Threat to World Stability and What to Do About It. Citigroup & Center for Strategic and International Studies. Global Aging Initiative. doi:10.1111/1468-0440.00187

Khan, H. &. L. Y. (2008). Globalization and the WTO Dispute Settlement Mechanism: Making a Rules-based Trading Regime Work. *(MPRA Paper 7613).* University Library of Munich, Germany.

Krugman, P. (2012). Is the United States like Greece? Not even close. *ADN.* https://www.adn.com/2012/03/13/2368710/krugman-is-the-united-states-like.html

Lombardi, N. W. (2006). Uneven patterns of governance: how developing countries are represented in the IMF. *Review of International Political Economy, 13*(3), 480-515.

Michael, D. Bordo, B. E. D. A. I. (1999). *Is Globalization Today Really Different than Globalization a Hunderd Years Ago?* (NBER Working Paper No. 7195) NBER.

Mikesell, R. F. (1994). The Bretton Woods debates. A memoir. Essays in International Finance, 192, 76.

Milanovic, B. (2007). *An even Higuer inequality than previously though: a note on global inequality calculations using the 2005 ICP results.* (World Bank Policy Research Working Paper Series). World Bank.

Nick Malkoutzis, N. (2011). Greece – A Year in Crisis. *Examining the Social and Political Impact of an Unprecedented Austerity Programme.*

OECD. (2013). OECD Employment Outlook 2013. OECD.

País, E. E. (2013). Depresión profunda. *EL PAÍS, 25.* https://elpais.com/elpais/2013/01/24/opinion/1359059699_473851.html

Palley, T. I. (2007). *Financialization: what it is and why it matters.* (Working Papers). The levy Economics Institute.

Peters, A. (2011). The Constitutionalisation of International Trade Law. The Prospects Of International Trade Regulation: From Fragmentation To Coherence, (pp. 69-102). Cambridge University Press.

Read, C. (2009). *Global Financial Meltdown: How We Can Avoid the Next Economic Crisis. Basingstoke* [England]. Palgrave Macmillan. doi:10.1057/9780230595187

Rodrik, D. (2001). *Trading in Illusions. Foreign Policy.* Washingtonpost.Newsweek Interactive, LLC. https://www.jstor.org/stable/3183155

Sachs., W. (1993). *Global Ecology and the Shadow of Development.* Zed Books.

Sachs & Huizinga. (1987). *U.S. Commercial Banks and the Developing Country Debt Crisis.* (NBER Working Paper No. 2455). NBER.

Spanu, V. (2003). Liberalization of the international trade and economic growth: implications for both developed and developing countries. Harvard University.

Spanu, V. (2003). *Liberalization of the international trade and economic growth: implications for both developed and developing countries.* Harvard University.

Stiglitz, J. (2004). Capital-market Liberalization, Globalization, and the IMF. *Oxford Review of Economic Policy, 20*(1), 57–71. doi:10.1093/oxrep/grh004

Stiglitz, J. (2006). *Making Globalization Work: Making Trade Fair.* Norton & Company. Ltda.

Stiglitzt, J. (2004). Capital-market Liberalization, Globalization, and the IMF. *Oxford Review of Economic Policy, 20*(1), 57–71. doi:10.1093/oxrep/grh004

Subramanian, & Wei, S.-J. (2007). The WTO promotes trade, strongly but unevenly [May. s.l.:s.n.]. *Journal of International Economics, 72*(1), 151–175. doi:10.1016/j.jinteco.2006.07.007

Swedberg, R. (1986). The Doctrine of Economic Neutrality of the IMF and the World Bank. *Journal of Peace Research, 23*(4), 377-390.

Thacker, S. C. (1999). The High Politics of IMF Lending. *World Politics, 52*(1), 38–75. doi:10.1017/S0043887100020025

Treanor, J. (2011). World's wealthiest people now richer than before the credit crunch. *The Guardian. Co.*

Wade, R. H. (2003). *The World Trade Organization and the schrinking of the development space.* (Working Paper No.31). London School of Economics.

Wade, R. H. (2004). Is Globalization reducing Poverty and Inequality. *World Development, 32*(4), 567–589. doi:10.1016/j.worlddev.2003.10.007

Walton, J., & Ragin, C. (1990, December). J. a. C., 1990. Global and National Sources of Political Protest: Third World Responses to the Debt Crisis. *American Sociological Review*, *55*(6), 876–890. doi:10.2307/2095752

Weintraub, R. E. (1984). International debt: Crisis and Challenge. Cato Journal, 4.

Wihlborg, W. Z. (2010). *The euro crisis: It isn´t just fiscal sn it doesn´t just involve Greece. Claremont McKenna College.* Robert Day School.

Woods & Lombardi. (2006, August). Uneven patterns of governance: How developing countries are represented in the IMF [s.l.:s.n.]. *Review of International Political Economy*, *13*(3).

World Bank. (1978). *World Development Report*. World Bank.

World Bank. (1979). *World Development Report*. World Bank.

World Bank – AA. (1945). *Articles of Agreement. Article I. Purposes.* World Bank.

ENDNOTES

1 On June 15th, 2012, Spain's public debt reached its highest level since 1913, exceeding by 17.4% the peak settled by the EU Stability and Growth pact (1998/1999). Up to January 2013, after more than one year of the new political administration (conservative), and the deepening of an austerity program of about $65b, levels of unemployment in Spain reach historical peak levels of 26%-, with 60% youth unemployment (País, 2013). For the time being, Greece is implementing the highest historical spending cuts in history, while Germany gives the green light for a rescue packet of 49.1 billion Euros intended to increase competitiveness and economic growth. As of February 2013, Italy's public debt accounted for about 130% of its GDP –the biggest stock in the Euro zone-, while real GDP per capita is expected to be lower than in 1999. In (The Economist., 2013).

2 Krugman has attempted to call it "the US lost decade".

3 Some of them such as the capacity of a single country (United States) of running enormous account deficits due to the demand of emerging countries to accumulate reserves, the asymmetric distribution and participation of peripheral economies in the executive bodies of the FMI and the WTO, the veto power of core territories to marginalize peripheral economies in the operational committees that gave birth to the institutions back in 1943, or the influence of big economies in processes of decision-making procedures taken by votes at the Board of Governors and the executive Board of the IMF and the WB.

4 "It is well known that one of the quintessential aspects of modernity is the separation of social life into functional spheres (the economy, the polity, society, culture, and the like), each with laws of its own. This is, strictly speaking, a modern development. As a separate domain, the economy had to be given expression by a proper science". (Escobar, 1995, p. 60)

5 The concept of capital exporting countries, rather than being part of a recent discursive construction to exemplify financial relations, or interaction of low capital backed economic structures with highly economic backed ones; makes part of a conception commonly inserted and recognized in the official literature of the World Bank in the first half of the 20th century. The last time it was used in

a yearly official document was by Robert McNamara, former World Bank president between 1968 and 1981. From the first year in which the World Development report of the Board of Direction of the World Bank, was made public in 1978, the concept of capital exporting countries were not used again historically. In McNamara, R. (1978) Chapter 8th (World Bank, 1978).

6 "Including the restoration of economies destroyed or disrupted by war"... See (World Bank - AA, 1945).

7 At this point it is possible to stress that the third purposive target of the Bank, which aims to "promote the long-range balanced growth of international trade (…) thereby assisting in raising productivity", is not possible to be fulfilled. This is because in absence of institutions of redistributive justice, market profitability boosts increasingly unequal relations between capital exporting and capital importing nodes.

8 USA (17.5% percent of the total IMF quotas), Japan (6.3%), Germany (6.1%), France (5.1%), UK (5.1%), Saudi Arabia (3.3%), China (3.0%), and Russia (2.8%).

9 Such as protectionist measures in high income territories. See (Chang, 2002).

10 Even in recognition of the risks faced by peripheral economies, levels of market volatility secured under the current global regulation, assured fundamental structural crisis associated with lagged economies during a great part of the second half of the twentieth century. As a matter of fact, is important to acknowledge, that it is just with the geographical reallocation of burdens that have taken place since the recession of 2007, and the overall evolution of processes of repricing of financial instruments, that policies to contain the volatility effects of global financial markets have led to suggest in high income territories (EU) tax schemes on financial transactions (Tobin tax). On volatility and domestic shocks to increase productivity. See (Stiglitz, 2004).

11 (Jackson, 2002). A detailed contemporary analysis can be found in (International Monetary Fund, 2012).

12 In the recent three decades this case has been particularly acute in the United States.

13 In the relation between life courses and resource flows on present day welfare states, see; (Frericks et. al., 2010)

14 See (Campbell, 1998). For the case of the United States, ideological tensions are represented on the discussion between government intervention vs supply side economics.

15 One can say customary contemporary ideological trends of electoral politics oscillate between redistributive politics (Keynesianism) and deregulation (German school). While at the national level such political trends are ideologically embraced by parties, globally they are framed by the boundaries of institutional regulation.

16 For the most recent prognosis about the evolution of such setting in both low and high industrialized countries, see (OECD, 2013). In accordance with the report, "Over the past decade, and particularly since the crisis, OECD countries have tended to reduce the strictness of employment protection legislation – the rules covering the hiring and firing of workers – especially regarding collective and individual dismissals".

17 The same setting is applied in western industrialized countries. By July 2013, OECD recovery prognoses of the 2008 financial crisis remained despairing while like Greece and Portugal faced young unemployment rates of 60% and 40%. According to the organization, "people on short term contracts were often the first to be fired at the beginning of the crisis" (Groom, 2013).

18 What is peculiar about this approach is the fact that many of the structures of governance and wage remuneration of peripheral economies with strong ties with core economies, particularly those in Africa, were inherited from the colonial laws, traditions and regulations.

19 This case has been highly documented in Escobar studies about development and particularly in the historical evolution of the role of rural or peripheral population into new nontraditional sectors that boost economic growth according to market demands. Paraphrasing Lewis he adds; "the central fact of economic development is rapid capital accumulation (including knowledge and skills)(…), The means to achieve this feat also follows: to use the traditional sector to fuel the modern one. This would require moving the rural underemployed, who, because of their large numbers, can be removed from the countryside without reducing agricultural output (…) because the marginal productivity of labour in agriculture is negligible or zero. This surplus labour would be hired at near-subsistence wages by the new industries set up with additional savings and foreign capital. (Escobar, 1995, p. 79). From a different perspective, this assumption explains why levels of unemployment are systematically high even in industrialized countries such as the United States. See more in (OECD, 2013, p. 29) (Escobar, 1995).

20 Even in highly industrialized countries, rather than experiencing a decrease, this tendency has consolidated as a customary policy to reduce burdens of unemployment. On September 2012, for instance, the percentage of citizens in the United States receiving food stamps to balance nutritional needs were 15%. Reaching an historical peak of 47 million people. In such case, the amount of people living on state subsistence expenditures, exceeds the population of 89% of the countries in the world.

21 In (Michael D. Bordo, 1999, p. 14) . See also (Wade, 2003) (Wade, 2004)

22 In the recent decades however, this shift has mixed in peculiar nations that combine in a single political territory vast numbers of unemployed or poor population, with increasing levels of investment in technology intensive ventures such as India, Indonesia, China or Brazil. All of them among the most unequal and populated countries in the world.

23 As it is acknowledge by Bordo in Krugman analysis, "A century ago U.S. trade with Latin American and Asian economies consisted of agricultural commodities that the United States did not produce in quantity, such as sugar, coffee, tea, etc. Today the U.S. is more likely to be importing manufactured goods from those countries. A classic instance is Mexico: currently over 80 percent of U.S. imports from Mexico are manufactured goods; a century ago the figure was less than ten percent". See also (Michael D. Bordo, 1999, p. 15).

24 Unilaterally led by the United States after Richard Nixon's decision to unpeg the dollar from the gold.

25 Such as the case of Asia.

26 Among them, the United States, Canada, Western Europe, Japan, Australia and New Zealand.

27 As it has been expressed; „Statist and redistributive approaches gave way to the liberalization of trade and investment regimes, the privatization of state-owned enterprises, and policies of restructuring and stabilizing under the control of the ominous International Monetary Fund (IMF). There was, indeed, a noticeable policy reversal. Reagan's "magic of the market" speech, delivered at the North-South conference in Cancún in 1981, publicly announced this turn" (Escobar, 1995, p. 93).

28 See annex No. 1.

29 Particularly in the US airline industry.

30 See Annex No. 2.

31 In the case of the US.

32 In a great extent caused by the prices of oil and the fragility of the markets after the fall of the Bretton Woods convertibility system.

33 The first one signed on February 2008 by President George Bush for an amount of $168 billion. The second one signed by President Barack Obama (American Recovery and Reinvestment Act) on February 2009 for an amount of $787 billion.

34 That up to now has not been completely reversed.

35 After the credit crunch, levels of inequality in the world increased substantially. Two years after the crash, "global richest have (…) recouped the losses they suffered after the 2008 banking crisis". While the big majority of the population resulted hardly affected by the meassures, top managers of financial corporations benefited extensively from the crisis. Indeed, at December 2012, corporations made historical record profits in the US (Records kept since 1946). With $1,75 Trillion, "up to 18,6% from a year ago" (Treanor, 2011). See also (Treanor, 2011) (Garofaldo, 2012).

36 Just as from 1985 the United States has increasingly accumulated a deficit in the balance of trade with China. A country that upon the elimination of western "civil liberties" has endured to become a node for investment and profitability for former western capital.

37 Source: World Bank Release: World Development Indicators . Units: Index, Not Seasonally Adjusted. Frequency: Annual

Chapter 8
Institutional Justice and the Ethical Dimension of the Norm of Modern Development at the Bretton Woods Institutions

ABSTRACT

The present chapter reconstructs historically how the notion of institutional justice was embedded within the normative construction of modern development. The chapter draws on contributions on critical constructivism, to tease out how in the evolution of late modern social system, the idea of justice was gradually legitimated within contractual governance architectures, that further normalized relations aroused on highly asymmetric agent environments, such as the World Bank or the International Monetary Fund. By depicting the concept of institutional justice, the goal of the chapter is to shed lights on the ideological dimension of the norm of modern development at the Bretton Woods Institutions, and the transposition of rather conflicting arrangements in the normative landscape of the conventional ethical dimension of the international system.

INTRODUCTION

In the course of defining how political asymmetries affect global structures of governance, little value has been given to its role in shaping socially constructed norms. From an historical perspective, this phenomenon has molded social principles and procedures that just upon the inclusion of otherwise disregarded views, appear as problematic or conflictive. A glimpse into the background of this antagonistic character of socialization, reveals that, over time, social practices become norms, and upon the legitimation of this symbolic constructions on structures of authority, they tend to acquire a somehow mandatory institutional category. From an international Relations perspective, such cases can be seen on organizations that regulate political relations by guidelines and discourses that acquire meaning

DOI: 10.4018/978-1-6684-9794-4.ch008

when put into practice, despite been highly contested in terms of procedures, foundational settings and normative outcomes.

In the task of steering framed spheres of international relations, the Bretton Woods Institutions reveal themselves as strategic nodes of normative meaning. Their ongoing allusion to an idea of development by the regulation of framed realms of political and economic relations, has further created a narrative of "global justice" hardly refuted over time. As such, the idea of "global justice" has transposed its semantic value into an institutional arrangement. In this scenario, it´s role as a virtuous principle for the mediation of interests on an international sphere, acquire a sense of legitimacy scarcely antagonized in today politics, but problematic when grasped from a more democratic or ethical perspective. In sum, in the global process of modern development, the idea of justice as a functional governance category has meticulously been transferred from the social to the contractual sphere. This shift has been triggered by the increasing levels of sophistication of societies, which upon the necessity of regulate relations, have posit on institutions the burdens derived from tensions of complex contemporary social systems.

Taking into account the role of historic contingencies in the birth process, formation, maturation and legitimation of institutions, as well as contributions of communicative action theory and critical constructivism, the present chapter presents a theoretical approach upon which at the Bretton Woods institutions, this concept of *modern contractual justice* can be grasped coherently. The working hypothesis of this argument, is that in contemporary structures of asymmetric governance, fundamental social norms evolve conflictively, acquiring institutional meaning that replace functionally and systemically the deontological attributes and claims for legitimacy of institutional practices.

In the present chapter, I reconstruct the idea of global justice and its institutional category at the Bretton Woods Institutions upon two features of the institutions. First an historical one, in which the contributions of historic institutionalism and critical constructivism, explain how the development of social systems, is gradually joined by the creation and implementation of steering structures. In such circumstance, the construction of norms is reached by making customary use in societies of constitutive traditions, some of them that further acquire a semantic content upon language and the sharing of fundamental symbolic expressions such as the idea of *justice*. The concept of *justice*, rather than having a de facto meaning, is made upon context and socialization. Both represent circumstances that on a governance level, attribute legitimacy to the institutional practice, while at the same time, suggest the inclusion of world perspectives otherwise disadvantaged or underrepresented on scenarios of unbalanced or asymmetric governance.

Secondly, In the case of the Bretton Woods institutions, my assumption is that such process acquires an institutional, rather than a democratic or dialogical content. This situation is explained by the existence of consistent asymmetries at the operational level of the institutions, further entrenched on executive committees, overall regulation, and the uneven distribution of burdens and benefits of political relations. I argue that such state of affairs is exemplified upon contractual approaches to international relations and politics, some of them increasingly contested in the recent years. Although the scope of this debate covers numerous theoretical positions, in accordance with the present research it fundamentally holds an origin on the contributions of contractual political science, carried out specially during the recent decades in the philosophical work of John Rawls and his "theory of justice". This construction, however, set loose and detached from other contributions supported on philosophy of law, communicative action theory (Habermas) or political economy (Amartya Sen). In short, this is because the increasing reconstruction of justice from an entirely institutional framework, neglects the role that context and communication hold as functional assemblies upon which such symbolic construction arise. On the case of the Bretton woods institutions, these phenomena carry a problematic consequence in view of the normative outcome of an idea of modern development, as well as the role of an institutional justice in legitimating political relations of a highly unbalanced international environment.

This chapter is divided into four parts. First, drawing from sociology and philosophy of law, it makes a descriptive account of a concept of justice built in the process of development of contemporary social systems. This part sets the background for the shift of this discursive construction upon the interventions of highly influential international organizations such as the Bretton Woods Institutions. Second, it stresses the tensions between the role of structures of governance that disjointed the legal validity of norms and their approach to fundamental symbolic construction such as the idea of justice. Third, it describes historically how the Bretton Woods Institutions, upon the idea of "modern development" addressed historically a legitimation of institutional justice that reveal highly conflicting consequences between core and periphery actors on a global level. The chapter argues that this situation, is due to the fact that such symbolic institutional production has been made upon conditions of strong political asymmetry, which in turn provides a narrow ground for agent contestation. Finally, the chapter depicts how the process of legitimation of institutional justice on a global level nurtured ideologically from theoretical approaches to contractual philosophy of law, derived most recently from the contributions of John Rawls.

1. History and the symbolic construction of justice in social systems

In the study of the process of construction of norms, it is necessary to stress the role that societies play in assuming cultural practices that are further typified into normative commonalities. While in contemporary social systems, norms have acquired meaning through processes of social interaction, in early stages of organization, they have been nurtured from symbolic constructions upon which individuals rationalize their role on an unexplored environment. With higher stages of coordination, societies tend to generate interaction upon such constructions, assigning meaning to phenomenon in the material world. From a local perspective, these sequences of events have been described from recent contributions on sociology where the role of language and communication has allowed the evolution of a theory of society upon which cognition, language, and interaction play a pivotal role.

On a global perspective, the contributions of constructivist international relations scholars have increasingly associated the early contributions on science to the study of institutions and the international system. In this fashion, they have been able to articulate how on a global level, symbolic and normative constructions endure over time upon processes of "intersubjective understanding[;] culture, identity, and other social features of political life" (Finnemore, 1996, p. 326). In recent decades, this line of research has provided the ground to explain how the same mechanisms settled the construction of fundamental symbolic expressions and social norms of nation states. Thereby, the production of domestic norms, and the further formalization within formal regulation of the modern nation state, has been the origin from which the development of a contemporary international society nurtures semantically. Likewise, this has been also the case of the idea of *justice*.

A customary explanation of the idea of justice as a symbolic construction of developing social systems, embraces by definition the notion of an "appropriate distributions of benefits and burdens over individuals" (Hockett, 2005, p. 96). In Hocket analysis, this means the inclusion into norms of a) variables that account what is fair according to a defined context; b)which kind of actors make part of such distributions of benefits and burdens; and c)the origin of the authority from which the distribution of burdens and benefits is determined[1] (Hockett, 2005, p. 96).

In the dilemma of societies to set standards to allocate benefits and burdens of social relations, practices of communication increase the self-awareness of individuals to rationalize the necessary variables to embrace this deliberatory practices. Upon such circumstance, communicative interaction sets the ground for the construction of constitutive symbolic expressions to manage the demands of customary collaboration. In the development of the definition of "just" arrangements, societies embrace the construction of utterances upon which the notion of justice acquire a sense of coherence, further legitimated by practices of socialization. This social feature holds truth even amidst diverse backgrounds and different levels of cognition, where some symbolic constructions of such principle remained equal even to social systems isolated from each other. This is why on modern contributions to sociology and linguistic "'[c]oncepts such as truth, rationality, and justification play the same role in every language community, even if they are interpreted differently and applied in accordance with different criteria'" (Johnson, 2008, p. 83).

In social structures therefore, language and cognition set the ground for the construction of a "thin" normativity in which early systems of values acquired a sense of *correctness* and *rightness* if coped with fundamental symbolic constructions of each social entity. In the ordinary practice of social organization, *justice* as a normative practice entails the assumption that the "norm" once discussed collectively, kept a sense of "truth". That is, it nurtures semantically and symbolically from early normative arrangements internalized along the process of development of social systems.

The practice of communication, and the increasing sophistication of linguistic constructions expressed through utterances, has been widely explored in the study of *values and beliefs* of social systems. In the creation of meaning, they enhanced the possibility of semantic analysis of sentences upon which persons interact in even higher levels of rationalization and formal institutionalization of normative practices. They can be considered as "descriptive sentences, which serve[d] to ascertain facts in the broadest sense(…); normative sentences (or ought-sentences), which serve to regulate actions, from the stand- point of the rightness (or *justice*) of a way of acting; evaluative sentences (or value judgments) (…) and explications, which serve to explain operations" (Habermas, 1984, p. 39).

The adoption of a *praxis of justice*, in each singular social context, unleashes the development of *value-standards* that allowed to social entities to avoid incurring in practices that violated their normative expectations; following patterns of distribution of burdens and benefits that cope their moral or ethical demands. With the assembly of formal structures of power, *value-standards* formed the principles by which individuals relate to each other on institutionalized forms of life. In sum, the translation of cultural constructions into structures of organization with local boundaries and similar claims to "truth" and "rightness".

The single most fundamental form of such evolution, takes place upon the constitution of regulatory frameworks that by making use of written law, define the boundaries of private and public relations. In the rationalization [modernization] of the diverse social spheres, these phenomena appeared together with the systematic erosion of figures of authority and mediation, and the emergence of personal instructed in the process of administration of "justice". As a matter of fact, in previous contributions of social science, this transition was legitimized discursively, attributing to such events a sense of legitimacy within the praxis of administration of justice. This is how classical approaches to sociology defend such transition as valid due to its "systematic" character. In such perspectives:

"Modern law is in a particularly high degree jurist law. With legally trained judges and officials, the administration of justice and public administration became professionalized. Not only the application of law but the enactment of law became increasingly bound to formal procedures and thereby to the

specialized mind of jurists. This situation promoted the systematization of legal propositions, the coherence of legal doctrine, that is to say, the rationalization of law according to internal, purely formal criteria of analytic conceptual structure, deductive rigor, principled explanation and justification, and the like"[2] *(Habermas, 1984, p. 256)* .

While the legitimacy of such transition is not a matter on discussion on the present section, it is worth to say that the translation from the social to the institutional realm didn't necessary represented the will of societies. This is why in many cases; law was signaled by a disturbing interaction with normative constructions, which in turn stressed the standardization upon the use of violence or "legal" coercion. On the other hand, on social analysis, these events have been characterized as an historical circumstance that emerged upon the influence of the Roman Law tradition, further entrenched into the modern positivist school of thinking. The adoption of such structures of administration however, spread from the local to the national level, composing the regulatory framework of administration of justice of the contemporary nation state.

From the contemporary nation state entity to the global realm, the shift of the administration of justice can be characterized as a phenomenon that took place upon two stages. On the one hand, the increasing levels of sophistication of public international law through the nation-state, which mayor historical cornerstone along the western world can be found in the Westphalia Treaty of 1648. Secondly, The Versailles Peace Conference that took place in Vienna after the end of the First World War, and the constitution of the League of Nations. As Thompson and Snidal have described this event;

"Under Article 16 of the League Covenant, all member states were required to come to the aid of a member that was the victim of military aggression. The League was overwhelmingly concerned with fostering peace, though economic and social issues did receive secondary attention. The Covenant further established the Permanent Court of International Justice, the first attempt to create a global forum of justice and predecessor to today's International Court of Justice" (Thompson & Snidal, 2013, p. 695).

From an historical view, both evolutionary stages determined the structures upon which the formalization of institutional justice departed from the national, to the international level. On the one hand, the constitution of the modern nation-state highlighted the configuration of a formal structure subject of international responsibilities and rights under the rule of law. Secondly, the apparently unfruitful creation of the League of Nations with the establishment of the Permanent Court of International Justice (1922), set the ground for the constitution of global regulatory bodies conceived to administer power and political relation globally. In this manner, normative expectation of social systems, were discreetly transposed into a global realm, to an organization with a defined international regulatory framework. With the disappearance of the Permanent Court of Justice, its functions were adopted by the contemporary International Court of Justice, established in June 1945 by the Charter of the United Nations. It was however just until 1946 when this functional shift of the international system took effect.

The existence of formal structures of administration of justice, however effective they may be, is not guaranty of the existence of *justice* in social affairs. From a systemic perspective, the transposition of systems of values and normative guidelines in law -and further into formal structures such as courts or international organizations-, just allowed the articulation of fundamental political spheres along the production of specialized regulation. This is how such institutional shift, rather than clear overall normative expectations, represented the articulation of functional spheres of social systems that endorsed mechanisms of coordination upon the compliance of a specialized regulatory framework (such as private or administrative law, human rights or humanitarian law, and criminal law among others). Justice consequently, as a symbolic construction of the global realm embodied along international structures of mediation and a written common law, acquired a functional[3] (Chimni, 2006, p. 212) rather than a deontological category. This is why from a constructivist perspective, Institutions such as the International Court of Justice, adhered *political efficiency* to the realm of interaction of a global level, though its legitimacy, scope or the validity of their decisions, can be subject to strong criticism. As Wiener puts it:

"Political efficiency, justice and security require generally accepted norms, rules and principles. The challenge for achieving the highest possible degree of general acceptance increases with the absence of formal government structures. After all, in contexts beyond the state norm acceptance and, more specifically, compliance with norms depend more decisively on the shared recognition of norms <u>than on their formal validity</u>*" (Wiener & Pueter, 2009, p. 4).*

As such, at the point in which member states of the organizations recognize justice as a composite of institutional arrangement, it's definition represented a shared believe or moreover an ethical construction internalized into the norm of social development legitimized by defined organizations on the international arena.

2. The tensions between law and global justice

In contemporary research on international relations, the events that determined the development of the idea of justice to an institutional level, are frequently a reason for controversy. This is because, on a highly asymmetric global environment, the demands for recognition of local normative constructions into the global realm are regularly isolated according to the regulatory framework of international organizations. In such circumstance, the idea of global justice is contested on a regular basis. This can be explained by the fact that, as a normative construction, it can be confined to a biased narrative that limits their own capacity of fulfilling legitimate expectations of the global society. As such, on a global asymmetric environment, it can represent a symbolic construction unable to cope genuine claims[4] (Chimni, 2006, p. 214). for recognition, redistribution of burdens or representation of periphery members of a highly unbalanced global order.

From a sociological perspective, the political character of an organization is not compulsory given by it foundational regulation. This reason holds true for the case of international institutions, which with the process of societal rationalization of contemporary societies, aimed to apply to a supranational level, the scope of local bureaucracy and the goal of administration via legal institutions. In modern social systems, this process took place upon overlapped stages of regulatory sophistication, that built robust structures of governance by normativity further embodied into law. At any stage of maturation of law as a social phenomenon, this character of norms tends to acquire a sense of legitimacy supported by formal structures of power –such as international institutions-. This condition however, stresses the antagonistic character of law with social claims for legitimacy, a phenomenon highly studies by Habermas contributions on philosophy of law. In his own words:

In the legal mode of validity, the facticity of the enforcement of law is intertwined with the legitimacy of a genesis of law that claims to be rational because it guarantees liberty. The tension between these two distinct moments of facticity and validity is thus intensified and behaviorally operationalized (Habermas, 1996, p. 28).

This explains why in that same theoretical approach -as well as in political science and international relations-, claims for legality of law are increasingly prone to be contested upon demands for its inherent legitimacy. In essence, the internal conjunction between these two phenomena [legality and legitimacy], are up to now a matter of concern in the scrutiny of the validity of normative and institutional constructions. This demand is further articulated with a paradox that can even go back to the very use of language and communication, and can be exemplified as the tension between normative expectations and formal structures of governance. While social systems evolve functionally through socialization and interaction upon subjective world perspectives and knowledge, their normative constitutive traditions remain equal due to their ontological character. In this regard, while the idea of justice can be extensively differentiated from strictly semantic perspectives assigned to subjects (individual-state-organizations-figures of authority), it´s ultimate validation remains in the realm of reason and the capacity of being openly contested by those to whom the norm is exerted upon. This last statement has one fundamental attribution, it means that the legitimacy of the notion of justice, responds to a collective dialogical construction, and thus, it can only be draw upon the active practice of socialization and communicative interaction.

Following this approach, it is possible to say that calls for a sense of justice as a social construction, indicate nothing more than the appeals of societies for the existence of regulatory legitimacy. This explains why the sociological force and origin of modern law -which in according to Habermas "steps in to fill the functional gaps in social orders whose integrative capacity are overtaxed" (Habermas, 1996, p. 42) cannot attend the claims for justice that arouse spontaneously in social entities in which a broad part of their inherent contradictions, are steered with de facto structures of power[5].

From a global perspective, this singularity acquires a functional and political (ideological) differentiation. Functionally, with more complex variables to deal with[6]; international institutions steer less categories of interaction, with a lower intensity than that attributed to nation state structures. Moreover, global structures of governance operate making use of few mechanisms of coercive power, a situation that warns their tragic nature when demanding increasing international law adherence. Moreover, from a strictly political perspective, this problem stresses the conflicting character of modern law, which upon practice and recognition has become a normative construction that legitimate asymmetric relations of power, and the maintenance of highly undemocratic institutions of global governance.

The legal mode of justice, which performs a functional role in the modern social system, is explained sociologically as an outcome of the evolutionary demands of social integration, colonized increasingly by money and administrative power. This justification however, triggers the potential of philosophy, to pursue an alternative line of discussion which has been embraced in contemporary contributions on philosophy of law. The main argument is that previous sociological approaches ignored the fact that the institutional dimension of social systems, cannot be addressed from the outset, therefore, cannot be grasped as an historical reconstruction of processes of rationalization (Weber), nor as a functional contractual agreement of social systems (Rawls). On the one hand, Weber approach takes to a higher level the fact that symbolic constructions further converted into normative patterns, can be always redeemed by accounting how they emerge into defined settings and typical situations. Finally, if such subjective character is disjointed from the justificatory legacy from which institutions nurtured symbolically, they fall as empty constructions of societies, and therefore cannot be considered as an outcome of the rationalization of the social sphere.

In according to Habermas; "By confining the reconstruction of meaning and validity within the narrow disciplinary boundaries of legal doctrine, Weber emphasizes the contrast between those two methodological perspectives. By virtue of this feature (i.e., the legal and the sociological) (…) legal orders are "legitimate orders" that, "although certainly not fitting ideas seamlessly together with interests, do interpret interests through ideas, thereby making reasons and validity claims factually effective" (Habermas, 1996, p. 70). While the difficulties of Rawls contractual approach are to be discussed in the following part of this chapter, it is worth to say, that his view in embedded in a cultural character attached to an idea of constitutionalism in which the concept of "fairness" is openly embraced. On the other hand, it entails a transition from technocratic approaches to social systems to a "normative self-understanding of constitutional democracy"[7] (Habermas, 1996) . By its nature, this represent a problematic approach, due to its potential capacity to excuse social pathologies that emerge on highly asymmetric environments.

In recent decades, the institutionalization of the idea of justice upon a formal institutional narrative has acquired a normative dimension, embraced discursively by influential international organizations such as the World Bank, or the International Monetary Fund. While at the level of the state, claims for legitimacy are frequently steered or tamed by administrative dependencies via redistributive measures, a formal structure of legal violence, or check and balances of liberal "democracies"[8], on a global level, this same claims fall into isolated and highly asymmetric administrative and executive boards. At the level of the Bretton Woods Institutions, this situation carries also the adoption of defined practices in fundamental spheres of international, further internalized and rationalized in the symbolic construction of the norm of "modern development". In an attempt to describe the consequences of such norm, and the rationalization of the institutional approach to justice at the Bretton Woods Institutions, the next section includes a briefly historical approach to such historical phenomena, followed by an exploration of the effects of this normative category.

3. The Bretton Woods institutions and the notion of regulation as justice.

The Bretton Woods conference, that took place at the end of the Second World War, exemplified the most ambitious attempt to transfer the regulatory nature of national structures of governance to a global level. In the limitations of managing a transition from the pre to the post war period, the urgency of the situation made possible the junction of political motivations and interests of representatives to agree in the construction of a global regulatory framework directed to steer selected social spheres of late modern societies. Over the scope for regulatory measures, the institutions were built upon the idea of increasing global coordination on monetary, financial and trade policy. At the time, the limitations of the nation-state in steering the increasing interaction and dependency of global markets, enabled the disarticulation of law into functional spheres upon which justice was to be administered according to framed guiding rationalities[9] (Finnemore, 1996, p. 1006). Therefore, the idea of establishing a global structure of governance appeared as a coherent step in the process of expansion of the productive global enterprise, slightly regulated in accordance with the principles of economic liberalism.

The institutional architecture of the Bretton Woods Institutions was conceived following the guidelines of western core economies. After the Second World War, there were arguably two fundamental political necessities that justified the constitution of the organizations. On the one hand the demands from Europe to recover from the consequences of the war, secondly, the necessity of global economic actors to adopt a common monetary, financial and economic regulatory framework for reestablishing international trade. While discursively, the institutions were announced as a new step in the Universalist project of global governance, their executive and administrative boards remained bounded to the interests, participation and representation of a limited group of countries, selected upon their position in the global economy or their role during the war. Moreover, during the second half of the 20th century, the level of legitimation of the institutions was consistently "overshadow" by the cold war and the opposite interests of core and periphery economies (Thompson & Snidal, 2013, p. 697).

In the limitations to cope the natural demands for legitimation of a highly uneven global environment, the appeals for impartiality at the Bretton Woods institutions were steered upon their level of influence in articulating a robust narrative of justice along the normative construction of development. The asymmetric representation, voting power and influence of the signatories of the agreement however, problematized attempts to discuss both the legal, as well as the more "democratic" procedures inside both the World Bank and the International Monetary Fund. Amidst the increasing distrust of capital importing countries in setting balanced conditions for the signatories, the final legal framework for participation excluded demands of low income territories. Thereby, this decision was further implemented along three operational practices; 1)regulatory settings that discouraged periphery economies to demand sanctions on influential countries, 2)the conservation of unbalanced representative bodies and a 3)systemic defined narrative on "institutional justice".

1) The limitations and pressures of periphery economies to impose economic or regulatory sanction against unfair practices of highly influential economic nodes, led to a systemic acceptance of political relations determined by power and money. With the robust tendency of the market to isolate social systems incapable of coping global demands for competitiveness a production –most of them under highly imbalanced conditions-, capital importing countries found themselves in the compulsory path of withstanding the blows of a global economy led by highly industrialized structures of production, while at the same time, improving their productive, institutional, political and cultural architecture. Although historically this phenomenon remained situated upon the geographical and political boundaries of the nation state, since the 70´s; it experienced a new geo-reallocation. In fact, within this decade the increasing levels of the global monetary base enhanced by the crash of the Bretton Woods convertibility system, boosted up the international money supply. These phenomena eased up the investment on former isolated territories, and reconfigured gradually the burdens and benefits of the global economy. Finally, this change was characterized by the annexation of new countries in the process of global production, while levels of global inequality between capital importing and capital exporting nodes increased sharply.

The necessities of capital importing nodes to approve the conditions of investment of financial capital, led to a gradually acceptance of the structure of distribution of the market as "fair". As such, this problematic interaction was considered for the organization as a "just" contractual relation, as far as it enhanced commercial relations between market suppliers and the communities in "need" of increasing its horizon of consumption of goods and services (Moore, 1985).

With the increasing levels of inequality, the operational *hinges* that maintained such state of affairs as "just" revealed itself as highly conflictive. However, the systematic relations of dependency of the system between capital exporting nodes and global south agents, maintained the conditions established upon the regulatory framework of the Bretton Woods Institutions as "fair"[10]. In essence, the erosion of the capacity of the nation state to control the functional gaps coped by economic relations, boosted up the capability of private actors to take the lead in defining the conditions upon which investment was granted in areas on need. Since in the current global architecture, there are no other institutions to guarantee trade relations under symmetric distribution of burdens and benefits, and numerous nation states lack the capacity of steering trade or exchange relations ruled by private law, depredatory activities became a customary practice (Chang, 2002).

2) From an institutional level, the idea of justice was granted by a discursive practice that even under conditions of highly unbalanced participative and executive boards, was presented as functional according to the regulatory framework and the routinary practices of the institutions. While demands for modifications of the voting structure, or for inclusion of isolated countries in the executive bodies remained, the distribution of administrative, political or legislative positions at the institutions perpetuated structurally and institutionally (Barro, 2005) .

Furthermore, overrepresentation of influential agents, boosted up the maintenance of power relations that frequently entailed benefits in terms of loans, treatment, information, position, voice and adaptation of representatives of core economies (Cha & Lee, 2010 B) (Cha & Lee, 2010 A). Since the constitution of the Bretton Woods institutions, the customary publication of the executive boards consistently addressed the problem of representation as a challenge for increasing the levels of democratic practices at the organizations. At the institutional and academic discussion however, is frequently ignored the fact that the voting structures of the institutions, and the distribution of positions in the administrative dependencies, doesn't just favor disproportionately the interests of core economies, but at the same time, operationalizes an institutional construction of "justice" upon which perspectives of periphery actors are frequently put off the table. Upon such circumstances, the very normative construction of modern development endorsed by official publication such as the World Bank Development Report, adhere to a notion of development in which customary conditions of political asymmetry at the institutions are transplanted from the institutional to the social realm. Such settings indeed, create the idea, that overrepresentation of overpowered of highly industrialized actors at the institutions, while not "just", are "fair" according to the customary institutional practice and political demands.

3) Finally, the maintenance of conditions of justice under highly asymmetric political relations of members, is preserved by the production of an institutional narrative upon which practices of the institutions are legitimized in the normative construction of "modern development". Modernity, among other attributes, holds for the World Bank and the International Monetary Fund the capacity of societies and national structures of governance to overcome the demands of a global economic environment. Upon this principle, the structural arrangements endured by peripheral societies are not only part of the necessity of the global economy to achieve economic growth, but more over, "modern economic growth"[11] (World Bank, 1978). In such perspective, policies on fertility reduction[12] (World Bank, 1984, p. 8), the enhancements of processes of massive migration of population from rural to urban areas[13] (World Bank, 1984, p. 60), education according to wage market demands[14] (World Bank, 1984, p. 89) and penetration of "efficient financial systems" for "market-based decision-making" (World Bank - FS, 1989), hold a sense of coherence with an official narrative to be imposed in areas isolated from the central structure of capital. As such, in the limitations of ensuring mechanisms of balanced interaction, the Bretton Woods Institutions transposed the deliberative dilemma of "justice praxis" into the sphere of a formal institution[15] (World Bank, 2011, p. XVI). This shift is characterized by the articulation of ideology with regu-

latory and operative systems that have barely being modified during the last seven decades. With the sophistication and increasing interdependence of global economic interaction, this functional structure provided a mixture of unbalance but robust economic growth that gradually strengthened relations of dependence between capital exporting and capital importing nodes, and an increasing level of submission of the nation-state to the global economic order.

In the sphere of commercial relations between countries, this features of the norm of development acquired the form of a discourse on liberalization, that rather than restoring the role of a deliberative field, ensured the acceptance of an equal treatment upon highly unequal social, economic and political nodes. This feature boosted up the appearance of double standards in which highly industrialized countries, with extensively capital backed production apparatuses, occupied dominantly the sphere of trade[16] (Frericks et.al., 2009). Thereby, the asymmetries revealed upon the regulatory framework of the institutions, were further boosted up by the idea that social tension aroused due conditions of scarcity, are to be steered in the long term by the increasing levels of global production. In practice however, this assumption falls short in explaining the strong correlations of the system between wealth and preferentialism[17] of core players by the current economic and commercial regulation (Cha & Lee, 2010 B) (Cha & Lee, 2010 A). By definition, the singularity of this phenomena led to the reconfiguration of the discourse of justice on an economic narrative. In this narrative, indebtedness (Spanu, 2003) of scarce capital countries, is presented as a consequence of failed fiscal policy or public administration measures, thus, asymmetric burdens of the system are warranted for the decades to come.

The administrative role of national normative regulatory bodies is transposed into a global scope upon the assumption of the limitations of establishing global structures of normative law. This event represents a phenomena of fragmentation of law between normative and "cognitive expectations" regulation. This assumption[18] (Teubner & Fischer-Lescano, kein Datum) is supported by the contributions of Teubner & Liscano, who drawing upon classical contributions on system theory suggest that from a social theory perspective:

Such problems are caused by the fragmented and operationally closed functional systems of a global society, which, in their expansionist fervor, create the real problems of the global society, and who at the same time make use of global law in order normatively to secure their own highly refined sphere logics (Teubner & Fischer-Lescano, kein Datum, p. 1007)

In practice, such shift represents the limitations of addressing on a global sphere the same regulatory measures to steer social relations that can be taken on the realm of the nation state. This idea of institutional "Justice" thus, operate upon defined epistemic communities and disjointed jurisprudence that overlap between nations in according to a global regulative framework. At the level of the Bretton Woods Institutions, the regulative function is acquired in line with the conditions established in the *World Trade Organization Dispute Settlements Mechanisms*, whose function is to provide a global trade regime regulation. The scheme however, allows the reproduction of power relations that stem from a highly asymmetric economic and political environment, upon which high financial and legal resource costs, legal provisions and pressure from the participatory and executive bodies of the World Trade Organization, fractures the final outcomes of the disputes settled. Even when peripheral economies are favored by sanctions, their enforcement capabilities are frequently limited. In turn, sanctions favoring global south economies can eventually lead the country to absorb retaliations from core countries. As it has been highly documented:

Though the DSU provisions are not biased literally, developing countries are not able to fully take advantage of the DSM in practice, even if certain provisions are supposed to favor them in principle. Since they do not have adequate financial and legal expertise resources, they can hardly bear the high costs of settling disputes through the DSM. Because of the unevenness of political power between developed states and developing countries, the latter group is in a disadvantageous position in the DSM given the political pressures they may suffer outside the WTO. The developing countries' lower status is also due to their inadequate capability to enforce the dispute settlement results, even if the outcomes are favorable to them (Khan, 2008).

With the reproduction of legal and political gaps that inhabit the regulatory settings of the Bretton Woods Institutions, "Justice" therefore is frequently presented not as politically biased, but as "institutionally inadequate". The global undisputed authority of the institutions that arouse from asymmetric agents however, is transposed into the universalization of a norm of development that signatories should commit themselves to comply with. This behavior is stressed as to ensure foreseeable consequences, and thus, "confidence" about the evolution of trade and economic affairs. On the other hand, the settlement of international disputes in accordance with the arrangements established by the WTO, confers a constitutional character to the resolution of trade disagreements upon a common normative framework. As Anne Peters puts it;

The constitutionalization of international law has been lopsided. The process has so far been adjudicative rather than deliberative. This is most visible in the WTO and the related microconstitutionalization debate. What has been identified by some scholars as constitutionalization of the WTO boils down to the legalization of the dispute settlement mechanism, judge-made principles, and constitutional techniques applied by the panels and the Appellate Body. The WTO's capacity for legislative response is muted by the unanimity requirement (Peters, 2009, p. 408)(Peters, 2011).

This aspect of international law, which is configured upon the Dispute Settlements mechanism, addresses only a limited sphere of social relations, isolating human rights concerns into world trade law. This critique, inspired fundamentally in *rights based* constitutionalism, puts back into relevance the role of legitimacy in the constitutional arena (Peters, 2011, p. 77). Furthermore, in philosophy of law, this dispute has been addressed as the structural limitations of a global regime not accountable, with essential democratic flaws. In this regard, "justice" as a principle embraced in the ideal of equality, became rather a problematic category in the effort of embracing it as a cornerstone for "development"[19]. Later on, these values are to play a key role when incorporated on institutions meant to rationalized and steer relations in highly complex social systems. Indeed, the weak "democratization" of international organizations such as the Bretton Woods Institution (Peters, 2011, p. 78), play a contradictory role in the constitutional process upon which via participation, organizations aim to attribute to policy outcomes a sense of legitimacy fulfilling social appeals for justice.

At present, even favoring periphery countries after a settle dispute, the political restrictions of the mechanisms of the WTO brings these countries to a situation upon which they need to adopt measures that threaten domestic arrangements for post contractual justice (democratic). This single event can happen when economic policies that tend to favor strategic sectors of highly industrialized countries are penalized, further carrying consequences to small economies in necessity to cope internal demand. At the same time, these effects take place when core economies don´t agree in lifting the protectionist measures of their own agricultural industries, further unleashing retaliatory policies on peripheral economies and making the dispute settlement mechanism riskier than submission (Rodrik, 2001) (Rodrick, 2002). Indeed, the unenforceability of obligations -supposedly to be carried voluntarily by highly industrialized countries-, boost up the asymmetries between the core and the periphery. This is explained by the fact that since while the agreements cover both kind of actors, the practice of enforceability can be exerted just upon "developing" areas[20] (Wade, 2003, p. 625) (Chimni, 2006).

In an attempt to articulate a narrative of institutional justice upon the functional limitations of an asymmetric global environment, the notion of justice is at the level of the Bretton Woods institutions disjointed from its global context and articulated into the realm of the nation state. This shift is characterized particularly with the use of the term *justice* as a composite of economic growth, transforming it in to an institutional category of local governance. Among the official publications of the Bretton Woods Institutions, the World Development Report highlights the predominant official record in which the concept of justice is addressed as a composite of modern development. In the narrative, the idea of "justice" becomes a functional composite of local governance, in line with other cost-effective priorities such as jobs[21] (World Bank, 2011, p. 145), competitiveness and overall economic growth. On an international perspective, the attempts to address the role of justice as a normative category, falls frequently into appreciations about the need to improve current mechanisms of distribution of roles and responsibilities of a highly inequitable political and economic global system, thus replicating consistent inequality in the treatment of actors[22] (Milanovic, 2009) (Sutcliffe, 2004) (IPCC/07, 2007) (United Nations Conference on Trade and Development, 2010, p. VI).

While the discussion over equal representation at the executive boards of the International Monetary Fund, the World Bank and the World Trade Organization, remain isolated from the institutional record, the unbalanced levels of bargaining and voting power are historically (Mikesell, 1994) and systematically (Eichengreen, 2004) (Eichengreen, 2008) (Leech, 2004) reinforced upon the governance system of the Institutions. In this fashion, the notion of *justice* as an outcome constructed upon participative or deliberative mechanisms, is entangled into highly undemocratic procedures that favor voting power of core participants both in the World Bank as well as in the IMF. This state of affairs has historically been maintained by the internal procedures defined to grant votes and shares[23]. They have been during the recent decades consistently denounced as "bizarre", by structural weaknesses, resulting in "a severe democratic imbalance with the distribution of voting power being massively biased against "developing" and poor countries". Furthermore, this "dominance by the industrialized countries has been criticized" for "leading the organization to adopt policies that have taken insufficient notice of the interests of" already broken economies (Leech, 2012).

4. Modern development and the contractual construction of Justice. (RAWLS)

While nowadays exist broad disagreement about the extent to which global redistributive measures should be implanted, at the Bretton Woods Institutions this discussion is rarely taken into account, or openly ignored. In the recent decades, this political opinion has been stressed even more upon two main circumstances. On the one hand, the increasing levels of reallocation of capital have diminished the role of the nation state as a legitimate representative of social interests in the political arena. This is because former inequalities between countries have been transplanted in inequalities between populations around the world[24]. Moreover, in many cases the interests of national representatives are more aligned with the interests of highly influential economic actors, rather than populations. This situation has reduced the levels of pressure of representatives of nation states to address at the executive boards of the Bretton Woods Institutions, modifications to contemporary regulation on trade. Indeed, the reallocation of capital in nodes of production and investment, since the 70´s, is not more configured in capital exporting and capital importing countries, but in nodes of investment, and nodes of dependency for investment. On the process of increasing profitability, representatives of nation states frequently ignore demands of periphery populations, since many of the arrangements of the international free trade system, doesn´t any more affect elites of periphery countries as during the past decades. Secondly, because in recent decades, contributions on philosophy and politics -mainly from the American school of political science-, have increasingly influenced the ideological construction of the idea of justice as "fairness", rather than as a category of equality or democratic social arrangements. This discursive practice, inspired in the contributions of contractualism, technocracy, and misrepresentations of German libertarianism, has been in recent decades endorsed systematically as an ideological provision to maintain practices that benefit extensively the preservation of rights and privileges of capital exporting nodes.

CONTRACTUALISM AND RAWLSIAN JUSTICE

In an attempt to renew the debate about the idea of justice on philosophy, during the 70s, John Rawls presented an alternative approach to the "classical utilitarian and intuitionist" conception. His theory fundamentally rested upon two principles and one fundamental assumption. For Rawls, in a social system; 1) "each person is to have an equal right to the most extensive basic liberty compatible with a similar liberty for others", and "social and economic inequalities are to be arranged so that they are both a) reasonably expected to be to everyone's advantage, and b) attached to positions and offices open to all (Rawls, 1971, p. 11)". This proposition come into being with the assumption that in society, each member must accept that before being part of the social system, ignoring his origin, and, hence, covered with a "veil of ignorance" that should accept to favor such social contract.

On a global level, this discursive construction of justice is addressed by international institutions that rather to favor democratic or participative conceptions of the idea of justice, favor efficient or post contractual (institutional) approaches to the concept. The reason by which the approach acquires an outstanding dimension in positivist academia, is because it favors the existence of contemporary relations of dependency and asymmetries. As such, the ideology endorses to the idea that formal arrangements of asymmetric power within institutions is an unalterable condition of today's contractual global agreement, and in essence; a natural setting of social systems. Accordingly, the fulfillment of the desires of individuals comes not from the capacity of those individuals to achieve them, but rather from the capacity of those individuals to accept that given a set of defined conditions of their society, his efforts can reach reasonable enough results according to their context of origin. The idea of reasonability, is given by the fact that in contemporary social systems, historical arrangements that distribute unequally opportunities, responsibilities and privileges are institutionally warranted. In such context, the idea of "justice as fairness", rather than entering into the discussion concerning scenarios for redistribution of privileges or reallocation of factors, support the maintenance of such measures as a given condition of late modern social systems, customarily ignoring the real demands of people who are to be part of the social contract. In such circumstance, what is "fair" may not necessarily always favor what is equal or proportionate, but simply what is possible for an actor within a structure without disadvantaging others. For this situation to work, it is required that each one of the members of the social contract accept and ignore the position they will occupy in a post contractual sphere. If each one of the members of the social contract ignores the role they will occupy in a highly asymmetric post contractual environment, and if none of them is capable to favor one position rather than other, each one of them may find reasonable to participate in the natural process of societies to assign a role. Since none of them can define their role on a pre-contractual stage, all of them agree in the role they will acquire in the post contractual stage. As a consequence, all of them assume the arrangement not as ideal, but as "fair". Such "veil of ignorance"[25] guaranty that further reflections about the impartiality of an action, don't account the pre contractual arrangements of the system, but the post contractual possibilities of each one of the members of the social system to achieve their wishes "freely", without affecting the whishes or the "liberty" of others. In such circumstance, the actions of the individuals are just directed to achieve their own goals according to their given conditions, rather to set new conditions prone to modify the circumstances or the arrangements in which they agree to participate during the pre-contractual stage.

When it comes to the idea of global justice, the institutional approach implies fundamentally two problematic conceptions. On the one hand, the idea of a "veil of ignorance" contradicts the right of each country to demand, or to suggest that rather than a contractual agreement, global arrangements were aroused upon historical circumstances that benefited extensively a selected groups of actors with higher "social goods". Moreover, allocation of social goods in a global as well as in a local level, under market conditions, entailed the maintenance and enforcement of relations of political asymmetry in the system, therefore, and increasingly unequal redistribution of benefits and burdens. Secondly, on a global level, the limitation of any contractual agreement rather than that established upon the conditions of the free market economy, frequently suggest that rights of redistributive justice are determined by the setting of the market. Till now, both ethical consideration besides the contractual approach of justice are out of the table for the World Bank and the International Monetary Fund. Moreover, during the recent decades, the processes of maturation of both institutions have internalized the progression of normative global "development" to a point in which further discussions concerning the voting power or influence of the actors within the organizations are considered as trivial, or simply ignored along grey literature of the executive boards. As a consequence, any further attempt to problematize functional settings of the ethical dimension of the international system, is eroded systematically in absent of a transnational body directed to steer the asymmetric allocation of privileges and burdens of the political architecture of both the IMF as well as the World Bank.

CONCLUSION

Following previous contributions on the cognitive sphere of the norm of "modern development", this chapter draws pivotal assumptions to understand it from the normative construction of justice as contractualism or fairness. The chapter particularly draws conclusions on the role international organizations such as the World Bank and the International Monetary Fund had in addressing an institutional approach to justice that evolved functionally over the economic and political scope of the nation state. On the one hand, the chapter has depicted extensively how the institutionalization of justice acquired a functional dimension on the process of development of late modern social systems. This process has been exerted by the increasing spheres of influence of the state over the life spheres of societies, and has been particularly boosted up by positivism and contractualist theories. Secondly, in late modernity, the chapter stresses how such process took place along the debate between legitimacy and the legal validity of normative constructions, and its relation with the norm of modern development. For highlighting this character of the system, the chapter has described how such historical shift took place along the institutional role of the Bretton Woods Institutions, and how it has been permeated by historical settings of political asymmetry along these institutions. Finally, the chapter has explained how much recently the legitimation of such representation of the idea of justice has acquired even more deeper roots by drawing on modern contractual philosophy of law. By depicting the concept of Institutional Justice, the goal of the chapter is to shed lights on the ideological dimension of the norm of modern development at the Bretton Woods Institutions, and the transposition of rather conflicting arrangements in the normative production of a defined ethical dimension of the international system. As expected, the chapter addresses such endeavor by contributing to the analysis of the meaning of institutional or contractual justice is late modern societies, and the way, during the recent decades, it has *colonized* the informational sphere of contemporary global south nation-states.

REFERENCES

Barro, R. J. (2005). *IMF Programs: Who Is Chosen and What Are the Effects?* Department of Economics, Harvard University. Department of Economics, Korea University. April.

Cha, M.-Y., & Lee, J. W. (2010). Patterns of International Trade and a Nation's Wealth. *Policies and Institutions for Economic Development in Historical Perspective, ISBN-10*, 1843310279.

Cha & Lee. (2010). Patterns of International Trade and a Nation's Wealth. Department of Physics, Inha University.

Chimni, B. (2006). *A just world under law: A view from the south.* American Society of International Law.

Eichengreen, B. (2004). Global Imbalances and the Lessons from Bretton Woods. *National Bureau of Economic Research.*

Eichengreen, B. (2008). *Globalizing Capital:A History of the International Monetary System* (2nd ed.). Princeton University Press. doi:10.2307/j.ctt7pfmc

Finnemore, M. (1996). Norms,culture, and world politics: insights from sociology's institutionalism. *Intemational Organization 50.*

Frericks, P. (2009). Toward a Neoliberal Europe?: Pension Reforms and Transformed. *Administration & Society.* doi:10.1177/0095399708328874

Habermas, J. (1984). The Theory of Communicative Action: Vol. 1. *Reason and the Rationalization of Society* (T. McCarthy, Trans.). Beacon Press.

Habermas, J. (1996). *Habermas Jürgen. Between Facts and Norms. Contributions to a Discourse Theory of Law and Democracy.* Massachusetts Institute of Technology. doi:10.7551/mitpress/1564.001.0001

Hockett, R. (2005). Three (potential) pillars of transnational economic justice: The Bretton Woods institutions as guarantors of global equal treatment and market completion. *Metaphilosophy, 36,* 93-127.

IPCC/07. (2007). *Synthesis Report. An Assessment of the Intergovernmental Panel on Climate Change.* IPCC Plenary XXVII, Valencia, Spain.

Johnson, P. (2008, February). Globalizing Democracy. Reflections on Habermas's Radicalism. *European Journal of Social Theory, 11*(1), 71–86. doi:10.1177/1368431007085288

Khan, H. (2008). *Globalization and the WTO Dispute Settlement Mechanism: Making a Rules-based Trading Regime Work.* (MPRA Paper 7613). University Library of Munich, Germany.

Leech, D. (2004). Voting Power and Voting Blocs. *The Warwick Economics Research Paper Series (TWERPS) 716.* University of Warwick, Department of Economics.

Leech, D. L. R. (2012). A New Analysis of A Priori Voting Power in the IMF: Recent Quota Reforms Give Little Cause for Celebration. WARWICK ECONOMIC RESEARCH PAPERS. No 1001. The University of Warwick.

Mikesell, R. F. (1994). The Bretton Woods debates. A memoir. Essays in International Finance, 192, 76.

Milanovic, B. (2009). *Global inequality and global inequality extraction ratio: The story of the last two centuries.* World Bank. https://mpra.ub.uni-muenchen.de/16535/

Moore, B. (1985). Authority and Inequality under Capitalism and Socialism. Oxford Press.

Peters, A. (2009). The merits of Global Constitutionalism. [©Indiana University Maurer School of Law — Bloomington.]. *Indiana Journal of Global Legal Studies, 16*(2), 397–411.

Peters, A. A. K. M. K. (2011). The Constitutionalisation of International Trade Law. *The Prospects Of International Trade Regulation: From Fragmentation To Coherence,* (pp. 69-102). Cambridge University Press.

Rawls, J. (1971). *A Theory of Justice.* Harvard University Press.

Rodrick, D. (2002). *Feasible Globalizations.* (NBER Working Paper No. 9129). NBER.

Rodrik, D. (2001). *The Global governance of Trade. As if development really mattered. United Nations Development Programm. Social Development Group.* Bureau for Development Policy.

Spanu, V. (2003). Liberalization of the international trade and economic growth: implications for both developed and developing countries. Harvard Press.

Sutcliffe, B. (2004). World Inequality and Globalization. Oxford Review of Economic Policy, 20. Oxford University Press. doi:10.1093/oxrep/grh002.

Teubner, G. & Fischer-Lescano, A. (2004). Regime-Collisions: The Vain Search for Legal Unity in the Fragmentation of Global Law. *Michigan Journal of International Law, 25*(4), 999-1046.

Thompson, A., & Snidal, D. (2013). International Organization. 9800. University of Chicago. In B. Bouckaert & G. DeGeest (Eds.), *Encyclopedia of Law and Economics* (pp. 692–722). https://encyclo.findlaw.com/9800book.pdf

United Nations Conference on Trade and Development. (2010). *The Least Developed Countries Report, Embargo Copy Edition*. UN.

Wade, R. H. (2003). *The World Trade Organization and the schrinking of the development space.* (Working Paper No.31). London School of Economics.

Wiener & Pueter. (2009). The quality of Norms is what actors make of it. Critical constructivism research on norms. *Journal of International Law and International Relations, 5*(1).

World Bank – FS. (1989). Report Presentation. *Financial systems and development: an overview*. World Bank.

World Bank. (1978). *World Development Report.* World Bank.

World Bank. (1984). *World Development Report.* World Bank.

World Bank. (2011). *World Development Report.* World Bank.

ENDNOTES

1 Justice concerns "an account of what shall count for purposes of justice as relevant benefits or burdens (…), of the individuals whose benefits and burdens will concern justice. And (…) about how we are to determine the propriety of the distribution". (Hockett, 2005, p. 96)

2 In Habermas. T of Communicative Action. S, 256. (Habermas, 1984, p. 256)

3 "the creation of a "just world" is not the task of international law at all and that its role should be confined to simply ensuring a "world under law." (Chimni, 2006, p. 212)

4 "Following Nancy Fraser, (…) there are three kinds of legitimate claims that constitute the idea of global justice which can help establish a global law of welfare in the matrix of international human rights law. (…)claims for redistribution,(…)recognition, and claims for representation". In (Chimni, 2006, p. 214).

5 Money, administrative positions, social stratification, asymmetries of information, and so on.

6 Such as culture, language, geographical extension or population.

7 From Rehg William. S, xxi. In (Habermas, 1996)

8 Such as the distinction between the judiciary, executive and legislative branch.

9 In according to Teubner, the "process [was] not confined to markets alone but also encompasse[d] science, culture, technology, health, the military, transport, tourism and sport, as well as, albeit in a clearly somewhat retarded form, politics, law and welfare; each of whose current developmental logic has today carved out an autonomous global system". (Finnemore, 1996, p. 1006)

10 A position clearly adopted from periphery actors to avoid flows of capital.

11 Robert McNamara in (World Bank, 1978)

12 WDR. 1984. S, 8. (World Bank, 1984, p. 8)

13 WDR. 1984. S, 60. (World Bank, 1984, p. 60)

14 WDR. 1984. S, 89. (World Bank, 1984, p. 89)

15 According to the 2001 World Development Report, the concept of justice has to be fundamentally with two spheres. Firstly the one that belong to the notion of fairness, " a universally identifiable

concept [that] carries the notion of fair process and due outcomes in the distribution of political power, resources, opportunities, and sanctions". Secondly, as an identificatory vector for functional operation in which "institutions (...) are central to resolving conflicts arising over alleged violations or different interpretations of the rules that societies create to govern members' behavior; and that, as a consequence, are central to strengthening the normative framework (laws and rules) that shapes public and private actions" (courts, coercive apparatuses, prosecution, etc). (World Bank, 2011, p. XVI)

16 A report of the OECD, describes how by the year 2004, 59 years after the foundation of the Bretton Woods Institutions, the top 20 exporting countries accounted for about 80% of exports, while the least industrialized for less than 1% (Frericks et.al., 2009)

17 Both conditions can be inferred from this regulatory structure, on the one hand, trade volumes and wealth are unevenly distributed and tend to correlate according to the levels of wealth of the importing countries. It means that increasing levels of trade tend to be more justified for capital backed countries. On the second hand, trade capital flows are acutely reallocated into core global economies. See (Cha & Lee, 2010 B) (Cha & Lee, 2010 A)

18 Normative regulation is to be related with politics, morality, law, etc. Cognitive expectations regulation with specialized law such as economy, science, intellectual property or technology, among others. See more on (Teubner & Fischer-Lescano, kein Datum)

19 This is because even in contemporary societies, foundational values of liberty and equality are frequently considered to be part of the discourse of modernity.

20 That explain why to date "No developing country has taken a developed country to the dispute settlement mechanism for not transferring technology. [Why not?] Because a)the costs of mounting a case are high for a developing country, b)the US and the EU may threaten reprisals, and c) the obligations of developed countries with regard to technology transfer and everything else are vague" (Wade, 2003, p. 625). See also; (Chimni, 2006).

21 Section 5th, 2010 "Development" report. (World Bank, 2011, p. 145)

22 The recognition of the pathologies of the system is blatant in the operational goals of the Institutions. They represent functional appendices of the United Nations structure of governance. The internalization of the asymmetries are further incorpored into formal scenarios of institutional discussion, in which the United Nations Conference on Sustainable Development" have taken the dominant role. These scenarios frequently take place since 1972, with the UN Conference on the Human Environment in Stockholm, followed up by the "1992 first UN Conference on Environment and Development" (UNCED), the "2002 World Summit on Sustainable Development" (WSSD), and the 2013 "Rio +20 Conference on Sustainable Development". However, 40 years after the first meeting, and particularly since the 70´s decade, levels of inequality in the world have increased acutely (Milanovic, 2009) (Sutcliffe, 2004), "global GHG emissions due to human activities have grown since pre-industrial times, with an increase of 70% between 1970 and 2004" (IPCC/07, 2007) and deforestation have increased acutely. In fact, the "2010th Least Developed Countries Report of the United Nations", warned that by 2010 "the number of people living in extreme poverty in LDCs has continued to increase throughout the past 30 years, including during the boom years, and by 2007 it was twice as high as in 1980" (United Nations Conference on Trade and Development, 2010, p. VI).

23 The last slightly attempt to reform the settings was conducted by former managing director of the IMF, Dominique Strauss Kahn in 2010.

24 Some of them very acute even in highly industrialized countries such as the United States.

25 As it is named by Rawls.

Chapter 9
Land Acquisition and the Semantic Context of Land Within the Normative Construction of "Modern Development":
A Historical Case Study at the Bretton Woods Institutions

ABSTRACT

This chapter aims to analyze how, historically, normative interventions on the idea of "development" at the Bretton Woods Institutions have defined a theoretical bias from which land and land acquisition has been represented. On the one hand, the chapter proposes a framework from which representations of land, land acquisition, and land ownership can be contextualized within scholarly literature on the concept of development. The second part of the chapter carries out an empirical case study on linguistic analysis to highlight how increasing levels of land concentration go hand in hand with normative interventions built at the top of the executive boards of an international architecture. The chapter reveals that rather than a coincidence, policies and recommendations on large scale land acquisition have made part of a highly institutionalized and ideologically defined discourse that has evolved semantically within selected periods of the history of these institutions.

DOI: 10.4018/978-1-6684-9794-4.ch009

INTRODUCTION

Large Scale Land Acquisition (LSLA) has become in recent decades a critical issue in political science and postcolonial analysis of international relations. While during the 20th century, most part of the phenomena has been linked with international dynamics of concentration of wealth and therefore of land as a global medium term venture asset, the normative landscape of LSLA has being rather isolated from the political debate. Such background has carried out the legitimation of practices that led to critical arrangements like increasing deforestation, urban encroachment of forest areas, industrial development of livestock farm, water sources contamination and depletion, human diasporas, food insecurity and food prices speculation among others. In such settings, the goal of the present chapter is to argue that rather than a coincidence, the historical representation of LSLA have made part of a highly institutionalized discourse of modern development, ingrained in customary publications of influential organizations such as the World Bank or the International Monetary Fund. The paper focuses in the role institutional grey literature has had in historically shaping the way land and territory has been understood by global institutions. It makes use of a theoretical approach to the study of land and development, and an empirical case study on linguistic analysis, to demonstrate how increasing levels of land concentration, go hand with hand with normative interventions built at the top of the executive boards of an international architecture.

THE ROLE OF LAND WITHIN THE IDEA OF DEVELOPMENT

Land acquisition and land ownership concentration has become in recent decades a topic of increasing research in post-colonial studies. This has been often linked with the fact that the phenomena tends to be seen as an arbitrary consequence of modern processes of urbanization, industrial agricultural expansion, commodification of land, and global asymmetries in access to financial capital. These settings have in turn created a historical shift in the quality, conditions and dimensions of acquisition of land, making it part of a subtle reality lead in the backdrop by private investors that aim to acquire low cost physical assets beyond national frontiers.

While during the recent years, research on land acquisition has been increasingly linked to trends of land concentration in capital scarce territories such as Africa, Asia or Latin America (Ronald, 2014, p. 193) (Schutter, 2011) (Shutter, 2011 a) (Cotula, 2014, p. 40), notorious clues show that land ownership concentration belongs to a global dynamic that in some capital abundant territories reach similar proportions to that of Brazil, Colombia, and the Philippines, known as territorially unequal countries. This in turn reveals that rather than a coincidence, land concentration belongs to an international process of commodification and concentration of property, bounded with numerous phenomena of inequality that expose acute trends within the recent decades. While most part of the industrialized world show little over foreign processes of Large Scale Land Acquisition, the importance of the topic has been boosted up in capital scarce nations that often rely on the role of land to renew domestic processes of food and water supply, residential autonomy, and defined cultural interests (Meinzen-Dick, 2014). Indeed, with a few exceptions and due to the political events of the 20th century, global land distribution by country remained unequal for most of the industrialized territories with the exclusion of the United States and Russia[1] (Skyner, 2001). This in turn, slowly revealed the importance of land as a customary systemic asset for a process of national "development", boosting up the depletion of domestic natural resources on most of the industrialized world, and therefore increasing the value of land and natural resources in capital scarce areas of the planet.

From an entirely political perspective, degraded forms of land acquisition have been progressively entitled as processes of land grabbing (Berhe, 2014) (Schutter, 2011) (Shutter, 2011 a) (Cotula, 2009) (Via, 2011). This phenomenon reveals global disparities and massive arbitrariness on access to land, signaled by large scale international investments in African, Latin - American, Middle Eastern, West European or Asian territories. This has further aggravated the scale of global land concentration, deepening processes of displacement of populations, and facilitating dominance on access to land of influential, extractive, real state and industrial transnational companies. During the recent years this trend have spread globally, and by today just within the borders of the EU, "the large farms (100 hectares and above) that only represent 3 percent of the total number of farms, control 50 percent of all farmed land" (TNI, 2013, p. 6).

At the global level, purchase of ownership rights over land acquire however a different connotation. This is how it has become a critical security concern of populations living in rural areas that often lack the institutional shelter of an abundant capital, or sophisticated nation state. On the other hand, legislation on institutional procedures concerning Large Scale Land Acquisition, often lack the necessary level of cohesion to join processes of land acquisition with sustainable practices of urbanization, and inclusive processes of industrial development. This phenomenon is clear in regions prone to marginalize former crop landowners. During the recent decades, such situation has led to the production of research directed to reveal the ambiguity of legislation than tends to regulate land acquisition practices within different jurisdictions, cultures, and overall institutional capacities of countries. This is how a long chain of contemporary research, focuses on inquiry over the "public purpose" of land within processes of "development", often argued as the reasons behind entrepreneurial or public interventions directed to occupy land. Despite the intensity of the debate, at the moment, increasing levels of land concentration continue being customarily globally reported both in industrialized as well as in non-industrialized territories.

The often difficult conditions to make a rigorous systemic diagnosis about the consequences of concentration of land, has been a matter of discussion in post-colonial studies. On the one hand, processes of land acquisition in industrialized countries have often go hand in hand with communitarian transitions to urban settlement schemes, boosting up levels of sophistication of societies, and easing up the burdens of lower sectors of the population to reach basic self-sufficiency requirements. Moreover, after the industrial revolution, modern urbanization entailed the expansion of agro industrial production, making use of procedures based upon concentration of land to increase efficiency, and providing to large parts of the population the possibility to enroll in occupations beyond survival nourishment. The discussion however lies in the distribution of burdens between actors that regularly encounter in asymmetric bargaining scenarios of appropriation of land. Therefore, it has been precisely in the interests that caused conflicts between large scale land seekers and medium or small owners –and communities-, that critical approaches to LSLA have found original ground. To exemplify this transition, the present research proposes three theoretical approaches which are based on the way and semantic context in which land and processes of land acquisition has been represented within normative constructions on the concept of "development". Namely and institutional, a sociological and a systemic developmentalism approach. The question each approach aims to resolve is: how problems derived from land acquisition are interpreted in scholarly research, and what is the role of land and the territory for communities and systems that strive for increasing levels of "development"?.

Institutional Developmentalism

Institutional developmentalism represents the single most used approach to study root causes, patterns and consequences of land acquisition within processes of development. It is characterized for considering land occupation and private large scale land acquisition as a conventional process of social organization; isolating non-mainstream schemes of domestic and global development. It shed lights on the political, legal, institutional and humanitarian implications of processes of land acquisition taking place mainly in rural areas or medium or low income territories. The focus however ignores the global and systemic dimension of the process, as well as the vast limitations of institutional approaches to the concept of development. It embraces critical discussions concerning social difficulties that follow processes of agro industrial maturation (José Luis Ramos, 2009), the scope or rural poverty within processes of massive land acquisition and urbanization (Verdeja, 2001) (Tokman, 1999), public order conflicts that arouse in the midst of massive land appropriation (Kombe, 2010) (German, 2011.) (Marulanda Gómez, 2002) (Sanchez, 2010), implications on food security and the political economy behind and acquisition for food commerce (De Zoysa, 2013) (Correa, 2009) (Ganho, 2011), land acquisition and compensation (Odame, 2008) (Ghatak & Mookherjee, 2011) (Mamonova, 2011), or law compliance and legality of LSLA within jurisdictions (Goswami, 2012), among others.

Institutional developmentalism highlights the domestic nature of processes of land acquisition that takes place in selected territories of the globe, taking for granted international structures of political, systemic and social organization. It stresses the validity of customary arrangements concerning the distribution and operationalization of land that has a reference point in capital abundant nodes. Such theoretical practice has indeed ended up making land a customary commodity within processes of global capital expansion.

Most literature on the Institutional Developmentalism approach to processes of land acquisition, aims to record the impact of large scale appropriations within a concept of development defined by international institutions such as the World Bank or the International Monetary Fund, and the history of influential territories such as the United States or Europe. Instead of focusing in the causes of the global expansion of patterns of concentration of land, it aims to account the consequences along selected geographies. Nowadays, the approach focusses predominantly on regions such as Latin-America, Africa and Asia. In Latin America, it tends to register the historical waves of peasant dispossession and resistance. In the case of Colombia, literature of the approach has focuses on events within the 1950-2010 period; where farmers of coffee, cotton or tobacco crops experienced highly traumatic transitions. Though in Colombia, more critical approaches to mainstream institutional settings led to massive processes of appropriation of land, whose picks took place during the decade of the 70´s with more than 800 civil occupations in one day (February 21st 1970) (Sanchez, 2010, p. 14), by now, levels of concentration of territory in the country account as one of the highest in the world. Indeed, just by 2012 the country registered the highest progression of granting of land titles for mining exploitation -with more than 9000 allowances-. Such policy increased in more than 4,8 million hectares of the territory the supply of land for acquisition for domestic or international capital. In the country, the approach also accounts practices of ownership of oil and mineral deposits (Ponce, 2012), diagnostics concerning the politization of protests by farmers, deliberations concerning the ownership of the land, the consequences of processes of colonization and violence, marginalization waves and conflicts within the "Haciendas" -plantations- (Palacios, 2011), processes through which land acquisition can boost up the production of basic agricultural products (José Luis Ramos, 2009, p. 78), the role of European NGO´s after rural forced displacement processes (Carlos, et al., 1998, p. 123), or the validity of the approaches to *development and land* of armed groups inside the country (Marulanda Gómez, 2002, p. 240). In México the studies focus on the analysis of the role of land acquisition within processes of agricultural development (Cordeiro, 2007) or the historical evolution of rural extreme poverty and its relation with urbanization dynamics along the territory (Verdeja, 2001, p. 76) (Tokman, 1999, p. 40). In Venezuela, Brazil, Chile, and Ecuador, it includes diagnostics about mining and land (Ponce, 2012, p. 121), the "modernization" of the agro industrial production, "alternatives" to the use of land in contrast with neo-liberal policies (Correa, 2009, p. 31) or the historical attempts to institutionalize continental and domestic land reforms, among others (Díaz, 2006, p. 26).

The same focus of the approach repeats in African or Asian territories, including research on the relation of urbanization and capital investment in countries like China (Sachs, 2005), rehabilitation of settlements, compensation and legal acquisition of land or jurisdictions and rights of settlers in India (Ghatak & Mookherjee, 2011) (Goswami, 2012), dynamics on Land grabbing, investment and water resources in Subsaharian Africa (Ganho, 2011) (German, 2011.), large scale land acquisition and food crops in Ethiopia (De Zoysa, 2013), emerging conflicts and socio political implications in Tanzania (Kombe, 2010), national policies on rehabilitation, "development" and land acquisition on Bangladesh (Al Ataha, 2013), or compensation and consultation in countries like Mali or Ghana, among many others (Odame, 2008) (Nolte & Voget-Kleschin, 2013).

The Sociological Approach

Sociological developmentalist approaches focus on analyzing the significance of land as a cultural topic in which notions of the role, connotation, use and value of territory conflict between societies. In the case of Latin-America, it aims to justify the cultural, economic and political existence of farmers and the farm life as a substantial prism from which land should be embraced (De Janvry, et al., 1991, p. 28). In this endeavor, the theoretical approach stresses the importance of the discussion about the reasons behind the commodification of land. It highlights the sociological dimension of modern processes of interaction of the population with the territory, stressing how it often left behind alternative communitarian structures, racial and tribal settings, or cultural and metaphysic beliefs (Marini, 2008., p. 235). In Colombia, for instance, it focuses on the scope and validity of indigenous initiatives in the organization, protection and definition of the use of land (Idárraga, et al., 2010, p. 178), the social and "emotional" sustainability of processes of concentration of land, and the disappearance of the indigenous culture due to the progression of the agricultural industrial culture (Palacios, 2011, p. 130). The approach problematizes massive land acquisition as a cultural byproduct of processes of institutionalized development that marginalize land use conceptions beyond the influence of late capitalist dynamics (Bucheli, 2006). Within the approach, land and land acquisition embrace a symbolic component (Guerra, 2007), different from plain institutional recommendations about the drama behind LSLA. Land tenure[2] (Suárez, 2012, p. 37) (Ordóñez, 2012, p. 115)., thereby, is something more than a market outcome of private property rights or dynamics of urbanization and operationalization of production of urban crops; it is a right derived from post-colonial reservation privileges, that entitled settlers to make use of territory beyond alien forms of commodification's of the ground (Mejía, 2007, p. 43). Within the continent, including through Paraguay (Ortiz, 2008), Mexico (Cordeiro, 2007, p. 15) or Venezuela (Hurtado, 2008), sociological approaches to land acquisition and development highlight the semantic differences or land and its role according to each community, disentangling the ambiguity of customary representation and mainstream scholarly views, and avoiding discussions over the systemic and political consequences of institutional approaches to land and land acquisition.

The Systemic Approach

A contemporary framework that examines the way land and land acquisition is represented within a process of development, can be exemplified by the systemic approach. It aims to avoid the customary critic of bargaining dynamics or the sociological background of processes of LSLA. Instead, the approach focuses on the global material restrictions of current processes of land concentration, while emphasizing the systemic limitations of customary institutional representations of the idea of development. It yields that, processes of development that commodify land and make it an asset prone to be a customary good for domestic or transnational profit, are likely to obey a structural architecture that by now, spreads normatively denying current shortages on supply of strategic minerals (Ponce, 2012, p. 68), critical geothermic global margins, massive biodiversity crises, decreases of the productivity of non-treated land (Cordeiro, 2007, p. 217), non-sustainable urban settlements, unaffordable consequences of deforestation, and the limitations of institutional constructions on the use of the territory and the notion of sustainability (Figueredes, 1999). Indeed, prognosis concerning entirely the socio-political consequences of processes of large Scale Land acquisition, avoids its natural binding with a global systemic reality that just at the beginning of the second half of the twentieth century, reveals critical events that enhance the understanding and conception of contemporary social system. This is why customary institutional constructions that aim to legitimate processes of concentration of land, reinforcing the market value of the environment, ignore the scientific value of the nature, the ecosystem and thermic equilibrium demands of the globe, and the inner systemic value of non-urbanized non-industrialized territory, making even redistributive land policies a biased and outdated framework to contextualize the consequences of processes of mercantilization and large scale acquisition of land (Ahumada, 2007) (Arcila, 2011).

CASE STUDY

Land and Development Since the Beginning of the Bretton Woods Institutions

This section makes use of empirical methods on linguistic analysis and social constructivism, to account how increasing processes of land concentration and transnational land acquisition, go hand in hand with normative constructions built at the top of the decision making boards of selected international institutions. It aims further to exemplify, how at the institutional level of a highly influential international architecture, the idea of land relates with one of the above mentioned approaches to development. It makes use of the contributions on historical institutionalism to explore how and within which periods; discourses on land acquisition have increasingly made a transition from an entirely economic character to an entirely political and institutional one. In this task, the section makes use grey literature from three historical periods of discourse production on the concept of development at the World Bank, and the International Monetary Fund. Rather than attempting explicitly to conduct reconstruction of discursive interventions, our approach is focused on analyzing how at the level of international institutions, normative interventions on land acquisition and land concentration, have been entrenched in a notion of modern "development", semantically understood and produced on the historical record. For this reason, we prefer to frame original publications on "development" at the level of the Bretton Woods Institutions in four variables: time frame, extension, character and qualitative features of linguistic interventions. Then we proceed to account our findings, and to contextualize it within the above mentioned three theoretical approaches to land and development.

The foundational period is located within the decade 1945-1955. It covers the establishment of the institutions as well as the beginning of the implementation of their operational functions, such as the distribution of loans within a discourse on development. Since very early on the history of these institutions, customary publications describing the result, expectations and operational activities per year, established symbolic differentiations between "developed" and "underdeveloped" countries. The institutional material to cover the representation of development within the first decade of operation is represented by the Agreement of the International Monetary Fund and the articles of agreement for the International Bank for Reconstruction and Development (22 July 1944), the General Agreement on Trade and Tariffs (1947), and the "Development Prospects Reports" of the World Bank between 1953 and 1958.

The transitional period covers the decade after the end of the Bretton Woods Convertibility systems, which took place between the years 1971 till 1973. This period is characterized by three intertwined phenomena; first, the unilateral decision of the former US president Richard Nixon to declare publicly the unpegging of the dollar from gold, (2) the enhancement of the capacity of all nations to expand the money supply according to their own monetary policies. (3) And the replacement of the "Development Prospects" of the World Bank by the "World Bank Development Report" -issued every year since 1978-. The discursive interventions to be analyzed within the decade 1973-1983, are formed upon the prospects of the period 1973-1976 (see Annex), plus the following World Bank Reports.

The contemporary period is formed by the Development Reports of the World Bank for the years 2003-2013, and the Executive Reports of the International Monetary Fund for the same decade.

THE METHOD

Though the present chapter is a section of further studies on the analysis of normative constructions, it sets an example to conduct additional studies on how meaning of normative interventions, is created, and how it keeps relation with defined sociopolitical topics. In the present study linguistic representations of the role of land within communities are embedded in a norm of development defined by keywords, dimensions, policy fields, and intensity of the thematization carried by international institutions. This case study aims to thematize the content of selected grey literature of the World Bank and the International Monetary Fund, revealing the context in which the notions of "land" and "development" are operationalized in the historical record of the Bretton Woods institutional discourse, and how it evolves throughout time.

Drawing upon the contributions of CDA as a theoretical approach to the analysis of language as a social practice, the study implies that the scrutiny of discursive interventions can contextualize the emergence of representations, roles, dominion, resistance, ideology and overall hierarchical dimensions within which representations of the role of land in societies has evolved historically. This analysis is conducted by studying the text as a discursive practice rather than as a linguistic device. For this task, the case study reveals within the text topical structures, concordance and clusters formation of concepts such as land, food, food security, agriculture, crops, land compensation, environment, ecosystem, biodiversity, displacement, droughts, deforestation, vacant lots, industrial agriculture, large scale land acquisition and so on. The assumption for further research on symbolic representations of land is that the gathering of the context allows the further implementation of CDA as an approach to extract the meaning of normative interventions.

The production of topical structures is a mechanism of syntactic production upon which phrases and linguistic constructions acquire diverse interpretations, boundaries and roles onto semantic structures. The customary questions given on the analysis of these structures are: Which topics do institutions produce knowledge about when they refer to land? In which manner they impose theoretical, philosophical, political or systemic limitations when it comes to represent the way in which land concentration, land acquisition, and free trade (among others) affect the very nature of land as a systemic asset, transposing it into a highly demanded commodity? In answering questions such as these, the chapter explores how over history, linguistic constructions have defined the intensity, the style, the treatment and overall grammatical strategies to present ant to represent discourse on the topic of land acquisition, and how it fits within the above mentioned theoretical approaches to land and development.

SOME CONSIDERATIONS ON THE THEMATIZATION OF NORMATIVE CONSTRUCTIONS

Thematization carries out the focalization of discourse on structures of representation of the "objective" world. These phenomena are customarily present in social systems aiming to arrange their own normative constructions by discursive interventions embraced politically, culturally and institutionally. In the analysis of how societies reproduce their own traditions, thematization plays a fundamental role in ensuring representations upon cognitive frames that aim to steer potentially contradictory[3] (Habermas, 1984, p. 395), easing the path to strengthen necessary communicative patterns to avoid misinterpretation or confusion. Finally, it reduces levels of dissension, playing a fundamental role in how knowledge and identification about the outside world ought to be embraced, and making it a device for the production of "behavior stabilizing" certainties (Habermas, 1996, p. 36) .

Throughout thematization, the text producer holds the role of create "reality" via language. This process is carried by the interrelation of a defined selection of themes, and the boundaries of the experiential content upon which actor's representations aim to describe something in the outside world. Inquiry on formal thematization of discourse, rather than focusing on the psychological processes that take place along a corpus creation, turns to the "linguistic outcome" of such process, that is, to the analysis of the compendium of symbolisms and the "Iconicity" (McCabe & Alonso, 2001) of the content of the linguistic product.

The present study holds the necessity of thematizing the original text corpus into semantic fields within which the norm of "modern development" is customarily represented. Such vector fields are given by conducting corpus linguistics and data driven analysis of selected institutional material of the Bretton Woods Institutions. This process takes place by running multiplatform tools focused on exploring and produce first and foremost the semantic properties of the text, as well as concordance lines, linguistic clusters, collocation or search terms, keyword lists and n-gram linguistic sequences for further exploration. In the current case study the process implies fundamentally to operationalize the method through which semantic and text analysis inquiry is to be carried out.

SEMANTIC ANALYSIS

In order to conduct the semantic analysis of the corpus, the methodology embraced in this research makes use of two interrelated tools. On the one hand, the USAS semantic Tag set[4], used and developed since 1990 on projects directed to conduct "content tag" of contemporary English. The tag set is composed by a structure that includes 21 major discourse fields, such as science and technology; the environment, social actions, states and processes; money & commerce; food and farming; or education, among others. Each one of the discourse fields is composed by multilevel subdivisions composed by prototypical word units. The lexicon contains over 37.000 words, with a template list of over 16.000 multi-word units (Archer et. al., 2002). Second; the web-based corpus tool Wmatrix, which provides an interface for the automatization of USAS and "CLAWS" -which is a complementary speech (POS) tagging software for English text-. Wmatrix can conduct not only a computer based process of tagging of uploaded text corpus, but also customary linguistic methods of corpus analysis such as frequency lists and concordance (Rayson, 2008) (Rayson, 2003). Finally, it provides the possibility of conducting semantic and keywords frequency comparisons between corpus, which in turn allows the researcher to recognize the differences and most significant key fields of the semantic structures of the text, and to provide statistical analysis of the tag frequency profiles.

Within the process of semantic analysis, this chapter focuses in three Semantic Fields of the USAS semantic tag set: "Food and Farming"; "World and Environment"; and "Money, commerce and Industry". Since land and land acquisition are not among the defined semantic categories of the semantic tag set, "food and farming" is considered to be the single most relevant category to define its role within the production of institutional discourse on development[5]. "World and Environment" aims to reveal the importance of representations of development that fit within the previously defined systemic approach to LSLA and development. Finally, "Money, Commerce and Industry" reveals the importance of the category along institutional international historical interventions on the concept of development, and its further relation with "Food and Farming", "World and Environment" tags.

TEXT ANALYSIS

Results Per Period

In the present study, text analysis contributes to accessory processes of discourse examination. It is carried out by the operationalization of three strategies of exploration of the linguistic corpus; Frequency of words, representative N-grams of linguistic sequences and concordance of highly frequent words into plots belonging to each one of the three periods of study; namely the post World War II period, the decade after the end of the convertibility system, including the publication of the "development" reports, and the last decade.

The outcome of the semantic analysis reveals a strong thematization of the concept of development with the systemic category of "Money, Commerce and Industry". On the highly institutional policy focus of the corpus, within the period 1947- 1957, discussions over land and land ownership remains as a marginalized topic of the literature.

A concordance plot on the selected corpus[6] of the period demonstrates that occurrences of text concerning land and land ownership are highly scarce. Indeed, the text shows a total of just 11 instances where discussions over land were included in the reports of the International Monetary Fund and the World Bank. Some of these consist of descriptions of agricultural achievements in Japan (World Bank, 1957), where after the end of the Second World War, the cropped area for cultivation of the country expanded "despite the encroachment of the urban population on the available cultivable land". The report also mentions the capacity of the country -by making use of "land reclamation" and double cropping processes-, to maintain levels of food production on average despite acute increase of the population. Indeed "while the area of agricultural land actually declined from an average of 6,01,721 cho (1 cho = 0.992 hectares) in 1933-35 to 5,446,189 in 1553-55, the area (destined) to crops actually increased from 7,539,,031 to 7,948,023 cho"[7] (World Bank, 1957).

Within the period, the World Bank includes also land diagnostics about Colombia and Mexico, written after official visits conducted by the Department of Operations for the Western Hemisphere of the institution. In the case of Colombia, considerations regarding the use of land, reveal a significant contrast with Japan´s diagnosis of the economy as a whole, therefore land was considered as one of the single most important assets for economic growth. Suggested policies indeed, aimed to boost the capacity of the country to improve agriculture, which formerly "lag(ged) behind other sectors of the economy" (World Bank, 1958). Such approaches hold truth for a country that despite its comparatively big land extensions and climates, presented difficult progresses in agricultural production. The reasons, according to the Bank, where given by the "low productivity of the small farm and the fact that large parts of the fertile valley lands (were) taken up by cattle-grazing"[8] (World Bank, 1958), making total agricultural production to "barely kept" with the increase of the population. In the reforms, the IBRD mission suggested the transition of cultivation from the mountain slopes to the rich valleys of Colombia, particularly the Bogota Sabana and the Cauca Valley, which in just one year expected to increase landownership concentration of about 40,000 hectares of the national most fertile land.

In the case of Mexico, processes of administration of land ownership were determined by the topography and big extension of the territory, developing necessary transportation roots within the country. Despite this condition, the Bank avoids to further develop the depth of the diagnosis, highlighting the agricultural development of the country, whose production growth between 1950-54 was 8% per annum (World Bank, 1958).

In conclusion, institutional approaches to land and land ownership at the level of the BBBWW institutions during the first period reveal a clear avoidance of sociological or systemic approaches. Indeed, semantic analysis of the text corpus shows that just about 0,36% of the thematic scope of the institutional reports, kept relation with considerations regarding land acquisition, land use, or land role in systemic approaches to development and physical territory.

Compared with the 1947-1957 period, the 1973-1983 period reveals a substantial increase in the role of land, food and farming as a component of the semantic production of a norm on "modern development". While in the first text corpus, the thematic scope of land and territory amounted a 0.36% of the content, by the decade after 1973, it accounted for almost 1.4% of it. Within the five years before the publication of the World Bank Development Report, this semantic shift was mainly given by the inclusion of the topic of land on institutional case studies of countries such as Malaysia, Rwanda, Ethiopia, Burma and Philippines, among others.

In the case of Malaysia, the Bank highlighted the former availability of "vast areas of virgin land" for implementing processes of industrial production of food. This policy moreover was bounded with the interests of the former "Federal Land Development Authority", which aimed to marginalized involvement of smallholders, imposing strong measures for promotion of large scale land acquisition for industrial production, and further increasing domestic and foreign land ownership concentration (World Bank, 1973). Indeed, the scheme aimed to provide land to the lowest income groups of the society but at no "great financial cost to the government". In turn, it made difficult for peasants or small land holders to develop industrially.

In Rwanda, the institutional reports emphasized the reasonable fair distribution of land ownership within the population, but the difficult soil characteristics and the acceptance of rudimentary agricultural techniques, which represented the work method over 98% of the cultivated land used for the "production of subsistence crops". This situation contrasted with the use and ownership concentration of land of expatriate farmers, that just in the case of Tea Gardens, by the end of 1972 hold 13% of the national cultivated area (World Bank, 1974). In the case of Ethiopia, the Bank highlighted the massive state ownership of land. According to the 1975 report, the model acquired by the country was determined by the "declaration of the Provisional Military Government of Ethiopia (1974), called "Ethiopian Socialism". Such policies included the nationalization of all rural land, making former commercial farms to turn over to "smallholders (…) or being operated as cooperatives or state farms", receiving indeed "acceptance by the majority of the Ethiopian population (World Bank, 1975). Indeed, just in December of 1974, about 30,000 university and senior secondary school students were sent to a one-year program for rural development to rural areas of the country. From that moment on however, self-sufficiency of the country to avoid famines during upcoming periods deteriorated.

During the 70´s decade, it is clear that further normative constructions on development and land ownership of the World Bank follow the same theoretical approach as in previous years. This is how in the semantic constructions of land and land ownership in the 1979 World Development report, the Bank insists on the necessity of countries to allow processes of concentration of land, to reduce costs. This, according to the Bank, is due to the fact that "small farms typically use more labor per unit of land than large farms". As the report pointed out; "In 1960, Colombian farms of less than three hectares used 20 times as much labor per hectare as farms in the range of 50 to 500 hectares" (World Bank, 1979, p. 50).

Following previous insights concerning processes of discourse production of a norm of development linked with the use of land and land ownership, it is finally possible to say that the 1973-1983 period of the text corpus, reveals a substantial change in the thematization of the topic. This in turn is also noteworthy in a cross frequency profile of the semantic role of food and farming, revealing a substantial increase in the role of land as a food and farming asset within a process of development.

Semantic analysis directed to reveal the thematization of discourse production on the norm of modern development and its relation with land and territory, reveals during the 2003-2007 period a substantial differentiation with the former two previous periods of the text corpus. Such variations however remain constant over time, giving higher connotations to semantic categories such as "Food and Farming", and "World and Environment". This transition reveals clearly a different connotation of the role of land and development, within the discursive interventions of institutions such as the World Bank or the International Monetary Fund. The shift demonstrates a new connotation of the role of land, not just from an economic to a sociological and political perspective, but also to a global systemic perspective; in which contemporary global crisis concerning current patterns of urban and social organization, are acknowledged as problematic and unsustainable in the short term.

When it comes to the thematization of land and land ownership within the period, plots of keywords clusters, reveal a constant pattern within the institutional reports between the years 2003 -2012; acutely decreasing in importance on the World Development Report of the year 2013. The peak of the topic is presented in the 2012 report, "Gender Equality and development", which accounts detailed analysis in rights of "ownership and control over land and assets" (World Bank, 2012, p. XXI). In terms of policies concerning land acquisition as a chain of customary processes of industrial development, the 2008 report –Agriculture for development- stresses that processes of land concentration "contributes to asset squeeze on smallholders and landless household" (World Bank, 2008, p. 85). Considering the very high levels of inequality of non-industrialized countries, and the difficulties on access to credit of capital scarce segments of the population, such statements conflict with Bank policies that highlight the fact that many countries lack competitive advantage on export oriented assets due to "limits on land acquisition or other features of the agrarian structure (where) small holders remain as dominant suppliers for export firms" (World Bank, 2008, p. 131). Indeed, the report focuses on selected case studies in countries such as Uganda, Kenya or Senegal, where according to the Bank, the suggested policies allowed Senegal during the last 15 years to reduce poverty by about 12 percentage points and extreme poverty by half, while increasing supply of agricultural products to foreign territories.

Within the evolution of discourse production of land and development at International Institutions such as the World Bank, it is worth to note the transition that semantic categories such as "world and environment" have played in reconstituting what the role of land is in the development of contemporary social systems. The results of the 2003-2013 period, reveal a sociological and political trend that aims to enhance the semantic horizon in which land, territory and the overall physical environment has been customarily represented. While in the present research it is not possible to assume that such trend is going to be maintained, nor the institutional or social implications of it over increasingly complex processes of global industrialization, it is worth to note that this study shed lights on patterns that can be further embraced academically and politically.

SUMMARY

The present study aims to reveal how institutional representations on land acquisition and land, rather than being deprived from ideological or theoretical bias, fit in a defined theoretical approach to development that has evolved within the last 80 years. In this endeavor, the chapter reveals substantial semantic evolutions on the concept of land and land ownership concentration, and its relation to a normative construction of development entrenched in the publications of institutions such as the World Bank or the International Monetary Fund. It also stresses a theoretical approach from which normative constructions on development, exemplify and give meaning to selected structures of contemporary social systems, such as the distribution and the role of land. Finally, it raises questions about the extent to which international institutions construct reality via discourse, further operationalizing it with policies created on asymmetric political architectures. The chapter reveals that rather than a coincidence, domestic interventions on land, land acquisition and land ownership keep a strong relation with symbolic constructions developed on international institutions. It also highlights how grey literature of normative interventions on development, rather than being absent from ideological bias, fit in a defined theoretical framework from which land and development have been historically represented.

REFERENCES

Ahumada, C. (2007). *Movimientos sociales, biodiversidad y libre comercio en la Amazonía. Universidad Javeriana.* Fundacion Cultural Javeriana de Artes Gráficas.

Al Ataha, S. (2013). Development Project, Land Acquisition and Resettlement in Bangladesh; A Quest for Well Formulated National Resettlement and Rehabilitation Policy. *International Journal of Humanities and Social Science*, *3*(7).

Archer, D. (2002). *Introduction to the USAS category system.* Lancs. http://ucrel.lancs.ac.uk/usas/usas%20guide.pdf.

Arcila, O. (2011). *La Amazonía colombiana urbanizada. Un análisis de sus asentamientos urbanos.* Instituto amazónico de investigaciones científicas.

Berhe, M. G. (2014). *A Delicate Balance. Land Use, Minority Rights and Social Stability in the Horn of Africa.* Institute for Peace and Security Studies, Addis Ababa University.

Bucheli, M. (2006). Curas, campesinos y laicos como gerentes de desarrollo. *La construcción de un modelo de desarrollo emergente en Colombia.*. EDISOCIAL.

Carlos, T., Jimenéz, D., Grando, L. & Zuluaga, Y. (1998). *El desplazamiento por la violencia en Colombia. Experiencias, análisis y posibles estrategias de atención en el Departamento de Antioquia.*. Pastoral Social ACNUR.

Cordeiro, J. L. (2007). El Desafío Latinoamericáno y sus cinco grandes retos. McGraw Hill.

Correa, R. (2009). *Ecuador: de Banana Republic a la No república.* Nomos Impresores.

Cotula, L. (2014). *Foreign Investmente, law and sustainable development. IIED Natural Resources Issues.* International Institute for Environment and Development.

Cotula, L. (2009). *Land grab or development opportunity? Agricultural investmente and international land deals in Africa.* IIED/FAO/IFAD.

De Janvry, A., Fajardo, D., Errazuriz, M. & Balcazar, F. (1991). *Campesinos y desarrollo en América Latina.* Fondo DRI.

De Zoysa, R. (2013). *The implications of large scale land acquisitio on small landholder`s food security.* (DPU WORKING PAPER NO. 156). DPU.

Díaz, A. (2006). *La reforma agraria en Colombia, Venezuela y Brasil. Nuestra costa caribe y el problema agrario.* D´vinni Ltda.

Figueredes, J. M. (1999). *Centroamérica en el camino hacia el desarrollo sostenible.*. Universidad de los Andes.

Ganho, W. (2011). *Is Water the Hidden Agenda of Agricultural Land Acquisition in sub-Saharan Africa?* University of Manchester.

German, L. S. G. M. E. (2011). *Contemporary processes of largescale land acquisition by investors: Case studies from sub-Saharan Africa.* (CIFOR Occasional Paper No.68).

Ghatak, M., & Mookherjee, D. (2011). *Land acquisition for industrialization and compensation of displaced farmers.* World Institute for Development Economics Research.

Goswami, A. (2012). *Land Acquisition, Rehabilitation and Resettlement: Law and Politics.* IIHS.

Guerra, W. (2007). *El poblamiento del territorio.*

Habermas, J. (1984). The Theory of Communicative Action, Volume 1: Reason and the Rationalization of Society. Boston: Beacon Press.

Habermas, J. (1996). Between Facts and Norms: Contributions to a Discourse Theory of Law and Democracy. Massachusetts Institute of Technology. doi:10.7551/mitpress/1564.001.0001

Hurtado, S. (2008). *Ecología, agricultura, comunidad.* Universidad Central de Venezuela. Ediciones de la Biblioteca.

Idárraga, A., Muñoz, D. A., & Vélez, H. (2010). Conflictos socio-ambientales por la extracción minera en Colombia: Casos de la inversión británica. Amigos de la Tierra.

Kombe, W. (2010). *Land acquisition for public use: emergin conflicts and their socio-political implications.* (Working paper No. 82). ARDHI University.

Mamonova, V. (2011). *Large-scale land acquisitions in the former Soviet Union. A study of rural social movements and land conflicts.* LANDac project.

Marini, R. M. (2008). *América Latina, dependencia y globalización..* Siglo del Hombre Editores.

Marulanda Gómez, O. (2002). *Labranza de Paz. Producción sostenible en el campo para la reconstrucción de la comunidad rural..* Editorial Norma.

McCabe & Alonso. (2001). Theme, transitivity and cognitive representation in Spanish and English written texts. *Circle of linguistics applied to communication. Revista Canaria de Estudios Ingleses.*

Meinzen-Dick, R. (2014). Property rights and sustainable irrigation: A developing country perspective. *Agricultural Water Management, 145*, 23–31. doi:10.1016/j.agwat.2014.03.017

Mejía, W., (2007). Presencia Embrea en el área metropolitana centro occidente. *Fundación cultural germinando.* Cristina Uribe Ediciones.

Nolte, K., & Voget-Kleschin, L. (2013). *Evaluating Consultation in Large-scale Land Acquisition.* (LDPI Working Paper). LDPI.

Odame, W. (2008). Compulsory Land Acquisition and Compensation in Ghana: Searching for alternative policies and strategies. *FIG/FAO/CNG International Seminar on State and Public Sector Land Management.* FAO.

Ordóñez, F. (2012). Zonas de reserva campesina: contribución a la democratización del acceso y la propiedad sobre la tierra y construcción alternativa del territorio desde el campesinado. En Propuestas, visiones y análisis sobre la política de desarrollo rural en Colombia. OXFAM, Colombia.

Ortiz, L. A. (2008). *Cultivar y cambiar. La cultura campesina ante la mercantilización de los espacios rurales en Paraguay.* FLACSO México.

Palacios, M. (2011). *De quien es la tierra? Propiedad, politización y protesta campesina en la década de 1930.* Universidad de los Andes. .

Ponce, A. (2012). *El desalentador panorama de la minería en Colombia.*. Random House Mondadori.

Rayson, P. (2003). *Matrix: A statistical method and software tool for linguistic analysis through corpus comparison.* [Ph.D. thesis, Lancaster University].

Rayson, P. (2008). From key words to key semantic domains. International Journal of Corpus Linguistics, 13(4), 519-549. . doi:10.1075/ijcl.13.4.06ray

Ronald, M. A. (2014). Land Grabbing in Uganda: Are pastoarlists second class citizens? In A delicate Balance. Land Use, Minority Rights and Social Stability in the Horn of Africa. Institute of Peace and Security Studies, Addis Ababa University.

Sachs, J. (2005). *El fin de la pobreza.* Vinni Ltda.

Sanchez, G. (2010). *La tierra en disputa. Memorias del despojo y resistencias campesinas en la costa caribe 1960 - 2010.* Ediciones Semana.

Schutter, O. D. (2011, Summer). The Green Rush: The Global Race for Farmland and the Rights of Land Users. *Harvard International Law Journal, 52*(02).

Shutter, O. D. (2011a, March). How not to think of land-grabbing; three critiques of large-scale investments in farmland. *The Journal of Peasant Studies, 38*(2), 249–279. doi:10.1080/03066150.2011.559008

Skyner, L. (2001, November). Political Conflict and Legal Uncertainty: The Privatisation of Land Ownership in Russia. *Europe-Asia Studies, 53*(7), 981–999. doi:10.1080/09668130120085001

Suárez, A. (2012). Es el derecho de superficie un instrumento para el desarrollo rural en Colombia? En "Propuestas, visiones y análisis sobre la política de desarrollo rural en Colombia." OXFAM Colombia.

TNI. (2013). Transnational Institute (TNI) for European Coordination Via Campesina and Hands off the Land network. *Land concentration, land grabbing and people struggles in Europe*. TNI.

Tokman, V. G. O. (1999). *Pobreza y desigualdad en América Latina.* Paidos.

Verdeja, J. (2001). *Tres décadas de pobreza en México.* Instituto Politecnico Nacional - México.

Verdeja, J. (2001). *Trés décadas de pobreza en México.* Instituto Politécnico Nacional.

Via, E. D. (2011). The Politics of "Win-Win" Narratives: Land Grabs as Development Opportunity? Cornell University IDS, University of Sussex, UK.

World Bank. (1957). *International Bank for reconstruction and development. The development and prospects of Japan´s economy. Report No. FE-2a. July 25.*

World Bank. (1958). International bank for reconstruction and development. *Recent economic developments and prospects of Colombia, Report No. WH-75a.* World Bank.

World Bank. (1958). International Bank for Reconstruction and Development. Recent economic developments and prospects of Mexico. *Report No. WH, 80t*(November), 24.

World Bank. (1973). *Development problems and prospects of Malaysis*. World Bank.

World Bank. (1974). Recent econoic development and proxpects of Rwanda. *Volume II: Annexes. Report No. 422a - RW*. World Bank.

World Bank. (1975). *Ethiopia recent economic development and current prospects*. World Bank.

World Bank. (1979). *World Development Report*. World Bank.

World Bank. (2008). World Development Report. *Agriculture for Development*.

World Bank. (2012). *World Development Report. Gender equality and development*. World Bank.

ENDNOTES

1 On Russia see also (Skyner, 2001)

2 On the discussion of the right of land tenure in the country, see also (Suárez, 2012, p. 37) (Ordóñez, 2012, p. 115).

3 Worldviews (Habermas, 1984, p. 395)

4 For more information about the project, see https://ucrel.lancs.ac.uk/usas/

5 The semantic category is mainly composed by words such as agricultural, food, agriculture, fields, cereals, forestry, fisheries, crop, trimmings, among others. This indeed suggest the often industrial connotation of the use of land within the institutional literature of the World Bank and the IMF. Such approach is further crossed with the results of the additional two semantic categories to analyze the extent to which approaches to land and its role in 20th century processes of industrialization, play a role on discursive interventions on development.

7 Ibid. (World Bank, 1957).

8 Ibid. (World Bank, 1958).

APPENDIX

Table 2(a). Preliminary results; Corpus 1947-1957

Money Commerce and Industry (_I)				
Summary information:				
Number of types shown: 379				
Total frequency of types shown: 4793 (7.99%)				
Total frequency overall: 60008				
Number of items shown with a given frequency:				
Frequency	**Types**		**Tokens**	
1	169	(44.59%)	169	(3.53%)
2	46	(12.14%)	92	(1.92%)
3	17	(4.49%)	51	(1.06%)
4	14	(3.69%)	56	(1.17%)
5	10	(2.64%)	50	(1.04%)
6	10	(2.64%)	60	(1.25%)
7	11	(2.90%)	77	(1.61%)
8	4	(1.06%)	32	(0.67%)
9	6	(1.58%)	54	(1.13%)
10	8	(2.11%)	80	(1.67%)
> 10	**84**	**(22.16%)**	**4072**	**(84.96%)**

Continued on following page

Table 2(a). Continued

Food and Farming (_F)				
Summary information:				
Number of types shown: 51				
Total frequency of types shown: 133 (0.22%)				
Total frequency overall: 60008				
Number of items shown with a given frequency:				
Frequency	**Types**		**Tokens**	
1	32	(62.75%)	32	(24.06%)
2	7	(13.73%)	14	(10.53%)
3	3	(5.88%)	9	(6.77%)
4		(0.00%)		(0.00%)
5	5	(9.80%)	25	(18.80%)
6		(0.00%)		(0.00%)
7	1	(1.96%)	7	(5.26%)
8		(0.00%)		(0.00%)
9		(0.00%)		(0.00%)
10		(0.00%)		(0.00%)
> 10	**3**	**(5.88%)**	**46**	**(34.59%)**

Continued on following page

Table 2(a). Continued

World and Environment (_W)				
Summary information:				
Number of types shown: 27				
Total frequency of types shown: 83 (0.14%)				
Total frequency overall: 60008				
Number of items shown with a given frequency:				
Frequency	**Types**		**Tokens**	
1	16	(59.26%)	16	(19.28%)
2	2	(7.41%)	4	(4.82%)
3	2	(7.41%)	6	(7.23%)
4	4	(14.81%)	16	(19.28%)
5	1	(3.70%)	5	(6.02%)
6		(0.00%)		(0.00%)
7		(0.00%)		(0.00%)
8		(0.00%)		(0.00%)
9		(0.00%)		(0.00%)
10	1	(3.70%)	10	(12.05%)
> 10	**1**	**(3.70%)**	**26**	**(31.33%)**

Words identified within the USAS Tag Field: 60,008
Selected Semantic sequences profiles

Table 2b. Preliminary results; Corpus 1947-1957

Money Commerce and Industry (_I)				
Summary information:				
Number of types shown:			579	
Total frequency of types shown:			7004	(6.70%)
Total frequency overall:			104539	
Number of items shown with a given frequency:				
Frequency	**Types**		**Tokens**	
1	262	(45.25%)	262	(3.74%)
2	63	(10.88%)	126	(1.80%)
3	28	(4.84%)	84	(1.20%)
4	25	(4.32%)	100	(1.43%)
5	30	(5.18%)	150	(2.14%)
6	16	(2.76%)	96	(1.37%)
7	13	(2.25%)	91	(1.30%)
8	9	(1.55%)	72	(1.03%)
9	7	(1.21%)	63	(0.90%)
10	8	(1.38%)	80	(1.14%)
> 10	**118**	**(20.38%)**	**5880**	**(83.95%)**

Table 2c. Preliminary results; Corpus 1947-1957

Food and Farming (_F)				
Number of types shown:			**140**	
Total frequency of types shown:			1021	(0.98%)
Total frequency overall:			104539	
Number of items shown with a given frequency:				
Frequency	**Types**		**Tokens**	
1	56	(40.00%)	56	(5.48%)
2	**28**	**(20.00%)**	**56**	**(5.48%)**
3	18	(12.86%)	54	(5.29%)
4	4	(2.86%)	16	(1.57%)
5	1	(0.71%)	5	(0.49%)
6	1	(0.71%)	6	(0.59%)
7	3	(2.14%)	21	(2.06%)
8	3	(2.14%)	24	(2.35%)
9	6	(4.29%)	54	(5.29%)
10	3	(2.14%)	30	(2.94%)
> 10	17	(12.14%)	699	(68.46%)

Table 2d. Preliminary results; Corpus 1947-1957

World and Environment (_W)				
Summary information:				
Number of types shown:			96	
Total frequency of types shown:			403	(0.39%)
Total frequency overall:			104539	
Number of items shown with a given frequency:				
Frequency	**Types**		**Tokens**	
1	49	(51.04%)	49	(12.16%)
2	14	(14.58%)	28	(6.95%)
3	8	(8.33%)	24	(5.96%)
4	6	(6.25%)	24	(5.96%)
5	2	(2.08%)	10	(2.48%)
6	3	(3.12%)	18	(4.47%)
7	4	(4.17%)	28	(6.95%)
8	2	(2.08%)	16	(3.97%)
9	1	(1.04%)	9	(2.23%)
10				

Preliminary Results; Corpus 1973-1983
Words identified within the USAS Tag Field: 104,539
Selected Semantic sequences profiles

Table 3a. Preliminary results; Corpus 2003-2007

Money Commerce and Industry (_I)				
Summary information:				
Number of types shown:			664	
Total frequency of types shown:			8612	(3.92%)
Total frequency overall:			219887	
Number of items shown with a given frequency:				
Frequency	**Types**		**Tokens**	
1	262	(39.46%)	262	(3.04%)
2	77	(11.60%)	154	(1.79%)
3	58	(8.73%)	174	(2.02%)
4	31	(4.67%)	124	(1.44%)
5	19	(2.86%)	95	(1.10%)
6	20	(3.01%)	120	(1.39%)
7	12	(1.81%)	84	(0.98%)
8	21	(3.16%)	168	(1.95%)
9	7	(1.05%)	63	(0.73%)
10	14	(2.11%)	140	(1.63%)
> 10	**143**	**21.54%**	**7228**	**(83.93%**

Table 3b. Preliminary results; Corpus 2003-2007

Food and Farming (_F)				
Summary information:				
Number of types shown:			191	
Total frequency of types shown:			1589	(0.72%)
Total frequency overall:			219887	
Number of items shown with a given frequency:				
Frequency	**Types**		**Tokens**	
1	84	(43.98%)	84	(5.29%)
2	23	(12.04%)	46	(2.89%)
3	16	(8.38%)	48	(3.02%)
4	8	(4.19%)	32	(2.01%)
5	10	(5.24%)	50	(3.15%)
6	4	(2.09%)	24	(1.51%)
7	6	(3.14%)	42	(2.64%)
8	5	(2.62%)	40	(2.52%)
9	1	(0.52%)	9	(0.57%)
10	2	(1.05%)	20	(1.26%)
> 10	**32**	**16.75%**	**1194**	**(75.14%**

Table 3c. Preliminary results; Corpus 2003-2007

World and Environment (_W)				
Summary information:				
Number of types shown:			206	
Total frequency of types shown:			3884	(1.77%)
Total frequency overall:			219887	
Number of items shown with a given frequency:				
Frequency	**Types**		**Tokens**	
1	71	(34.47%)	71	(1.83%)
2	30	(14.56%)	60	(1.54%)
3	15	(7.28%)	45	(1.16%)
4	15	(7.28%)	60	(1.54%)
5	9	(4.37%)	45	(1.16%)
6	10	(4.85%)	60	(1.54%)
7	5	(2.43%)	35	(0.90%)
8	5	(2.43%)	40	(1.03%)
9	1	(0.49%)	9	(0.23%)
10	4	(1.94%)	40	(1.03%)
> 10	**41**	**(19.90%)**	**3419**	**(88.03%)**

Words identified within the USAS Tag Field: 219,887

Chapter 10
Normative Constructions of the Corporate Role of Multilatinas and Multiasians:
Within the Institutional Approach to Development at the Bretton Woods Institutions

ABSTRACT

This chapter analyzes how, historically, international institutions such as the World Bank and the International Monetary fund issued normative constructions that defined institutionally the evolution of corporations on the global south, particularly multiasians and multilatinas. The chapter carries out a single historical case study to analyze how within selected periods of the 20th century, normative interventions on development excerpted on customary official publications of both institutions, defined the character, role, and overall influence of multilatinas and multiasians on selected sectors of a global highly deregulated economy. The chapter sheds lights on how thematization and the evolution of ideological representations of the of the corporate role of multinational corporations in defined regions can be found noticeably within selected periods of time of the study.

INTRODUCTION

This chapter analyzes how historically, international institutions such as the World Bank and the International Monetary fund, issued normative constructions that defined institutionally the evolution of corporations on the global south, particularly multiasians and multilatinas. It carries out a single historical case study to analyze how within selected periods of the 20th century, normative interventions on development excerpted on customary official publications of both institutions, predefined the character,

DOI: 10.4018/978-1-6684-9794-4.ch010

role, scope and overall influence of multilatinas and multiasians in selected sectors of a global highly deregulated economy.

Making use of the contributions of historical institutionalism (Thelen, 1999), the first section highlights the fundamental settings through which the World Bank and the international monetary fund, defined further conditions for multiasians and multilatinas to strive in selected sectors and investment areas of the global economic system. It describes how through decades, south based institutions lost preeminence over the influence of global market relations, stressing a character of a norm on development that faded the principle of economic sovereignty. Such shift explains how back at the end of the Second World War, relations between nations experienced a political transition characterized by a shifting from countries recognizing each other as actors with a similar political autonomy, to one in which they view each other as components of a global market, openly affected by norms and regulations present on institutional publications at the executive level of the World Bank and the IMF. In such context, corporate mutual predation of defined economic areas, such as land investment, agriculture, services, raw material or minerals, became increasingly necessary. The section further explains how after the foundation of the Bretton Woods Institutions, the increasing pre-eminence of global financial capital over the settings of the global south, stressed the use of the market to acquire political or economic advantages and to increase profit margins, ensuring the adjustment of both multilatinas and multiasians, as well as the domestic social structures of those two regions. Finally, the section addresses the task to briefly schematize the theoretical approaches to the corporate global South, defining three fundamental approaches to the corporate role within the literature, a a)political economy approach, a b)domestic institutional approach and a c)globalizing approach; further including such framework into a single case study.

After offering a theoretical approach to multinational corporations and the global south, the second part of this chapter carries out a single case study, stressing the way in which normative interventions on development of this institutions, thematized and framed the roll and influential capacity of multilatinas and multiasians along three periods of history, namely; the decade after the end of the second world war, the decade after the end of the dollar convertibility system, and the last decade. For this goal the section conducts linguistic and critical discourse analysis to reveal to which extent and in which areas, corporations of the global south played a role in a process of global development, defined normatively by international organizations such as the World Bank and the IMF.

HISTORICAL DEPICTION AND NORMATIVE CONSTRUCTION OF THE GLOBAL SOUTH MULTINATIONAL ECONOMIC ARCHITECTURE

With the foundation of the Bretton Woods Institutions and the new regulatory framework of the global economy, the roles of multinational corporations and their influence over the social landscape acquired a leading political character. It was precisely after the agreements of New Hampshire, that lender and debtor countries configured a new defined financial and economic settings through which social and political relations where to be contextualized in the decades to come (Thacker, 1999). The prominent role of multinational corporations boosted up the conception and expansion of a new regulatory framework to the concept of "global development" (Dickens et al, 1949) (Rodrik, 2001) (Sachs, 1993), as well as a new depiction of "modernity" (Escobar, 2008). Indeed, the new setting revealed clearly that in the decades to come "poor countries, with low levels of institutionality" will be openly "weak in comparison to transnational megacorporations" (Berron, 2014), which stressed the new normative landscape of global political interaction.

The construction of a process of development embedded in the notion of the modern economy was for the Bretton Woods Institutions a fundamental assumption for rising contemporary social systems (Alacevich, 2007) (Alacevich, 2008) (Beyen, 1944). This global idea of modernity rather than a social category was established within the influence of governance structures shaped by nodes of social production (Black., 1960), and thus the creation of multinational corporations able to lead a strategic role on the global economy (Bradshaw & Huang, 1991) (Das, 2010) (Eichengreen, 2008). This explains why "modernity" for the World Bank, didn´t embrace the supposition of the nation state as a total political category, but rather as a byproduct of the market economy, presenting increasing levels of global inequality not as a structural problem of social systems, but rather as an externality that coexisted with modernity (Galbraith, 2008) (Milanovic, 2007) (Milanovic, 2006) (Sutcliffe., 2004). It is precisely in this setting, in which three major operational discourses to the role of multinational corporations on the global economy can be extracted from the executive and grey literature of the IMF and the World Bank, such as the World Trade Development report: namely a **a)political economy approach, a b)domestic institutional approach and a c)globalizing approach.**

The Political Economic Approach

From a "*Political economic approach*", processes of liberalization endorsed to the competitive capacities of national social systems to participate in a global scheme of production (Spanu, 2003) (Leiteritz & Moschella, 2010). This assumption was embraced because historically and since the Bretton Woods meeting, a global structure of redistribution of wealth -such as the nation state- has been absent from the system. This is why at the end of the Second World War, the poor capacity of Multilatinas and Multiasians to strive into the economic system, eased relations of dominant position of capital exporting nodes which frequently adhere to monopolistic or protectionist practices (Chang, 2002) (Stiglitz, 2004) (Stiglitz, 2002). While on the one hand customary economic theory demonstrates the lack of competitiveness that arise from monopolistic or dominant position practices of actors into market encounters, at the level of the Bretton Woods Institutions, such relations with corporations of the global south were not addressed as a fundamental problem of the global market architecture (Boughton, 2002) (Easterly, 2000) (IMF, 1944). As a consequence, development at the level of international politics, institutionalized a defined secondary role for multiasians and multilatinas, benefiting corporations and actors at the top of executive bodies of international organizations.

The Institutional Approach

From an "*Institutional approach*", asymmetries of the system are customarily taken apart from the set of economic or politic indicators of the World Bank. This perspective assumes that compliance with symmetric conditions of trade liberalization and therefore fair settings for multinationals of the global south are secondary for a healthy interinstitutional coordination. During the recent decades, and especially since the official publications of the "WB Development Report" (WBDR), the approach grows along the annual reports on the "state" of the global economy issued by the World Bank. (World Bank, 2009) Indeed, the development of those anomalies are depicted as a functional pattern of a "modern economy" that enhanced at higher levels the transformation of Multilatinas and Multiasians as byproducts of global flows of capital (Correa, 2002) (Cordeiro, 2007) (Zamberi & Kitchen, 2008); and specially those taking place in Latin America on the first half of the 1990 and on Asia during the 1980 (Clifton & Revuelta, 2010) (Pray, 1985) (Santiso, 2007). The institutional approach, also, rather than describing the global trends of flows of capital and the role of multinationals of the global south on the global economy, highlights the domestic features of processes of economic development on capital scarce countries (Figueredes, 1999) (José Luis Ramos, 2009). Furthermore, the approach has been further addressed in the customary grey literature of both the World Bank and the IMF. Among other issues, it addresses since early institutional publications how integration of social systems with the global economy intensified rather than decreased social exclusion generating a displacement of labor and poverty for a long period of the 20th century, yet such arrangements have been necessary for modernization. In accordance with the bank, in such social systems, the poorest members of the population were "unlikely to share economic growth" (…) therefore, by 1978, "the incomes and consumption levels of the poorer half of the population (…) stagnated [and] in countries where agriculture has expanded more slowly than population (…) the incomes of some of the rural population have (…) declined" (WDR, 1978, p. 7). On the other hand, whereas institutional research on peripheral economies addressed domestic rather than international problems, at the level of highly industrialized countries domestic pathologies are customarily isolated, highlighting the global character of their economies (Rueda, 2013). In contrast with the depiction of Asian and Latin America processes of industrialization, institutional literature regarding the "development" of highly industrialized economies, stress regularly their character as global leaders and role models.

Finally, a fundamental feature of the institutional perspective, is given by the influential role of the reports on "development" of the World Bank since 1978, when assumptions about how the global south was supposed to overcome their lags in the global economy, were contextualized as a non-relevant outcome off the "historical experience"[1] (WDR 1978. S, 7). These policies exacerbated in Latin America the necessity to address structural problems making use of "Cepalistic"[2] domestic approaches to processes of economic development (Berry, et al., 1986). In contrast, in South East Asia, more autonomous domestic measures disrupted in the economic success of the 1880 decade in countries such as Singapore, Malaysia, Thailand, Indonesia, the Philippines and Hong Kong, which back then embodied "the region with the highest economic growth in the World" (Frith, 1988, p. 4).

The Globalizing Approach

Finally, and especially during the recent decades, the role of Multinational corporations of the global South has been depicted as a complementary asset of the international economy. This new construction is explained by the fact that both Multilatinas and Multiasians, share increasingly important influence on the global economy. This approach, can be considered as a *"Globalizing approach"*, whose theoretical features depicts the increasing rise and interdependence of Multiasians and Multilatinas (Collinson & Rugman, 2007), their development as expanding international financial and economic conglomerates (Zamberi & Kitchen, 2008), the evolution of a global emerging multinational network of markets such as Brazil, India China or Mexico (Santiso, 2008), or processes of internationalization of formerly scarce capital countries or value-added activities of Latin-American firms, among others (Cuervo-Cazurra, 2007) (Cuervo-Cazurra, 2007).

MULTILATINAS, MULTIASIANS AND THE NORMATIVE CONSTRUCTION OF MODERN DEVELOPMENT WITHIN THREE PERIODS OF HISTORY

The following section of this chapter carries out a single case study to reveal how and to which extent, grey literature of the global economic architecture that goes back to the end of the Second World War, thematized the role of Multiasians and Multilatinas within selected periods of history. The section carries out a single case study on linguistic analysis to depicts the way in which normative constructions of the concept of development, represent the theoretical approach, character, scope and overall participation of multinational corporations headquarted in Asia and Latin America during the decade after the Second World War, the decade after the end of the Bretton Woods convertibility system, and the last decade. Making use of a method of analysis on thematization of discourse (Rueda, 2015), the section provides an empirical depiction of semantic fields and normative constructions through which international institutions such as the World Bank and the International Monetary Fund, rather than approaching objectively multinational corporations of the global south, carried out a defined cultural baggage that further affected Latin-American and Asian participation. Finally, the study aims to stress how such situation further provided bias in the way in which regulation, intra state relations and overall international policies on the promotion and development of multilatinas and multiasians where addressed globally.

As described, the goal of the present chapter is to study the thematization of normative constructions by revealing ideological bias of institutional literature through the examination of language[3].

Following previous research directed to the study of language, especially in the thematizacion of normative constructions in text corpora (Rueda, 2015), this section aims to reveal the extent to which grey literature of the World Bank and the International Monetary Fund framed and represented the corporate role of Asia and Latin-America within the three abovementioned approaches to corporate roles in global development; a) the political economic, b) the institutional and c) the globalizing approach. For this objective, the chapter makes use of three Semantic Fields of the USAS semantic tag set: "Money Commerce & Industry"; "Government & Public"; and "Social Actions".

I. Money Commerce & Industry brings out the semantic representation of the global south as an economic asset of global economic development. This semantic field is chosen due to the fact that it represents global south corporations as satellites of the economy, unable to ask for more equitable conditions of international competition from the market demands. This field aims to characterize the extent to which a *"political Economic approach"* to the corporate role on global development is represented on grey literature on the Institutions, thematizing discourse by stressing the role of the economy over the political relations in multi agents structures such as the World Bank of the IMF.
II. "Government and Public" semantic field joints the institutional importance of corporations with a global institutional architecture for development, and therefore is used to measure the extent to which International Institutions have a higher role in regulating both development as well as corporate global relations. This semantic field fits within the *"Institutional approach"* to the corporate global role on development, decreasing the significance of corporations in contrast with institutions, and stressing their role as established governance assets.
III. Finally, the "Social Action" semantic field depicts the level of dependence, interaction and interdependence of Global south actors within a highly increasing globalized world. This chosen field is bounded with the theoretical representations of the *"Globalizing approach"* to the corporate

role of Multilatinas and Multiasians, highlighting the role that social relations have over strictly economic or institutional arrangements.

Finally, text analysis contributes to the process of discourse examination, carrying out if necessary three strategies of exploration of the corpus linguistic: Frequency of words, representative N-grams of linguistic sequences and concordance of highly frequent words into plots belonging to each one of the three periods of study; the post-World War II period, the decade after the end of the convertibility system, including the publication of the "development" reports, and the last decade.

Figure 1. Results per periods 1947 – 1957

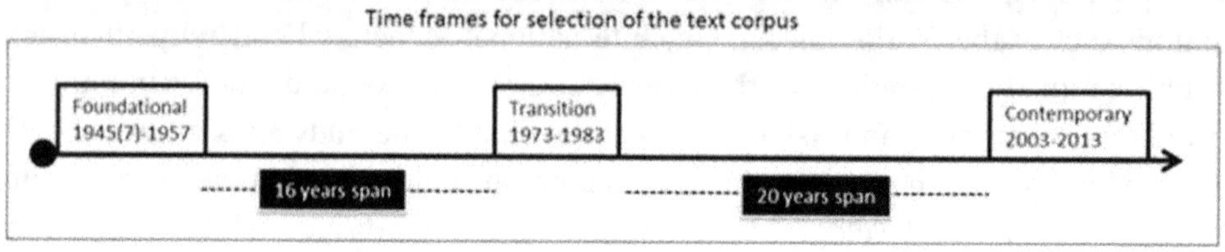

Figure 2. Money commerce and industry, government and public, and social actions states and processes

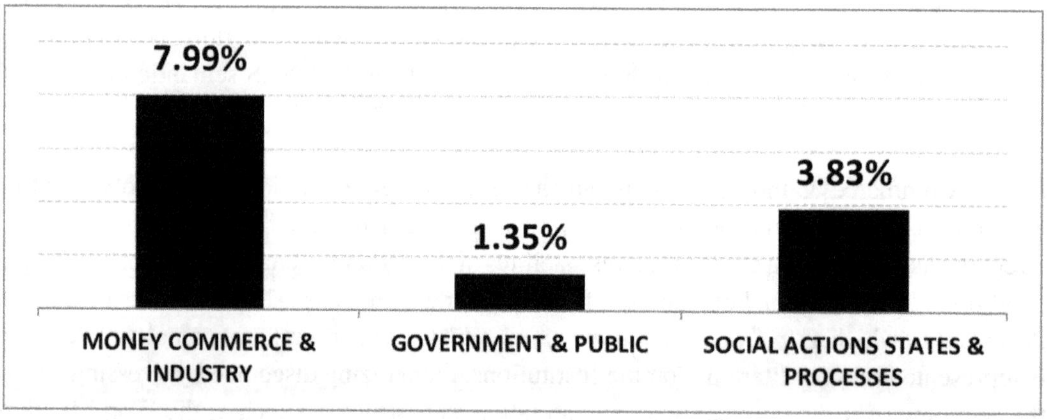

The text corpus of the period 1947-1957 reveals a noticeable relevance of the semantic field "Money, Commerce & Industry", in contrast with "Social Actions" and "Government & Public". This tendency can be also found on the evolution of the semantic field within the upcoming two periods. In contrast with the other semantic fields, the tendency exposes a highly relevant economic approach of the selected grey literature of the World Bank and the IMF, framing and thematizing how development is framed extensively within a market structure, and therefore, how global south actors should play a role within institutions in which they are vastly underrepresented.

Figure 3. Money commerce and industry

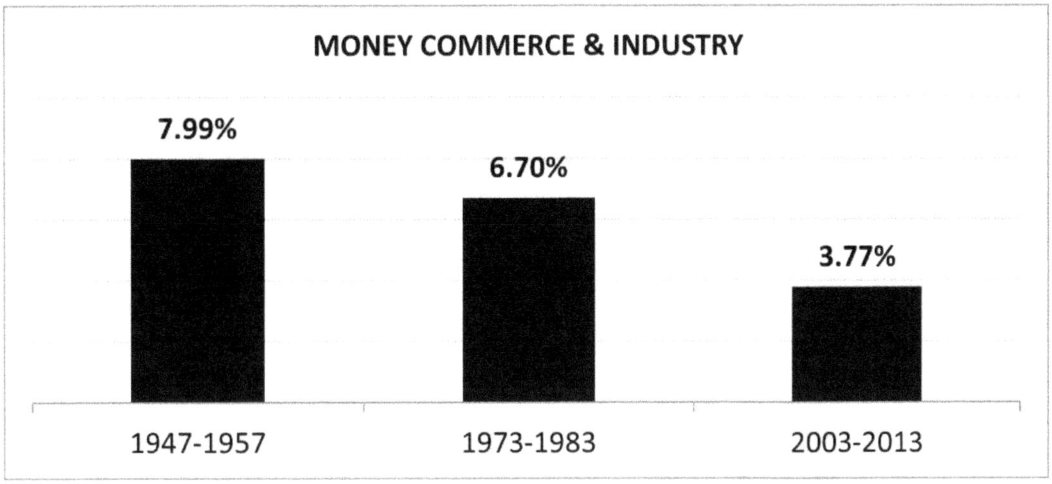

A concordance search of the text corpus in the selected period reveals a highly diminished role of Latin America and Asia as fundamental actors of the corporate global environment within which the Bretton Woods Institutions represented global development. Indeed, among the selected text corpus, the word "Asia" presents no occurrences along a list of more than 60.000 instances. In contrast, "Latin America" is mentioned on a scarce total of 18 occurrences, in which it is possible to address the way in which Latin America corporate role is represented. Within the 14th openly expressed ocurrences of the geographic area, Latin America is mentioned 11 times as a strategic Great Britain supplier of "primary products" (International Bank for Reconstruction and Development, 1953, p. 58), revealing how during those years while the "British imports increased considerably, the value of British imports from Latin America actually declined and there (were) no expansion in British exports to the area". Indeed, however, the approach of the documentation, stresses clearly an entirely British perspective to the commercial relations with Latin America since such commercial interaction of the 1952 British surplus with Latin America was considered a "temporary phenomenon which would disappear as soon as British imports from the area were resumed". Moreover, the situation for England represented a *non* "healthy development considering how much Britain needed the primary products available in Latin America".

In this period, it is worth to note that the commercial strategies of England to maintain surplus with their commercial European counterparts included the adoption of pressures to short imports of Britain from the former OEEC (Organization for European Economic Co-operation). This institution just by 1961 included United States and Canada; becoming the well-known OECD (Organization for Economic Cooperation and Development). Such strategy however, was to be found unable in the case of Latin America, since a shortage of sterling or dollars in the region, represented a decline in British exports, institutionalizing a dependency of Latin America of capital generated in the *common wealth*. Indeed, within the period, as the former Bank for Reconstruction & Development report revealed, a "sharp decline in British imports from these countries *(Latin America)* which took place in 1952 (… was) accompanied by a steady decline in British exports" (International Bank for Reconstruction and Development, 1953, p. 77) .

In conclusion, institutional representations of the corporate role of Latin America and Asia within the concept of development, reveals during the 1947 – 1957 period a submissive and secondary position. On the other hand, among the corpus, there are coincidences illustrating Latin America or Asia in first person, nor the future necessary strategies of the region to strive in a highly asymmetric institutional environment. Finally, the scarce yet valuable content found in the selected institutional text corpora, depicts clearly how a "political economic approach" to the corporate role of Latin America and Asia, may well explain better south north relations of the period and the way in which further interactions with Latin America and Asia were to be represented and addressed.

Figure 4. Period 1973 – 1983 word search

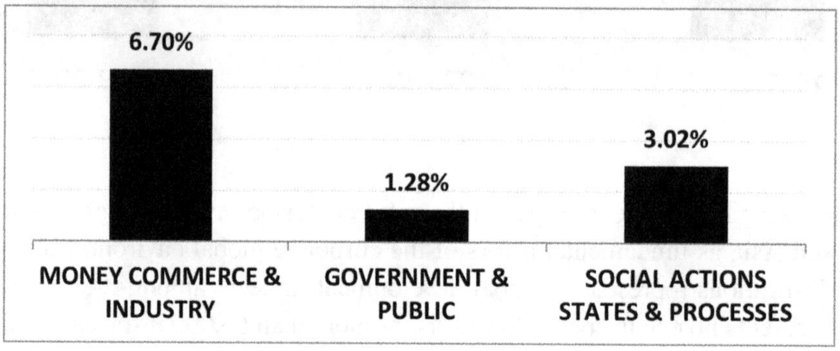

From a preliminary view, the decade 1973 – 1983 shows a similar tendency to that presented in the previous research period. This is explained by the distribution of the three semantic fields selected from the UCREL semantic tag set. The similarity on the distribution however is valuable considering how the 1973-1983 period corpora didn't include the institutional foundational documentation of the World Bank and the International Monetary Fund, while at the same time almost doubles in extension the corpora selected for the 1947 – 1957 period, yet keeping the original thematic structure.

In contrast with the previous period, the 1973-1983 decade reveals an inversion in the tendency Latin America and Asia role was addressed within the selected corpora. This trend is explained by the fact that occurrences within search terms reveal cero (0) frequencies of the term "Latin" or "Latin" referred to the geographical region, yet a total of 9 "Asia" and 5 "Asia" search occurrences. This results makes clear a shift in references to both geographical regions and its role as a corporate node of global development. In such cases, the development reports account the increasing role of South East Asia, highlighting how by 1970, Malaysia excelled as the most prosperous developing country of the region, maintaining "fairly high rates of growth of CNP in constant prices (…and) averaging about 6 percent per annum during" the decade (World Bank, 1973). The content also stresses the outstanding historical role Singapore and Hong Kong presented during the decade, highlighting how for instance, the corporate sector of South Asia played a key role in the development process, yet in the case of Malaysia a big share was owned by foreign investors. Indeed, by the 70s "the corporate sector of the share of Malaysia" was "only about 2 percent of total assets; (…while) foreigners own as much as 62 percent" (World Bank, 1973, p. 2). In fact, within the World Bank reports, the corporate role of South Asian companies played a key function in political relations in the region and especially with China, which was by the time viewed as a potential geopolitical key actor. In this settings, companies such as the Malaysian Airlines System, the International Shipping corporation, PERNAS, the Urban Development Authority, SEDS´s State Development Corporations and others, were taken into account as strategic nodes of the economy of the region, even when paradoxically "foreigners dominated the (...share of) manufacturing and commercial sectors" (World Bank, 1973, p. 39).

Among Hong Kong, Malaysia, Indonesia and Thailand, the reports of the Bank also highlight the evolution and corporate role of the Philippines and Burma within the region. On the one hand, Philippine's corporate sector –and especially early manufacturing industry- is presented as a rising premature productive niche, considering by the 1970s decade, that "overall performance in both domestic and export markets appears to have fallen short of potential, and compares unfavorably with that of industry in some other countries which share common characteristics with it" (World Bank, 1974). In contrast with the decade after the Second World War, the reports of the Bank in this case focuses more in the state of the industry and the strategic further measures the country should adopt to improve its performance. In this approach, the document suggests numerous measures to be taken for instance in the footwear industry –favoring the prospects of the country against region competitors such as Japan, Korea, Taiwan and Hong Kong -, the textile, Garment, general manufacture and embroidery sector-, the finance corporate sector, the raw material sector –special interest put into the raw wood pulp-, the transportation and construction sector, and even in the infant shipping building sector. This last one in which the country most advanced rivals were South Korea and Japan.

Overall the approach to the role of the corporate Asian sector within the normative construction of the concept of development, is found to be as a strategic within the local requirements of the continent. Along the occurrences over the text search, references to corporations of the global north or representations of the role of countries at the executive level of institutions such as the World Bank or the IMF are relatively scarce in the diagnosis focused in the corporate role of Asia.

Figure 5. Period 2003 – 2013

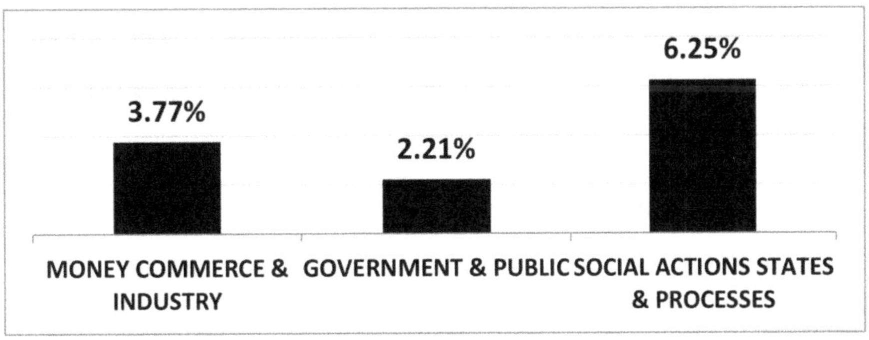

Semantic analysis directed to reveal the thematization of discourse production on the corporate role of the concept of development, shows a significant change on the period 2003-2013 in comparison with previous periods. During the decade and rather as a highly surprising shift, the content of the corpus presents a higher connotation of the "Social actions States & Processes" semantic tag field, in comparison with "Money Commerce & Industry" or "Government & Public". This preliminary result in turn allows us to associate a value laden thematization of the corpora to the above mentioned "Globalizing approach" to the corporate role of Asia and Latin America.

The result of a tag search of coincidences of the word "Latin" or "Asia" within the 2003-2013 text corpora, present an outstanding outcome in comparison with previous periods. In total, the search for the case of "Asia" presents 99 occurrences; and in the case of the *Latin* region a total of 184 occurrences. This shows a clear predisposition of the institutional grey literature of the organizations to incorporate within the text corpora, semantic areas that turn to the analysis of Latin America or Asia as a relevant corporate role within the norm of "development".

Overall, the concordance plots of the selected period shows a similar presentation of the corporate role of Asia and Latin America to that presented in the period 1973-1983. Since no other relevant depiction of the corporate role of this two regions within the text corpora can be included without further research, it is possible to address that the thematization of the corporations of the global south within the text, presents a "Social Actions" semantic frequency profile, with a complementary clear assimilation of the Latin America and Asia region, and therefore can be considered part of a "globalizing approach" to the corporate role of global south corporations.

CONCLUSION

Thematization of the normative construction of development has played an historical key role in the way in which corporate Latin America and Asia have been depicted within grey literature of the World Bank and the International Monetary Fund. This paper addresses this issue by making use of a rather alternative CDA theoretical and empirical approach. From a theoretical perspective the chapter operationalizes three approaches to the corporate role of the normative construction of development; a "*political economic approach", an "institutional approach" and a "globalizing approach"*. Later on the chapter carries out a single case study to analyze the extent to which this approaches can be found along three periods of this institutions, and within three semantic Fields of the USAS semantic tag set: "Money Commerce & Industry"; "Government & Public"; and "Social Actions" respectively. In conclusion the chapter addresses that thematization of the corporate role of Multiasians and Multilatinas can be found noticeably within three periods of time. A political economic approaches corresponds with the result of the 1947 – 1957 period; a globalizing approach matches with the result of the 2000-2013 decade, and potentially and institutional approach or a value laden shift to it matches with the semantic thematization and depiction of the corporate role of Multiasians and Multilatinas along the 1973-1983 decade

REFERENCES

Alacevich, M. (2007). *Early Development Economics Debates*. World Bank.

Alacevich, M. (2008). *The World Bank's Early Reflections on Development: A Development Institution or a Bank?* World Bank. https://openknowledge.worldbank.org/handle/10986/6840 doi:10.1596/1813-9450-4670

Berron, G. (2014). Economic power, democracy and human rights. A new international debates on human rights and corporations. *Sur. International Journal on Human Rights*.

Berry, A., Thoumi, F. E., & Zerda, A. (1986). Crecimiento y políticas económicas en Colombia: 1970-1984. *Colombia beyond the National Front*. West View Press.

Beyen, J. W. (1948). The International Bank for Reconstruction and Development. *International Affairs*, 24.

Black, E. R. (1960, June). The age of economic development. *Economic Journal (London)*, *70*(278), 266–276. doi:10.2307/2228727

Boughton, J. M. (2002). Why White, Not Keynes? Inventing the Postwar International Monetary System. *IMF Working Paper*. IMF.

Bradshaw, Y. W., & Huang, J. (1991, Autumn). Intensifying global dependency: Foreign Debt, Structural Adjustment and Third World Underdevelopment. *The Sociological Quarterly*, *32*(3), 321–342. doi:10.1111/j.1533-8525.1991.tb00162.x

Chang, H. J. (2002). Kicking away the ladder. [Anthem World History]. *Policies and Institutions for Economic Development in Historical Perspective*, *ISBN-10*, 1843310279.

Clifton, J. & Revuelta, J. (2010). *"Multilatinas" in the American dynamics of nation champion policy and asymmetric behaviour.* Revista Internacional de Organizaciones. RIO. No.04.

Collinson, S., & Rugman, A. (2007). The regional character of Asian multinational Enterprises. [Springer.]. *Asia Pacific Journal of Management*, *24*(4), 429–446. doi:10.100710490-006-9035-y

Cordeiro, J. L. (2007). El Desafío Latinoamericáno y sus cinco grandes retos. McGraw Hill.

Correa, R. (2002). Structural reforms and economic growth in Latin America: a sensitivity analysis. *CEPAL review*. CEPAL.

Cuervo-Cazurra, A. (2007). Sequence of value-added activities in the multinationalization of developing country firms. *Journal of International Management*, *13*(3), 258–277. doi:10.1016/j.intman.2007.05.009

Cuervo-Cazurra, A. (2007). The Multinationalization of Developing contry MNEs: The case of Multilatinas. Sonoco International Business Department. *Journal of International Management*.

Das, D. K. (2010). *Financial Globalization: Growth, Integration, Innovation, and Crisis*. Palgrave Macmillan. doi:10.1057/9780230289949

Dickens. (1949, June). Private Foreign Investments: A Means of World Economic Development. [Jun.]. *Political Science Quarterly*, *64*(2), 211–244.

EasterlyW. (2000). The Effect of IMF and World Bank Programs on Poverty. SSRN. https://ssrn.com/abstract=256883 or doi:10.2139/ssrn.256883

Eichengreen, B. (2008). *Globalizing Capital:A History of the International Monetary System* (2nd ed.). Princeton University Press. doi:10.2307/j.ctt7pfmc

Escobar, A. (2008). The Problematization of Poverty; the tale of three worlds and development. In *The development reader* (pp. 131–140). MPG, Books Ltd. Bodmin.

Figueredes, J. M. (1999). *Centroamérica en el camino hacia el desarrollo sostenible.*. s.l.:Universidad de los Andes. Colombia. ISBN. 958-695-029-8.

Frith, K. (1988). *More than we bargained for: The impact of consumer culture in South East Asia. Department of Journalism and Mass comunication*. Iowa State University.

Galbraith, J. K. (2008). *Inequality and Economic and Political Change*. (UTIP Working Paper). UTIP.

IMF. (1944). Articles of Agreement of the International Monetary Fund. New Hampshire, IMF.

International Bank for Reconstruction and Development. (1953). *The position of the world economy on the eve of the outbreak of the Koren War and the post-korean developments and prospects*. International Bank.

José Luis Ramos, R. A. (2009). *Transformacion productiva y desarrollo tecnologico. El caso de la region caribe Colombiana.*. Ediciones Uninorte.

Leiteritz & Moschella. R. J. M. (2010). The IMF and capital account liberalization: a case of failed norm institutionalization. In Susan Park & Antje Vetterlein. Owning Development. Creating Policy Norms in the IMF and the WB. Cambridge University Press.

Milanovic, B. 2006. *Global income inequality: What it is and why it matters*. World Bank.

Milanovic, B. (2007). An even Higuer inequality than previously though: a note on global inequality calculations using the 2005 ICP results. *World Bank Policy Research Working Paper Series*. ICP.

Pray, C. (1985). *Private sector research and technology transfer in Asian agriculture: report on phase 1 aid grant OTR 0091-G-SS-4195*. Unniversity of Minnesota..

Rodrik, D. (2001). *The Global governance of Trade. As if development really mattered. United Nations Development Programm. Social Development Group*. Bureau for Development Policy.

RuedaR. 2013. Social Crisis and global repricing of financial instruments. (July 24, 2013). SSRN. https://ssrn.com/abstract=2297893 or doi:10.2139/ssrn.2297893

Rueda, R. (2015). Land Acquisition and the Semantic Context of Land within the Normative Construction of Modern Development. In Handbook of Research on In Country determinants and implications with Foreign Land Acquisitions. IGI GLobal.

Sachs, W. (1993). Global Ecology and the Shadow of "Development". in Global Ecology: A New Arena of Political Conflict. London and New Jersey: Zed Books.

Santiso, J. (2007). *The emergence of latin multinationals*. (OECD Emerging Markets Network Working Paper). OECD.

Santiso, J. (2008). The emergence of Latin Multinationals. *CEPAL Review*, *95*(August).

Spanu, V. (2003). *Liberalization of the international trade and economic growth: implications for both developed and developing countries*. John F. Kennedy School of Government.

Stiglitz, J. (2002). Globalization and its Discontents. Norton & Company.

Stiglitz, J. (2004). Capital-market Liberalization, Globalization, and the IMF. *Oxford Review of Economic Policy*, *20*(1), 57–71. doi:10.1093/oxrep/grh004

Sutcliffe, B. (2004). World Inequality and Globalization. Oxford Review of Economic Policy, 20. Oxford University Press. . doi:10.1093/oxrep/grh002

Thacker, S. C. (1999). The High Politics of IMF Lending. *World Politics, 52*(1), 38–75. doi:10.1017/S0043887100020025

Thelen, K. (1999). Historical Institutionalism in Comparative Politics. *Annual Review of Political Science, 2*(1), 369–404. Retrieved (https://www.annualreviews.org/doi/abs/10.1146/annurev.p

WDR. (1978). *World Development Report.* World Bank.

World Bank. (1973). International Bank for Reconstruction and Development. *Development Prospects of Malaysia, 1.* World Bank.

World Bank. (1974). Bank for Reconstruction and Development. International Development Asociation. *Industrial Development Probelms and Prospects in the Philippines.* World Bank.

World Bank. (2009). Reshaping economic geography. *World Bank World Development Report.* World Bank.

Zamberi, S. & Kitchen, J. P. (2008). Transnational corporations from Asian developing countries: The internationalisation characteristics and business strategies of Sime Darby Berhad. *Journal of Business Science and Applied Management, 3*(2).

ENDNOTES

1 Ibid.

2 Guidelines from the Economic Commission for Latin America (ECLA) or CEPAL in Spanish.

3 See chapter 4.

APPENDIX

Table 1. Preliminary results; Corpus 947-1957

MONEY COMMERCE & INDUSTRY				
Number of types shown: 379				
Total frequency of types shown: 4793 (7.99%)				
Total frequency overall: 60008				
Number of items shown with a given frequency:				
Frequency	**Types**		**Tokens**	
1	169	(44.59%)	169	(3.53%)
2	46	(12.14%)	92	(1.92%)
3	17	(4.49%)	51	(1.06%)
4	14	(3.69%)	56	(1.17%)
5	10	(2.64%)	50	(1.04%)
6	10	(2.64%)	60	(1.25%)
7	11	(2.90%)	77	(1.61%)
8	4	(1.06%)	32	(0.67%)
9	6	(1.58%)	54	(1.13%)
10	8	(2.11%)	80	(1.67%)
> 10	**84**	**(22.16%)**	**4072**	**(84.96%)**

GOVERNMENT & PUBLIC				
Number of types shown: 151				
Total frequency of types shown: 813 (1.35%)				
Total frequency overall: 60008				
Number of items shown with a given frequency:				
Frequency	**Types**		**Tokens**	
1	70	(46.36%)	70	(8.61%)
2	32	(21.19%)	64	(7.87%)
3	13	(8.61%)	39	(4.80%)
4	5	(3.31%)	20	(2.46%)
5	6	(3.97%)	30	(3.69%)
6	2	(1.32%)	12	(1.48%)
7	5	(3.31%)	35	(4.31%)
8	2	(1.32%)	16	(1.97%)
9		(0.00%)		(0.00%)
10		(0.00%)		(0.00%)
> 10	**16**	**(10.60%)**	**527**	**(64.82%)**

SOCIAL ACTIONS STATES & PROCESSES				
Number of types shown: 402				
Total frequency of types shown: 2300 (3.83%)				
Total frequency overall: 60008				
Number of items shown with a given frequency:				
Frequency	**Types**		**Tokens**	
1	173	(43.03%)	173	(7.52%)
2	68	(16.92%)	136	(5.91%)
3	40	(9.95%)	120	(5.22%)
4	19	(4.73%)	76	(3.30%)
5	11	(2.74%)	55	(2.39%)
6	19	(4.73%)	114	(4.96%)
7	9	(2.24%)	63	(2.74%)
8	10	(2.49%)	80	(3.48%)
9	6	(1.49%)	54	(2.35%)
10	3	(0.75%)	30	(1.30%)
> 10	**44**	**(10.95%)**	**1399**	**(60.83%)**

1973 - 1983

MONEY COMMERCE & INDUSTRY				
Number of types shown: 579				
Total frequency of types shown: 7004 (6.70%)				
Total frequency overall: 104539				
Number of items shown with a given frequency:				
Frequency	**Types**		**Tokens**	
1	262	(45.25%)	262	(3.74%)
2	63	(10.88%)	126	(1.80%)
3	28	(4.84%)	84	(1.20%)
4	25	(4.32%)	100	(1.43%)
5	30	(5.18%)	150	(2.14%)
6	16	(2.76%)	96	(1.37%)
7	13	(2.25%)	91	(1.30%)
8	9	(1.55%)	72	(1.03%)
9	7	(1.21%)	63	(0.90%)

GOVERNMENT & PUBLIC				
Number of types shown: 178				
Total frequency of types shown: 1336 (1.28%)				
Total frequency overall: 104539				
Number of items shown with a given frequency:				
Frequency	**Types**		**Tokens**	
1	91	(51.12%)	91	(6.81%)
2	22	(12.36%)	44	(3.29%)
3	15	(8.43%)	45	(3.37%)
4	7	(3.93%)	28	(2.10%)
5	10	(5.62%)	50	(3.74%)
6	6	(3.37%)	36	(2.69%)
7	3	(1.69%)	21	(1.57%)
8	2	(1.12%)	16	(1.20%)
9	1	(0.56%)	9	(0.67%)

SOCIAL ACTIONS STATES & PROCESSES				
Number of types shown: 600				
Total frequency of types shown: 3161 (3.02%)				
Total frequency overall: 104539				
Number of items shown with a given frequency:				
Frequency	**Types**		**Tokens**	
1	295	(49.17%)	295	(9.33%)
2	83	(13.83%)	166	(5.25%)
3	55	(9.17%)	165	(5.22%)
4	27	(4.50%)	108	(3.42%)
5	22	(3.67%)	110	(3.48%)
6	22	(3.67%)	132	(4.18%)
7	6	(1.00%)	42	(1.33%)
8	12	(2.00%)	96	(3.04%)
9	7	(1.17%)	63	(1.99%)

Continued on following page

Table 1. Continued

MONEY COMMERCE & INDUSTRY					GOVERNMENT & PUBLIC					SOCIAL ACTIONS STATES & PROCESSES				
10	8	(1.38%)	80	(1.14%)	10	3	(1.69%)	30	(2.25%)	10	5	(0.83%)	50	(1.58%)
> 10	**118**	**(20.38%)**	**5880**	**(83.95%**	**> 10**	**18**	**(10.11%)**	**966**	**(72.31%)**	**> 10**	**66**	**(11.00%)**	**1934**	**(61.18%)**
2003 - 2013														
MONEY COMMERCE & INDUSTRY					GOVERNMENT & PUBLIC					SOCIAL ACTIONS STATES & PROCESSES				
Number of types shown: 1052					Number of types shown: 797					Number of types shown: 1859				
Total frequency of types shown: 21949 (3.77%)					Total frequency of types shown: 12888 (2.21%)					Total frequency of types shown: 36402 (6.25%)				
Total frequency overall: 582060					Total frequency overall: 582060					Total frequency overall: 582060				
Number of items shown with a given frequency:					Number of items shown with a given frequency:					Number of items shown with a given frequency:				
Frequency	**Types**		**Tokens**		**Frequency**	**Types**		**Tokens**		**Frequency**	**Types**		**Tokens**	
1	416	(39.54%)	416	(1.90%)	1	314	(39.40%)	314	(2.44%)	1	665	(35.77%)	665	(1.83%)
2	122	(11.60%)	244	(1.11%)	2	112	(14.05%)	224	(1.74%)	2	260	(13.99%)	520	(1.43%)
3	78	(7.41%)	234	(1.07%)	3	59	(7.40%)	177	(1.37%)	3	136	(7.32%)	408	(1.12%)
4	47	(4.47%)	188	(0.86%)	4	38	(4.77%)	152	(1.18%)	4	104	(5.59%)	416	(1.14%)
5	33	(3.14%)	165	(0.75%)	5	34	(4.27%)	170	(1.32%)	5	59	(3.17%)	295	(0.81%)
6	37	(3.52%)	222	(1.01%)	6	21	(2.63%)	126	(0.98%)	6	61	(3.28%)	366	(1.01%)
7	24	(2.28%)	168	(0.77%)	7	19	(2.38%)	133	(1.03%)	7	40	(2.15%)	280	(0.77%)
8	21	(2.00%)	168	(0.77%)	8	13	(1.63%)	104	(0.81%)	8	38	(2.04%)	304	(0.84%)
9	21	(2.00%)	189	(0.86%)	9	12	(1.51%)	108	(0.84%)	9	37	(1.99%)	333	(0.91%)
10	18	(1.71%)	180	(0.82%)	10	9	(1.13%)	90	(0.70%)	10	28	(1.51%)	280	(0.77%)
> 10	**235**	**(22.34%)**	**19775**	**(90.10%)**	**> 10**	**166**	**(20.83%)**	**11290**	**(87.60%)**	**> 10**	**431**	**(23.18%)**	**32535**	**(89.38%)**

CONCLUSION

In recent decades, the idea of asymmetry, rather than inequality, has been avoided of being adequately formulated for conducting research in political science, international relations theory and social sciences. One of the main reasons behind this evolution of modern research has to do with the ontological dichotomy between social science scholars. Hence, unable to offer a coherent depiction of the factual and subjective relations that drive politics and societies, they have further endorsed single ontological categories for explaining social phenomena. These events have later created a bifurcation between materialist and constructivist, unable to be adequately bounded for the study and comprehension of norms and their evolution. Finally, within single ontological categories, it has not been possible to effectively contextualize and comprehend the way norms unfold within late modern social systems, affecting the appropriate understanding of the phenomena that lays beneath actors' relations in multi-agent environments, such as international organizations. In offering a coherent solution to this historical problem, the present book has introduced the *theory of political asymmetry*; aiming to contribute to the adequate understanding of the inner processes taking place in governance architectures, and looking forward to track and to contextualize the detailed evolutions of norms produced within them in contemporary societies.

The *theory of political asymmetry* contextualizes the evolution of norms within defined settings of contemporary late modern social systems. It stresses the material role of individuals as both strategic and subject-oriented actors, aiming to rationalize processes of social coordination among formal institutions. As such, the development of societies has been permanently bounded by these two rather contradictory features of agents, further replicated at the level of the nation state on international institutions such as the World Bank and the International Monetary Fund. The theory, therefore, stresses both the instrumentalist character and the cognitive dimension of asymmetry, and how these two features are further framed, distorted, bordered and surrounded by institutional arrangements that take place in concrete temporal processes.

THE THEORY AND THE CONTEXT OF NORMS PRODUCTION ON LATE MODERN INTERNATIONAL INSTITUTIONS

For presenting an articulated description of how contemporary international institutions operate within the process of production of meaning of norms, the *theory of political asymmetry* has selected the use of six theoretical thinking tools. From a sociological perspective, the theory highlights how norms on late modern social systems must be clearly contextualized within the 1) properties of economic relations over contemporary normative constructions, must stress the 2) relevance of subtle formal structures on discourse production, and must conceive that 3) "norms" and "normative constructions" are a practice of symmetric interaction. From an institutional perspective, the theory highlights the fact that norms production on multi-agent environments, such as international institutions, must stress the role of 4) concrete temporal processes and the development of discourse, the permanent 5) relation between institutions and superstructures, such as the global economy, and must highlight the symbiotic relation between 6) institutional values (culture and epistemic communities) and meaning.

These tools draw on previous contributions of historical institutionalism and critical constructivism. They explain and put into context how contemporary international institutions 1) are not absent from the progression of the global capitalist enterprise, and 2) are *utterly* subjected to well-defined biographical events that have further affected global processes of societal development. As such, a coherent depiction of norms, and particularly of the "norm of modern development", rather than avoiding such two variables must stress them so as to reveal the extent to which asymmetric architectures distort, reproduce, self-referentiate and frame normative meaning.

THE CASE OF *MODERN DEVELOPMENT* AND THE EVOLUTION OF MEANING OF ASYMMETRIC ENVIRONMENTS

In the selection of the case study, the *theory of political asymmetry* reveals that, consistently, asymmetric political environments are characterized by an *extraordinary* aversion to change over time. Hence, normative meaning produced at the executive and administrative level of international institutions is hardly contested, and remains almost unchanged even after several decades. This, in turn, exposes that if substantive reconfiguration of the institutional architectures where flows of information between agents take place is not exerted, norms produced within asymmetric settings are not able to be disputed, refuted, challenged, changed or regulatively modified over several generations.

In the case of the norm of "modern development", this book depicts the material consequences of such settings. In doing so, it approaches both the ideological and power dimension of asymmetry, as well as its cognitive aspect. For the ideological (power) dimension, the book describes the transmutation of its ethical or deontological character into the normalization of a contractual approach to justice, depicting the evolution of the institutional turn to ethics, and the functional normalization of social crisis within the historical progression of the norm. From a cognitive dimension, the theory reveals the almost unchallenged evolution of their approach on salient features of contemporary social systems, such as the role of land in processes of human settlements and urban organization, or the historical representation of global south corporations within grey literature of both multi-agent environments, the WB and the IMF.

The *theory of political asymmetry* is also an attempt to understand and to put into context the relation and evolution within structures of governance of the cultural backgrounds of agents and their inner individual interests. It highlights, through the biographical stages of the WB and the IMF, the norms that developed within formal executive boards of governance institutions, which remain essentially uncontested over time. In this regard, nation-states, as individual agents, are not able to realize such problematic features of the international system, even after numerous replacements of professional staff at the executive level of international institutions. As such, this feature of asymmetry in international organizations is hardly contested unless the architectures through which communication processes take place, opens up channels of dialogical interaction, or endorse institutionally, or with new mandatory character, a different ideological, legal or epistemic approach. This last cognitive dimension of institutions, reveals the odd semantic horizons within which epistemic communities reproduce overtime, *recycling* permanently the same constitutive *contractual* traditions.

POLITICAL ASYMMETRY AND THE *NARCISSIST* CHARACTER OF ASYMMETRIC GOVERNANCE

From the 2008 global economic downturn to the discussions on climate change, immigration, terrorism, energetic security or global resource depletion, the incremental level of global interdependence makes necessary the definition of channels of dialogical coordination through which domestic political and economic efforts can fill the informational gap left by asymmetric structures of governance. In this regard, the attempt to tease out the limitations of the current governance architecture, rather than stressing the political character of these events, points to the necessity to put into context the scientific nature of global politics, and the informational and overall cognitive limitations of agents within asymmetric structures.

Along these features, the book aims to clearly bring to the fore the mutual relation between power and cognition that evolves along the governance boards of international organizations. With this aim, the theory highlights on the one hand, how asymmetries map the reality of the ideological and social relations between non-industrialized and industrialized territories. As such, historical social shock measures have not only shifted from periphery to core countries, but have also been adopted and normalized in the latter one, eroding attempts to construct social projects isolated from global flows of capital. Furthermore, it has revealed how, over time, normative constructions such as the idea of modernity, have recreated a single subjective ethical dimension, excerpted contractually, transposing rather conflicting arrangements along the concept of institutional justice, and colonizing the dialogical sphere of global politics.

On the other hand, it has shown over defined biographical periods of the World Bank and the International Monetary Fund, the semantic and overall informational evolution of ideological or theoretical bias, and its relation with grey influential literature on *development*. As such, it revealed how organizations operationalize asymmetric reality via discourse, fitting defined theoretical frameworks on environmental and economic features of late modern social systems. Intrinsically, over time, they tend to reproduce perspectives of influential agents that take decisions by embracing value-laden assumptions, in absence of functional channels of contestation.

The research aims to expose the rather self-referential thinking process of epistemic communities—or the narcissistic character of global politics—, and their limitations in better contextualizing and comprehending global contemporary urgencies. As such, the concrete temporal events that shaped the institutional biography of these institutions have distorted both, global political interaction and dialogical coordination between countries that agree to follow the conditions given in the foundational process of the WB or the IMF. Finally, the case study on the "norm of modern development" reveals how the current global political architecture has, within the Bretton Woods institutions, trapped the multidisciplinary character of development, framing over decades the semantic dimension of the concept within functional boundaries of institutions that *mimic* patterns of agents that interacted back in 1945.

Table 18. 50 Main key field

	Key words	TF. Keine Zeichen	Vlookup	Semantic preeminence
1	64386	Z5	Grammatical bin	a
2	8576	Z99	Unmatched	a
3	6130	N1	Numbers	a
4	5338	Z8	Pronouns etc.	a
5	5169	Z2	Geographical names	a
6	4068	A3	Being	a
7	3908	M7	Places	a
8	2982	A2.1	Affect: Modify, change	a
9	2923	P1	Education in general	a
10	2839	A1.1.1	General actions, making etc.	a
11	2578	S5	Groups and affiliation	b
12	2472	A7	Definite (+ modals)	b
13	2432	T3	Time: Old, new and young; age	b
14	2266	Z1	Personal names	b
15	2209	N5	Quantities	b
16	2151	A2.2	Affect: Cause/Connected	b
17	2149	S2	People	b
18	2103	A9	Getting and giving; possession	b
19	2102	S8	Helping/hindering	b
20	2084	I1.1	Money: Affluence	b
21	1880	M6	Location and direction	c
22	1714	N5	Quantities	c
23	1690	X7	Wanting; planning; choosing	c
24	1647	I3.1	Work and employment: Generally	c
25	1535	M1	Moving, coming and going	c
26	1505	G1.1	Government etc.	c
27	1502	Q2.2	Speech acts	c
28	1433	A9	Getting and giving; possession	c
29	1420	W3	Geographical terms	c
30	1343	S7.1	Power, organizing	c
31	1335	A6.1	Comparing: Similar/different	d
32	1255	A13.3	Degree: Boosters	d
33	1247	N5	Quantities	d
34	1126	W1	The universe	d
35	1120	A5.1	Evaluation: Good/bad	d
36	1079	T1.3	Time: Period	d
37	1053	S1.1.1	General	d
38	1027	W5	Green issues	d

Continued on following page

Table 18. Continued

	Key words	TF. Keine Zeichen	Vlookup	Semantic preeminence
39	1023	Z6	Negative	d
40	1022	S6	Obligation and necessity	d
41	1022	A11.1	Importance: Important	e
42	983	S4	Kin	e
43	947	F4	Farming & Horticulture	e
44	942	X2.2	Knowledge	e
45	938	N3.2	Measurement: Size	e
46	900	O2	Objects generally	e
47	890	N5	Quantities	e
48	844	A6.2	Comparing: Usual/unusual	e
49	844	Y2	Information technology and computing	e
50	829	Z3	Other proper names	e

Table 19. 50 main key field

	Key words	TF. Keine Zeichen	Vlookup	Semantic preeminence
1	150770	Z5	Grammatical bin	a
2	30775	Z99	Unmatched	a
3	24116	N1	Numbers	a
4	20841	Z2	Geographical names	a
5	12061	M7	Places	a
6	11729	Z1	Personal names	a
7	9331	A2.1	Affect: Modify, change	a
8	8992	Z8	Pronouns etc.	a
9	8050	A3	Being	a
10	7710	F4	Farming & Horticulture	a
11	7248	A1.1.1	General actions, making etc.	b
12	6686	S5	Groups and affiliation	b
13	5380	A2.2	Affect: Cause/Connected	b
14	5323	N5	Quantities	b
15	5321	A7	Definite (+ modals)	b
16	5298	S8	Helping/hindering	b
17	5051	I1.1	Money: Affluence	b
18	4941	M6	Location and direction	b
19	4730	G1.1	Government etc.	b
20	4657	X7	Wanting; planning; choosing	b
21	4326	I2.2	Business: Selling	c
22	4231	A9	Getting and giving; possession	c
23	4032	A9	Getting and giving; possession	c
24	3939	Z3	Other proper names	c
25	3740	M1	Moving, coming and going	c
26	3736	A6.1	Comparing: Similar/different	c
27	3678	Q2.2	Speech acts	c
28	3674	N5	Quantities	c
29	3552	S7.1	Power, organizing	c
30	3354	W3	Geographical terms	c
31	3308	O2	Objects generally	d
32	3232	W1	The universe	d
33	2824	T1.3	Time: Period	d
34	2684	X2.4	Investigate, examine, test, search	d
35	2600	I2.1	Business: Generally	d
36	2593	A11.1	Importance: Important	d
37	2443	N5	Quantities	d
38	2433	N5	Quantities	d

Continued on following page

Table 19. Continued

	Key words	TF. Keine Zeichen	Vlookup	Semantic preeminence
39	2401	F1	Food	d
40	2385	N3.2	Measurement: Size	d
41	2383	S6	Obligation and necessity	e
42	2356	X4.2	Mental object: Means, method	e
43	2342	I3.1	Work and employment: Generally	e
44	2242	S2	People	e
45	2174	A5.1	Evaluation: Good/bad	e
46	2164	A4.1	Generally kinds, groups, examples	e
47	2100	I1	Money generally	e
48	2098	G2.1	Crime, law and order: Law & order	e
49	2085	W4	Weather	e
50	2025	M2	Putting, taking, pulling, pushing, transporting &c.	e

Table 20.

	Format conventions	Final list of reports to be included in the text corpus			
		Reports in French			
	Doc Name	**Document Date**	**Report Number**	**Country**	**Pages**
11	Mauritius - Recent economic developments and prospects (English)	FEB 28, 1974	268	Mauritius	**45**
12	Philippines - Industrial development problems and prospects (Vol. 2): Review of selected sub-sectors (English)	MAR 15, 1974	280	Philippines	111
13	Philippines - Industrial development problems and prospects (Vol. 1 of 2): General issues (English)	MAR 19, 1974	280	Philippines	**91**
14	Fiji - Current economic position and prospects (Vol. 2 of 2): A review of agricultural development (English)	MAR 27, 1974	376	Fiji	131
15	Sri Lanka - Recent economic developments and current prospects (English)	APR 30, 1974	407	Sri Lanka	219
16	Rwanda - Recent economic development and prospects (Vol. 2 of 3): Annexes (French)	JUN 24, 1974	422	Rwanda	FR
17	Rwanda - Recent economic development and prospects (Vol. 1 of 3): Main report (English)	JUL 24, 1974	422	Rwanda	**51**
18	Rwanda - Recent economic development and prospects (Vol. 2 of 3): Annexes (English)	JUL 24, 1974	422	Rwanda	**65**
19	Rwanda - Recent economic development and prospects (Vol. 3 of 3): Statistical appendix (English)	JUL 24, 1974	422	Rwanda	79
20	Rwanda - Recent economic development and prospects (Vol. 1 of 3): Rapport principal (French)	JUL 24, 1974	422	Rwanda	FR
21	Rwanda - Recent economic development and prospects (Vol. 3 of 3): Annexe statistique (French)	JUL 24, 1974	422	Rwanda	FR
22	Prospects for developing countries (English)	JUL 31, 1974	477	World	82
23	Nigeria - Current economic position and prospects (Vol. 2 of 3): Recent economic development and prospects (English)	AUG 05, 1974	416	Nigeria	95
24	Niger - Current economic position and development prospects (Vol. 1 of 3): Main report (English)	AUG 20, 1974	487	Niger	161
25	Niger - Current economic position and development prospects (Vol. 2 of 3): The agricultural sector (main report) (English)	AUG 20, 1974	487	Niger	147
26	Niger - Current economic position and development prospects (Vol. 3 of 3): The agricultural sector (annexes) (English)	AUG 20, 1974	487	Niger	116
27	Niger - Current economic position and development prospects (Vol. 1 of 3): Rapport principal (French)	SEP 06, 1974	487	Niger	FR
28	Niger - Current economic position and development prospects (Vol. 2 of 3): Le secteur agricole (rapport principal) (French)	SEP 06, 1974	487	Niger	FR
29	Niger - Current economic position and development prospects (Vol. 3 of 3): Le secteur agricole (annexes) (French)	SEP 06, 1974	487	Niger	FR
30	Burundi - Recent economic development and prospects: Burundi - Evolution recente et perspectives de l'economie (French)	JAN 14, 1975	504	Burundi	FR
31	Malawi - Recent economic development and prospects (English)	JAN 31, 1975	560	Malawi	105
32	Burundi - Recent economic development and prospects (English)	JAN 31, 1975	504	Burundi	121
33	Sri Lanka - Recent economic developments and current prospects (English)	FEB 28, 1975	622	Sri Lanka	130
34	Guatemala - Memorandum on recent economic development and prospects (English)	MAR 31, 1975	681	Guatemala	115
35	Tanzania - Industrial and mining sector survey (Vol. 2 of 3): Current status and development prospects of the mining sector (English)	MAR 31, 1975	647	Tanzania	**75**
36	Tanzania - Industrial and mining sector survey (Vol. 3 of 3): Current status and development prospects of engineering and basic metal industries and current status and development prospects of the textile industry (English)	MAR 31, 1975	647	Tanzania	98

Continued on following page

Table 20. Continued

	Format conventions	Final list of reports to be included in the text corpus			
		Reports in French			
37	Indonesia - Development prospects and needs - basic economic report (Vol. 1 of 2): Main volume (English)	APR 15, 1975	708	Indonesia	100
38	Indonesia - Development prospects and needs - basic economic report (Vol. 2 of 2): Statistical annex (English)	APR 15, 1975	708	Indonesia	75
39	Botswana - Development strategy in a mineral-led economy - basic economic report (Vol. 1 of 2): Current economic position and prospects (English)	MAY 15, 1975	735	Botswana	119
40	Nepal - A review of major issues related to development prospects (English)	MAY 31, 1975	677	Nepal	107
41	Upper Volta - Current economic position and development prospects: Haute Volta - Situation economique et perspectives de developpement (French)	JUL 07, 1975	564	Burkina Faso	FR
42	Upper Volta - Current economic position and development prospects (English)	JUL 31, 1975	564	Burkina Faso	157
43	Somalia - Recent economic developments and current prospects (Vol. 1 of 2): The main report (English)	AUG 20, 1975	702	Somalia	129
44	Somalia - Recent economic developments and current prospects (Vol. 2 of 2): Annexes (English)	AUG 20, 1975	702	Somalia	222
45	Thailand - Current economic prospects and development issues (Vol. 1 of 2): Main report (English)	NOV 14, 1975	924	Thailand	118
46	Thailand - Current economic prospects and development issues (Vol. 2 of 2): Statistical appendix (English)	NOV 14, 1975	924	Thailand	87
47	Ethiopia - Economic development and current prospects (Vol. 1 of 2): Development policy issues (English)	DEC 01, 1975	790	Ethiopia	**27**
48	Ethiopia - Economic development and current prospects (Vol. 2 of 2): Recent economic developments (English)	DEC 01, 1975	790	Ethiopia	**71**
49	Pakistan - Recent trends and development prospects (English)	MAR 31, 1976	1023	Pakistan	146
50	Philippines - Priorities and prospects for development: basic economic report (Vol. 1 of 3): Summary and conclusions, an overview of development prospects in the Philippines, statistical appendix (English)	MAY 05, 1976	1095	Philippines	**88**
51	Philippines - Priorities and prospects for development: basic economic report (Vol. 2 of 3): The sectors (English)	MAY 05, 1976	1095	Philippines	314
52	Philippines - Priorities and prospects for development: basic economic report (Vol. 3 of 3): Investments & resource management (English)	MAY 05, 1976	1095	Philippines	167
53	Papua New Guinea - Economic situation and development prospects (English)	JUL 31, 1976	1150	Papua New Guinea	198
54	Burma - Development in Burma: issues and prospects (English)	JUL 31, 1976	1024	Myanmar	**129**
55	Philippines - Priorities and prospects for development: basic economic report (English)	JUL 31, 1976	PUB1095	Philippines	N/A
56	Prospects for developing countries: 1977-85, a staff study (English)	SEP 30, 1976	37591	World	260
57	Ecuador - Industrial development problems and prospects (English)	OCT 31, 1976	1186	Ecuador	**96**
58	Madagascar - Economic memorandum on current position, prospects, and selected development issues: Madagascar - Situation et perspectives economiques et questions principales relatives au developpement (French)	DEC 20, 1976	1099	Madagascar	FR
59	Madagascar - Economic memorandum on current position, prospects, and selected development issues (English)	DEC 31, 1976	1099	Madagascar	238
60	Tunisia - Economic position and prospects: review of the fifth development plan 1977-1981: Tunisie - Situation economique et perspectives: etude du cinquieme plan de developpement (1977-81) (French)	MAY 02, 1977	1539	Tunisia	153
61	Tunisia - Economic position and prospects: review of the fifth development plan 1977-1981 (English)	MAY 31, 1977	1539	Tunisia	N/A
62	Nigeria - Recent economic developments and short-term prospects (English)	DEC 31, 1977	1690	Nigeria	**77**

Continued on following page

Table 20. Continued

	Format conventions	Final list of reports to be included in the text corpus			
		Reports in French			
63	Papua New Guinea - Its Economic situation and prospects for development (English)	1977			237
64	COFFEE COCOA DEVELOPMENT LENDING	1977			**148**

Table 21. UCREL semantic analysis system[1] (McArthur, 1981)

					[1] Tom McArthur's Longman Lexicon of Contemporary English (McArthur, 1981) and others.	Semantic field	Tag Code
GENERAL & ABSTRACT TERMS	A		MONEY & COMMERCE	I		Participation	S1.1.3
General	A1		Money generally	I1		Deserve etc.	S1.1.4
General actions, making etc.	A1.1.1		Money: Affluence	I1.1		Personality traits	S1.2
Damaging and destroying	A1.1.2		Money: Debts	I1.2		Approachability and Friendliness	S1.2.1
Suitability	A1.2		Money: Price	I1.3		Avarice	S1.2.2
Caution	A1.3		Business	I2		Egoism	S1.2.3
Chance, luck	A1.4		Business: Generally	I2.1		Politeness	S1.2.4
Use	A1.5		Business: Selling	I2.2		Toughness; strong/weak	S1.2.5
Using	A1.5.1		Work and employment	I3		Sensible	S1.2.6
Usefulness	A1.5.2		Work and employment: Generally	I3.1		People	S2
Physical/mental	A1.6		Work and employment: Professionalism	I3.2		People: Female	S2.1
Constraint	A1.7		Industry	I4		People: Male	S2.2
Inclusion/Exclusion	A1.8		ENTERTAINMENT, SPORTS & GAMES	K		Relationship	S3
Avoiding	A1.9		Entertainment generally	K1		Relationship: General	S3.1
Affect	A2		Music and related activities	K2		Relationship: Intimate/sexual	S3.2
Affect: Modify, change	A2.1		Recorded sound etc.	K3		Kin	S4
Affect: Cause/Connected	A2.2		Drama, the theatre & show business	K4		Groups and affiliation	S5
Being	A3		Sports and games generally	K5		Obligation and necessity	S6
Classification	A4		Sports	K5.1		Power relationship	S7
Generally kinds, groups, examples	A4.1		Games	K5.2		Power, organizing	S7.1
Particular/general; detail	A4.2		Children's games and toys	K6		Respect	S7.2
Evaluation	A5		LIFE & LIVING THINGS	L		Competition	S7.3
Evaluation: Good/bad	A5.1		Life and living things	L1		Permission	S7.4
Evaluation: True/false	A5.2		Living creatures generally	L2		Helping/hindering	S8
Evaluation: Accuracy	A5.3		Plants	L3		Religion and the supernatural	S9
Evaluation: Authenticity	A5.4		MOVEMENT, LOCATION, TRAVEL & TRANSPORT	M		TIME	T
Comparing	A6		Moving, coming and going	M1		Time	T1
Comparing: Similar/different	A6.1		Putting, taking, pulling, pushing, transporting &c.	M2		Time: General	T1.1
Comparing: Usual/unusual	A6.2		Movement/transportation: land	M3		Time: General: Past	T1.1.1
Comparing: Variety	A6.3		Movement/transportation: water	M4		Time: General: Present; simultaneous	T1.1.2
Definite (+ modals)	A7		Movement/transportation: air	M5		Time: General: Future	T1.1.3
Seem	A8		Location and direction	M6		Time: Momentary	T1.2
Getting and giving; possession	A9		Places	M7		Time: Period	T1.3
Open/closed; Hiding/Hidden;	A10		Remaining/stationary	M8		Time: Beginning and ending	T2
Finding; Showing			NUMBERS & MEASUREMENT	N		Time: Old, new and young; age	T3

Continued on following page

Table 21. Continued

					[1] Tom McArthur's Longman Lexicon of Contemporary English (McArthur, 1981) and others.	Semantic field	Tag Code
Importance	A11		Numbers	N1		Time: Early/late	T4
Importance: Important	A11.1		Mathematics	N2		THE WORLD & OUR ENVIRONMENT	W
Importance: Noticeability	A11.2		Measurement	N3		The universe	W1
Easy/difficult	A12		Measurement: General	N3.1		Light	W2
Degree	A13		Measurement: Size	N3.2		Geographical terms	W3
Degree: Non-specific	A13.1		Measurement: Distance	N3.3		Weather	W4
Degree: Maximizers	A13.2		Measurement: Volume	N3.4		Green issues	W5
Degree: Boosters	A13.3		Measurement: Weight	N3.5		PSYCHOLOGICAL ACTIONS, STATES & PROCESSES	X
Degree: Approximators	A13.4		Measurement: Area	N3.6		General	X1
Degree: Compromisers	A13.5		Measurement: Length & height	N3.7		Mental actions and processes	X2
Degree: Diminishers	A13.6		Measurement: Speed	N3.8		Thought, belief	X2.1
Degree: Minimizers	A13.7		Linear order	N4		Knowledge	X2.2
Exclusivizers/particularizers	A14		Quantities	N5		Learn	X2.3
Safety/Danger	A15		Entirety; maximum	N5.1		Investigate, examine, test, search	X2.4
THE BODY & THE INDIVIDUAL	B		Exceeding; waste	N5.2		Understand	X2.5
Anatomy and physiology	B1		Frequency etc.	N6		Expect	X2.6
Health and disease	B2		SUBSTANCES, MATERIALS, OBJECTS & EQUIPMENT	O		Sensory	X3
Medicines and medical treatment	B3		Substances and materials generally	O1		Sensory: Taste	X3.1
Cleaning and personal care	B4		Substances and materials generally: Solid	O1.1		Sensory: Sound	X3.2
Clothes and personal belongings	B5		Substances and materials generally: Liquid	O1.2		Sensory: Touch	X3.3
ARTS & CRAFTS	C		Substances and materials generally: Gas	O1.3		Sensory: Sight	X3.4
Arts and crafts	C1		Objects generally	O2		Sensory: Smell	X3.5
EMOTIONAL ACTIONS, STATES & PROCESSES	E		Electricity and electrical equipment	O3		Mental object	X4
General	E1		Physical attributes	O4		Mental object: Conceptual object	X4.1
Liking	E2		General appearance and physical properties	O4.1		Mental object: Means, method	X4.2
Calm/Violent/Angry	E3		Judgement of appearance (pretty etc.)	O4.2		Attention	X5
Happy/sad	E4		Colour and colour patterns	O4.3		Attention	X5.1
Happy/sad: Happy	E4.1		Shape	O4.4		Interest/boredom/excited/energetic	X5.2
Happy/sad: Contentment	E4.2		Texture	O4.5		Deciding	X6
Fear/bravery/shock	E5		Temperature	O4.6		Wanting; planning; choosing	X7
Worry, concern, confident	E6		EDUCATION	P		Trying	X8
FOOD & FARMING	F		Education in general	P1		Ability	X9
Food	F1		LINGUISTIC ACTIONS, STATES & PROCESSES	Q		Ability: Ability, intelligence	X9.1

Continued on following page

Table 21. Continued

					[1] Tom McArthur's Longman Lexicon of Contemporary English (McArthur, 1981) and others.	Semantic field	Tag Code
Drinks	F2		Communication	Q1		Ability: Success and failure	X9.2
Cigarettes and drugs	F3		Communication in general	Q1.1		SCIENCE & TECHNOLOGY	Y
Farming & Horticulture	F4		Chapter documents and writing	Q1.2		Science and technology in general	Y1
GOVT. & THE PUBLIC DOMAIN	G		Telecommunications	Q1.3		Information technology and computing	Y2
Government, Politics & elections	G1		Speech acts	Q2		NAMES & GRAMMATICAL WORDS	Z
Government etc.	G1.1		Speech etc: Communicative	Q2.1		Unmatched proper noun	Z0
Politics	G1.2		Speech acts	Q2.2		Personal names	Z1
Crime, law and order	G2		Language, speech and grammar	Q3		Geographical names	Z2
Crime, law and order: Law & order	G2.1		The Media	Q4		Other proper names	Z3
General ethics	G2.2		The Media: Books	Q4.1		Discourse Bin	Z4
Warfare, defence and the army; Weapons	G3		The Media: Newschapters etc.	Q4.2		Grammatical bin	Z5
ARCHITECTURE, BUILDINGS, HOUSES & THE HOME	H		The Media: TV, Radio & Cinema	Q4.3		Negative	Z6
Architecture, kinds of houses & buildings	H1		SOCIAL ACTIONS, STATES & PROCESSES	S		If	Z7
Parts of buildings	H2		Social actions, states & processes	S1		Pronouns etc.	Z8
Areas around or near houses	H3		Social actions, states & processes	S1.1		Trash can	Z9
Residence	H4		General	S1.1.1		Unmatched	Z99
Furniture and household fittings	H5		Reciprocity	S1.1.2			

Compilation of References

Aggarwal, V., Keohane, R., & Yoffie, D. (1987, June). The Dynamics of Negotiated Protectionism. *The American Political Science Review*, *81*(2), 345–366. doi:10.2307/1961956

Ágh, A. (1998). *From Democratization to Modernization in Hungary: The Political Preconditions for the Full Membership in the European Union Final Report*. NATO Fellowships Programme.

Ahumada, C. (2007). *Movimientos sociales, biodiversidad y libre comercio en la Amazonía. Universidad Javeriana.* Fundacion Cultural Javeriana de Artes Gráficas.

Akerlof, G. A. (1970, August). The Market for "Lemons". Quality Uncertainty and the Market Mechanism. [s.l.:s.n.]. *The Quarterly Journal of Economics*, *84*(3), 488–500. doi:10.2307/1879431

Al Ataha, S. (2013). Development Project, Land Acquisition and Resettlement in Bangladesh; A Quest for Well Formulated National Resettlement and Rehabilitation Policy. *International Journal of Humanities and Social Science*, *3*(7).

Alacevich, M. (2007). *Early Development Economics Debates Revisited*. World Bank, Washington, DC. https://openknowledge.worldbank.org/handle/10986/7565

Alacevich, M. (2007). *Early Development Economics Debates*. World Bank.

Alacevich, M. (2008). *The World Bank's Early Reflections on Development: A Development Institution or a Bank?* World Bank. https://openknowledge.worldbank.org/handle/10986/6840 doi:10.1596/1813-9450-4670

Alonso Et Al, S. J. K. W. M. (2011). *Introduction. The Future of Representative Democracy*. Cambridge University Press. doi:10.1017/CBO9780511770883

Archer, D. (2002). *Introduction to the USAS category system.* Lancs. http://ucrel.lancs.ac.uk/usas/usas%20guide.pdf.

Archer., D. A. W. P. R. (2002). *Introduction to the USAS category system.* UCREL. http://ucrel.lancs.ac.uk/usas/usas%20guide.pdf

Arcila, O. (2011). *La Amazonía colombiana urbanizada. Un análisis de sus asentamientos urbanos.* Instituto amazónico de investigaciones científicas.

Arenal, C. d. (1984). *Introducción a las relaciones Internacionales. Introductions to the International Relations*. Tecnos.

Arendt, H. (1972). *Crises of the Republic: Lying in Politics; Civil Disobedience; On Violence; Thoughts on Politics and Revolution*. Harcourt Brace Jovanovich.

Aristotle, B. J. (2000). *Politics*. Dover Publications.

Baker, P. (2006). Using Corpora in Discourse Analysis. Continuum. doi:10.5040/9781350933996

Balkin, J. M. (2011). *Living Originalism. Equality before the law.* Harvard University Press.

Barnett & Duvall, M. (2005). *Power in International Politics, 59*(1). Cambridge. , doi:10.1017/S0020818305050010

Barro, R. J. (2005). *IMF Programs: Who Is Chosen and What Are the Effects?* Department of Economics, Harvard University.

Barro, R. J. (2005). *IMF Programs: Who Is Chosen and What Are the Effects?* Department of Economics, Harvard University. Department of Economics, Korea University. April.

Barro, R. J. (2005). *IMF Programs: Who Is Chosen and What Are the Effects?* Department of Economics, Korea University.

Barro, R. J. a. J.-W. L. (2005). IMF Programs: Who Is Chosen And What Are The Effects?. *Journal of Monetary Economics, 7*(52), 1245-1269.

Barro, R. J. a. J.-W. L., 2005. IMF Programs: Who Is Chosen And What Are The Effects?. *Journal of Monetary Economics,* 7 October, Volume 52, pp. 1245-1269.

Barro, R. J., 2005. and Jong-Wha Lee. IMF Programs: Who Is Chosen and What Are the Effects?. Department of Economics, Harvard University. Department of Economics, Korea University. April.

Berhe, M. G. (2014). *A Delicate Balance. Land Use, Minority Rights and Social Stability in the Horn of Africa.* Institute for Peace and Security Studies, Addis Ababa University.

Berron, G. (2014). Economic power, democracy and human rights. A new international debates on human rights and corporations. *Sur. International Journal on Human Rights.*

Berry, A., Thoumi, F. E., & Zerda, A. (1986). Crecimiento y políticas económicas en Colombia: 1970-1984. *Colombia beyond the National Front.* West View Press.

Beyen, J. W. (1948). The International Bank for Reconstruction and Development. *International Affairs*, 24.

Bird, G., & Rowlands, D. (2006). IMF quotas: Constructin an international organization using inferior building blocks. *The Review of International Organizations*, *1*(2), 153–171. doi:10.100711558-006-8342-x

Bird-Pollan, S. M.-D. a. S., 2010. *Nation state, capitalism, democracy: Philosophical and political motives in European Journal of Social Theory. 13: 443 the thought of Jürgen Habermas DOI:* .. s.l.:s.n. doi:10.1177/1368431010382759

Black, E. R. (1960, June). The age of economic development. *Economic Journal (London)*, *70*(278), 266–276. doi:10.2307/2228727

Blommaert, J. (2005). *Discourse: A Critical Introduction. Key topics in sociolinguistics.* Cambridge University Press. doi:10.1017/CBO9780511610295

Blommaert, J., & Bulcaen, C. (2000). Critical Discourse Analysis. Annual Review of Anthropology, *29*, 447–466.

Blommaert, J., & Bulcaen, C. (2000). Critical Discourse Analysis. Annual Review of Anthropology. *VOl.*, *29*, 447–466.

Boughton, J. M. (2002). *Why White, Not Keynes? Inventing the Postwar International Monetary System.* (IMF Working Paper). IMF.

Boughton, J. M. (2002). Why White, Not Keynes? Inventing the Postwar International Monetary System. *IMF Working Paper*. IMF.

Boughton, J. M. 2002. Why White, Not Keynes? Inventing the Postwar International Monetary System. *IMF Working Paper,* March.pp. 1-25.

Bradshaw, Y. W., & Huang, J. (1991, Autumn). Intensifying global dependency: Foreign Debt, Structural Adjustment and Third World Underdevelopment. *The Sociological Quarterly*, *32*(3), 321–342. doi:10.1111/j.1533-8525.1991.tb00162.x

Brantly, W. (2006). *China and Vietnam The Politics of Asymmetry*. Cambridge University Press.

Brown, V. (2011). *The Reflectivist Critique of Positivist IR Theory*. Cardiff University. http://www.e-ir.info/2011/02/27/the-reflectivist-critique-of-positivist-ir-theory/.

Brown, V. (2011). *The Reflectivist Critique of Positivist IR Theory*. EIR. http://www.e-ir.info/2011/02/27/the-reflectivist-critique-of-positivist-ir-theory/

Brown, V. 2011. The Reflectivist Critique of Positivist IR Theory. Cardiff University. http://www.e-ir.info/2011/02/27/the-reflectivist-critique-of-positivist-ir-theory/, February 27.

Buchanan, J. M. (1977). Democracy in Deficit: The Political Legacy of Lord Keynes. In *The Collected Works of James M. Buchanan in 20 vols* (pp. 1999–2002). Liberty Fund.

Bucheli, M. (2006). Curas, campesinos y laicos como gerentes de desarrollo. *La construcción de un modelo de desarrollo emergente en Colombia.*. EDISOCIAL.

Burca, G. d. (2009). The European Court of Justice and the International Legal Order After Kadi. [s.l.:s.n.]. *Harvard International Law Journal*, *1*(51).

Buzan, B. (2004). *From International to World Society.* Cambridge Studies in International Relations.

Campbel, J. L. (2002). Ideas, politics, and public policy. [s.l.:s.n.]. *Annual Review of Sociology*, *28*(1), 21–38. doi:10.1146/annurev.soc.28.110601.141111

Campbell, J. L. (1998). *No. 3 (Jun., 1998)* (Vol. 27). Institutional Analysis and the Role of Ideas in Political Economy. Theory and Society. Springer. https://www.jstor.org/stable/657900

Carlos, T., Jimenéz, D., Grando, L. & Zuluaga, Y. (1998). *El desplazamiento por la violencia en Colombia. Experiencias, análisis y posibles estrategias de atención en el Departamento de Antioquia.*. Pastoral Social ACNUR.

Carthy, M. (1984). Introduction. The theory of communicative action, 1(1). Beacon Press.

Carthy, M. (1984). Introduction. The theory of communicative action. Boston: Beacon Press.

Cass, D. (2001). The "Constitutionalization" of International Trade Law: Judicial Norm-Generation as the engine of constitutional development on international trade. The Constitutionalisation of International Trade Law (2011). *European Journal of International Law*, *12*(1), 39–75. doi:10.1093/ejil/12.1.39

Cha & Lee. (2010). Patterns of International Trade and a Nation's Wealth. Department of Physics, Inha University, Incheon.

Cha & Lee. (2010). Patterns of International Trade and a Nation's Wealth. Department of Physics, Inha University.

Cha & Lee. (20100. Patterns of International Trade and a Nation's Wealth. Department of Physics, Inha University, Incheon, 402-751.

Cha, M.-Y. & Lee, J. W. (2010). *Wealth dinamics in world trade (Moon-Yong Cha a, Jae Woo Leea – Patterns of International Trade and a Nation's Wealth.*. Cornell University Press.

Cha, M.-Y. & Lee, J. W. (2010). Wealth dinamics in world trade (Moon-Yong Cha a, Jae Woo Leea – Patterns of International Trade and a Nation's Wealth.. *Journal of the Korean Phys ical Society, 56*(3), p. 998 - 1002.

Cha, M.-Y., & Lee, J. W. (2010). Patterns of International Trade and a Nation's Wealth. *Policies and Institutions for Economic Development in Historical Perspective, ISBN-10,* 1843310279.

Chang, H.-J. (2002). Kicking Away the Ladder. Development Strategy in Historical Perspective. Anthem Press.

Chang, H. J. (2002). Kicking away the ladder. [Anthem World History]. *Policies and Institutions for Economic Development in Historical Perspective, ISBN-10,* 1843310279.

Chang, H.-J. (2002). *Kicking Away the Ladder. Development Strategy in Historical Perspective*. Anthem Press.

Checkel, J. (1998, January). The Constructivist turn in International Relations Theory. Review Article. *World Politics, 50,* 324–348. doi:10.1017/S0043887100008133

Cheng. (2005). *Notes on equilibrium in symmetric games*. University of Michigan Artificial Intelligence Lab..

Chimni, B. (2006). *A just world under law: A view from the south.* American Society of International Law.

Clifford, B. 2009. *New human rights issues. Understanding their contentious rise. Colombia Internacional 69, ene - jun 2009, Pp 228, ISSN 0121-5612, Bogotá, Pp. 14 - 35.* s.l.:s.n.

Clifton, J. & Revuelta, J. (2010). *"Multilatinas" in the American dynamics of nation champion policy and asymmetric behaviour.* Revista Internacional de Organizaciones. RIO. No.04.

Collinson, S., & Rugman, A. (2007). The regional character of Asian multinational Enterprises. [Springer.]. *Asia Pacific Journal of Management, 24*(4), 429–446. doi:10.100710490-006-9035-y

Convention, P. (1788). *The Constitution of the United States.* National Archives.

Cooper & Truman. (2007). *The IMF Quota Formula: Linchpin of Fund Reform. Harvard University.* Peterson Institute for International Economics.

Cordeiro, J. L. (2007). El Desafío Latinoamericáno y sus cinco grandes retos. McGraw Hill.

Cordeiro, J. L. (2007). El Desafío Latinoamericáno y sus cinco grandes retos. McGraw Hill.

Correa, R. (2002). Structural reforms and economic growth in Latin America: a sensitivity analysis. *CEPAL review*. CEPAL.

Correa, R. (2009). *Ecuador: de Banana Republic a la No república.* Nomos Impresores.

Cotula, L. (2009). *Land grab or development opportunity? Agricultural investmente and international land deals in Africa.* IIED/FAO/IFAD.

Cotula, L. V. S. L. R. K. J. (2009). *Land grab or development opportunity? Agricultural investmente and international land deals in Africa.* IIED/FAO/IFAD, London/Rome.

Cotula, L. (2014). *Foreign Investmente, law and sustainable development. IIED Natural Resources Issues.* International Institute for Environment and Development.

Crespino, J. (2003). The History of Jim Crow; Remembering Jim Crow. [s.l.:s.n.]. *The Journal of American History, 90*(2), 750–752. doi:10.2307/3659600

Crocier & Huntington. (1973). The crisis on democracy. The trilateral comission. New York University Press.

Cuervo-Cazurra, A. (2007). Sequence of value-added activities in the multinationalization of developing country firms. *Journal of International Management, 13*(3), 258–277. doi:10.1016/j.intman.2007.05.009

Cuervo-Cazurra, A. (2007). The Multinationalization of Developing contry MNEs: The case of Multilatinas. Sonoco International Business Department. *Journal of International Management.*

Das, D. K. (2010). *Financial Globalization: Growth, Integration, Innovation, and Crisis.* Palgrave Macmillan. doi:10.1057/9780230289949

David Rueda, J. P. (2000). *Wage Inequality and varieties of capitalism.* Cambridge University Press.

De Janvry, A., Fajardo, D., Errazuriz, M. & Balcazar, F. (1991). *Campesinos y desarrollo en América Latina.* Fondo DRI.

De Zoysa, R. (2013). *The implications of large scale land acquisitio on small landholder`s food security.* (DPU WORKING PAPER NO. 156). DPU.

Dennis Leech, R. L. (2004). Voting Power in the Bretton Woods Institutions. (*Warwick Economic Research Papers).*

Dennis Leech, R. L. (2004). *Voting Power in the Bretton Woods Institutions.* (Warwick Economic Research Papers). Warwick Economic.

Dennis Leech, R. L., 2004. Voting Power in the Bretton Woods Institutions. *WARWICK ECONOMIC RESEARCH PAPERS*, November, Issue 718.

Deutch, J., Arnold, K., Ernest, M. & Daniel, P. (2004). Making the World Safe for Nuclear Energy. *Survival, 46*(4), 65-79. Routledge, part of the Taylor & Francis Group..

Diamond, W. (1956). Economic Problems of Foreign Trade and Investment in Underdeveloped Countries. *Ohio State Law Journal, 17*, 254.

Díaz, A. (2006). *La reforma agraria en Colombia, Venezuela y Brasil. Nuestra costa caribe y el problema agrario.* D´vinni Ltda.

Dickens. (1949, June). Private Foreign Investments: A Means of World Economic Development. [Jun.]. *Political Science Quarterly, 64*(2), 211–244.

Dijk, T. A. (2002). *Critical Discourse Studies: A Sociocognitive approach. Rewritten version of the author's contribution.*

Dijk, T. A. v. (1980). *MACROSTRUCTURES. An Interdisciplinary Study of Global Structures in Discourse.* Interaction, and Cognition.

Dijk, T. v. (1994). *Cuadernos. Nº2, Año 2.* Octubre -Maestría en Lingüística. Escuela de Ciencia del Lenguaje y Literaturas.

Djik, T. (1994). Discurso, poder y cognicion social. Escuela de Ciencia del Lenguaje y Literaturas.

Djik, T. (1997). Discurso cognicion y sociedad. *Van Djik -En Signos 8*(22), 66-74.

Djik, T. (1997). Handbook of Discourse Analysis (pp. 352-371). Oxford: Blackwell.

Djik, T. A. (1993). Principles of critical discourse analysis. Discourse & Society, Sage.

Djik, T. A. v. (2008). Critical Discourse Analysis. In D. Schiffrin, D. Tannen, & H. E. Hamilton (Eds.), *The Handbook of Discourse Analysis.* Blackwell Publishers Ltd. doi:10.1002/9780470753460.ch19

Dowrick, S. (2005). CONTRADICTORY TRENDS IN GLOBAL INCOME INEQUALITY: A TALE OF TWO BIASES. *Review of Income and Wealth, 51*(2), 201 - 229.

Dreher et. al., A. &. J.-E. S., 2010. *Do the IMF and theWorld Bank influence voting in the UN General Assembly. Public Choice. DOI* .. s.l.:s.n. doi:10.1007/s11127-010-9750-2

Duangkamon Chotikapanich, R. V. D. R. (1997). Global and Regional Inequality in the Distribution of Income: Estimation with Limited and Incomplete Data. *Empirical Economics*, *22*(4), 533–546. doi:10.1007/BF01205778

Easterly, W. (2000). The effect of IMF and World Bank programs on poverty. *Social Science Research Network Electronic Paper Collection*, (December), 31.

EasterlyW. (2000). The Effect of IMF and World Bank Programs on Poverty. SSRN. https://ssrn.com/abstract=256883 or doi:10.2139/ssrn.256883

Eckstein, H., & Apter, D. 1963. *Comparative Politics. Glencoe, Free Press.* s.l.:s.n.

Ehrenfeld, W. (2012). *Climate Innovation - The Case of the Central Chemical Industrie. April 2012. No. 2.* IWH-Diskussionspapiere.

Eichengreen, B. (2004). *Global Imbalances and the Lessons from Bretton Woods.* National Bureau of Economic Research.

Eichengreen, B. 2004. Global Imbalances and the Lessons from Bretton Woods. *National Bureau of Economic Research*, May, Volume Working Paper No. 10497, p. 39.

Eichengreen, B. (2004). Global Imbalances And The Lessons Of Bretton Woods.National Bureau Of Economic Research. *Working Paper*, *10497*, 2004. https://www.nber.org/papers/w10497

Eichengreen, B. (2008). *Globalizing Capital:A History of the International Monetary System* (2nd ed.). Princeton University Press. doi:10.2307/j.ctt7pfmc

Eichengreen, B. (2012). *Exorbitant Privilege: The Rise and Fall of the Dollar and the Future of the International Monetary System.* Oxford University Press.

Elliott, M. N. (2009). *The US Financial and Economic Crisis: Where Does It Stand and Where Do We Go From Here?*

Encyclopædia Britannica. (2013). *Encyclopædia Britannica Online Academic Edition.* Encyclopædia Britannica Inc.

Escobar, A. (1995). *Encountering Development. The making and unmaking of the third world.* Princeton University Press.

Escobar, A. (2008). The Problematization of Poverty; the tale of three worlds and development. In *The development reader* (pp. 131–140). MPG, Books Ltd. Bodmin.

Fairclough & Chouliaraki. (1999). Discourse in Late Modernity. Rethinking Critical Discourse Analysis. Edimburgh University Press.

Fairclough & Chouliaraki. N. a. L., 1999. Discourse in Late Modernity. Rethinking Critical Discourse Analysis. Edimburgh University Press. Cambridge. ISBN. 0-7486-1082-0.

Farrel & Finnemore. (2009, February). H. a. M., 2009. Ontology, methodology and causation in the American school of international political economy. George Washington University,Washington, DC, USA. *Review of International Political Economy*, *16*(1), 58–71.

Farrel & Finnemore. (2009, February). Ontology, methodology and causation in the American school of international political economy. George Washington University,Washington, DC, USA. *Review of International Political Economy*, *16*(1), 58–71.

Figueredes, J. M. (1999). *Centroamérica en el camino hacia el desarrollo sostenible..* Universidad de los Andes.

Figueredes, J. M. (1999). *Centroamérica en el camino hacia el desarrollo sostenible..* s.l.:Universidad de los Andes. Colombia. ISBN. 958-695-029-8.

Fink, G., & Yolles, M. (2015). Collective emotion regulation in an organization - a plural agency with cognition and affect. *Journal of Organizational Change Management*, *28*(5), 832–871. doi:10.1108/JOCM-09-2014-0179

Finnemore & Barnett. (1999). The politics, power and pathologies of International Organizations. International Organization 53(4).

Finnemore & Barnett. (1999). The politics, power and pathologies of International Organizations. International Organization, 53(4).

Finnemore & Barnett. M. &. M., 1999. The politics, power and pathologies of International Organizations. International Organization 53. 4, Autumn, pp. 699-732. By the IO Fundation and the Massachusetts Institute of Technology. s.l.:s.n.

Finnemore & Sikkin, M. a. K., 1998. International Norm Dynamics and Political Change. nternational Organization 52, 4, Autumn 1998, pp. 887-917 . 1998 by The 10 Foundation and the Massachusetts Institute of Technology..

Finnemore & Sikkin. (1998). International Norm Dynamics and Political Change. *International Organization 52*(4).

Finnemore & Sykkink. (2001). TAKING STOCK: The Constructivist Research Programin International Relations and Comparative Politics. Annual Review of Political Science, 4, 391-416 doi:10.1146/annurev.polisci.4.1.391

Finnemore, M. (1994). International organizations as teachers of norms: the United Nations Educational, Scientific, and Cutural Organization and science policy. *Intemational Organization 47*, 4.

Finnemore, M. (1994). International organizations as teachers of norms: the United Nations Educational, Scientific, and Cutural Organization and science policy. *International Organization, 47*(4), 565-597.

Finnemore, M. (1996). Norms,culture, and world politics: insights from sociology's institutionalism. *Intemational Organization 50*(2).

Finnemore, M. (1996). Norms,culture, and world politics: insights from sociology's institutionalism. *Intemational Organization 50.*

Finnemore, M. (1996). Norms,culture, and world politics: insights from sociology's institutionalism. *IntemationalOrganization 50*(2)..

Finnemore, M., 1994. International organizations as teachers of norms: the United Nations Educational, Scientific, and Cutural Organization and science policy. ntemational Organization 47, 4, Autumn 1993, pp. 565-597 ?3 1994 by The 10 Foundation and the MIT.

Finnnemore & Sikkink, M. &. K., 2001. *TAKING STOCK: The Constructivist Research Programin International Relations and Comparative Politics. Annu. Rev. Polit. Sci. 2001. 4:391–416 Copyright c ©2001 by Annual Reviews.* s.l.:s.n.

Fontana, B. (1993). *Hegemony and Power. In the relation between Gramsci and Machiavelly.* Univ Of Minnesota Press.

Frericks et.al., P. (2009). Toward a Neoliberal Europe?: Pension Reforms and Transformed. *Administration & Society, 41*(135). doi:10.1177/0095399708328874

Frericks, P. (2010). *Patricia Frericks, Mark Harvey and Robert Maier The 'paradox of the shrinking middle': The central dilemma of European social policy. Critical Social Policy.* Sage. doi:10.1177/0261018310367671

Frericks. (2010). Capitalist Welfare Societies' Trade-Off Between Economic Efficiency And Social Solidarity *European Societies, 12*(5), 719–741. doi:10.1080/14616696.2010.483010

Frith, K. (1988). *More than we bargained for: The impact of consumer culture in South East Asia. Department of Journalism and Mass comunication.* Iowa State University.

Frith, K. (1988). *More than we bargained for: The impact of consumer culture in South East Asia. Department of Journalism and Mass comunication.* Iowa State University.

GAAT. (1947). *The general agreement on tariffs and trade ("GATT 1947").* World Trade Organization.

Galbraith, J. K. (2008). *Inequality and Economic and Political Change.* (UTIP Working Paper*).* UTIP.

Galbraith, J. K. (2008). *Inequality and Economic and Political Change.* UTIP Working Paper No. 51). UTIP.

Galbraith, J. K. (1988, April - June). 1998. The Political Asymmetry of Economic Policy. *Eastern Economic Journal, 14*(2), 125–128.

Gandara, P. 2007. *The Role of Energy for Regional Integration in the EMP:Working Paper Number 0712.* Berlín: Jean Monnet Centre of Excellence.Freie Universität Berlin. Germany. Date: 31/12/2007. The Sixth Framework Programme. Contract No. 028386.

Ganho, W. (2011). *Is Water the Hidden Agenda of Agricultural Land Acquisition in sub-Saharan Africa?* University of Manchester.

Garofaldo, P. (2012). *Corporate Profits Hit Record High While Worker Wages Hit Record Low. December 3th. Think progress.* Think Progress. https://thinkprogress.org/economy/2012/12/03/1270541/corporate-profits-wages-record/?mobile=nc

German, L. S. G. M. E. (2011). *Contemporary processes of largescale land acquisition by investors: Case studies from sub-Saharan Africa.* (CIFOR Occasional Paper No.68).

Ghatak, M., & Mookherjee, D. (2011). *Land acquisition for industrialization and compensation of displaced farmers.* World Institute for Development Economics Research.

Gialdino, I. V. (2009). Ontological and Epistemological Foundations of Qualitative Research. *Advances in Qualitative Research in Ibero America , 10*(2).

Gibbs, J. P. (1965). *No. 5 (Mar. 1965)* (Vol. 70). Norms: The Problem of Definition and Clasiffication. American Journal of Sociology. The University of Chicago Press. https://www.jstor.org/stable/2774978

Goldgeier, J. M., & Tetlock, P. E. (2001). Psycology and International Relations Theory. [Annual Reviews.]. *Annual Review of Political Science, 4*(1), 67–92. doi:10.1146/annurev.polisci.4.1.67

Goswami, A. (2012). *Land Acquisition, Rehabilitation and Resettlement: Law and Politics.* IIHS.

Gourinchas, P.-O., & Rey, H. (2005). *From world banker to world venture capitalist: us external adjustment and the exorbitant privilege.* National bureau of economic research.

Greif, A. (1994). On the Political Foundations of the Late Medieval Commercial Revolution: Genoa During the Twelfth and Thirteenth Centuries. The Journal of Economic History. *53rd Annual Meeting of the Economic History Association.* Springer.

Groom, B. (2013). OECD jobless rates forecast to remain stubbornly high. *Financial Times, 16.* http://www.ft.com/cms/s/0/5d7c8300-ede4-11e2-816e-00144feabdc0.html#axzz2dl8t6Nz2..

Guerra, W. (2007). *El poblamiento del territorio.*

Guijarro & Yus. (2009). The origin of chirality in the molecules of life. A revision from awareness to the current theories and perspectives of this unsolved problem. University of Alicante, The royal society of Chemistry.

Guilhot, N. (2008). The realist Gambit: Postwar American Political Science and the Birth of IR Theory. International Studies Association. *International Political Sociology, 2*(4), 281–304. doi:10.1111/j.1749-5687.2008.00052.x

Haas, P. (1992). Introduction: Epistemic Communities and International Policy Coordination. *International Organization, 46*(1), 1-35.

Haas, E. B. (1964). *Beyond the Nation-State. Functionalism and International Organization*. Stanford University Press. Stanford. California.

Haas, P. (1992). Introduction. Epistemic communities and international policy coordination. *International Organization*, 46(1), 1–35.

Haas, P. (1992). Introduction. Epistemic communities and international policy coordination. MIT Press. International Organization. *Knowledge, Power, and International Policy Coordination*, (Winter), 1–35.

Habermas, J. (1984). The Theory of Communicative Action, Volume 1: Reason and the Rationalization of Society. [T. McCarthy, trans.]. Boston: Beacon Press.

Habermas, J. (1984). The Theory of Communicative Action, Volume 1: Reason and the Rationalization of Society. [T. McCarthy]. Boston: Beacon Press

Habermas, J. (1984). The Theory of Communicative Action, Volume 1: Reason and the Rationalization of Society. Boston: Beacon Press.

Habermas, J. (1984). The Theory of Communicative Action, Volume 1: Reason and the Rationalization of Society. Translated by Thomas McCarthy. Boston: Beacon Press.

Habermas, J. (1996). Between Facts and Norms. Contributions to a Discourse Theory of Law and Democracy. [W. Rehg, trans.] Massachusetts Institute of Technology. doi:10.7551/mitpress/1564.001.0001

Habermas, J. (1998). The Inclusion of the Other Studies in Political Theory. The MIT Press.

Habermas, J. (2001). Why Europe Need a Constitution. *New Left Review, 11*.

Habermas, J. 1988. Legitimation Crisis. British Library Cataloguing in Publication Data. ISBN 0-7456-0609-1. First published in Great Britain by Heinemann Educational Books 1976.First published by Polity Press.: s.n.

Habermas, J., 2001. Why Europe Need a Constitution. New Left Review 11 sep oct 2001-5.

Habermas, J., 2006. Between Naturalism and Religion. Entre Naturalismo y Religión. Ediciones Paidós Ibérica, S. A..

Habermas, J. (1984). The Theory of Communicative Action: Vol. 1. *Reason and the Rationalization of Society* (T. McCarthy, Trans.). Beacon Press.

Habermas, J. (1985). Theory of communicative action.: Vol. 2. *Lifeworld and System. A critique of functionalist reason* [T. McCarthy, Trans.]. Beacon Press.

Habermas, J. (1992). *Legitimation Crisis*. Polity.

Habermas, J. (2000). *The Postnational Constellation* (M. Pensky, Trans.). MIT Press.

Habermas, J. (2008). Freedom and Determinism. In *Between Naturalism and Religion: Philosophical Essays. Ciaran Cronin (trans.)*. Polity Press.

Habermas, J. 1984. *The Theory of Communicative Action, Volume 1: Reason and the Rationalization of Society. Translated by Thomas McCarthy. Boston: Beacon Press*, s.l.:s.n.

Hadi, M. A. (1998). *Dialogue on Jerusalem*. Palestinian Academic Society for the Study of International Affairs.

Haig, E. (2001). A study of the application of Critical Discourse Analysis to ecolinguistics and the teaching of eco-theory. Studies in language and culture (Nagoya University).

Haig, E. (2006). *A Critical Discourse Analysis of News about Youth Crime in British Radio Programmes and Online Message Boards*. Lang. https://www.lang.nagoya-u.ac.jp/tagen/media/journal/200803/haig.pdf

Hall & Taylor. P. a. R., 1996. Political Science and the new three Institutionalisms. Political Studies Association. XLIV. 936-957. Blackwell publishers.

Hansen, A. H. (1944). World Institutions for Stability and Expansion. *Foreign Affairs, 22*, 248–255... doi:10.2307/20029821

Hansen, L. (2011). Theorizing the image for Security Studies: Visual securitization and the Muhammad Cartoon Crisis. *European Journal of International Relations, 17*(1), 51–74. https://ejt.sagepub.com/cgi/doi/10.1177/1354066110388593. doi:10.1177/1354066110388593

Harjes, T. (2007). Globalization and Income Inequality: A European Perspective. International Monetary Fund.

Heat, J. 2010. *'Legitimation crisis' in the later work of Jürgen Habermas. In* https://philpapers.org/rec/HEALCI. *University of Montreal. 15-04.* s.l.:s.n.

Heath, J. (2009). Habermas and analytical Marxism. *Philosophy & Social Criticism, 35*(8). http://www.sagepub.co.uk/journalsPermissions.nav

Herrmann, V., Voss, J. F., Schooler, T. Y. E., & Ciarrochi, J. (1997). Images in International Relations: An Experimental Test of Cognitive Schemata. [September.]. *International Studies Quarterly, 41*(3), 403–433. doi:10.1111/0020-8833.00050

Hockett, R. (2005). Three (potential) pillars of transnational economic justice: The Bretton Woods institutions as guarantors of global equal treatment and market completion. *Metaphilosophy, 36,* 93-127.

Hopf, T. (1998, Summer). The Promise of Constructivism in International Relations Theory. [MIT Press.]. *International Security, 23*(1), 171–200. doi:10.1162/isec.23.1.171

Horvath, J. (n.d.) *Critical Discourse Analysis of Obama´s Political Discourse.*

Huckin, T. A. J. &. C.-L. J. (2012). Critical discourse analysis and rhetoric and composition. *College Composition and Communication,* •••, 107–129.

Hurtado, S. (2008). *Ecología, agricultura, comunidad.* Universidad Central de Venezuela. Ediciones de la Biblioteca.

Hurtado, S. (2008). *Ecología, agricultura, comunidad.* Universidad Central de Venezuela.

Idárraga, A., Muñoz, D. A., & Vélez, H. (2010). Conflictos socio-ambientales por la extracción minera en Colombia: Casos de la inversión británica. Amigos de la Tierra.

IMF. (1944). Articles of Agreement of the International Monetary Fund. International Monetary Fund.

IMF. (1944). Articles of Agreement of the International Monetary Fund. New Hampshire, IMF.

IMF. (2012). International Monetary Fund. *Executive Board Report*. International Money Fund.

International Bank for Reconstruction and Development. (1953). *The position of the world economy on the eve of the outbreak of the Koren War and the post-korean developments and prospects*. International Bank.

International Monetary Fund. (2012). *Global Financial Stability Report. A Report by the Monetary and Capital Markets Department on Market Developments and Issues*. IMF.

IPCC/07. (2007). *Synthesis Report. An Assessment of the Intergovernmental Panel on Climate Change.* IPCC Plenary XXVII, Valencia, Spain.

Jackson, R. (2002). *The Global Retirement Crisis.* The Threat to World Stability and What to Do About It. Citigroup & Center for Strategic and International Studies. Global Aging Initiative. doi:10.1111/1468-0440.00187

Johnson, P. (2008). Globalizing Democracy: Reflections on Habermas's Radicalism. *European Journal of Social Theory, 11*(1), 71–86. https://est.sagepub.com/content/11/1/71. doi:10.1177/1368431007085288

José Luis Ramos, R. A. (2009). *Transformacion productiva y desarrollo tecnologico. El caso de la region caribe Colombiana.*. Ediciones Uninorte.

Kahler, M. (1985, July). European Protectionism in Theory and Practice. [Cambridge University Press.]. *World Politics, 37*(4), 475–502. doi:10.2307/2010341

Kant, I. (1793). *Prolegomena.* University of Washington.

Keller, R. (2006). Analysing discourse: An approach from the sociology of knowledge. *Historical Social Research (Köln), 31*, 2.

Keohane & Raustiala. (2008). *Toward a Post-Kyoto Climate Change Architecture: a Political Analysis.* The Harvard Project on International Climate Agreements.

Kessler, A. S. L. C. M. G. M., Lülfesmann, C., & Myers, G. M. (2003). (2003), Economic versus political symmetry and the welfare concern with market integration and tax competition *Journal of Public Economics, 87*(5-6), 847–865. doi:10.1016/S0047-2727(01)00155-4

Khan Haider, Y. L. (2008). Globalization and the WTO Dispute Settlement Mechanism: Making a Rules-based Trading Regime Work. (MPRA Paper 7613). University Library of Munich, Germany.

Khan Haider, Y. L. (2008). Globalization and the WTO Dispute Settlement Mechanism: Making a Rules-based Trading Regime Work. University Library of Munich, Germany.

Khan Haider, Y. L. 2008. "Globalization and the WTO Dispute Settlement Mechanism: Making a Rules-based Trading Regime Work". MPRA Paper 7613, University Library of Munich, Germany, revised.: s.n.

Khan, H. &. L. Y. (2008). Globalization and the WTO Dispute Settlement Mechanism: Making a Rules-based Trading Regime Work. *(MPRA Paper 7613).* University Library of Munich, Germany.

Khan, H. (2008). *Globalization and the WTO Dispute Settlement Mechanism: Making a Rules-based Trading Regime Work.* (MPRA Paper 7613). University Library of Munich, Germany.

Kitcher, P. (2001). *Science, Truth, and Democracy.* Oxford Studies in the Philosophy of Science. doi:10.1093/0195145836.001.0001

KjaerP. (2006). Systems in Context. On the outcome of the Habermas/Luhmann-debate. ANCILLA IURIS (anci.ch). SSRN.

Koch, R. (1995). The case of Latour. *Configurations, 3*(3), 319–347. doi:10.1353/con.1995.0020

Kojeve, A. (1969). *Introduction to the reading of Hegel.* [J. H. Nichols. Jr., trans.]. Cornell University Press.

Kombe, W. (2010). *Land acquisition for public use: emergin conflicts and their socio-political implications.* (Working paper No. 82). ARDHI University.

Konrad, Z. (1980). *The Origin of the German Social Market Economy. The leading ideas and their intellectual roots.* Adam Smith Institute.

Kratochwil, D. (2000). Constructing a New Orthodoxy? Wendst's Social Theory of International Politics and the Constructivist Challenge. Milennium – *Journal of International Students*, *29*, 73.

Kratochwil, D. (2000). Constructing a New Orthodoxy? Wendst's Social Theory of International Politics and the Constructivist Challenge. Milennium. *Journal of International Students*, *29*, 73.

Kratochwil, F. (1993). The embarrassment of changes: Neorealism as the science of Realpolitik without politics. *Review of International Studies*, *19*(1), 63–80. doi:10.1017/S0260210500117346

Krugman, P. (2012). Is the United States like Greece? Not even close. *ADN*. https://www.adn.com/2012/03/13/2368710/krugman-is-the-united-states-like.html

Lang, A. F. (2005). *Hannah Arendt and International Relations: Readings Across the Lines. New York: Palgrave Macmillan.*

Lawson, G., (2012). The eternal divide?: history and International Relations. *European journal of International Relations.*

Leech, D. &. L. R., 2004. "Voting Power and Voting Blocs," The Warwick Economics Research Paper Series (TWERPS) 716, University of Warwick, Department of Economics.

Leech, D. (2004). Voting Power and Voting Blocs. *The Warwick Economics Research Paper Series (TWERPS) 716*. University of Warwick, Department of Economics.

Leech, D. (2004). Voting Power in the Bretton Woods Institutions. *Warwick Economic Research Paper*. Warwick Economic Research Group.

Leech, D. L. a. R., 2012. A New Analysis of A Priori Voting Power in the IMF: Recent Quota Reforms Give Little Cause for Celebration. WARWICK ECONOMIC RESEARCH PAPERS. No. 1001..

Leech, D. L. R. (2012). A New Analysis of A Priori Voting Power in the IMF: Recent Quota Reforms Give Little Cause for Celebration. WARWICK ECONOMIC RESEARCH PAPERS. No 1001. The University of Warwick.

Leiteritz & Moschella. (2010). The IMF and capital account liberalization: a case of failed norm institutionalization. In S. Park & A. Vetterlein (eds.) Owning Development. Creating Policy Norms in the IMF and the WB. Cambridge University Press.

Leiteritz & Moschella. (2010). The IMF and capital account liberalization: a case of failed norm institutionalization. In S. Park & A. Vetterlein (eds.) Owning Development: Creating Policy Norms in the IMF and the WB. Cambridge University Press.

Leiteritz & Moschella. R. J. M. (2010). The IMF and capital account liberalization: a case of failed norm institutionalization. In Susan Park & Antje Vetterlein. Owning Development. Creating Policy Norms in the IMF and the WB. Cambridge University Press.

Lewis, N. (2011). 1971: Bretton Woods And The Four-Decade Trauma Of Its Collapse. *Forbes*. https://www.forbes.com/2011/07/07/bretton-woods-collapse.html. 2011.

Lewis, N. 2011. 1971: Bretton Woods And The Four-Decade Trauma Of Its Collapse. https://www.forbes.com/2011/07/07/bretton-woods-collapse.html. 2011.

Lombardi, N. W. &. D. (2006). Uneven patterns of governance: how developing countries are represented in the IMF. *Review of International Political Economy, 13*(3), pp. 480-515.

Lombardi, N. W. &. D., 2006. Uneven patterns of governance: how developing countries are represented in the IMF. *Review of International Political Economy,* August, 13(3), pp. 480-515.

Lombardi, N. W. (2006). Uneven patterns of governance: how developing countries are represented in the IMF. *Review of International Political Economy, 13*(3), 480-515.

Lord, E. (2013). *Symmetry and Pattern in Projective Geometry.* Springer.

Luban, D. (1979). On Habermas on Arendt on Power. *Philosophy and Social Criticism, 6*(1).

Luke, A. (2008). Theory and Practice CDA. L. Saha (ed) *International Encyclopedia of the Sociology of Education.* Elsevier Science Ltd.

Mamonova, V. (2011). *Large-scale land acquisitions in the former Soviet Union. A study of rural social movements and land conflicts.* LANDac project.

Marini, R. M. (2008). *América Latina, dependencia y globalización..* Siglo del Hombre Editores.

Mariotti, M. (2000). Maximal symmetry and the Nash solution. *Social Choice and Welfare, 17*(1), 45–53. doi:10.1007/PL00007174

Marulanda Gómez, O. (2002). *Labranza de Paz. Producción sostenible en el campo para la reconstrucción de la comunidad rural..* Editorial Norma.

Maxwell, J. A. (1996). Applied Social Research Methods Series: Vol. 41. *Qualitative Research Design. An interactive Approach. Sage Publications, Inc.*

McCabe & Alonso. (2001). Theme, transitivity and cognitive representation in spanish and english written texts. *Circle of linguistics applied to communication.* Revista Canaria de Estudios Ingleses.

McCabe & Alonso. (2001). Theme, transitivity and cognitive representation in Spanish and English written texts. *Circle of linguistics applied to communication. Revista Canaria de Estudios Ingleses.*

McCright, A., & Dunlap, R. (2011). The politicization of climate change and polarization in the american public's views of global warming, 2001–2010. The Sociological Quarterly, 52(2).

Meinzen-Dick, R. (2014). Property rights and sustainable irrigation: A developing country perspective. *Agricultural Water Management, 145*, 23–31. doi:10.1016/j.agwat.2014.03.017

Mejía, W., (2007). Presencia Embrea en el área metropolitana centro occidente. *Fundación cultural germinando.* Cristina Uribe Ediciones.

Mendelson, J. (1979). The Habermas-Gadamer Debate. *New German Critique, 18,* 44–73. . doi:10.2307/487850

Michael, D. Bordo, B. E. D. A. I. (1999). *Is Globalization Today Really Different than Globalization a Hunderd Years Ago?* (NBER Working Paper No. 7195) NBER.

Mikesell, R. F. (1994). The Bretton Woods debates. A memoir. Essays in International Finance, 192, 76.

Mikesell, R. F. (1994). The Bretton Woods debates. A memoir. Essays in International Finance, 192, 76.

Mikesell, R. F. (1994). The Bretton Woods debates. A memoir. Essays in International Finance, 192.

Mikesell, R. F. 1994. The Bretton Woods debates. A memoir. Essays in International Finance, March, Volume 192, p. 76.

Milanovic, B. (2006). *Global income inequality: What it is and why it matters.* Washington: (World Bank Policy Research Working Paper 3865). World Bank.

Milanovic, B. (2007). *An even Higuer inequality than previously though: a note on global inequality calculations using the 2005 ICP results.* (World Bank Policy Research Working Paper Series). World Bank.

Milanovic, B. (2007). An even Higuer inequality than previously though: a note on global inequality calculations using the 2005 ICP results. *World Bank Policy Research Working Paper Series.* ICP.

Milanovic, B. (2007). An even Higuer inequality than previously though: a note on global inequality calculations using the 2005 ICP results. *World Bank Policy Research Working Paper Series.* World Bank.

Milanovic, B. (2009). *Global inequality and global inequality extraction ratio: The story of the last two centuries.* World Bank, University of Maryland.

Milanovic, B. (2009). *Global inequality and global inequality extraction ratio: The story of the last two centuries.* World Bank. https://mpra.ub.uni-muenchen.de/16535/

Milanovic, B. 2006. *Global income inequality: What it is and why it matters.* World Bank.

Moore, B. (1985). Authority and Inequality under Capitalism and Socialism. Oxford Press.

Moore, B. 1985. Authority and Inequality under Capitalism and Socialism. Oxford(Brasenose College): s.n.

Morgenthau, H. J. (1950). *Politics among nations: the struggle for power and peace. New York: Knopf.* s.l.:s.n.

Morris, R. T. (1956). A typology of Norms. *American Sociological Review, 21*(5), 610-613. American Sociological Association. https://www.jstor.org/stable/2089098.

Nandy, A. (1989). Science as a Reason of State. *Science as Culture, 1*(7), 69–83. doi:10.1080/09505438909526260

Nick Malkoutzis, N. (2011). Greece – A Year in Crisis. *Examining the Social and Political Impact of an Unprecedented Austerity Programme.*

Niiniluoto, I. (1991). *No. 1. Scientific knowledge and Scientific Practice (Oct., 1991)* (Vol. 89). Realism, relativism and constructivism. Synthese. Springer.

Nixon, R. (1971). Address to the Nation Outlining a New Economic Policy: 'The Challenge of Peace.' *Public Papers of the Presidents, Richard Nixon, Containing the Public Messages, Speeches, and Statements of the President.*

Nolte, K., & Voget-Kleschin, L. (2013). *Evaluating Consultation in Large-scale Land Acquisition.* (LDPI Working Paper). LDPI.

North, D. C. (1991). Institutions. *The Journal of Economic Perspectives, 5*(1), 97–112. doi:10.1257/jep.5.1.97

O'Neill Surber, J. P. (2003). The "End of History" Revisited: Kantian Reason, Hegelian Spirit, and the History of Philosophy. In Hegel's History of Philosophy. New Interpretations. State University of New York Press.

Odame, W. (2008). Compulsory Land Acquisition and Compensation in Ghana: Searching for alternative policies and strategies. *FIG/FAO/CNG International Seminar on State and Public Sector Land Management.* FAO.

OECD. (2013). OECD Employment Outlook 2013. OECD.

Olmstead, C. J. (1964). *Foreign aid as an effective means of persuasion.* American Society of International Law.

Ordóñez, F. (2012). Zonas de reserva campesina: contribución a la democratización del acceso y la propiedad sobre la tierra y construcción alternativa del territorio desde el campesinado. En Propuestas, visiones y análisis sobre la política de desarrollo rural en Colombia. OXFAM, Colombia.

Ortiz, L. A. (2008). *Cultivar y cambiar. La cultura campesina ante la mercantilización de los espacios rurales en Paraguay.* FLACSO México.

País, E. E. (2013). Depresión profunda. *EL PAÍS, 25.* https://elpais.com/elpais/2013/01/24/opinion/1359059699_473851.html

Palacios, M. (2011). *De quien es la tierra? Propiedad, politización y protesta campesina en la década de 1930.* Universidad de los Andes. .

Palley, T. I. (2007). *Financialization: what it is and why it matters.* (Working Papers). The levy Economics Institute.

Park & Vetterlein. (2010). Do policy norms reconstitute global development? In S. Park & A. Vetterlein (eds.) Owning Development: Creating Policy Norms in the IMF and the WB. Cambridge University Press.

Park & Vetterlein. S. a. A., 2010. Do policy norms reconstitute global development? In Susan Park & Antje Vetterlein. Owning Development. Creating Policy Norms in the IMF and the WB. Cambridge University Press.

Passmore, J. (1965). *The idea of a history of philosophy. History and Theory: The historiofraphy of the historiy of philosophy.* Wiley-Blackwell for Wesleyan University.

Paterson, M. (1996). *Global warming and Global Politics.* Taylor & Francis Group.

Peters, A. (2011). The Constitutionalisation of International Trade Law. The Prospects Of International Trade Regulation: From Fragmentation To Coherence, (pp. 69-102). Cambridge University Press.

Peters, A. 2011. The Constitutionalisation of International Trade Law (2011). THE PROSPECTS OF INTERNATIONAL TRADE REGULATION: FROM FRAGMENTATION TO COHERENCE, pp. 69-102, Cambridge University Press.

Peters, A. A. K. M. K. (2011). The Constitutionalisation of International Trade Law. *The Prospects Of International Trade Regulation: From Fragmentation To Coherence*, (pp. 69-102). Cambridge University Press.

Peters, A. (2009). The merits of Global Constitutionalism. [©Indiana University Maurer School of Law — Bloomington.]. *Indiana Journal of Global Legal Studies, 16*(2), 397–411.

Pettenger, M. E. (2008). The Social Construction of Climate Change: Power, Knowledge, Norms, Discourses. *Journal of Environmental Law, 20*(3), 486–489. doi:10.1093/jel/eqn016

Piketty, T. (2014). Capital in the Twenty-First Century. *The Belknap Press.*

Polanyi, K. (2001). *The Great Transformation. Beacon Press Books. 1944 - 2001.* Foreword by Joseph E. Stiglitz.

Ponce, A. (2012). *El desalentador panorama de la minería en Colombia..* Random House Mondadori.

Pray, C. (1985). *Private sector research and technology transfer in Asian agriculture: report on phase 1 aid grant OTR 0091-G-SS-4195.* Unniversity of Minnesota..

Rapaczynski, A. (1996). The roles of the State and the Market in Establishing Property Rights. *Journal of Economic Perspectives, 10*(2).

Rasminsky, L. (1944, July). International Credit and Currency Plans. *Foreign Affairs, 1.* https://www.foreignaffairs.com/articles/70355/louis-rasminsky/international-credit-and-currency-plans

Rasmussen M, D., 1976. *Advanced Capitalism and Social Theory: Habermas On the Problem of Legitimation: DOI: Philosophy Social Criticism 1976 3: 349.* s.l.:s.n. doi:10.1177/019145377600300402

Rawls, J. (1971). *A Theory of Justice.* Harvard University Press.

Rawls, J., 1971. *A Theory of Justice. 0674017722, 9780674017726. Harvard University Press.* s.l.:s.n.

Rayson, P. (2003). *Matrix: A statistical method and software tool for linguistic analysis through corpus comparison.* [Ph.D. thesis, Lancaster University].

Rayson, P. (2008). From key words to key semantic domains. *International Journal of Corpus Linguistics, 13*(4). . doi:10.1075/ijcl.13.4.06ray

Read, C. (2009). *Global Financial Meltdown: How We Can Avoid the Next Economic Crisis. Basingstoke* [England]. Palgrave Macmillan. doi:10.1057/9780230595187

Riehl, J. P. (2010). *Mirror-image asymmetry. An introduction to the origin and consequences of chirality.* John Wiley & Sons, Inc. doi:10.1002/9780470588888

Riles, A. (2010). *Collateral Expertise: Legal Knowledge in the Global Financial Markets.* The Wenner-Gren Foundation for Anthropological Research.

Riles, A., 2010. *Collateral Expertise: Legal Knowledge in the Global Financial Markets. The Wenner-Gren Foundation for Anthropological Research. All rights reserved. 0011-3204/2010/5106-0006..* s.l.:s.n.

Rodrick, D. (2002). Feasible Globalizations. *(NBER Working Paper No. 9129).* NBER.

Rodrick, D. 2002. *Feasible Globalizations. NBER Working Paper No. 9129. JEL No. F0. September.* s.l.:s.n.

Rodrik, D. (2001). *Trading in Illusions.* Foreign Policy. No. 123 (Mar. – Apr), pp. 54-62. Washingtonpost.Newsweek Interactive, LLC. https://www.jstor.org/stable/3183155

Rodrik, D. (2001). *Trading in Illusions. Foreign Policy.* Washingtonpost.Newsweek Interactive, LLC. https://www.jstor.org/stable/3183155

Rodrik, D. (2001). *Trading in Illusions.* Washingtonpost.Newsweek Interactive, LLC. https://www.jstor.org/stable/3183155

Rodrik, D., 2001. *Trading in Illusions. Foreign Policy. No. 123 (Mar. – Apr., 2001), pp. 54-62. (article consists of 9 pages). Published by: Washingtonpost.Newsweek Interactive, LLC. Stable URL:* https://www.jstor.org/stable/3183155. s.l.:s.n.

Rodrik, D. (2001). *The Global governance of Trade. As if development really mattered.* Bureau for Development Policy.

Rodrik, D. (2001). *The Global governance of Trade. As if development really mattered. United Nations Development Programm. Social Development Group.* Bureau for Development Policy.

Ronald, M. A. (2014). Land Grabbing in Uganda: Are pastoarlists second class citizens? In A delicate Balance. Land Use, Minority Rights and Social Stability in the Horn of Africa. Institute of Peace and Security Studies, Addis Ababa University.

Rosen, J. (2008). *Symmetry Rules. How science and nature are founded on symmetry.* Frontiers Collection.

Rosenfeld, M. (2001). *The rule of law and the construction of constitutional democracy.* Jacob Burns Institute for Advanced Legal Studies.

Rueda, C. R. (2013). Global Crisis and History Repeating: Three Historical Stages of the Norm of "Modern Development" within the Regulatory Framework of the Bretton Woods Institutions. SSRN Scholarly Paper.

Rueda, C. R. 2013. Global Crisis and History Repeating: Three Historical Stages of the Norm of „Modern Development" within the Regulatory Framework of the Bretton Woods Institutions. SSRN Scholarly Paper. Rochester, NY: Social Science Research Network, 24. Juli.

Rueda, R. (2015). Land Acquisition and the Semantic Context of Land within the Normative Construction of Modern Development. In Handbook of Research on In Country determinants and implications with Foreign Land Acquisitions. IGI GLobal.

RUEDA. (2013). *R.* POLITICAL ASYMMETRY.

RuedaR. 2013. Social Crisis and global repricing of financial instruments. (July 24, 2013). SSRN. https://ssrn.com/abstract=2297893 or doi:10.2139/ssrn.2297893

Sachs & Huizinga. (1987). *U.S. Commercial Banks and the Developing Country Debt Crisis.* (NBER Working Paper No. 2455). NBER.

Sachs, J. (2005). *El fin de la pobreza.* Vinni Ltda.

Sachs, J. D. (2006). The End of Poverty: Economic Possibilities for Our Time. London: Penguin (Non-Classics).

Sachs, W. (1993). Global Ecology and the Shadow of "Development". in Global Ecology: A New Arena of Political Conflict. London and New Jersey: Zed Books.

Sachs, W. (1993). Global Ecology and the Shadow of Development in Global Ecology: A New Arena of Political Conflict. Zed Books.

Sachs., W. (1993). *Global Ecology and the Shadow of Development.* Zed Books.

Sachs., W., 1993. *Global Ecology and the Shadow of „Development".. in Global Ecology: A New Arena of Political Conflict, pp3 – 21 Wolfgang Sachs (ed), London and New Jersey: Zed Books..* s.l.:s.n.

Sanchez, G. (2010). *La tierra en disputa. Memorias del despojo y resistencias campesinas en la costa caribe 1960 - 2010.* Ediciones Semana.

Santiso, J. (2007). *The emergence of latin multinationals.* (OECD Emerging Markets Network Working Paper). OECD.

Santiso, J. (2008). The emergence of Latin Multinationals. *CEPAL Review, 95*(August).

Schouten, P. (2008). 'Theory Talk #3: Alexander Wendt on UFO's, Black Swans and Constructivist International Relations Theory.' *Theory Talks.* http://www.theory-talks.org/2008/04/theory-talk-3.html.

Schutter, O. D. (2011, Summer). The Green Rush: The Global Race for Farmland and the Rights of Land Users. *Harvard International Law Journal, 52*(02).

Sheyholislami, J. (2001). *Yesterday's "separatists" are today's "resistance fighters": A critical discourse analysis of the representations of the Iraqi Kurds in the NY Times and the Globe and Mail.* [Thesis, Carleton University].

Shutter, O. D. (2011a, March). How not to think of land-grabbing; three critiques of large-scale investments in farmland. *The Journal of Peasant Studies, 38*(2), 249–279. doi:10.1080/03066150.2011.559008

Skyner, L. (2001, November). Political Conflict and Legal Uncertainty: The Privatisation of Land Ownership in Russia. *Europe-Asia Studies, 53*(7), 981–999. doi:10.1080/09668130120085001

Spanu, V. (2003). Liberalization of the international trade and economic growth: implications for both developed and developing countries. Harvard Press.

Spanu, V. (2003). *Liberalization of the international trade and economic growth: implications for both developed and developing countries.* Harvard University

Spanu, V. (2003). Liberalization of the international trade and economic growth: implications for both developed and developing countries. Harvard University.

Spanu, V. (2003). Liberalization of the international trade and economic growth: implications for both developed and developing countries. John F. Kennedy School of Government, Harvard University.

Spanu, V. (2003). *Liberalization of the international trade and economic growth: implications for both developed and developing countries.* John F. Kennedy School of Government.

Spanu, V. 2003. Liberalization of the international trade and economic growth: implications for both developed and developing countries. John F. Kennedy School of Government. 79 Kennedy Street. Harvard University. Cambridge, MA 02138 May.: s.n.

Srivastava, J., 2011. *Norm" on Sustainable Development. Predicament and the Problematiqze. India Quarterly: A Journal of International Affairs June 2011 vol. 67 no. 2. 93-110..* s.l.:s.n. doi:10.1177/097492841006700201

Steinhoff, U., 2009. *"Communicative" versus Purposive Rationality. 2009 Print ISBN-13: 9780199547807 Published to Oxford Scholarship Online: September 2009 DOI: ..* s.l.:s.n. doi:10.1093/acprof:oso/9780199547807.001.0001

Stewart, I. (2008). Why Beauty Is Truth: The History of Symmetry. New York; London: BasicBooks.

Stiglitz, J. (2002). Globalization and its Discontents. Norton & Company.

Stiglitz, J. (2006). *Making Globalization Work: Making Trade Fair.* Norton & Company. Ltda.

Stiglitz, J. E. (2001). Nobel Prize Lecture, December 8, 2001, Information And The Change In The Paradigm In Economics. Columbia Business School, Columbia University.

Stiglitz, J., 2003. *Globalization and Its Discontents.* Penguin; Auflage: New Ed (3. April 2003). ISBN-10: 014101038X. ISBN-13: 978-0141010380.: s.n.

Stiglitz, J. (2004). Capital-market Liberalization, Globalization, and the IMF. *Oxford Review of Economic Policy*, *20*(1), 57–71. doi:10.1093/oxrep/grh004

Sturm, A. D. (2006). Do IMF and World Bank Influence Voting in the UN General Assembly? (CESifo Working Paper Series 1724). CESifo Group Munich.

Suárez, A. (2012). Es el derecho de superficie un instrumento para el desarrollo rural en Colombia? En "Propuestas, visiones y análisis sobre la política de desarrollo rural en Colombia." OXFAM Colombia.

Subramanian, & Wei, S.-J. (2007). The WTO promotes trade, strongly but unevenly [May. s.l.:s.n.]. *Journal of International Economics*, *72*(1), 151–175. doi:10.1016/j.jinteco.2006.07.007

Sutcliffe, B. (2004). World Inequality and Globalization. Oxford Review of Economic Policy Limited. Oxford Press. . doi:10.1093/oxrep/grh002

Sutcliffe, B. (2004). World Inequality and Globalization. Oxford Review of Economic Policy, 20. Oxford University Press. doi:10.1093/oxrep/grh002.

Swedberg, R. (1986). The Doctrine of Economic Neutrality of the IMF and the World Bank. *Journal of Peace Research, 23*(4), 377-390.

Swedberg, R. (1986). The Doctrine of Economic Neutrality of the IMF and the World Bank. *Journal of Peace Research, 23*(4), pp. 377-390.

Swedberg, R., 1986. The Doctrine of Economic Neutrality of the IMF and the World Bank. *Journal of Peace Research,* December, 23(4), pp. 377-390.

Taylor, P. A. H. R. R. (1996). Political Science and the Three New Institutionalism. *Polilical Studies Associalion, XLIV,* 936–957.

Tenorio, E. H. (2011). Critical Discourse Analysis, an Overview. *Nordic Journal of English Studies, 10*(1), 183–210. doi:10.35360/njes.247

Teubner, G. & Fischer-Lescano, A. (2004). Regime-Collisions: The Vain Search for Legal Unity in the Fragmentation of Global Law. *Michigan Journal of International Law, 25*(4), 999-1046.

Teubner, G. (2004). Fischer-Lescano, Andreas. Regime-Collisions: The Vain Search for Legal Unity in the Fragmentation of Global Law. *Michigan Journal of International Law, 25*(4).

Thacker, S. C. (1999). The High Politics of IMF Lending. *World Politics, 52*(1), 38–75. doi:10.1017/S0043887100020025

Thelen, K. (1999). Historical Institutionalism in Comparative Politics. *Annual Review of Political Science 2*(1), 369–404. https://www.annualreviews.org/doi/abs/10.1146/annurev.p

Thelen, K. (1999). Historical Institutionalism in Comparative Politics. *Annual Review of Political Science, 2*(1), 369–404. Retrieved (https://www.annualreviews.org/doi/abs/10.1146/annurev.p

Thelen, K. 1999. "Historical Institutionalism in Comparative Politics" edited by Sven Steinmo, Kathleen Thelen, and Frank Longstreth. Annual Review of Political Science 2(1):369–404. Retrieved (https://www.annualreviews.org/doi/abs/10.1146/annurev.p

Thelen, K. (1999). Historical Institutionalism in Comparative Politics. *Annual Review of Political Science, 2*(1), 369–404. doi:10.1146/annurev.polisci.2.1.369

Thomas, T. L. (2001). Deciphering Asymmetry's Word Game. Academic journal article from Military Review, 81(4).

Thomas, C. (2001). *Knud Erik Jørgensen, u. A. W., 2001. The Social Construction of Europe*. SAGE.

Thompson, K. (2003). Systematicity and Experience: Hegel and the Function of the History of Philosophy. In.*Hegel's History of Philosophy. New Interpretations.* State University of New York Press.

Thompson, A. (1999). Alexander Thompson and Duncan Snidal. The History of International Organizations. *University of Chicago., 9800*, 692–722.

Thompson, A., & Snidal, D. (2013). International Organization. 9800. University of Chicago. In B. Bouckaert & G. DeGeest (Eds.), *Encyclopedia of Law and Economics* (pp. 692–722). https://encyclo.findlaw.com/9800book.pdf

TNI. (2013). Transnational Institute (TNI) for European Coordination Via Campesina and Hands off the Land network. *Land concentration, land grabbing and people struggles in Europe*. TNI.

Tokman, V. G. O. (1999). *Pobreza y desigualdad en América Latina.* Paidos.

Treanor, J. (2011). World's wealthiest people now richer than before the credit crunch. *The Guardian. Co.*

UK War Cabinet 338, I., 1944. Memorandum by the Chancellor of the Exchequer. The Proposed United Nations Bank for Reconstruction and Development. Secret. W.P. (44) 338. 20th June, 1944. S, 27679.

UK War Cabinet 45, I., 1945. War Cabinet Document. Confidential Annex. W.M. (45) 9th conclusions. Minute 4. International Monetary Fund. 25th January, 1945 – 5,30 p.m. S,1 (35). Copy No. 10..

UK War Cabinet 45b, I., 1945. W.P. (45) 96. Commercial Policy; Article VII. Memorandum by the Chancelor of the Exchequer. 24th February, 1945. S, 2.

UK War Cabinet 83, I., 1944. War Cabinet 83 (44). Conclusions of a Meeting of the War Cabinet held in the Cabinet War Room on Wednesday, 28th June, 1944, at 6 pm.

United Nations Conference on Trade and Development. (2010). *The Least Developed Countries Report, Embargo Copy Edition*. UN.

United Nations. (1983). *Process of preparation of the Environmental Perspective to the Year 2000 and Beyond*. Resolution 38 / 161. UN.

United Nations. (1983). Process of preparation of the Environmental Perspective to the Year 2000 and Beyond. *Resolution 38*(161).

United Nations. (2009). *Global Compact International Yearbook*. UN.

US State Department. (1945). *Proposals for Expansion of World Trade and Employment*. Federal Reserve Bank.

Van Dijk, T. (1980). *MACROSTRUCTURES - An Interdisciplinary Study of Global Structures in Discourse, Interaction, and Cognition*. Lawrence Erlbaum Associates, Publishers.

Van Dijk, T. (2014). Discourse & Knowledge - A sociocognitive approach. *Universitat Pompeu Fabra, Barcelona.*

Van Dijk, T. (1993). Principles of Critical Discourse Analysis. *Discourse & Society*, *4*(2), 249–283. https://das.sagepub.com/cgi/doi/10.1177/0957926593004002006. doi:10.1177/0957926593004002006

Verdeja, J. (2001). *Trés décadas de pobreza en México*. Instituto Politécnico Nacional.

Verdeja, J. (2001). *Tres décadas de pobreza en México*. Instituto Politecnico Nacional - México.

Vetterlein, & Associates. P. (2010). Owning Development: Creating Policy Norms in the IMF and the World Bank. Cambridge: Cambridge University Press.

Vetterlein, S. P. a. A., 2010. Owning development: creating policy norms in the IMD and the World Bank..

Vetterlein., & Associates. P., 2010. Owning Development: Creating Policy Norms in the IMF and the World Bank. Cambridge: Cambridge University Press.

Via, E. D. (2011). The Politics of "Win-Win" Narratives: Land Grabs as Development Opportunity? Cornell University IDS, University of Sussex, UK.

Wade, R. H. (2003). *The World Trade Organization and the schrinking of the development space.* (Working Paper No.31). London School of Economics.

Wade, R. H., 2003. *The World Trade Organization and the schrinking of the development space. Working Paper No.31. London School of Economics. Development Research Center.*. s.l.:s.n.

Wade, R. H. (2003). What strategies are viable for developing countries today? The World Trade Organization and the shrinking of 'development space.' *Review of International Political Economy*, *10*(4), 621–644. http://www.in. doi:10.1080/09692290310001601902

Wade, R. H. (2004). Is Globalization reducing Poverty and Inequality. *World Development*, *32*(4), 567–589. doi:10.1016/j.worlddev.2003.10.007

Walton, J., & Ragin, C. (1990, December). J. a. C., 1990. Global and National Sources of Political Protest: Third World Responses to the Debt Crisis. *American Sociological Review*, *55*(6), 876–890. doi:10.2307/2095752

WDR. (1978). *World Development Report*. World Bank.

Weaver, C. (2010). The strategic social construction of the World Bank's gender and development policy norm. In *Susan Park & Antje Vetterlein. Owning Development. Creating Policy Norms in the IMF and the WB*. Cambridge University Press. doi:10.1017/CBO9780511762710.005

Weber, M. (2001). *The Protestant Ethic and the Spirit of Capitalism*. [T. Parsons, trans.] Routledge Classics.

Weintraub, R. E. (1984). International debt: Crisis and Challenge. Cato Journal, 4.

Wendt, A. (1992). Anarchy is what states make of it: The social construction of power politics. *International Organization, 46, 391-425.*.

Wendt, A. (1999). Social Theory of International Politics. *Social Theory of International Politics*. Cambridge University Press. doi:10.1017/CBO9780511612183

Wiener & Pueter, A. &. U., 2009. *The quality of Norms is what actors make of it. Critical constructivism research on norms. Journal of International Law and International Relations. Introduction. Volume 5, issue 1. Winter 2009. Special issue. Contested Norms iin International law and IR*. s.l.:s.n.

Wiener & Pueter. (2009). The quality of Norms is what actors make of it. Critical constructivism research on norms. *Journal of International Law and International Relations*, *5*(1).

Wiener, A. (2006). Constructivist Approaches in International Relations Theory: Puzzles and Promises. *The Constitutionalism Web-Paper*. University of Bath, Department of European Studies and Modern Languages. http://ideas.repec.org/p/erp/conweb/p0025.htm

Wiener, A. (2007). *Constructivist Approaches in International Relations Theory: Puzzles and Promises Constitutionalism Webpapers, ConWEB No 5/2006*. Queen's University Belfast.

Wiener, A. (2007). The Dual Quality of Norms and Governance beyond the State: Sociological and Normative Approaches to 'Interaction'. *Critical Review of International Social and Political Philosophy*, *10*(1), 47-69.

Wiener, A. (2007). The Dual Quality of Norms and Governance beyond the State: Sociological and Normative Approaches to 'Interaction'. *Critical Review of International Social and Political Philosophy*, *10*(1), pp. 47-69.

Wiener, A. (2008). The Invisible Constitution of Politics. Contested Norms and International Encounters. Cambridge University Press. doi:10.1017/CBO9780511490408

Wiener, A. (2014). *A Theory of Contestation*. Springer Berlin Heidelberg.

Wiener, A., (2007). *Contested Meanings of Norms: A Research Framework. Comparative European Politics*. Palgrave Macmillan.

Wiener, A., 2007. *Constructivist Approaches in International Relations Theory: Puzzles and Promises Constitutionalism Webpapers, ConWEB No 5/2006. Queen's University Belfast. Rivista Italiana di Scienza Politica.*. s.l.:s.n.

Wiener, A., 2007. *Contested Meanings of Norms: A Research Framework. Comparative European Politics, 2007, 5, (1–17). Palgrave Macmillan Ltd 1472-4790/07*. s.l.:s.n.

Wiener, A., 2014. *A Theory of Contestation. Springer Berlin Heidelberg.*. s.l.:s.n.

Wiener, A. (2007). *Constructivist Approaches in International Relations Theory: Puzzles and Promises Constitutionalism Webpapers, ConWEB No 5/2006*. Queen's University.

Wiener, A. (2008). *The invisible constitution of politics. Contested norms and international encounters. Cambridge University Press.* Cambridge.

Wight, C. (2007, March). A manifesto for Scientific Realism in IR: Assuming the Can-Opener Won't Work. *Millennium, 35*(2), 379–398. doi:10.1177/03058298070350021601

Wihlborg, W. Z. (2010). *The euro crisis: It isn´t just fiscal sn it doesn´t just involve Greece. Claremont McKenna College.* Robert Day School.

Williams, J. H. (1944). Currency Stabilization: American and British Attitudes. *Foreign Affairs, 22*, 2... doi:10.2307/20029820

Wodak & Koller. (2010). Handbook of communication in the public sphere. Walter de Gruyter.

Wodak & Krzyzynowski. (2008). Qualitative Discourse Analysis in the Social Sciences. Palgrave McMillan.

Wodak & Meyer. (2009). Methods of critical discourse analysis. (pp. 62-85). London Sage..

Wodak, F. (1997). *Discourse Studies. CDA Discourse studies. A Multidisciplinary Introduction.* Teun A. van Djik - CDA.

Womack, B. (2006). China and Vietnam: The Politics of Asymmetry. Cambridge University Press.

Woods & Lombardi. (2006, August). Uneven patterns of governance: How developing countries are represented in the IMF [s.l.:s.n.]. *Review of International Political Economy, 13*(3).

World Bank – AA. (1945). *Articles of Agreement. Article I. Purposes.* World Bank.

World Bank - EDP (1969). K*enya - Economic development prospects (Vol. 1 of 2): Main report (English).* World Baannk.

World Bank - EDP. (1970). *Tanzania - Economic development and prospects (Vol. 1 of 2): Main report (English).* World Bank.

World Bank - EDP. (1976). *Philippines - Priorities and prospects for development: basic economic report (Vol. 3 of 3): Investments & resource management (English).* World Bank.

World Bank – FS. (1989). Report Presentation. *Financial systems and development: an overview.* World Bank.

World Bank. (1957). *International Bank for reconstruction and development. The development and prospects of Japan´s economy. Report No. FE-2a. July 25.*

World Bank. (1958). International bank for reconstruction and development. *Recent economic developments and prospects of Colombia, Report No. WH-75a.* World Bank.

World Bank. (1958). International Bank for Reconstruction and Development. Recent economic developments and prospects of Mexico. *Report No. WH, 80t*(November), 24.

World Bank. (1973). *Development problems and prospects of Malaysia.* World Bank.

World Bank. (1973). International Bank for Reconstruction and Development. *Development Prospects of Malaysia, 1.* World Bank.

World Bank. (1974). Bank for Reconstruction and Development. International Development Asociation. *Industrial Development Probelms and Prospects in the Philippines.* World Bank.

World Bank. (1974). Recent econoic development and proxpects of Rwanda. *Volume II: Annexes. Report No. 422a - RW.* World Bank.

World Bank. (1975). *Ethiopia recent economic development and current prospects.* World Bank.

World Bank. (1978). *World Development Report.* World Bank.

World Bank. (1979). *World Development Report.* World Bank.

World Bank. (1980). *World Development Report.* World Bank.

World Bank. (1984). *World Development Report.* World Bank.

World Bank. (2006). *World Development Report.* World Bank.

World Bank. (2008). World Development Report. *Agriculture for Development.*

World Bank. (2009). Reshaping economic geography. *World Bank World Development Report.* World Bank.

World Bank. (2011). *World Development Report.* World Bank.

World Bank. (2012). *World Development Report. Gender equality and development.* World Bank.

World Bank. 1978. World Development Report. World Bank. Library of Congress Catalog Number: 78-67086.

Wray, B. (2001). *Science, Biases, and the Threat of Global Pessimism.* University of British Columbia.

Wray, B. (2001). *Science, Biases, and the Threat of Global Pessimism.* University of British Columbia. Philosophy of Science.

Zamberi, S. & Kitchen, J. P. (2008). Transnational corporations from Asian developing countries: The internationalisation characteristics and business strategies of Sime Darby Berhad. *Journal of Business Science and Applied Management, 3*(2).

About the Contributors

Renny Rueda Castañeda is an assistant professor and former chair of the Bachelor Program on Security and Strategic Studies at the American University in the Emirates. UAE. He is holds a PhD from the Faculty of Economy and Social Sciences of the University of Hamburg, Germany (Centrum für Globalisierung und Governance (CGG)) . He is an Economist with studies on Government, Management, and Public Affairs (Externado Colombian University, Columbia University of New York), Economic Analysis (University of Berkeley Extension Prog. USA), and MA on International Law & International Relations (Complutense University of Madrid, Spain). He has also been an economic advisor to the Inter-American Development Bank and has been a lecturer on international economy, international law, international relations, and political science in various Universities in Colombia. His doctoral research has been published by Taylor & Francis (Uk) and IGI (US), and deals with the construction of norms on scenarios of asymmetric governance, IR, norms and epistemic communities, cognitive governance and late modern market systems. Renny is also the founder of E-codemocracy, an organization that aims to enhance the implementation of decentralization technology and self-governance on autonomous civil interaction. He is an Advisory Board member of the Solonian Democracy Institute, in Ireland. Renny is also a media entrepreneur in Colombia, South America, and has served as an editorial director of numerous projects on political, antiterrorist, and economic journalism. He is fluent in Spanish, English, and German.

Index

L

M

N

O

S

W

www.ingramcontent.com/pod-product-compliance
Lightning Source LLC
LaVergne TN
LVHW080528300926
849162LV00007B/1565